FROMMER'S
EasyGuide
TO

W9-BUP-364

NEW ORLEANS

By
Diana Schram

Easy Guides are ✦ Quick To Read ✦ Light To Carry
✦ For Expert Advice ✦ In All Price Ranges

FrommerMedia LLC

Published by
FROMMER MEDIA LLC

Copyright © 2015 by Frommer Media LLC. All rights reserved. No part of this publication may be repro-
duced, stored in a retrieval system, or transmitted in any form or by any means, electronic, mechanical,
photocopying, recording, scanning or otherwise, except as permitted under Sections 107 or 108 of the
1976 United States Copyright Act, without the prior written permission of the Publisher. Requests to the
Publisher for permission should be addressed to support@frommermedia.com.

Frommer's is a registered trademark of Arthur Frommer. Frommer Media LLC is not associated with any
product or vendor mentioned in this book.

ISBN 978-1-62887-076-3 (paper), 978-1-62887-077-0 (e-book)

Editorial Director: Pauline Frommer
Editor: Billy Fox
Production Editor: Carol Pogoni
Cartographer: Roberta Stockwell
Indexer: Maro Riofrancos

For information on our other products or services, see www.frommers.com.

Frommer Media LLC also publishes its books in a variety of electronic formats. Some content that
appears in print may not be available in electronic formats.

Manufactured in the United States of America

5 4 3 2 1

AN IMPORTANT NOTE

The world is a dynamic place. Hotels change ownership, restaurants hike their prices, museums
alter their opening hours, and busses and trains change their routings. And all of this can occur
in the several months after our authors have visited, inspected, and written about these hotels,
restaurants, museums, and transportation services. Though we have made valiant efforts to keep
all our information fresh and up-to-date, some few changes can inevitably occur in the periods
before a revised edition of this guidebook is published. So please bear with us if a tiny number
of the details in this book have changed. Please also note that we have no responsibility or liabil-
ity for any inaccuracy or errors or omissions, or for inconvenience, loss, damage, or expenses suffered by anyone as a result of assertions in this guide.

CONTENTS

ABOUT THE AUTHOR

Diana Schram, writer and strategic marketing consultant, has authored five books, numerous articles, and scads of content about New Orleans. She followed a familiar path to the city: vacation; enrapture; return; return again; increased tolerance of fleur de lis iconography; homeownership; increased tolerance of everything else; weight gain. In her spare time she enjoys music, film, tennis, biking, watching videos of soldiers reuniting with their dogs, and breathing.

To Harch, because everything he do gonh be funky from now on. I just know it.

Many thanks to Arthur and Pauline Frommer for inspiration, wisdom, guts, and glory. Massive appreciation to the talented Billy Fox (killer editor, not death row killer), whose real name is Billy Fox; I owe you far more than a new box of red pencils. Infinite love to the city, the people, and the ghosts of New Orleans; its particular peculiarities and eternal mysteries; and its tellers of tales and truths—for they are as warm and essential to me as its air. Love to the Fat Pack (Chuck, Fiona, John, Nettie, Robin, Steve, and Wesly) and the Plumpettes (Gary, Linda, Mark, and Paula). With love to the Schwams, Beers, Dileos, Zuckerbergs, and to Moonpie, Scot, and Drew Brees. I love the North Rendon All Stars. How much do I love our house? About 6 degrees lower and to the right. Love ever to Dave and Mary, of course.

ABOUT THE FROMMER'S TRAVEL GUIDES

For most of the past 50 years, Frommer's has been the leading series of travel guides in North America, accounting for as many as 24% of all guidebooks sold. I think I know why.

Though we hope our books are entertaining, we nevertheless deal with travel in a serious fashion. Our guidebooks have never looked on such journeys as a mere recreation, but as a far more important human function, a time of learning and introspection, an essential part of a civilized life. We stress the culture, lifestyle, history and beliefs of the destinations we cover, and urge our readers to seek out people and new ideas as the chief rewards of travel.

We have never shied from controversy. We have, from the beginning, encouraged our authors to be intensely judgmental, critical—both pro and con—in their comments, and wholly independent. Our only clients are our readers, and we have triggered the ire of countless prominent sorts, from a tourist newspaper we called "practically worthless" (it unsuccessfully sued us) to the many rip-offs we've condemned.

And because we believe that travel should be available to everyone regardless of their incomes, we have always been cost-conscious at every level of expenditure. Though we have broadened our recommendations beyond the budget category, we insist that every lodging we include be sensibly priced. We use every form of media to assist our readers, and are particularly proud of our feisty daily website, the award-winning Frommers.com.

I have high hopes for the future of Frommer's. May these guidebooks, in all the years ahead, continue to reflect the joy of travel and the freedom that travel represents. May they always pursue a cost-conscious path, so that people of all incomes can enjoy the rewards of travel. And may they create, for both the traveler and the persons among whom we travel, a community of friends, where all human beings live in harmony and peace.

Arthur Frommer

THE BEST OF NEW ORLEANS

N ew Orleans should come with a warning label. No, no, not about hurricanes. Forget that. That's like solely identifying Hawaii with erupting volcanoes. No, this is about the city itself. See, there's this group of residents known as the "never lefts." They are the people who come to New Orleans as tourists, and the city worked its magic on them.

They become spellbound by the beauty of the French Quarter and the Garden District, and marvel that history is alive right beneath their feet. They listen to music flowing from random doorways and street corners—jazz, Cajun, blues, whatever—and find themselves moving to a languorous rhythm. They kiss beneath flickering gas lamps, and groove to a brass band in a crowded club long past their usual bedtime. They eat sumptuous, indulgent meals, and scandalously indulge yet again hours later, with 3am beignets at Café du Monde, where they watch the passing human parade. They'll catch the scent of jasmine and sweet olive (with a whiff of the Caribbean, and a garlic topnote, perhaps) wafting through the moist, honeyed air.

The air . . . aah, the New Orleans air. People say romance is in the air here. It's true, of course, because the air is dreamy. It's the dewy ingénue who grows up fast in the first act, softly whispering your name. And if you're meant to be together, you'll feel that undeniable flutter, the high-voltage spark that says *I'm in your heart forever.*

That's what happens to the never lefts. They came for Mardi Gras, for a festival, a conference, a tryst, a reunion—just came—and fell hard. New Orleans does that to people.

What is it about this place? Well, for one thing, New Orleans is where centuries commingle, perhaps not effortlessly but nowhere more fruitfully, as if nothing essential has passed between them. It's where a barstool or a park bench becomes the opening salvo in a conversation you may never forget—for raconteurship thrives here. It's where a masquerade party of old masters, modernists, and bohemian street artists fill the city's stunning mélange of museums and galleries. It's a city that actually has an *official cocktail*—which speaks volumes to its state of mind. It's where gumbo—the savory Creole stew that is often (over) used in describing the city's multicultural tableau—is actually an apt metaphor: It speaks of a place that's deep and mysterious, rich with flavor and plenty spicy, and so much more than the sum of its many disparate parts.

New Orleans, the most unique city in the United States, works its charms like a spell. But don't take our word for it. Go. See, hear, and taste for yourself. The best way to get inside New Orleans is to plunge right in. Don't just go for the obvious. Sure, we've met people who never left

Bourbon Street and had a terrific time, but the city has so much more to offer. Look over the advice that follows, and see if New Orleans casts its seductive spell on you. Perhaps you'll come to understand the never lefts. Perhaps you'll even become one.

THE most authentic NEW ORLEANS EXPERIENCES

- **Do Festivals, Big or Small:** Yes to Jazz Fest, Mardi Gras, or French Quarter Fest, but also the smaller fests in New Orleans and nearby towns. If one is on while you're visiting, seek it out. See p. 40.
- **Dress Up. Or Down:** At better restaurants, men wear jackets—including seersucker when in season—and un-ironic hats. Women can and do wear dresses (not just LBDs) and heels. It's required at the finest spots, optional but frequently done at the more moderate bistros (where jeans are also okay). Dressing down might mean cosplay, wacky wigs, whatever. You can get away with it here.
- **Frequent Dive Bars,** if that's your thang. For those whose thang it is, this town is siiick with good ones. See p. 178.
- **Tour the Swamps:** Don't discount this because you think it's too touristy (New Yorkers still go to Broadway, right?). It's an absolutely authentic, ecologically and historically fascinating, unique-to-the-region experience. See p. 156.
- **Ride a Bike:** New Orleans is flat and compact, and you can see a lot on two wheels that you might otherwise miss. See p. 234 for rentals and p. 160 for tours.
- **Cheer the Saints:** In the Dome, if possible—ain't nothing like it, nowhere. Or at least from a barstool, like everyone else who ain't in the Dome. See p. 165.
- **Eat Take-out from Corner Grocery Back Counters:** Traditionally done while leaning against a building or sitting on the curb (or on someone's stoop, which we probably shouldn't encourage). See p. 88.
- **Argue about the Best Po' Boy:** Which requires trying a few. See p. 27 or chapter 6.
- **Go to Church:** Despite the reputation for decadence, this is a pretty pious city. Going to church is a wonderful way to get some faith on, hear some astounding gospel, and mingle with the welcoming locals. See p. 137.
- **Check Out Freebie Concerts:** Spring through autumn, free shows bring the locals to Armstrong Park near the French Quarter (Thursdays; www.pufap.org); City Park in Mid-City (Thursdays; p. 142); and Lafayette Square in the CBD (www.wednesday atthesquare.com).
- **Stroll the Galleries:** There are openings with wine and low-key revelry the first Saturday eve of each month on Julia Street and second Saturdays on St. Claude Avenue (www.scadnola.com), but any time will do. See p. 134.
- **Eat Indulgent, Unhurried, Fancy Lunches:** Especially on Friday.
- **Chat:** Discuss. Debate. Banter. In restaurants, bars, or shops. With people you've just met. We'll give you topics: football, and city politics/ineptitude. Barring your expertise in those arenas, trading anecdotes about your observations as a tourist, discussing a recent meal, or asking for recommendations about your next meal (or other activity) gets the convo started.
- **Eat with Your Hands:** Specifically, peel shrimp and crawfish (in season), best done outdoors; and slurp oysters, best done standing at a bar and jiving with the shucker.
- **Join the Street Spontaneity:** If a wailing trumpet catches your ear, follow the sound till you find it. If the swing band playing in the middle of Royal Street moves you, give your partner a whirl (and drop a few bucks in their hat). And if you're

lucky enough to happen upon a second-line parade passing by, don't dare watch from the sidewalk. Jump in and high-step it down the street. It's New Orleans—it's what you do.

THE best PLACES TO EAT IN NEW ORLEANS

o **Best All-Around Dining Experience You Can Have in New Orleans:** No surprises here, they're world-famous for good reason: **Commander's Palace** (p. 106), hands down. At the other end of the spectrum, **Café du Monde** (p. 116). Somewhere in the middle: **Brigtsen's** (p. 108).

o **Best Classic New Orleans Restaurant:** Of the three old-line, fine-dining mainstays that have been enjoyed for generations, **Arnaud's** is our choice for food; **Galatoire's** (p. 77) for the overall experience; **Antoine's** (p. 82) for room after amazing room full of history.

o **Best Contemporary Creole:** We're awfully fond of **Herbsaint** (p. 101), **MiLA** (p. 102), and the lovely **Coquette** (p. 108).

o **Best Contemporary Cajun:** Pork-centric **Cochon** (p. 103), where you won't find yo mama's Cajun, and **K-Paul's** (p. 77), the originator and still a standard-bearer.

o **Best Italian: Irene's Cuisine** (p. 84) represents New Orleans's traditional Italian; **Domenica** (p. 104) carries the contemporary banner; and we fell hard for newcomer **Marcello's** (p. 102) nuovo Sicilian.

o **Best Neighborhood Restaurants:** New Orleans tucks away some shockingly good restaurants on unassuming residential streets. **Clancy's** (p. 105), **Elizabeth's** (p. 92), **Gautreau's** (p. 109), and **Liuzza's by the Track** show the range.

o **Best Neighbahood Restaurants:** In contrast to those above, these are old-school joints, where locals still ask, "Hey, dahwlin', wheah y'at?" We've gotta go wit da Creole Italian oldies, at **Mandina's** (p. 96) and **Liuzza's** (p. 95).

o **Most Innovative Restaurants:** The gastronomic trickery at **Root** (p. 103) and rich uncle **Square Root** (p. 103) aren't just sleight of hand. **Maurepas Foods** (p. 93) is right up there and **Killer Poboys** (p. 180) pushes the sammie boundaries.

o **Best Expense or Savings Account Blowouts: Restaurant R'evolution** (p. 80), **Emeril's** (p. 99), **August** (p. 99) and $150 prix-fixe **Square Root** (p. 103).

o **Best Bistro:** Tough choice, given the richness of this category, but **La Petite Grocery** (p. 110), **Annunciation** (p. 100), and **Sylvain** (p. 87) figure highly.

o **Best Outdoor Dining:** Start with the pretty courtyards at **Bayona** (p. 82), **Martinique** (p. 110), and **Café Amelie** (p. 86) on starry nights or balmy afternoons; or the scenic balconies at **Tableau** (p. 85) and **Dat Dog** (p. 114) on Frenchmen.

o **Best for Kids:** The no-brainers are **Café du Monde** (p. 116), for powdered sugar mess and mania; the counter at **Camellia Grill** (p. 113); and a **snoball** outing (p. 119). **Antoine's** (p. 82) offers a good fine-dining introduction.

o **Best Slightly Offbeat but Utterly New Orleanean Restaurants:** Definitely **Jacque-Imo's** (p. 109) and **Bacchanal** (p. 91). **Cochon Butcher** (p. 104) and the even fancier **Upperline** (p. 111) fit the category.

o **Best Seafood: GW Fins** sets a high bar (p. 83); **Peche** (p. 102) and **Borgne** (p. 100) are strong contenders; straight-up simple **Big Fisherman** (p. 113) covers the boiled seafood angle.

o **Best Desserts:** A meal at **Emeril's** (p. 99) is incomplete without its banana cream pie; ditto **Commander's Palace's** (p. 106) bread pudding soufflé. The Grill Room's

Japanese Pumpkin Cheesecake is a stunner, and the pastry chefs at **Lilette** (p. 110), **La Petite Grocery** (p. 110), and **Coquette** (p. 108) excel. Or head to a specialist at **Sucré** (p. 118) or **Angelo Brocato's** (p. 116).

- **Best Brunch: Ralph's on the Park** (p. 94) or **Dante's Kitchen** (p. 112) can't miss, while the jazz brunch at **Antoine's** (p. 82), **Arnaud's** (p. 82), and **Commander's Palace** (p. 106) are great fun. Long lines at the casual **Biscuits & Buns** (p. 97) and **Elizabeth's** (p. 92) are full of those in the know.

- **Restaurants with the Best Cocktail Programs:** From a looong list, we'll go with **Kingfish** (p. 84), **Dominique's,** (p. 109), **High Hat** (p. 112), and **Café Adelaide** (p. 101).

- **Best Wine Lists:** The extensive collection at **Emeril's** (p. 99), **Commander's Palace** (p. 106), and **Antoine's** (p. 82) cover every base. The lists at **Bayona** (p. 82) and **Gautreau's** (p. 109) are smaller but well-curated.

- **Best for Late-Night Eats:** Get 24-hour satisfaction at **Clover Grill** (p. 89), **Camellia Grill** (p. 113), and **Verti Marte** (p. 88). For heartier, sit-down fare, **La Boca** (p. 101), **St. Lawrence** (219 N. Peters St., www.saintlawrencenola.com), and **Yuki** (p. 93) serve late. There's always beignets from **Café du Monde** (p. 116) or **Morning Call** (p. 118).

THE best PLACES TO STAY IN NEW ORLEANS

This is a little like deciding on a scoop of ice cream—so many tasty options to choose from, and different people like different flavors. We've tried to narrow down the selections based on specific criteria.

- **Best Moderately Priced Lodging:** In general, you'll get the biggest bang in the **off-season** (including the heat of summer), when even luxury properties drop their rates to levels that are hard to pass up. In the Central Business District, the **Drury Inn** (p. 65) is surprisingly reasonable and an easy hop to the Quarter. In the B&B category, the **Chimes** (p. 67), a delightful family-owned guesthouse in the Garden District, has generated legions of loyal return guests.

- **Best Luxury Hotel:** At the intimate **Audubon Cottages** (p. 51), the luxury commences when your 24-hour butler greets you at the private, unmarked entrance. For sheer opulence, attention to your every need, and vast expanses of room, our vote goes to the **Windsor Court** (p. 64). A Club Level suite, of course.

- **Best Service:** All those in the "Luxury" category above excel in the service category. We're also continually impressed by the attentive **Loews** (p. 65). Of the more modest accommodations, the Campo family makes you feel at home at the **Villa Convento** (p. 58), as do the Uptown **Maison Perrier** (p. 67) and **Maison de Macarty** (p. 61) in the Bywater.

- **Most Romantic:** Romance is wherever you make it, but **Ashtons** (p. 62) encourages long, languid mornings. Stumbling distance from Napoleon House, the sweet exterior of the **St. Helene** (508 Chartres St.; www.hotelsthelene.com) belies its sexy, sleek rooms and near-private pool; and **The Saint's** outlandish, fiery Lucifer Suite was made for misbehavior (931 Canal St.; www.thesainthotelneworleans.com).

- **Best for Families:** It's not fancy, but we like the **Homewood Suites** (p. 65) for the spacious two-room suites, location, and freebie meals. The **Richelieu** (p. 58) and **Maison Dupuy** (p. 56) also offer easy comfort and swimming pools.

- **Best Faaabulous B&B:** A lot of B&Bs are crammed with over-the-top antiques, but at the **Antebellum** (p. 63), they all come with a story. We love the tawdry over-the-topness, hidden hot tub, and actual bordello bed.
- **Best for Hipness:** The elaborate **Melrose Mansion** (p. 62) is a Victorian mansion on the outside, an oasis of upscale cool inside. In the CBD, the innovative minimalist style and ultra-hip Loa Bar at the **International House** (p. 64) brings serious swag, as does the Quarter's violet-hued **Le Marais.**
- **Best Funky Little Spot:** We're fond of the sweetly oddball **B&W Courtyards** (p. 60), the Frenchmen-adjacent **Royal Street Inn** (p. 61), and the hodge-podgey but well-located ex-brothel now called the **Dauphine Orleans** (p. 54).
- **Best Hidden Gem:** Just beyond the French Quarter and veiled behind high walls is an enchanting cluster of old plantation buildings in the Tremé, the stunning **Jazz Quarters Bed & Breakfast** (p. 56). The **Claiborne Mansion's** superb suites and splendid pool are a serene oasis a block from the Frenchmen Street mayhem (p. 60).

THE best TRIP MEMENTOS

Nothing wrong with T-shirts, caps, Mardi Gras beads, and snow globes (except that you can get those anywhere). We offer some alternate ideas.

- **A Book from Faulkner House:** Pick up some reading material from this charming jewel on little Pirate's Alley, crammed with Louisiana-related tomes (p. 192). Many an author has tried, with varying success, to capture New Orleans on the page. Their efforts may help you know what it means to miss New Orleans. Check out our reading list in chapter 2.
- **A Photo or Art Book from A Gallery for Fine Photography:** The owner calls his impressive shop "the only museum where you can buy the art." A fine photograph from one of the many famous photographers represented here is a souvenir you can relish every day—not to mention a wise investment. If an original isn't feasible, consider a fine photo book. See p. 190.
- **A Southern Scent from Hové:** This classic perfumery creates its own perfumes and soaps. We got hooked on sachet-favorite vetiver, described as "smelling like the South." Locals also adore the scents made from the indigenous sweet olive, and the fine gentlemanly scents. See p. 196.
- **A Razor from Aidan Gill:** Manly and mannerly, the selection of hand-sculpted razors (and other accessories) will charm even the most diehard disposable dude and up his style quotient in a single stroke. Or just take home some smooth cheeks courtesy of an ultraluxe straight-razor shave. See p. 195.
- **A CD from Louisiana Music Factory:** New Orleans's soundtrack is as essential to your experience as her sights and tastes. A few CDs will keep the good times rolling back home. Check out our recorded-music recommendations in chapter 2; for details on the Louisiana Music Factory, see p. 197.
- **A Hat from Meyer:** We're mad about **Meyer the Hatter,** for the selection, the service, and the 100-year-plus history. You're in the South, *chère,* you can rock some class headgear. See p. 194.
- **A "be nice or leave" Sign:** Dr. Bob's colorful, bottle-cap-edged signs may have proliferated around the city, but they're still true, local works of folk art, handmade with found materials. Available in a variety of sizes, materials, and sentiments at **Pop City,** 940 Decatur St. (© **504/528-8559**); **Funrock'n,** 3109 Magazine St.

(*C* **504/895-4102**); but it's more fun to visit **Dr. Bob's Bywater studio,** 3027 Chartres St. (*C* **504/945-2225**), open "by chance or appointment." Make sure they still carry them.

o **Fleur-de-lis Jewelry:** Gold, silver, glass, cufflink, nose ring, pendant: The selection is unending. Wear it with pride; share it with a smile. Consider something from **Mignon Faget** (p. 196) or an inexpensive bauble from the flea-market stands at the **French Market** (p. 186).

o **Sazerac Glasses:** If you've taken a shine to the city's official cocktail, the gift shop at the **Roosevelt Hotel** (p. 64) has perfect reproductions of their original glasses.

o **Pralines:** The choice for office gifts. And for home. Maybe one for the plane or car on the way there . See p. 192 (and don't call them *pray*-lines).

THE best OF OUTDOOR NEW ORLEANS

Not exactly what you think of when you think Big Easy—it's not Yellowstone, after all. But there are some surprisingly wonderful outdoorsy things to do here that will only enhance the vacation you envisioned. Besides, it can't all be about dark bars and decadent meals. Oh wait, it's New Orleans. Yes, it can. Still . . . these experiences provide a fine counterpoint and a different perspective.

o **Kayak Bayou St. John:** A guided kayak tour of placid, pretty Bayou St. John is an entrancing way to see this historically significant waterway—and maybe work off a few bites of fried shrimp po' boy. See p. 133.

o **Do City Park:** Whatever your outdoor thing, it's probably doable somewhere in the glorious, 1,300-acre City Park, from pedal-boating to picnicking, birding to bicycling, mini-golfing to art-gazing. It's a great spot for a morning run; so is **Audubon Park** (p. 141) if you're staying Uptown. See p. 142.

o **Tour the Swamps:** The swamps are spooky, serene, and fascinating. The gators are spellbinding, and the guides are knowledgeable naturalists who will open your eyes to every flora and fauna in this unique ecoculture. See p. 156.

o **Ferry Cross the Mississippi:** It's not quite Huck Finn, but a brief "cruise" on the ferry to the historic Algiers neighborhood is an easy way to roll on the river and take in a different view. See p. 235.

o **See the City from Two Wheels:** Whether you rent a bike (p. 234), take a guided bike tour (p. 160), or roll through on a Segway (p. 161), seeing the flat, compact city via two wheels makes for a sweet ride.

o **Dine Alfresco:** We didn't say the best of *active* outdoor New Orleans, did we? A languid, courtyard dinner under the Southern stars (or lunch under an umbrella) at **Bayona, Martinique, Café Amelie, Bacchanal, Green Goddess,** or **Tableau** is an experience to be savored.

o **Do Yoga in the Besthoff Sculpture Garden:** We can't think of a more sublime way to start a Saturday. Especially when it's followed by beignets and coffee (just steps away at **Morning Call** cafe). A little yin, a little yang. Saturdays at 8am in City Park (p. 136; *C* **504/456-5000**).

o **Walk. Walk. And Walk Some More:** This city is made for walking. It's truly the best way to take in the captivating sights, appreciate the silken air, and ogle (or join) the goings-on you will undoubtedly encounter. We won't bring up the c-word benefits (calories. Oops, drat . . . sorry). No texting while walking, though—these old sidewalks require your full attention.

THE best MUSEUMS IN NEW ORLEANS

New York, Chicago, Paris, Rome . . . great museum cities, all. New Orleans isn't included in that list, but it's a surprisingly excellent museum city. Museums also make stellar retreats when the elements become overbearing.

- **New Orleans African American Museum:** Located in the historic Faubourg Tremé, the collection recounts the astounding historical and cultural contributions that emanated from this very neighborhood (and beyond). See p. 154.
- **Backstreet Museum:** To truly appreciate them, you really must see the Mardi Gras Indians' astounding beaded suits up close (if not in action, then in this collection), and learn about this unique tradition. See p. 134.
- **The Cabildo:** An extensive recollection of Louisiana and New Orleans history, including terrific Mardi Gras exhibits. And Napoleon's death mask. See p. 128.
- **The Insectarium:** Yes, it is what it sounds like. It's especially good for families, but unexpectedly captivating even for the bug-averse. See p. 125.
- **Louisiana Children's Museum:** There's so much hands-on, interactive fun to be had here (for all ages) that you don't even realize you're also learning. See p. 163.
- **New Orleans Museum of Art:** Consistently well-curated exhibits and an excellent permanent collection of all forms of fine art, housed in a stunning, neoclassical-meets-modernist building in the heart of beautiful City Park. See p. 135.
- **Ogden Museum of Southern Art:** A splendid collection of the art of the American South, new and old, in a modern atrium nestled between two historic buildings. See p. 136.
- **Pharmacy Museum:** Leeches and opium and Voodoo spells, oh my. A mightily worthwhile, off-the-wall diversion. See p. 131.
- **The Presbytère:** The excellent exhibit on hurricanes here captures their impact from all aspects; other rotating exhibits are consistently good. See p. 131.
- **Southern Food and Beverage Museum:** Unsurprisingly, given New Orleans' food and drink obsessions, this museum recently moved to much-expanded quarters. A great diversion for anyone with an interest beyond the next meal. See p. 136.
- **World War II Museum:** It's the best museum of its kind. Do not miss the world-class collection and interactive displays here. Period. See p. 135.

NEW ORLEANS IN CONTEXT

Throughout this book, we talk about the mystique of New Orleans and its intoxicating, ineffable essence. But first, it's time for some stats. The largest city in Louisiana (pop. 378,000) and one of the chief cities of the South, New Orleans is nearly 100 miles above the mouth of the Mississippi River system and stretches along a strip of land 5 to 8 miles wide between the Mississippi and Lake Pontchartrain. Surrounded by a river and a lake, the city is largely under sea level. The highest natural point is in City Park, a whopping 35 feet above sea level.

New Orleans has always been known for its jazz-infused joie de vivre, a place where antebellum-meets-bohemia in a high-stepping dance of life, lived fully and out loud. Its recent history, however, is marked by two horrific, well-known events: the Deepwater Horizon oil spill in the nearby Gulf of Mexico, and the failure of the levee system following Hurricane Katrina. But in this, the 10th anniversary year following that devastation, the city is rebounding so palpably that the air fairly prickles with its energy.

In this chapter, we briefly recount the area's rich history, starting with today and then reaching back to its foundation, to help explain how New Orleaneans got their resilient, life-affirming "yatitude" (from "Where y'at?"—the local version of "How ya doin'?").

NEW ORLEANS TODAY

Since Katrina, a new entrepreneurial drive and creative spirit have engulfed the city. Residency, tourism, and convention numbers have increased since a post-Katrina downturn. Construction cranes crisscross the airspace (particularly along Tulane Avenue, where construction of an ambitious new biomedical corridor is under way), and cameras and booms are seemingly everywhere as the local film industry is, well, booming. Rebuilding and startup projects helped protect New Orleans from the depths of the 2008 recession.

The hopping Frenchmen Street club scene shows no sign of stopping, and there are an astounding 600 more restaurants in the city than there were pre-Katrina. The HBO series *Tremé* portrayed authentic New Orleans with a (mostly) spot-on eye and a killer soundtrack, focusing a new fascination on the local culture.

Once untrammeled streets like Oak, Freret, and St. Claude have blossomed with business and activity (Oretha Castle Haley Blvd. is primed to join the list soon). The public schools, rebuilt largely as charters, have the test numbers to confirm that the possible is provable.

Still, all is not rosy. While the tourist zones show zero signs of ill wind, those venturing into certain neighborhoods will still find pristine, rebuilt homes next to abandoned blights. Redevelopment of the decimated Lower 9th Ward is sluggish. It's a massive tabula rasa cleared of its upended homes populated by a few pioneering resettlers and the architectural anachronisms of Make It Right homes (Brad Pitt's foundation). Yet amid their stark backdrop, these homes and their owners embrace their in-your-face presence, as if to proclaim, "Damn right we're here. And we've got *solar panels.*"

The grim images that focused the eyes of the world on New Orleans in August, 2005 are not easily erased, nor should they be. The category 5 storm was downgraded to a category 3 when it hit New Orleans, but the surge was too much for the city's federal levee system. Its failure flooded 80% of the city, causing 1,836 recorded deaths and all form of astounding, horrifying loss. Some 28,000 people took refuge in the Superdome, the ill-prepared refuge of last resort.

Four and a half years later, the Dome's home football team, the New Orleans Saints, at long last came marching in with their first-ever Super Bowl victory. The long-derided 'Aints restored what billions in rebuilding funds couldn't: civic pride.

It may seem trivial, even disrespectful, to cite a football game as a turning point in the city's rebirth—but it isn't. The effects of this real and symbolic victory reached far beyond the ecstatic, extended celebrations—and they cannot be understated. It was one of many high points in 2010: The *prior* week, Mitch Landrieu won the mayoral race with 66% of the vote, marking the end to the previous administration's fumbling, inertia, and corruption. The week *after* the Saints victory, the largest Mardi Gras crowds in 25 years watched the hyper-exultant parades roll. Two months later, a then-record half-million revelers packed the streets for the French Quarter Fest. The good times were rolling once again, at full speed.

And then, the whammy. One. More. Time. (Eye roll, headshake.)

The BP Deepwater Horizon oil spill hit, with potent imagery again painting New Orleans black with a wide, crude brush. In reality, New Orleans is some 150 miles from the spill, and those images of taint were far worse than the reality (though state-mates in the affected areas were hard-hit). New Orleans remained utterly unsullied, and much testing showed the sumptuous Gulf seafood was (and is) safe and plentiful.

Although locals will forever mark time as B.K. or A.K. (Before Katrina or After Katrina), New Orleanans just did what they do: proclaimed their undying love for their city; mixed a cocktail, and set to tidying up. Oh, and throw a few parties for half a million people, and host a Super Bowl, and earn top awards on umpteen "Best of" travel polls.

The indomitable spirit is intact. The oysters are still sweet, the jasmine air still sultry. Rebirth Brass Band still plays the Maple Leaf on Tuesdays, and parades erupt at random. New Orleans is still the best city in the United States, and the *bons temps*—like those beloved Saints of field and song—go marching in and on, and we're right there with them. You should be, too. Go, and be in that number.

HISTORY 101

In the Beginning

In 1682, explorer René-Robert Cavelier, Sieur de la Salle, claimed the region for France, as he had with lands northward to Canada. His navigational and leadership failures in later explorations resulted in his mutinous murder in Texas in 1687 by his own party, fed up with his life-risking demands. Next, at the turn of the 18th century, two French-Canadian brothers led an expedition from France to rediscover the mouth of the Mississippi. The expedition succeeded, and Pierre Le Moyne, Sieur d'Iberville, and 18-year-old Jean Baptiste Le Moyne, Sieur de Bienville, staked a claim at a dramatic bend in the river, near where La Salle had stopped almost 2 decades earlier. Iberville also established a fort at Biloxi. Brother Bienville stayed on there, becoming commanding officer of the territory while harboring thoughts of returning to the spot up the river to establish a new capital city.

In 1718 Bienville got his chance. The French monarch was eager to develop, populate, and garner the riches that Louisiana promised. Bienville was charged with finding a suitable location for a settlement, one that would also protect France's New World holdings from British expansion. Bienville chose the easily defensible high ground at the bend in the river. Although it was some 100 miles inland along the river from the Gulf of Mexico, the site was near St. John's Bayou, a waterway into Lake Pontchartrain. This "back door" was convenient for a military defense or escape, and as a trade route (as the Choctaw Indians had long known)—allowing relatively easy access to the Gulf while bypassing a perilous section of the Mississippi.

The new town was named La Nouvelle-Orléans in honor of the duc d'Orléans, then the regent of France. The "property development" was entrusted to John Law's Company of the West. Following the plan of a late French medieval town, a central square (the Place d'Armes) was laid out with streets forming a grid around it. A church, government office, priest's house, and official residences fronted the square, and earthen ramparts dotted with forts were built around the perimeter. A tiny wooden levee was raised against the river, which still flooded periodically and turned the streets into rivers of mud. Today this area of original settlement is known as the Vieux Carré (old square) and the Place d'Armes as Jackson Square.

A Melting Pot

In its first few years, New Orleans was a community of French officials, adventurers, merchants, slaves, soldiers, and convicts from French prisons, all living in crude huts of cypress, moss, and clay. These were the first ingredients of New Orleans's population gumbo. The city's commerce was mainly limited to trade with native tribes and to instituting agricultural production.

To supply people and capital to the colony, John Law's company essentially pulled the first real estate scam in the New World. The territory and the city were marketed on the continent as Heaven on Earth, full of immediate and boundless opportunities for wealth and luxury. The value of real estate soared, and wealthy Europeans, aristocrats, merchants, exiles, soldiers, and a large contingent of German farmers arrived—to find only mosquitoes, a raw frontier existence, and swampy land. The scheme nearly bankrupted the French nation, but New Orleans' population grew, and in 1723 it replaced Biloxi as the capital of the Louisiana territory.

The next year, Bienville approved the Code Noir, which set forth the laws under which African slaves were to be treated and established Catholicism as the territory's official religion. While it codified slavery and banished Jews from Louisiana, the code did provide slaves recognition and a very slight degree of legal protection, unusual in the South at that time.

Greater New Orleans

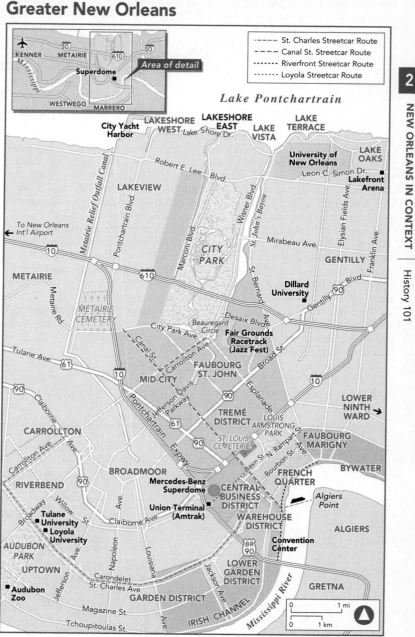

----- St. Charles Streetcar Route
----- Canal St. Streetcar Route
······ Riverfront Streetcar Route
········ Loyola Streetcar Route

KENNER METAIRIE
Superdome
Area of detail
WESTWEGO MARRERO

Lake Pontchartrain

LAKESHORE **LAKESHORE** **LAKE**
WEST **EAST** **TERRACE**
City Yacht Lake Shore Dr. **LAKE**
Harbor **VISTA**

LAKE
OAKS

University of
New Orleans
Leon C. Simon Dr. **Lakefront
Arena**

Robert E. Lee Blvd.

LAKEVIEW

Pontchartrain Blvd.

Wisner Blvd.

St. John's Bayou

Mirabeau Ave.

Franklin Ave.

Elysian Fields Ave.

To New Orleans
Int'l Airport

Metairie Relief Outfall Canal

Marconi Blvd.

**CITY
PARK**

St. Bernard Ave.

GENTILLY

Gentilly Blvd.

METAIRIE

Metairie Rd.

**METAIRIE
CEMETERY**

610

**Dillard
University**

Desaix Blvd.

Beauregard
Circle

City Park Ave.

Canal St.

Carrollton Ave.

Tulane Ave.

**Fair Grounds
Racetrack
(Jazz Fest)**

Broad St.

**FAUBOURG
ST. JOHN**

MID-CITY

Jefferson Davis Parkway

Esplanade

**LOWER
NINTH
WARD**

CARROLLTON

Carrollton Ave.

Claiborne Ave.

Pontchartrain Expwy.

**TREMÉ
DISTRICT**

LOUIS
ARMSTRONG
PARK

N. Rampart St.

Basin St.

Bourbon St.

**ST. LOUIS
CEMETERIES**

**FAUBOURG
MARIGNY**

BYWATER

RIVERBEND

Broadway

Willow St.

BROADMOOR

**Mercedes-Benz
Superdome**

**Union Terminal
(Amtrak)**

Claiborne Ave.

Napoleon Ave.

Louisiana Ave.

**FRENCH
QUARTER**

**CENTRAL
BUSINESS
DISTRICT**

**WAREHOUSE
DISTRICT**

**Convention
Center**

*Algiers
Point*

ALGIERS

**Tulane
University**
**Loyola
University**

**AUDUBON
PARK**

UPTOWN

**Audubon
Zoo**

Jefferson Ave.

Carondelet
St. Charles Ave.

Jackson Ave.

**LOWER
GARDEN
DISTRICT**

GARDEN DISTRICT

Magazine St.

Tchoupitoulas St.

IRISH CHANNEL

Mississippi River

GRETNA

0 .... 1 mi
0 .... 1 km

A lack of potential wives created a significant barrier to population and societal development. In 1727, a small contingent of Ursuline nuns were sent over and established a convent. While the nuns weren't exactly eligible, they did provide a temporary home and education to many subsequent shiploads of *les filles à la cassette*. The "cassette girls" or "casket girls"—named for the government-issue *cassettes* or casketlike trunks in which they carried their possessions—were young women of appropriate character sent to Louisiana by the French government to be courted and married by the colonists. (If we're to believe the current residents of the city, the plan was remarkably successful: Nearly everyone in New Orleans claims descent from the virtuous casket girls or from Spanish or French nobility. By insinuation, that means the colony's motley initial population of convicts and "fallen women" was wholly infertile. Hmm . . .)

John Law's company relinquished its governance of Louisiana in 1731, and the French monarch regained direct control of the territory. In the following decades, planters established estates up and down the river from New Orleans. In the city, wealthier society began to develop a courtly atmosphere on the French model. Amid their rough-and-tumble existence on their plantations, families competed to see who could throw the most opulent parties in their city townhouses.

During the 18th century, colonization of a different sort was taking place to the west, along the Gulf of Mexico. There, many French colonists, displaced by British rule from Acadia, Nova Scotia, made their way south from Canada and formed a rural outpost, where their descendants still live, farm, trap, and speak their unique brand of French to this day. These Acadians' name has been Anglicized, and we know them today as Cajuns.

Meanwhile, New Orleans commercial development was stymied by trading restrictions imposed by France: The colony could trade only with the mother country. To subvert the restrictions, smugglers and pirates provided alternative markets and transportation for the local crops, furs, bricks, and tar.

As the French saw it, the colony was costing them development money, and the return on investment wasn't paying off. In 1762, Louis XV traded the city and all of Louisiana west of the Mississippi to his cousin Charles III of Spain in the secret Treaty of

DATELINE

1682 La Salle stops near the present site while traveling down the Mississippi River from the Great Lakes region and plants a cross claiming the territory for Louis XIV.

1699 Pierre Le Moyne, Sieur d'Iberville, rediscovers and secures the mouth of the Mississippi—on Mardi Gras day.

1718 The first governor of Louisiana, Iberville's brother, Jean-Baptiste Le Moyne, Sieur de Bienville, founds New Orleans.

1723 New Orleans replaces Biloxi as the capital of Louisiana.

1752 Ursuline Convent completed.

1762 Louis XV secretly cedes New Orleans and all of Louisiana west of the Mississippi to Spain.

1768 French residents in New Orleans banish Spanish commissioner Don Antonio de Ulloa, proclaiming independence from Spain.

1769 The Spanish return.

1783 Treaty of Paris confirms Spanish possession.

Fontainebleau. It took 2 years for the news to reach a shocked New Orleans, and the Spanish took 2 more years to send a governor, Don Antonio de Ulloa. He made few friends among local residents, who eventually demanded Ulloa's removal. Some proposed the formation of a Louisiana republic. Ulloa was sent packing, and for a time, New Orleans and Louisiana were effectively independent of any foreign power. That came to a crashing end in 1769 when the Spanish sent forth Don Alexander "Bloody" O'Reilly and 3,000 soldiers. Local leaders of the relatively peaceful rebellion were executed, and Spanish rule was imposed again. With a Gallic shrug, French aristocracy mingled with Spanish nobility, intermarried, and helped to create a new "Creole" culture.

A devastating fire struck in 1788, destroying more than 850 buildings, and again in 1794 in the midst of rebuilding. From the ashes emerged a new architecture dominated by the proud Spanish style of brick-and-plaster buildings replete with arches, courtyards, balconies with their famed cast-iron railings, and, of course, attached slave quarters. Today you'll still see tile markers giving Spanish street names at French Quarter street corners.

The Spanish imposed the same kind of trade restrictions on the city that the French had, with even less success (making for good times for pirates and privateers like the infamous brothers Pierre and Jean Lafitte). Still, this was a period of intense imperial conflict and maneuvering between the Spanish, French, English, and Americans. Spain allowed some American revolutionaries to trade through the city in support of the colonists' fight against Britain, but France rallied and regained possession of the territory in 1800 with a surprisingly quiet transfer of ownership. They held on for 3 years while Napoleon negotiated the Louisiana Purchase with the United States for the paltry (as it turned out) sum of $15 million. For Creole society, the return to French rule was unpleasant enough because France had long been facing serious financial troubles. But a sale to uncouth America was anathema. To their minds, it meant the end of a European lifestyle in the Vieux Carré.

Thus, when Americans arrived in the city, the upper classes made it known that they were welcome to settle—away from the old city and Creole society across Canal Street (so named because a drainage canal was once planned along its route).

1788–94	Fires destroy much of the city; new brick buildings replace wood.	1812	The *New Orleans*, the first steam vessel to travel the Mississippi, arrives from Pittsburgh. Louisiana admitted as a U.S. state.
1794	Planter Etienne de Boré granulates sugar from cane for the first time, spawning a boom in the industry.	1815	Battle of New Orleans.
1795	Treaty of Madrid opens port to Americans; trade thrives.	1831	The first (horse-drawn) railway west of the Alleghenies is completed, linking New Orleans and Milneburg.
1800	Louisiana again becomes a French possession.	1832–33	Yellow fever and cholera epidemic kills 10,000 people in 2 years.
1803	France officially takes possession of the territory. United States then purchases it and takes possession.	1837	First newspaper coverage of Mardi Gras parade.
1805	New Orleans incorporates as a city; first elections are held.		

continues

And so it was that New Orleans came to be two parallel cities. The American section spread outward from Canal Street along St. Charles Avenue; business and cultural institutions centered in the Central Business District; and mansions rose in what is now the Garden District, which was a separate, incorporated city until 1852. French and Creole society dominated the Quarter for the rest of the 19th century, extending toward Lake Pontchartrain along Esplanade Avenue. Soon, however, the Americans (crass though they may have seemed) brought commercial success to the city, which quickly warmed relations—the Americans sought the vitality of downtown society, and the Creoles sought the profit of American business. They also had occasion to join forces against hurricanes, yellow-fever epidemics, and floods.

From the Battle of New Orleans to the Civil War

Perhaps nothing helped to cement a sense of community more than the Battle of New Orleans, during the War of 1812. The great turning point in Creole-American relations was the cooperation of Andrew Jackson and Jean Lafitte (and Choctaw Indians, and black soldiers, not incidentally). To save the city, Jackson set aside his disdain for the pirate, and Lafitte turned down offers to fight for the British, instead supplying the Americans with cannons and ammunition that helped swing the battle in their favor. When Jackson called for volunteers, some 5,000 citizens from both sides of Canal Street responded. At the battle on January 8, 1815, at Chalmette Battlefield (p. 142) a few miles downstream from the city, approximately 2,000 British troops and 20 Americans were killed or wounded. The course of history was changed, Louisiana was incorporated into the Union, and Jackson became a hero—though ironically neither he nor the British had been aware that a treaty concluding the war had been signed a full 2 weeks before, on December 24, 1814. Needless to say, fireworks are gonna fly for the Battle of New Orleans' bicentennial celebration in 2015. (See "New Orleans Calendar of Events," later in this chapter.)

From then until the Civil War, New Orleans was a boomtown. Colonial trade restrictions had evaporated with the Louisiana Purchase, and steam-powered river travel

---

1840 Antoine Alciatore, founder of Antoine's restaurant, arrives from Marseille. New Orleans is the fourth-largest city in the United States and is second only to New York as a port.

1850 Booming commerce totals $200 million; cotton accounts for 45% of total trade. City becomes largest slave market in the country.

1852 New Orleans annexes Lafayette.

1853–55 Yellow fever epidemic during the summer; 12% of the population killed in 1853 in roughly 2 months.

1861–62 Louisiana secedes from the Union; city captured by Admiral Farragut.

1865–77 Reconstruction; "carpetbaggers" swarm into the city, and tensions climax in clashes between the Crescent White League and government forces.

1884–85 Cotton Centennial Exposition (World's Fair) held at the present site of Audubon Park.

1890 Jelly Roll Morton born.

1890 Creole of color Homer Plessy gets arrested riding a train recently segregated by Jim Crow laws. He sues the state, culminating in

arrived in 1812. River commerce exploded, and by the 1840s New Orleans's port was on par with New York's. Cotton and sugar made many local fortunes (on the backs of slave labor); wealthy planters joined the city merchants in building luxurious townhouses and in attending festivals, opera, theater, banquets, parades, and spectacular balls (including "Quadroon Balls," where beautiful mulatto girls were peddled to the male gentry as possible mistresses). As always, politics and gambling were dominant pastimes of these citizens and visitors.

By the middle of the century, cotton-related business was responsible for nearly half of the total commerce in New Orleans, and the city housed a large and ruthless slave market to support it. Paradoxically, New Orleans also had an extensive, established population of "free men (and women) of color" in the American South. Furthermore, racial distinctions within the city became increasingly difficult to determine; people could often trace their ancestry back to two or even three different continents. Adding to the diversity, waves of Irish and German immigrants arrived in New Orleans during this period, supplying important sources of labor to support the city's growth.

The only major impediments to the development of the city in these decades were occasional yellow-fever epidemics, which killed thousands of residents and visitors. Despite the clearing of swampland, the mosquito-borne disease persisted until the final decades of the 19th century.

Reconstruction & Beyond

The boom era ended rather abruptly with the Civil War and Louisiana's secession from the United States in 1861. Federal troops marched into the city in 1862 and stayed until 1877, through the bitter Reconstruction period. Throughout the South, this period saw violent clashes between armed white groups and the state's Reconstruction forces.

After the war, the city went about the business of rebuilding its economic life—without slavery. Without a free labor base, some fortunes crashed, but the city persevered. By 1880, annexations had fleshed out the city limits, port activity had picked up, and railroads were establishing their economic importance. A new group of immigrants, Italians, came to put their unique mark on the city. Through it all, an

the landmark U.S. Supreme Court decision *Plessy v. Ferguson*.

1892 First electric streetcar operates along St. Charles Avenue.

1897 Sidney Bechet born. Storyville established.

1901 Louis Armstrong born.

1911 Razzy Dazzy Spasm Band performs in New York; another band takes its name, adjusting it to Razzy Dazzy Jazzy Band—first use of "jazz."

1917 Original Dixieland Jazz Band attains height of popularity.

1921 Inner-Harbor Navigational Canal built, connecting Lake Pontchartrain and the Mississippi.

1928 Colorful Huey P. Long elected governor of Louisiana; 4 years later he is elected to U.S. Senate.

1935 Long is shot dead.

1938 Tennessee Williams arrives in New Orleans. Huey P. Long Bridge built over Mississippi River.

1939 French Quarter Residents Association formed as an agent for preservation.

continues

undiminished enthusiasm for fun survived. Gambling thrived; there were hundreds of saloons and scores of "bawdy houses" engaged in prostitution (illegal, but uncontrolled). New Orleans was earning an international reputation for open vice, much to the chagrin of the city's polite society.

In 1897, Alderman Sidney Story moved all illegal (but highly profitable) activities into a restricted district along Basin Street next to the French Quarter, in an effort to improve the city's tarnishing image. Quickly nicknamed Storyville, the district boasted fancy "sporting palaces" with elaborate decor, musical entertainment, and a wide variety of ladies of pleasure. The *Blue Book* directory listed the names, addresses, and races of more than 700 prostitutes, working the swanky "palaces" down to the decrepit "cribs." Black musicians such as Jelly Roll Morton played in the more ornate bordellos, popularizing early forms of jazz. When the Secretary of the Navy decreed in 1917 that armed forces should not be exposed to so much open vice, Storyville closed down and disappeared—with nary a trace beyond its great cultural impact.

The 20th Century

The 20th century found the city's port becoming the largest in the United States and the second-busiest in the world (after Amsterdam), with goods coming in by barge and rail. Electrification and other modern technology kept the port whirring. Drainage problems were conquered by means of high levees, canals, pumping stations, and great spillways, which direct floodwater away from the city. Bridges were built across the Mississippi River, including the Huey P. Long Bridge, named after Louisiana's famous politician and demagogue. New Orleans's emergence as a regional financial center, with more than 50 commercial banks, led to the construction of soaring office buildings, mostly in the Central Business District. World War II grew a thriving shipbuilding business, which was replaced by the expansion of oil, gas, and petrochemical businesses after the war. Later in the 20th century, tourism became another primary economic driver.

Like most other American cities, the city's population spread outward, filling suburbs and nearby municipalities. A thriving community in New Orleans East was

---

1956 Lake Pontchartrain Causeway, world's longest bridge, completed.

1960 The city's public schools integrated.

1973 Parades banned in the Vieux Carré, changing the character of the city's observance of Mardi Gras.

1975 Superdome opens.

1976 Anne Rice publishes best-selling *Interview with the Vampire*, set in New Orleans.

1977 Ernest N. "Dutch" Morial becomes first African-American mayor.

1984 Louisiana World Expo draws disappointing crowds but spurs redevelopment of the riverside area.

1988 Anne Rice moves back to New Orleans, spawning a frenzy of fans flocking to her Garden District home.

1999 Harrah's opens new casino.

developed by Vietnamese refugees, who immigrated in the 1970s. Unlike other cities, however, New Orleans has been able to preserve its original town center and much of its historic architecture.

NEW ORLEANS IN POPULAR CULTURE

Books

You can fill many bookcases with New Orleans literature and authors, so consider the following list as just a starter kit. Get more recommendations at the fine bookshops listed in chapter 9.

GENERAL FICTION

There are many examples of early fiction that give a good taste of old-time New Orleans life. George Washington Cable's stories are revealing and colorful, as in *Old Creole Days* (1879). Perhaps the best writer to touch on the lives of the earliest Creoles is Kate Chopin, whose late-1800s works, including the revered *The Awakening,* are set in Louisiana.

Frances Parkinson Keyes lived on Chartres Street from 1945 to 1970. Her most famous works are *Dinner at Antoine's* and *Madame Castel's Lodger,* each with curious descriptions of life in the city at that time, along with excellent descriptions of food.

Ellen Gilchrist's contemporary fiction, including the short-story collection *In the Land of Dreamy Dreams,* portrays life in wealthy uptown New Orleans. Sheila Bosworth's wonderful tragicomedies perfectly sum up the city and its collection of characters—check out all-time favorites *Almost Innocent* or *Slow Poison.* Other possibilities are Nancy Lemann's delightful *Lives of the Saints* and Michael Ondaatje's controversial *Coming Through Slaughter,* a fictionalized account of Buddy Bolden and the early New Orleans jazz era.

Newer favorites include Moira Crone's sci-fi thriller *The Not Yet,* which sets the city in a future even stranger than the present; and Michael Zell's challenging but satisfying

2000	The National World War II Museum opens. Mardi Gras 2000 draws record crowds.		offshore spill in U.S. history—BP Deepwater Horizon despoils Gulf of Mexico.
2005	City floods when levees fail following Hurricane Katrina.	2012	Census shows city has reached 75% of its pre-Katrina population.
2010	"Who Dat" frenzy: underdog Saints win NFL Super Bowl championship for first time in the team's 43-year history. HBO's *Tremé* TV series debuts. Worst	2015	Bicentennial of Battle of New Orleans victory.
		2018	City of New Orleans' 300th anniversary.

thriller *Errata.* In the perennially popular, well-crafted series by James Lee Burke, misfit Cajun detective Dave Robicheaux keeps the bad guys running and the pages turning.

And then there is the cottage industry known as Anne Rice, who undeniably ignited the current era of pop vampire culture (bow to the master, *True Blood, Twilight,* and *Vampire Diaries*). Her now-classic *Vampire Chronicles* books expertly capture the city's spooky, elegant essence.

HISTORY

Lyle Saxon's *Fabulous New Orleans* is the most charming place to start learning about the city's past. (Saxon was director of the writer's program under the WPA.) From there, move on to his coauthored folk-tale collection, *Gumbo Ya-Ya.* Roark Bradford's novel, *Kingdom Coming,* covers Voodoo in the Civil War era. Mark Twain visited the city often in his riverboat days, and his *Life on the Mississippi* has a good number of tales about New Orleans and its riverfront life. *The WPA Guide to New Orleans* also contains excellent social and historical background and provides a fascinating picture of the city in 1938. *Beautiful Crescent,* by Joan Garvey and Mary Lou Widmer, is a solid reference book on the history of New Orleans. Those who loved *Gangs of New York* will be pleased to learn Herbert Asbury gave the same highly entertaining, not terribly factual treatment to New Orleans in *The French Quarter: An Informal History of the New Orleans Underworld.* New Orleans's favorite patroness, the Baroness de Pontalba, gets the biography treatment in Christina Vella's *Intimate Enemies.* In *The Last Madam: A Life in the New Orleans Underworld,* Christine Wiltz reveals a bawdy bygone era, conveyed through the words of Norma Wallace. The brothel owner recorded her memoirs before her 1974 suicide.

Three newer, eminently readable histories are Ned Sublette's *The World That Made New Orleans,* which focuses on the cultural influences of European, African, and Caribbean settlers; Lawrence Powell's *Accidental City,* a definitive look back at the city's scrappy evolution; and the elegantly entangled *Unfathomable City,* a coffee table atlas with essays by Rebecca Solnit and Rebecca Snedecker.

Of the many guides to Mardi Gras, Henri Schindler's *Mardi Gras New Orleans* account is that of a historian and a long-term producer of balls and parades. *Mardi Gras in New Orleans: An Illustrated History* is a concise history of the celebration from ancient times to 2001, produced by *Mardi Gras Guide* publisher Arthur Hardy.

Lovers of the lurid will enjoy *Madame LaLaurie,* a well-researched biography of the notorious, high-society murderess. Sara Roahen's charming *Gumbo Tales: Finding My Place at the New Orleans Table* leaves readers hungering for more of her uproarious outsider's insights, as the recent transplant to New Orleans discovers the culture through its distinctive food and drink.

Speaking of which, in *The Fish That Ate the Whale: The Life and Times of America's Banana King,* Rich Cohen recounts the rags-to-riches-to-revolution tale of local fruit magnate Sam Zemurray.

LITERATURE

William Faulkner came to New Orleans, lived on Pirate's Alley, and penned *Soldiers' Pay.* Several other Faulkner novels and short stories are set in New Orleans. Tennessee Williams became a devoted New Orleans fan, living in the city on and off for many years. It inspired him to write *A Streetcar Named Desire,* one of the best-known New Orleans tales. He also set *The Rose Tattoo* in the city.

Other notable New Orleans writers include Walker Percy and Shirley Ann Grau. Percy's novels, including *The Moviegoer* and *Love in the Ruins,* are classic portrayals of the idiosyncrasies of New Orleans and its residents. Grau's most famous novel, *The Keepers of the House,* won the Pulitzer Prize in 1964. John Kennedy Toole also received a Pulitzer, but he wasn't around to know about it, having committed suicide years before. At the time of his death, none of his works had even been published. Toole's *A Confederacy of Dunces* is a timeless New Orleans tragicomedy that'll have you laughing out loud.

Robert Penn Warren's classic novel *All the King's Men,* an exceedingly loose telling of the story of Huey P. Long, makes the list because it's so good—and because it gives a portrait of the performance art known as Louisiana politics.

A further notable modern writer is Robert Olen Butler, who won the Pulitzer in 1993 for his collection of stories, *A Good Scent from a Strange Mountain,* set primarily in New Orleans's Vietnamese community.

POST-KATRINA LITERATURE

It's true that from great tragedy comes great art, and the following help shape an image of pre- and post-flood New Orleans. Tom Piazza's *Why New Orleans Matters* is a love letter to and about the city and the number one choice for people trying to "get" New Orleans. His novel, *City of Refuge,* bisects Katrina through the experiences of two families. Rosemary James, of Faulkner House Books, edited *My New Orleans,* a collection of essays by locals ranging from writers to restaurateurs and raconteurs, attempting to pin down just what it is about this place that keeps them here, come hell or high water. Local historian Douglas Brinkley's meticulous *The Great Deluge* may not end up the definitive postmortem examination of Katrina, but it will be hard to top. *Times-Picayune* columnist Chris Rose collected his heartbreaking personal essays, written as he and his colleagues covered their flooded city, in *1 Dead in Attic,* while Pulitzer Prize-winning journalist Sherri Fink recounts the complexities of the tragic *Five Days at Memorial.*

Zeitoun, Dave Eggers' gripping narrative nonfiction, recounts the tale of one man's horror and a nation's injustice (look up Zeitoun's even more shocking post-publication story for a completely different perspective), while *New Yorker* columnist Dan Baum weaves together differing perspectives to illustrate how the multihued city unifies nine diverse narratives in *Nine Lives.*

Finally, fans of football and motivational memoirs may enjoy *Home Team* by Saints coach Sean Payton or Drew Brees' *Coming Back Stronger.*

BOOKS ABOUT MUSIC

Ann Allen Savoy's *Cajun Music Vol. 1* is a combination songbook and oral history featuring previously un-transcribed Cajun music with lyrics in French (including a pronunciation guide) and English. A labor of many years, it's a definitive work and invaluable resource.

For a look at specific time periods, people, and places in the history of New Orleans jazz, you have a number of choices. They include William Carter's *Preservation Hall;* John Chilton's *Sidney Bechet: The Wizard of Jazz;* Gunther Schuller's *Early Jazz: Its Roots and Musical Development;* the excellent *A Trumpet Around the Corner: The Story of New Orleans Jazz,* by Samuel Charters; *New Orleans Jazz: Images of America,* by Edward Branley; and *New Orleans Style,* by Bill Russell. Al Rose's *Storyville, New Orleans* is an excellent source of information about the very beginnings of jazz; while *Up From the Cradle of Jazz* tells its story post-WWII. *Songs of My Fathers* is Tom Sancton's fine retelling of his boyhood at the feet of the great Preservation Hall musicians.

If you prefer primary sources, read Louis Armstrong's *Satchmo: My Life in New Orleans,* or *Satchmo: The Wonderful World and Art of Louis Armstrong,* a bio by way of his own artworks. We also suggest Sidney Bechet's *Treat It Gentle,* and the story of Mac Rebennack's (aka Dr. John) wild life as reflected in *Under a Hoodoo Moon.* Ben Sandmel's exhaustively researched *Ernie K-Doe: the R&B Emperor of New Orleans* can't help but be entertaining, given the subject.

Film & Television

With atmosphere and mystery to spare, all forms of water and roadways, new and old architecture, and attractive tax incentives, film and TV production is nonstop here in "Hollywood South." The city isn't a character in all of them, but it's the heart of the highly authentic HBO series *Tremé.* If you come across the stellar, little-seen series *Frank's Place* (1987–88), don't miss it. *True Blood* is filmed mostly in Baton Rouge, but that's okay.

Consider these for some pre- or post-visit flavor: classics like Brando in *A Streetcar Named Desire* (1951); Betty Davis in *Jezebel* (1938); the kitschy but decent Elvis vehicle *King Creole* (1958); and counterculture Mardi Gras freak-out *Easy Rider.* *Belizaire the Cajun* (1986) tells of the violence between 19th-century Cajuns and English speakers; Tom Waits bums around the city, the countryside, and jail in the indie *Down by Law* (1986); and a young Brooke Shields navigates a Storyville childhood in Louis Malle's *Pretty Baby* (1978). Then there's the steamy but flawed (and locally derided) *The Big Easy.* Brad Pitt ages backwards in *The Curious Case of Benjamin Button* (2008) and goes fang to fang with Tom Cruise in *Interview with the Vampire* (1994). Nic Cage just goes all Nic Cage in *Bad Lieutenant: Port of Call New Orleans* (2009). The Oscar-nominated *Beasts of the Southern Wild* (2012) set its powerful magic realism in the Louisiana bayous. Lastly, for kids of any age, when *Abbott & Costello Go to Mars* (1953), they end up at Mardi Gras—an altogether different universe.

All of the late, very great Les Blank's documentaries on Louisiana are worthy, but start with *Always for Pleasure* (1978). Documentaries about the Katrina experience cover every angle, notably in Spike Lee's *When the Levees Broke;* the remarkable, Oscar-nominated *Trouble the Water;* the superb prize-winning *Faubourg Tremé: The Untold Story of Black New Orleans;* and Harry Shearer's exposé *The Big Uneasy.*

Recordings

Oh, boy. Well, the selections listed below should give you a good start, though we could fill pages more (and we're barely even touching on the many fine pop, rock, or folky contributions). Also see the names listed in the Nightlife section (p. 167), and for more advice or recommendations, consult the über-helpful know-it-alls at **Louisiana Music Factory** (see p. 197).

CROSS-GENRE ANTHOLOGIES

There are many collections and anthologies of New Orleans and Louisiana music available, including the 1990s Alligator Stomp series by Rhino Records. The most comprehensive, critically acclaimed *Doctors, Professors, Kings & Queens: The Big Ol' Box of New Orleans* is a four-disc package released in 2004 by Shout! Factory and the one collection that touches all the bases of the diverse musical gumbo that is the Crescent City. For a more modest taste, order up the *Tremé, Season 1* soundtrack, which covers a bit of the same fertile, funky ground, albeit just from recent years.

JAZZ

A classic New Orleans jazz collection starts with the originators: King Oliver, Kid Ory, Sidney Bechet, Original Dixieland Jazz Band, and Jellyroll Morton, say. Add some early Louis Armstrong, with his Hot Five and Hot Seven bands.

Ken Burns' Jazz box covers them and more from New Orleans and beyond, and the anthologies *New Orleans* (Atlantic Jazz), *Recorded in New Orleans Volumes 1 and 2* (Good Time Jazz), and *New Orleans Jazz* (Arhoolie) are good choices. Preservation Hall's *Preservation* covers the classics; Pete Fountain, Al Hirt (try *Honey in the Horn*), and Louis Prima (*The Wildest*) all swing things in a new direction.

Leaping forward, Wynton Marsalis, Terrance Blanchard, clarinetist Tim Laughlin and Harry Connick, Jr. build on those traditions, and trumpeters Irvin Mayfield and Nicolas Payton push them forward. Terrific old-time revivalists like the New Orleans Jazz Vipers, Meschiya Lake (check out *Lucky Devil*), the Smoking Time Jazz Band, Debbie Davies, and Aurora Nealand are well worth the cost of a disc or a download.

BRASS BANDS

The age-old tradition of brass-oriented street bands underwent a spectacular revival in the 1980s and 1990s with the revitalization of such long-term presences as the Olympia Brass Band and the arrival of newcomers like the Dirty Dozen Brass Band (try their monster anthology *This Is the Dirty Dozen Brass Band*). They inspired a younger and funkier generation, including Grammy winners Rebirth Brass Band, New Birth, the Hot 8, the Stooges, up-and-comers TBC, hybridists the Brass-a-Holics, and the Soul Rebels, perhaps the best of the crowd. It's all better live, so get ye to the clubs or try *The Main Event: Live at the Maple Leaf*, or the loose, bumping *Rock with the Hot 8*. Alternately, *I Am a Brass-a-Holic* is not live but is irresistibly bumping.

RHYTHM, BLUES & SOUL

First things first: Get your Fats on with *My Blue Heaven* or any "Best of" compilation. Then get Dr. John's *Gumbo* or *Mos Scocious: The Dr. John Anthology*. Round out your legends collection with Professor Longhair's *'Fess: The Professor Longhair Anthology* and fellow key wizard James Booker's *Classified: Remixed*. Go down funk road with the Meters' classic *Cissy Strut* and *The Wild Tchoupitoulas* for Mardi Gras Indian funk. Ivan Neville's Dumpstaphunk band is keeping the funk alive, while Galactic might be funk, might be jazz, could be rock or jam—but is never uninteresting. Start with *Ruckus*. Trombone Shorty rocks jazz, R&B, funk, and hip hop into his own thang, turning out monster hits like the recent *Say That to This*. We're true to hometown heroes the Neville Brothers' *Yellow Moon* and *Treacherous: A History of the Neville Brothers, 1955–1985*. *Songbook* shows why producer/writer Allen Toussaint is a true icon. Also get some soul crooners in, like Soul Queen Irma Thomas' *Time Is on My Side* and Johnny Adams' *Heart & Soul*. Worthwhile anthologies include *The Best of New Orleans Rhythm & Blues Volumes 1 and 2; Sehorn's Soul Farm;* and *The Mardi Gras Indians Super Sunday Showdown*.

HIP HOP & BOUNCE

New Orleans's distinctive hip hop and rap scene produced numerous stars and a home-grown subgenre: booty-dropping, second-line-influenced, twerk-propagating bounce.

It began with Big Freedia, who must be experienced live, but *Just Be Free* will do. Breakout dirty Southerner Juvenile's *400* is a classic, while hip hop star Lil Wayne's breakout flow on *Tha Carter II* still holds up massively. The risqué rhymes on Mystikal's eponymous debut broke musical ground before legal troubles sidelined his career.

EATING & DRINKING

Where oh where to start? Is there any other American city so revered, so identified with the glory of gluttony and the joy of the juice than New Orleans? Perhaps, but none with a truly indigenous cuisine (or two), none that lay claim (rightly or not) to inventing the cocktail, and surely none that goes about it with such unbridled gusto. As the oft-repeated homily goes: In most places, people eat to live; in New Orleans, people live to eat. Seriously, you're only visiting, so convince your tortured psyche that you can resume a sensible diet when you get home and immerse yourself in the local culture. In other words, *indulge*. It's so very worth it. A very strident vegan friend gave it up for a few days while here (yes, really), though most chefs, and certainly those in the better restaurants, are adept at adapting to any specified "isms" or dietary restriction. The single most important thing to know? *Make reservations.*

Chapter 11 has much more about Cajun and Creole food. Chapter 8 has cocktailing info. And chapter 6, "Where to Dine in New Orleans," points you to the top troughs.

WHEN TO GO

With the possible exception of July and August (unless you thrive on heat and humidity), just about any time is the right time to go to New Orleans. We love the warm, jasmine-infused nights and warmer days of mid-fall and spring best, and even relish the occasional high drama of a good summer thunderstorm.

It's important to know what's going on when, since the city's landscape, and hotel availability and rates, can change dramatically depending on what events or conventions are on. Mardi Gras is, of course, the hardest time of year to get a hotel room, but it can also be difficult during major festivals (French Quarter Fest, Jazz & Heritage Festival, Essence) and sporting events (BCS, Sugar Bowl, Saints and LSU Superdome games). New Orleans isn't recognized as a holiday destination, but in December it's gussied up with decorations, there are all kinds of holiday special events, and the weather is quite fine. Eager hotels often have good deals, and many restaurants offer special prix fixe "Réveillon" deals. Take advantage of it.

The Weather

The average mean temperature in New Orleans is an inviting 70°F (21°C), but it can drop or rise considerably in a single day. (It can be 40°F/4°C and rain one day, 80°F/27°C and humidity the next.) Conditions depend primarily on whether it rains and whether there is direct sunlight or cloud cover. Rain can provide slight and temporary relief on a hot day; it tends to hit in sudden (and sometimes dramatically heavy) showers, which disappear as quickly as they arrive. In unimpeded sun it gets much warmer. The high humidity can intensify even mild warms and colds. Still, the semitropical climate is part of New Orleans's appeal—the slight moistness makes for lush, sensual air.

If you can stand it, do consider braving the city in summer; the tourist business slows down a tad, which produces hotel bargains. On a recent July visit, high-end hotels were offering rooms from $89 to $129 (way, *way* below their regular rates), sometimes with additional perks thrown in. Plus, you can often get upgrades to fancy suites for a song—ask when you check in. In August, local restaurants run bargain, prix-fixe "**COOLinary**" specials (www.coolinaryneworleans.com). Yeah, it's hot and humid, bearable for some, miserable for others—but there are always plenty of air-conditioned respites to duck into.

New Orleans should be pleasant most of the year. During the muggy, bargain summer months, follow the natives' example: stay out of the midday sun and duck from one air-conditioned locale to another. June and September can still be humid and warm; early spring and mid-fall are glorious. Winter is mild by American standards—but don't expect Florida warmth—and punctuated by an occasional freeze-level cold snap. But *unpredictable* and *flexible* are the watchwords. The whims of the weather gods are at play, so be ready to adjust accordingly.

Hurricane season runs June 1 to November 30. Obviously, there are no guarantees, but despite the high drama of recent years, severe storms are fairly rare. In the height of summer, T-shirts, shorts, and tissue-weight fabrics are acceptable everywhere except the finest restaurants. In the spring and fall, something a little warmer is in order; in the winter, carry a mid-weight coat or jacket and pack a folding umbrella (though they're available everywhere, as are cheap rain ponchos for unexpected downpours). The biggest summertime climate problem can be the air-conditioning overcompensation that chills rooms—especially restaurants—to meat-locker-like temps, so bring those light wraps along even on warm nights.

New Orleans's Average Temperatures & Rainfall

	JAN	FEB	MAR	APR	MAY	JUNE	JULY	AUG	SEPT	OCT	NOV	DEC
HIGH (°F)	62	65	71	78	85	89	91	90	87	80	71	65
HIGH (°C)	17	18	22	26	29	32	33	32	31	27	22	18
LOW (°F)	43	46	52	58	66	71	73	73	70	60	50	45
LOW (°C)	6	8	11	14	19	22	23	23	21	16	10	7
DAYS OF RAINFALL	10	9	9	7	8	11	14	13	10	6	7	10

New Orleans Calendar of Events

For more information on **Mardi Gras, Jazz Fest, Festival Internationale,** and other major area events, see chapter 4, "Mardi Gras & Jazz Fest." For general information, contact the **New Orleans Metropolitan Convention and Visitors Bureau,** 2020 St. Charles Ave., New Orleans, LA 70130 (www.neworleanscvb.com, ℂ **800/672-6124** or 504/566-5011). For a list of other Louisiana festivals, visit www.laffnet.org.

JANUARY

Allstate Sugar Bowl Classic. First held in 1934, this is New Orleans's oldest yearly sporting occasion. The football game in the Superdome is the main event, but in the days just beforehand, look for a second line parade to kick off the festivities, and a massive Fan Fest in the French Quarter. www.allstatesugarbowl.org; ℂ **504/828-2440.** January 1, 2015.

Battle of New Orleans Bicentennial. Expect cannons to be fired, reenactors to be out in full force, and a comprehensive exhibit at the Presbytere Museum (p. 131) as the city celebrates its victory in the war of 1812. www.battleofneworleans2015.com; ✆ **504/589-4428.** January 9 to 11, 2015.

FEBRUARY

Lundi Gras. This tradition brings a free, outdoor music-and-food celebration to Spanish Plaza (Poydras St. at the river), with the big event at 6pm: the ceremonial, waterfront arrival of the Kings of Rex and Zulu, marking the beginning of Mardi Gras. They're welcomed by the mayor, fireworks, and much whoop-de-doo. ✆ **504/522-1555.** See also p. 42. Monday before Mardi Gras (Feb 16, 2015; Feb 8, 2016).

Mardi Gras. The culmination of the 2-month-long carnival season, Mardi Gras is the centuries-old annual blowout. Each year the eyes of the world are on New Orleans, as the entire city stops working and starts partying, and the streets are taken over by awe-inspiring parades. See chapter 4. Day before Ash Wednesday (February 17, 2015; February 9, 2016).

MARCH

St. Patrick's Day Parades. There are several, with dates (like the paraders) usually staggered. Instead of Mardi Gras beads, watchers are pelted with veggies, including the coveted cabbages. In 2015, a funky French Quarter parade kicks off at Molly's at the Market (1107 Decatur St.) on Friday, March 13, at 6pm. On St. Patrick's Day (Tuesday, March 17, 2015), the downtown parade begins at 6pm at Burgundy and Piety in the Bywater and stumbles along a route to Bourbon Street (www.stpatricksdayneworleans. com; ✆ **504/525-5169**).

St. Joseph's Day Parade. Another fascinating, little-known festivity. Italians venerate St. Joseph, patron saint of families and working men, on his saint's day (March 19) with a parade (usually the weekend before) and the creation of devotional altars. These moving, elaborate works of art feature food, candles, and statues and can be viewed at various churches and private homes (where you might also get fed), and at the American Italian Museum, 537 St. Peters St. Locations are listed in the *Times-Picayune* classifieds and on www.nola.com prior to the event. ✆ **504/522-7294.**

Super Sunday. This annual Mardi Gras Indians showdown takes place on the Sunday nearest St. Joseph's Day (March 19). The more organized "uptown" event is in A.L. Davis Park, Washington Avenue and LaSalle Street, from noon till late afternoon. Indian tribes garbed in full, feathered regalia gather to preen, parade, and engage in ritualized showdowns with traditional chants (with food booths and music, of course). The "downtown" Indians have a much looser street meeting, determined by weather or whim a few weeks or even months after St. Joseph's Day, usually on Bayou St. John at Orleans Avenue. Another Indian gathering, Big Sunday, is tentatively scheduled for March 19. Both are intentionally underannounced, but check with the Backstreet Museum (p. 134) or www.wwoz.org/inthe street. Mid-March. More on p. 43.

Tennessee Williams New Orleans Literary Festival. This 5-day series celebrates New Orleans's rich literary heritage with theatrical performances, readings, discussions, master classes, musical events, walking tours, and the ever-popular Stella Shouting Contest. It's not exclusive to Williams, and the roster of writers and publishers participating is impressive. Info at www.tennesseewilliams. net or ✆ **504/581-1144.** March 25 to 29, 2015.

APRIL

The Crescent City Classic. This 10k race from Jackson Square to Audubon Park brings an international field of top (and lesser) runners to the city. www.ccc10k.com; ✆ **504/861-8686.** Saturday before Easter. April 4, 2015.

French Quarter Festival. The 3½-day French Quarter Festival celebrates local music of the traditional jazz, brass band, Cajun/zydeco, or funk variety. The free event has become wildly popular (maybe too much so?): In 2014, 733,000 people attended. There are scores of outdoor concerts, food booths, art shows, children's activities, tours, and seminars set throughout the Quarter, making it easy to return to your hotel room for a rest, though some stages are at far-flung ends of the Quarter. Book travel early; this good time is becoming a victim of its own success. www.fqfi.org; ✆ **800/673-5725** or 504/522-5730. April 9 to 12, 2015.

Festival International de Louisiane. Some people split their festing between Jazz Fest and the popular (read: big) Festival International in Lafayette. The free, 5-day street fair, which focuses on French music and culture, overlaps with the first weekend of Jazz Fest so it dovetails nicely. See p. 48. www.festivalinternational.com; ✆ **337/232-8086.** April 22 to 26, 2015.

New Orleans Jazz & Heritage Festival presented by Shell (Jazz Fest). A 10-day event that draws musicians, cooks, and craftspeople and their fans to celebrate music and life, Jazz Fest rivals Mardi Gras in popularity. Much more information in chapter 4. www.nojazzfest.com; ✆ **504/410-4100.** April 24 to May 3, 2015.

MAY

Mid-City Bayou Boogaloo. Another weekend, another laid-back New Orleans music, art, and food fest. This one's themeless, with the pretty location along Bayou St. John (and the rubber-ducky derby) being the draw for the largely local crowd. Bring a blanket, a parasol, and cash for snacks and brews, and go now before it gets too huge. www.thebayouboogaloo.com; ✆ **504/488-3865.** May 15 to 17, 2015.

New Orleans Wine & Food Experience. Some 11,000 people attend this 4-day gourmandistic pleasure, at which 150 vintners, 75 restaurants, and myriad chefs feature their wines and wares via tastings, seminars, and vintner dinners. The culmination is a grand, 2-day tasting held in the Superdome, but the party might really hit its stride with the Royal Street Stroll, where revelers indulge their way from one tasting station to the next along the closed street. www.nowfe.com; ✆ **504/529-9463.** May 20 to 23, 2015.

Oyster Festival. Aw shucks, it's a weekend dedicated to slurping delicious gulf oysters and listening to live music while overlooking the Mississippi River. Local restaurants serve up their best bivalve recipes and pro shuckers compete, all to promote the centuries-old local oyster fishing industry. Admission is free. And it's still mostly a locals' fest. For now. www.neworleansoysterfestival.org; ✆ **504/888-7608.** May 30 to 31, 2015.

JUNE

Creole Tomato Fest. This sweet, smallish fest set in the French Market celebrates the 'mater with cooking demos, tastings, a Tomato Parade, and music of course. www.frenchmarket.org; ✆ **504/522-2621.** June 6 to 7, 2015.

Cajun Zydeco Festival. This growing, free fest sponsored by Jazz Fest recently relocated to Armstrong Park in the Tremé. Expect plenty of two-stepping, a few waltzes, lessons for both, arts markets, kids' activities, and yes, food booths with a seafood focus. www.jazzandheritage.org/cajun-zydeco; ✆ **504/558-6100.** June 13 to 14, 2015.

JULY

Essence Music Festival. This massive, 3-day event sponsored by *Essence* magazine consistently presents a stellar lineup of R&B, soul, and hip hop musicians (like Beyoncé, Kanye West, Mary J. Blige, Prince, Chaka Khan, and George Clinton) in evening concerts on a main stage and clublike "Super Lounges." During the day, this "party with a purpose" offers educational and empowerment seminars featuring A-list (Cosby! Oprah!) speakers and celebs, crafts, and trade fairs. In 2014, ticket prices started at $58 for a single day; $1,100 for VIP. www.essencemusicfestival.com. July 2 to 5, 2015.

Go Fourth on the River. The annual Fourth of July celebration begins in the morning along the French Quarter riverfront and culminates with a spectacular fireworks display at 9pm. www.go4ontheriver.com; ✆ **800/672-6124.** July 4.

Tales of the Cocktail. This 5-day mixtravaganza celebrates all things liquor. Based at the Monteleone Hotel but pouring over into other venues, it's a scholarly gathering of 20,000 hospitality professionals, serious mixologists, and admirers of the cocktail culture. (Read: If you make your own bitters and take 10 minutes to mix a drink, this might be for you. If your drink of choice is a PBR or whiskey neat, pass). The popular events, including "Spirited Dinners" (food and cocktail pairings at local restaurants), fill up fast. Go to www.talesofthecocktail.com. July 15 to 19, 2015.

AUGUST

Satchmo Summerfest. Louis Armstrong, hometown boy made very good, is celebrated with his own festival, held around his real birthday (he claimed to be born on July 4, but records prove otherwise). There's food, music, kids' activities, and seminars, with the emphasis on jazz entertainment and education to ensure that Satchmo lives on. www.fqfi.org; ✆ **504/522-5730.** July 31 to August 2, 2015.

The Rayne Frog Festival. Cajuns can always find an excuse to hold a party, and here the humble frog begets a *fais-do-do* (dance), waltz competition, and frog-racing, -jumping, and -eating contests. For the amphibian-deprived, there's even a Rent-a-Frog service. Gotta love it. www.raynefrogfestival.com; ✆ **800/346-1958** in the U.S., 800/543-5340 in Canada, or 337/232-3808. Mid-August.

SEPTEMBER

Southern Decadence. This multiday, multinight dance/party/raunchfest attracts more than 100,000 gay men (and some women) from around the world. The frenzied peak is during the bar-studded parade route. Book rooms early or get a weekend ticket package in advance to save line time; and even if *you're* not too hot for leather, September in New Orleans is. www.southerndecadence. net; ✆ **504/522-8047.** Labor Day weekend, September 3 to September 7, 2015.

OCTOBER

Festivals Acadiens & Creoles. Much smaller than the nearby Francophone-focused **Festival International** (see April), this Lafayette event doesn't conflict with Jazz Fest. It combines the **Bayou Food Festival,** the **Festival de Musique Acadienne,** and the **Louisiana Native Crafts Festival.** Players, bring your instruments—there's a jam tent. It's fun, easygoing, tasty, and free, so spend freely to help keep it going. www.festivalsacadiens.com; ✆ **800/346-1958** in the U.S., 800/543-5340 in Canada, or 337/232-3737. October 2015; call or check website for exact dates.

Crescent City Blues & BBQ Festival. A recent rash of credible BBQ restaurants might finally be changing the city's low profile in the pantheon of great BBQ destinations. They'll be strutting their stuff at this free fest, located in Lafayette Park in the Central Business District. Add two stages for blues tunes, a good line-up, and consider our folding chairs packed. This one is set to blow up. www.jazzandheritage.org/blues-fest; ✆ **504/558-6100.** October 16 to 18, 2015.

Halloween. Halloween is celebrated especially grandly here in the ghostly city, rivaling Mardi Gras for costume outrageousness. The French Quarter is Halloween central (especially for the LGBT crowd), but ghoulish action around the city includes Boo-at-the-Zoo (last 2 weekends in October) for kids; the spooky Mortuary Haunted House in Mid-City (www.themortuary.net); and the truly terrifying House of Shock on the outskirts of town (www.houseofshock.com). October 31 and surrounding days.

Ponderosa Stomp. This weekend celebration of early American rock is a mecca for fans and students of all things roots—blues, twang, swamp, thrash, or beyond—who attend scholarly daytime conferences, and nighttime concerts by seminal but largely unheralded performers. www.ponderosastomp.org; ✆ **504/810-9116.** Fall 2015; call or check website for exact dates.

Voodoo Music + Arts Experience. The monstrous 3-day Voodoo Fest draws 150,000 youngish people to the City Park festival grounds, where over 100 acts fill 6 stages and a huge dance space. The diverse lineup features major stars from Metallica to Macklemore and Skrillex to Snoop Dogg, plus up-and-comers and a solid crop of locals. Eclectic art and exotic performances, Halloween-costumed people-watching, and food and drink round out the available diversions. Tickets range from $125 to $1,000. www.worshipthemusic.com. October 30 to November 1, 2015.

NOVEMBER

Words & Music: A Literary Fest in New Orleans. This highly ambitious literary and music conference offers round-table discussions with eminent authors with varying connections to the city; original drama, poetry readings, master classes, and writing competitions. www.wordsandmusic.org; ✆ **504/586-1609.** Mid-November.

Po-Boy Festival. You could just go to the participating restaurants any other day of the year—surely the wait will be shorter—but there probably won't be a blessing of the po' boy. This one-day fest along Oak Street is crazy crowded, but there are indeed some dang deelish sandwiches and it's a fun locals' scene. www.poboyfest.com. Late November.

DECEMBER

Christmas, New Orleans Style. It's no surprise that the ever-celebratory New Orleaneans do Christmas really well. The town is decorated to a fare-thee-well and there are nightly concerts in St. Louis Cathedral and candlelit caroling in Jackson Square (Dec 20, 2015). Bonfires line the levees along the River Road on Christmas Eve (to guide Papa Noël, in his alligator-drawn sled), and house tours offer glimpses of stunningly turned-out residences. Lowered room rates and discounted "Réveillon" restaurant dinners also make this an economically attractive time to visit. www.neworleansonline.com/christmas; ✆ **504/522-5730.** Throughout December.

Celebration in the Oaks. Hundreds of thousands of lights illustrating holiday themes bedeck sections of City Park, and a walking and miniature-train tour lets you take in the charm and grandeur at your leisure. It's simple, affordable, nostalgic winter wonderment for the whole family. Plus there's ice skating and carousel and amusement park rides. www.neworleanscitypark.com; ✆ **544/482-4888.** Late November to early January.

New Year's Eve. The countdown party takes place in Jackson Square and, in the Southern equivalent of Times Square, revelers watch a lighted fleur-de-lis drop from the top of Jackson Brewery. Fireworks ensue. December 31.

RESPONSIBLE TOURISM

Responsible tourism in New Orleans may start as you leave the airport, since many airport shuttle vans and taxis are hybrids. Mardi Gras revelers will probably watch biodiesel-powered floats and catch beads on biodegradable string to help the strands fall from the tree branches. Many attractions are easily accessed by foot, streetcar, tour bus, or bike (rentals on p. 234).

Caloric intake in New Orleans can be decidedly *ir*responsible. You won't find many vegetarian or vegan options in the tourist areas, but nearly every restaurant offers options or accommodates dietary preferences (and Middle Eastern and Asian fallback restaurants are around). Further, almost every fine and contemporary dining establishment (and many simpler ones) have long embraced the lake-, river-, ocean-, and farm-to-table movement, sourcing from local ingredients and purveyors; some even have their own farms and gardens. A building's fragility and infrastructure, plus regulations that protect historic construction, can make green improvements difficult or prohibitive (especially in the French Quarter). New or recently rebuilt properties including the **Hyatt Regency** and the **Roosevelt** (p. 64) have incorporated significant smart-energy features. Most other hotels have instituted modest sustainability programs like recycling and on-demand linen replacement.

An ironic environmental upside to Hurricane Katrina and the Deepwater oil spill is increased awareness of the need to support locally-owned businesses as a means of rebuilding the local economy and maintaining the culture. The Urban Conservancy's **Stay Local** program (www.staylocal.org) has a good searchable directory of locally-owned businesses to patronize. Voluntourism is still popular, especially with groups. **Habitat for Humanity** accepts volunteers for a day, a year, or any term. The respected organization has created the Musicians Village for artists who lost their homes in the flood (www.habitat-nola.org; C **504/861-2077**). Or try **Common Ground** (www.commongroundrelief.org; C **504/218-1729**) and the **United Saints Recovery Project** (www.unitedsaints.org; C **504/895-2922,** ext. 108). **Youth Rebuilding New Orleans,** which rehabs homes primarily for teachers, is geared towards teens and even younger kids (service hours anyone?). They can do volunteer work with or without parents in tow (www.yrno.com; C **504/264-3344**). **America's Wetland Conservation Corps** focuses on vitally important wetlands restoration and sometimes has volunteer activities (www.americaswetland.com; C **504/293-2610**), as does **Groundwork New Orleans,** which builds rain gardens and other ecological improvements (www.groundworkNOLA.org).

Larger groups of travelers can also work through the **New Orleans Convention and Visitors Bureau** (p. 244) or **Projects with a Purpose** (www.projectswithapurpose.org; C **504/934-1000**). Allow 1 to 2 weeks to complete applications and paperwork. Volunteers may be responsible for certain expenses, equipment, and accommodations. **Volunteer International** (www.volunteerinternational.org) has a helpful tool to assess whether the type of work you intend is a good fit.

Given the tribulations that New Orleans and Louisiana have undergone, the most important act of responsible travel may simply be going, spending, enjoying, and encouraging others to do the same.

SUGGESTED ITINERARIES

It's easy to wander aimlessly through New Orleans with your eyes wide, your mouth agape, and your hand holding someone else's (or holding your Frommer's guide). It's truly unlike any place in the United States, so nearly everything you happen upon will be new and wondrous. It's equally easy to duck into a restaurant or watering hole, or take a meditative rest on a bench in Jackson Square or along the Mississippi River . . . and end up there for hours. Nothing wrong with that (we encourage it, in fact). But New Orleans has gobs of sites that can't be missed and countless curious little nooks that shouldn't be. The following itineraries are designed to help you make the most of your time as you navigate the city. If you have the time, take our **walking tours** (p. 199) or sign up for a **guided tour**—see our recommendations for the best on p. 151.

THE ICONIC QUARTER IN 1 DAY

You could spend days, weeks even, in the glorious, historic **French Quarter,** but even if you only have 1 day to explore, you can't go wrong here. This very full day includes all the requisites for an ideal New Orleans visit: eating, walking, drinking, soaking in some history, eating more, music, and dancing. *Tip:* As you stroll the neighborhood, check out the building exteriors: apart from the ironwork (mostly slave-made, originally), they're actually on the plain side. The Creoles saved the embellishments for their indoor living quarters. *Start: Along the riverfront at St. Louis Street.*

Hour 1: A Riverfront Stroll in Woldenberg Park ★★

Rise with the riverboats, and take a walk along **Woldenberg Park** (the pedestrian walkway adjacent to the river) toward the **Moonwalk** (named for former Mayor Moon Landrieu, not a dance step) overlooking **Jackson Square** (named for General/President Andrew, not Michael, King of Pop). Stop to notice some of the curious public art installations and take in the sights of the vessels rounding the curving crescent in Ol' Man River, much like they have for centuries.

New Orleans Itineraries

The Iconic Quarter in 1 Day

1. Woldenberg Park
2. Jackson Square
3. Café du Monde
4. St. Louis Cathedral
5. The Presbytère
6. The Cabildo
7. Central Grocery
8. M.S. Rau

9. Galatoire's 33
10. Pat O'Brien's
11. Bayona Restaurant
12. Preservation Hall
13. Felix's Restaurant & Oyster Bar
14. Irvin Mayfield's Jazz Playhouse

Beyond the Quarter in 1 Day

1. St. Charles Streetcar stop, Canal Street at Carondelet
2. Garden District Book Shop
3. Lafayette Cemetery No. 1

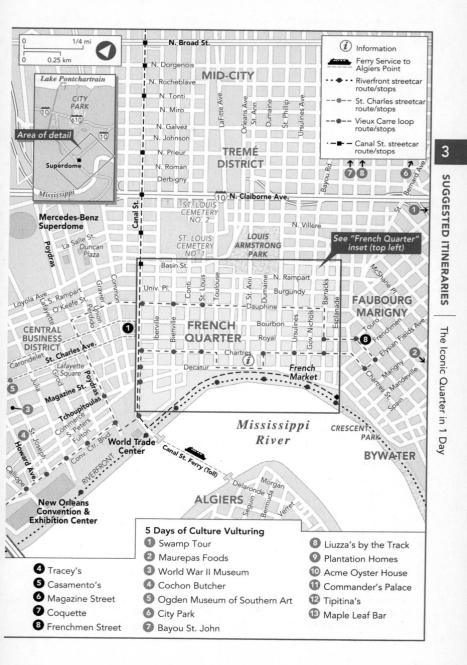

5 Days of Culture Vulturing
1 Swamp Tour
2 Maurepas Foods
3 World War II Museum
4 Cochon Butcher
5 Ogden Museum of Southern Art
6 City Park
7 Bayou St. John
8 Liuzza's by the Track
9 Plantation Homes
10 Acme Oyster House
11 Commander's Palace
12 Tipitina's
13 Maple Leaf Bar

4 Tracey's
5 Casamento's
6 Magazine Street
7 Coquette
8 Frenchmen Street

Hour 2: Café du Monde ★★★

Downing a cup of creamy, chicory-laced café au lait (coffee with milk) and savoring beignets covered in powdered sugar is the ideal way to start a New Orleans day. Watch this city come to lazy life as carriage drivers queue up across the street. If the line for a table is too long, go around back, get your beignets to go, and walk across to Jackson Square to enjoy them from a park bench. *Hint:* Dark clothes and powdered sugar don't mix. See p. 116.

Hour 3: St. Louis Cathedral ★

It's not the most inspiring ecclesiastical building, but it is the center of spiritual life for a town that is surprisingly devoutly Catholic (it's always a shock to note how many foreheads bear ashes the day after Mardi Gras' frantic antics). Legend has it that the serene garden in the back was a favorite haunt of good Catholic Marie Laveau—better known as the Voodoo Queen. Not even the infamous Pere Antoine, sent to New Orleans by the Office of the Inquisition, could convince Madame Laveau to forsake Voodoo. The imposing statue of Jesus lost a thumb to Katrina; at night its stunning shadow is otherworldly. See p. 125.

Hour 4: The Presbytère & the Cabildo ★★★

The former home of the priests who worked at St. Louis Cathedral has been turned into a museum housing a terrific "Living with Hurricanes" exhibit (p. 131). It's well worth an hour. If you still have time, the **Cabildo** museum (on the other side of St. Louis Cathedral; p. 128) is where the Louisiana Purchase was signed. Its exhibits illustrate New Orleans and Louisiana history and culture, including Mardi Gras. Our favorite item? Napoleon Bonaparte's death mask. See p. 129.

Hour 5: Muffuletta at Central Grocery ★

Ya gotta do it. Gotta get a muffuletta from **Central Grocery,** whose version of the celebrated Italian sandwich—filled with olive salad, Italian cold cuts, and cheese—is ginormous; half is more than enough for one person. Eat in at the tiny tables in back or thread your way through the buildings across the street to chow down along the banks of the Mississippi (p. 91).

Hour 6: Shops & Street Color on Royal Street ★★★

Royal Street is lined with swanky antiques, art, and clothing shops and has loads of antebellum eye candy, architecturally speaking. Be sure to browse the sublime and ridiculous collection at **M.S. Rau,** at 630 Royal (p. 188). The 100+ year-old antiques store welcomes gawkers. Several blocks of Royal are closed to vehicles from 11am to 4pm, and colorful street performers, from the talented to the tawdry, entertain for tips.

Hour 7: Bourbon Street ★

Dusk is the best time to do Bourbon, when it's not too tame and it's not too rowdy. Sure, Bourbon Street is gaudy, loud, and sometimes even gross. But before the sleaziness gets serious and the obnoxiousness sets in, when music pours out the doors and dancers and barmen hawk their wares, it's also seductive and exhilarating. Everyone has to do it once; some do it often. Have a pre-dinner cocktail at **Galatoire's 33** (p. 77), the new classic on the street, or a legendary Hurricane on the always-lively patio at **Pat O'Brien's** (p. 180).

Hour 8: Bayona Restaurant ★★★

Food is an intensely important part of your time in New Orleans, and you must dine well, several times daily. For your iconic French Quarter dinner, try **Bayona,** Chef Susan Spicer's iconic modern eatery, deservedly so. (p. 82).

Hour 9: Let the Good Times Roll ★★★

Nightlife is essential to your day. Do not miss **Preservation Hall** (p. 171)—it's affordable, and it's the real, traditional jazz McCoy. Late-night munchies? Head for **Felix's Restaurant & Oyster Bar** (p. 89) for a dozen raw. Still going? Slink into swanky **Irvin Mayfield's Jazz Playhouse** (p. 171), where the city's finest jazzmen and -women play. When you finally must, collapse in your bed. If you're exhausted, full, smiling, and anticipating tomorrow, your day has been a success.

BEYOND THE QUARTER IN 1 DAY

You've had your day of exploring the Quarter. Now get out of the Quarter, *get out of the Quarter,* **get out of the Quarter!** Got it? Today you must explore New Orleans beyond the French Quarter, and we send you to the other side of the city for a completely different perspective. It's another full day, packed with great stuff to see and do. And eat. *Start: St. Charles Streetcar line, Canal Street stop.*

Hour 1: St. Charles Avenue Streetcar ★★★

Hop on the oldest continuously operating wooden streetcar in the country. Expect breezes through open windows, not air-conditioning, so doing this in the cool of the morning is a good idea. Admire the gorgeous homes and sprawling oaks along the way, and remember which side of the car you rode on so that you can sit on the other side for the ride back. (*Tip:* Get a **JazzyPass,** good for a full day of streetcar and bus transportation.) See p. 236.

Hours 2–3: The Garden District ★★★

Aside from its historical significance, this neighborhood of fabulous houses and lush greenery is just plain beautiful. Contrast the plain exteriors of the "French" Quarter with these grand, ornamented "American district" spectacles. Follow the walking tour on p. 207 or take a guided tour from **Historic New Orleans Tours** (p. 152). Start at the **Garden District Book Shop** (p. 192), 2727 Prytania St. at Washington Ave.

Hour 4: Lafayette Cemetery No. 1 ★★

The "little cities of the dead" are part of the iconic landscape of New Orleans. This pretty cemetery catered to Uptown folks, and has more foliage and room than others. Notice the tombs with French or German writing, and the four matching mausoleums in the far left corner. They belong to four boyhood friends (one a Civil War vet) who once played together here. Like many of the city's cemeteries, Lafayette No. 1 is in great need of maintenance and lacking funds to do so. See p. 146.

Hour 5: Magazine Street Lunch Break ★

Two surefire lunch options are on nearby Magazine Street. For a cold beer and a very respectable roast beef po' boy, hit up **Tracey's,** just 2 blocks away on 2604 Magazine St. **Casamento's** (p. 113), about a mile up at 4330 Magazine, is about as classic as an oyster bar gets, and their bivalves are sublime. A cab or the no. 11 bus will get you there. Call ahead to make sure they'll be open.

Hour 6: Magazine Street Shopping ★★★

Explore the fab boutiques, antiques, and galleries along **Magazine Street** (p. 187), where even non-shoppers can enjoy the quirky mix of upscale-downscale, old-meets-new. The souvenir options trounce those of the Bourbon Street T-shirt shops. Use that JazzyPass to hop on and off the no. 11 bus (it runs about every 20 min.); cabs or feet also work.

Hour 7: Dinner at Coquette ★★★

Why are we so positively smitten with **Coquette?** Because it's perfect. Do make a reservation; don't skip dessert. See p. 108.

Hour 8: Frenchmen Street ★★★

Hit up the dozen clubs and bars of **Frenchmen Street** in the Quarter-adjacent Faubourg Marigny. Wander, mingle, people-watch, heed the music pouring forth, and then pick a club or three in which to work your mojo. See p. 171.

FIVE DAYS OF CULTURE VULTURING

A trip to New Orleans is not just about eating, drinking, dancing, and admiring fancy houses (although that's a big part of it). The city and surrounds are dripping with cultural coolness and historic eye-openers. Each of these five itineraries combines an enlightening or entertaining activity plus suggestions for nearby dining (and maybe another idea or two that we can't resist planting)—leaving time to discover the city as it's meant to be discovered, in serendipitous fashion. Do them all, or choose a couple of faves.

Day 1: Swamp Tour ★★★

We scoff at those who scoff at swamp tours because they're too "touristy." Unless you're from Florida, you need to do this. Everyone knows about the gators, and they're cool enough. But the swamps themselves are mystical and otherworldly, and their ecological, cultural, and economic relevance is fascinating. Get an early start so you have time for afternoon activities. Most tour companies can arrange round-trip transportation from your hotel. See p. 156.

After watching gators chowing down on food unlikely to be part of their natural diet, you're probably ready to do the same. Since you're already out exploring far-flung waterways, we're sending you to **Maurepas Foods** (p. 93) in the Bywater, a popular, newer spot in this artsy neighborhood with creative (but not experimental), locally-focused food and drink, at fair prices to boot.

Day 2: National World War II Museum ★★★

This remarkable historical jewel sprawls across several buildings, each jam-packed with thought-provoking exhibits. Make sure to listen to some of the potent, personal oral histories and if you see a veteran, volunteering or visiting, say thank you for us, please.

You could spend hours here, and you should. But you could also split your time appreciating the premier collection of Southern art in the country, traditional and modern, at the stylish, airy **Ogden Museum of Southern Art,** just a block away (p. 136).

Have lunch at **Cochon Butcher** (p. 104), an upscale Cajun-inflected deli 2 blocks from the museum. The cured meats stand out, but just about everything is stellar (we've never left without a side of their Brussels sprouts). If you liked the muffuletta from Central Grocery, you can do a comparison taste test here. It's debatable, but Butcher's might just be the best in town.

Day 3: City Park ★★★

The 1,300 acres here are as full of nature's glory as they are with activities, from the Spanish moss–draped giant live oaks to the splendid **New Orleans Museum of Art** (p. 135) to the outstanding **Sculpture Garden.** If you have kids in tow, take a ride in a pedal boat in the lake or visit the kids' amusement park and **Storybook Land.** The lush **Botanical Gardens** include the **Train Gardens,** a sort of melted Dr. Seuss replica of the city in miniature, complete with model trains (not to mention enormous lily pads). See p. 142.

Just outside the main entrance to City Park is **Bayou St. John,** a former bustling canal turned scenic body of water, and the sight of the city's origins. If you're up for more footwork, a stroll here is one of the lesser-known, more peaceful delights of the city. Or, point yourself down Esplanade Avenue and turn left on Lopez, where shivering-cold schooners of Abita and one of the city's best gumbos awaits at **Liuzza's by the Track** (p. 98). Also get the garlic oyster po' boy. You're welcome.

Day 4: River Road Plantation Homes ★

To see an altogether different, but vitally important side of the city's history, visit one or two of the **plantation homes along River Road** (p. 218). You'll need a car or tour company for this outing, a very worthwhile look at the pre– and post–Civil War eras, slavery, and Reconstruction. Afterwards, make a beeline for the French Quarter and get your slurp on at **Acme Oyster House** (p. 88). Don't neglect the charbroiled ones (gateway oysters for those who don't do them raw), and if it's in season get some boiled crawfish, too. Just for good measure.

Day 5: Commander's Palace ★

Your iconic cultural event today is a grand dining adventure at **Commander's Palace.** Choose a long, luxurious dinner or a languid, martini-laden lunch. The world-famous establishment never rests on its laurels, but continues to push Creole cuisine in new and exciting directions—while honoring its origins. It's fine dining done the New Orleans way: with a side of fun. Later, check out who's on at **Tipitina's** (p. 178) or the **Maple Leaf Bar** (p. 177), both pillars of stellar NOLA tuneage (yes, you can wear your fancy-pants clothes to a club; you won't be alone and besides, no one cares). This represents our perfect day in New Orleans: mixing high-society dining with down-and-dirty dancing, going from an elegant manse to an everyman's dive. Great food. Great music. Great time.

The City at a Glance

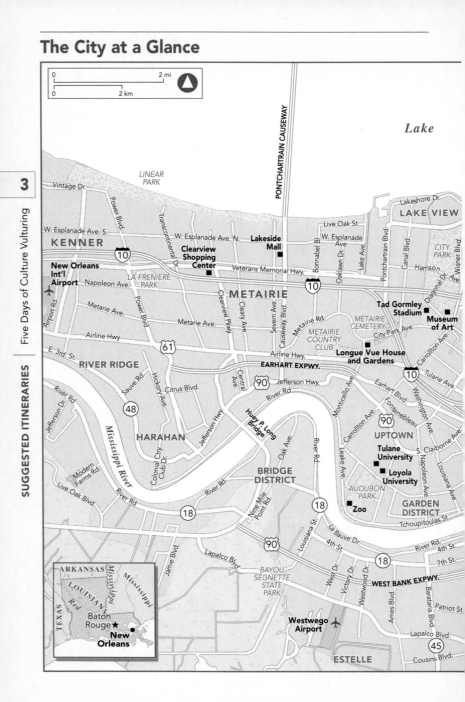

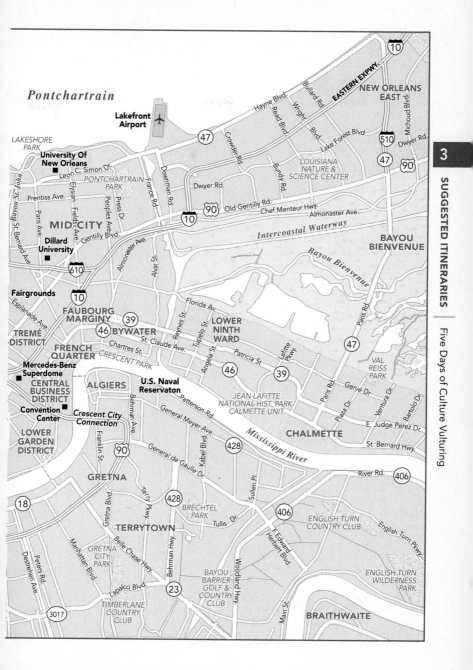

Orientation & Neighborhoods in Brief

"Where y'at?" goes the traditional local greeting. "Where" is straightforward in the French Quarter, a 13-block-long grid between Canal Street and Esplanade Avenue, running from the Mississippi River to North Rampart Street.

After that, fuggedaboutit. Because of the bend in the river (the "crescent" in the "Crescent City" moniker), the streets are laid out at angles and curves that render directions useless. Readjust your thinking to New Orleans's compass points: *lakeside, riverside, uptown,* and *downtown.* You'll catch on quickly if you keep in mind that North Rampart Street is the *lakeside* boundary of the Quarter and Canal Street is its *uptown* border. And by all means, use the maps provided—you'll need them.

Note that street names change when they cross Canal Street: Bourbon Street becomes Carondelet, and Royal becomes St. Charles, for example.

CITY LAYOUT

The French Quarter Made up of about 90 square blocks with Jackson Square at its center, this section is also known as the Vieux Carré (Old Square) and is bordered by Canal Street, North Rampart Street, the Mississippi River, and Esplanade Avenue. The Quarter (or FQ) is full of hotels, restaurants, clubs, bars, stores, residences, and museums. The most historic and best-preserved area in the city, it's the focal point for most first-time visitors. Explore the neighborhood in detail with our French Quarter walking tour (p. 199).

Faubourg Marigny Bordering the eastern edge of the French Quarter across Esplanade Avenue, the Marigny boasts the city's premier nightlife center: famed Frenchmen Street. Named for 6 rebellious French dudes who were hung here for promoting formation of a new government (in 1768—8 years before the Declaration of Independence), Frenchmen Street is a must-visit haunt for music lovers and anyone seeking a scene. This small Creole suburb is populated by old-time residents, young urban dwellers who've moved in recently, and a thriving LGBTQ community.

Bywater This riverside neighborhood past the Faubourg Marigny, a hotbed of renovation and gentrification, still has its share of modest and rundown homes set amid sparkling renovations and artily rehabbed shotgun shacks. Historically, the area was also home to immigrants, free people of color, and artisans; today many studios still dot the area, along with new hipster bars, cafes, celebs, and the freshly-minted Crescent Park (p. 143).

Mid-City/Esplanade Ridge Stretching north from the French Quarter to City Park, Esplanade Ridge hugs either side of Esplanade Avenue (once the grande avenue of New Orleans's Creole society, rivaling St. Charles Avenue). Crossing Esplanade is the historic **Bayou St. John** waterway, adjacent to the lovely **Faubourg St. John** neighborhood. Booming, popular **Mid-City** also encompasses **City Park,** and its residential neighborhoods stretch upward toward Lake Pontchartrain.

Faubourg Tremé Directly across Rampart Street from the French Quarter, this dense 19th-century Creole community is one of the oldest African-American neighborhoods in the country. Home to many of the city's best musicians, it is seeing some post-Katrina gentrification, but remains a dynamic, organic residential community, as highlighted in the HBO series named for the area. Once considered unsafe for tourists, it's much improved and more populated, though as in many parts of the city, it has its share of crime, and it is not advisable to walk through the area at night or solo.

Central Business District In the 19th century, **Canal Street** divided the French and American sections of the city. Historically New Orleans's main street, it's a far cry from the days of yore when white-gloved ladies and seersuckered men shopped this grand avenue. But several fine hotels, restaurants, and renovated theaters are evidence of

Canal's impending renewal. Uptown of Canal Street is the **CBD,** also roughly bounded by the elevated Pontchartrain Expressway (Business Rte. U.S. I-90) between Loyola Avenue and the Mississippi River. This hotbed of hip houses New Orleans's major business and government offices, along with some of the city's most elegant hotels, best restaurants, and the **Mercedes-Benz Superdome.** Within the CBD is the **Warehouse District,** which was just a heap of abandoned warehouses some 20-ish years ago. With the efforts of some dedicated individuals and institutions, it has evolved into a thriving residential and commercial neighborhood and is still growing madly. Besides cool loft conversions, terrific restaurants, and hot music clubs, the area also houses the city's lively **arts district,** with major museums and myriad galleries along **Julia Street** (see p. 134).

Uptown/The Garden District Bounded by St. Charles Avenue (lakeside) and Magazine Street (riverside) between Jackson and Louisiana avenues, the **Garden District (GD)** remains one of the most picturesque areas in the city. Originally the site of a plantation, it was subdivided and developed as a residential neighborhood for wealthy Americans who built elaborate homes and gardens, some still existing. See our Garden District walking tour on p. 207. The Garden District is *located* "uptown"; the neighborhood west of the Garden District is also *called* **Uptown** (the term is used for the *direction* and the *area,* just to confuse us). The **Lower Garden District (LGD)** refers to the segment between the Pontchartrain Expressway (I-90) and Jackson Avenue.

The Irish Channel The area bounded by Magazine Street and the Mississippi River, Louisiana Avenue, and the Central Business District got its name during the 1800s when more than 100,000 Irish immigrated to New Orleans and found (mostly blue-collar) work. Not much has changed. The quiet residential neighborhood, where the run-down mixes comfortably with the fixed up, is speckled with some amazing churches, a few good restaurants, a whole lotta good dive bars, and the occasional cobblestone street.

Algiers Point Directly across the Mississippi River and connected by ferry (p. 235), Algiers Point is another original Creole suburb, largely unchanged if a little less lively than it was during the once-booming days of the railroad and dry-docking industries.

MARDI GRAS & JAZZ FEST

For many people, what they know about New Orleans begins and ends with its parties: Mardi Gras—the biggest street blowout in America—or Jazz Fest, the grand-père of all other music fests and still the best music event in the country, despite copious spawn. In the place where anything is an excuse for a celebration (festivals center on swamps, gumbo, crawfish, frogs, tomatoes, daiquiris, pork, and on it goes), the first thing you need to bring is a rollicking, party-ready attitude. New Orleans pretty much does the rest.

This chapter gives you some background, foreground, and tips to help you get on your good foot for the biggies: Mardi Gras and Jazz Fest.

MARDI GRAS

The granddaddy of all New Orleans celebrations is Mardi Gras. Thanks to sensationalized media accounts that zero in on the salacious aspects of this Carnival, its rep as a "Girls Gone Wild"–style spring break persists, drawing masses of wannabes for decadent, X-rated action rather than tradition. If that's your thang, by all means go forth and par-tay (just remember, Facebook is *forever*).

But there is so much more to Carnival than the media-hyped wanton action. Truth is, Mardi Gras remains one of the most exciting times to visit New Orleans, for people from all walks. Yes, you can hang in the Bourbon Street fratmosphere till you're wholly hung, but you can also spend days admiring and reveling in the city's rich traditions, or have a fun, memorable family vacation beyond what any mouse could offer.

Knowing some of its long and fascinating history helps put matters in perspective. First of all, Mardi Gras is just one day: French for "Fat Tuesday," Mardi Gras is the day before Ash Wednesday, when Lent begins. Though many people *call it* Mardi Gras, "Carnival" is the correct term for the 5- to 8-week "season" stretching from Twelfth Night (Jan 6) to Fat Tuesday. The idea was that good Christians would massively indulge in preparation for their impending self-denial during Lent.

The party's origins can be traced to the Roman **Lupercalia** festival: 2 days when all sexual and social order disappeared, cross-dressing was mandatory, and the population ran riot (sound familiar?). The early Christian church was naturally appalled by this, but unable to stop it. So Lupercalia was grafted to the beginning of Lent, as a compromise to bribe everyone into observance.

4

Carnival (from a Latin word roughly meaning "farewell to flesh") and its lavish masked balls and other revels became popular in Italy and France, and the tradition followed the Creoles to New Orleans. The first Carnival balls occurred in 1743. By the mid-1800s, Mardi Gras mischief had grown so ugly (the harmless habit of tossing flour on revelers gradually turned into throwing bricks at them) that everyone predicted the end of the tradition.

The Birth of the Krewes

Everything changed in 1856. Tired of being left out of the Creoles' Mardi Gras, a group of Americans who belonged to a secret society called Cowbellians formed the Mystick Krewe of Comus (named after the hero of a John Milton poem). On Mardi Gras evening, they presented a breathtakingly imaginative, torch-lit parade. And so a new tradition was born, with new rituals and standards established. Mardi Gras marked the height of the social season for **"krewes,"** groups comprised of prominent society and business types.

After the Civil War put a temporary halt to things, two new enduring customs were added. Members threw trinkets to onlookers, and a queen reigned over their lavish balls.

As an elite Old South institution, Mardi Gras eschewed racial equality or harmony. African Americans participated in parades only by carrying torches to illuminate the route (the atmospheric if controversial *flambeaux,* as the torches are known). In 1909, a black man named William Storey mocked the elaborately garbed Rex (aka, King of Carnival) by prancing after his float wearing a lard can for a crown. Storey was promptly dubbed "King Zulu." Thus begat the Krewe of Zulu, which parodied the high-minded Rex krewe and mocked racial stereotypes. The Zulu parade quickly became one of the most popular aspects of Mardi Gras, famously crowning Louis Armstrong as King Zulu in 1949.

Unfortunately, most krewes still excluded blacks, Jews, and women even as late as the 1990s when anti-discrimination sentiment and laws (tied to parade permits) finally forced the issue. The mighty Comus, in a move that many old-liners still feel marked the beginning of the end of classic Mardi Gras, canceled its parade rather than integrate. Proteus and Momus followed. Proteus later relented and parades again; Momus parties but no longer parades.

Then as now, the krewes and traditions of Mardi Gras change. Today there are dozens of unofficial krewes and "sub-krewe" spinoffs, and more crop up like roadside wildflowers (or weeds), some with hilarious or subversive themes.

Spectacle & Beauty

Parades were always things of spectacle and beauty, but they grew bigger than the narrow Quarter streets could accommodate—and bigger yet. New "superkrewes" emerged, like Orpheus (founded by local musician and lifelong Mardi Gras enthusiast Harry Connick, Jr.), Bacchus, and Endymion, with nonexclusive memberships and block-long floats. The largest parades can have dozens of floats, celebrity guests, marching bands, dance troupes, motorcycle or scooter squads, and thousands of participants.

The trinkets known as **throws** fly thick and fast from the floats, to the traditional cry of "Throw me something, Mister!" The ubiquitous plastic beads were originally glass, often from Czechoslovakia. **Doubloons,** the oversize aluminum coins stamped with the year and the krewe's coat of arms, are collector's items for natives. Other throws include **stuffed animals, plastic krewe cups,** and especially the cherished **Zulu coconuts** and **Muses shoes.**

Kickin' Up Your Heels: Mardi Gras Activities

Mardi Gras can be whatever you want. The entire city shuts down (including schools and many businesses) so that every citizen can join in the celebrations. Families and friends gather on the streets, on their stoops, or on balconies. They barbecue in the neutral ground (median strip) along the route, and throw elaborate house parties. Bourbon Street is a parade of exhibitionism and drunkenness. Canal Street is a hotbed of bead lust. Royal and Frenchmen Streets are a dance of costumed free spirits and fantasies made real.

THE SEASON   The date of Fat Tuesday is different each year, but Carnival season always starts on **Twelfth Night,** January 6, when the Phunny Phorty Phellows kick things off with a streetcar party cruise.

Over the following weeks, the city celebrates, often with round, purple, green, and gold **king cakes.** Each has a tiny plastic baby (representing the Baby Jesus) baked right in. Getting the slice with the baby is a good omen, and traditionally means you have to throw the next King Cake party. For the high-society crowd, the season brings dozens of ritualized parties and **masked balls,** where krewes introduce their royal courts.

Two or three weeks before Mardi Gras itself, the parading (and parodying) begins. Adorable canines parade in the **Mystick Krewe of Barkus,** often with their humans in matching costumes. The riotous **Krewe du Vieux** outrages with un-family-friendly decadence. Sweetly insubordinate 'tit Rəx features itsy bitsy insurrectionary floats, shoebox-size stabs at the more established traditions (like those of *grande* Rex—'tit being an abbreviation of the French *petit,* meaning "wee"). For a slightly mellower Mardi Gras experience, consider coming for the weekend 10 days before Fat Tuesday. You can count on 10 to 15 small-to-midsize parades, and easily manageable crowds.

The following weekend the parades (15 of 'em) and the crowds are *way* bigger—the massive party is *on.*

LUNDI GRAS   n a tradition going back to 1874, King Zulu arrives by boat to meet King Rex on the Monday before Fat Tuesday (it's February 16 in 2015). With the mayor presiding, this officially welcomes Mardi Gras day. Nowadays, an all-day music and food fest along the riverfront celebrates the grand event (unsurprisingly). Events start by noon; the kings meet around 5pm; major fireworks follow. That night, **Proteus** and the **Krewe of Orpheus** hold their parades, and a good portion of the city pulls an all-nighter.

MARDI GRAS DAY   The two biggest parades, Zulu and Rex, run back to back to kick things off. Zulu starts near the Central Business District at 8:30am; Rex starts uptown at 10am. Across town, the bohemian Societé of St. Anne musters around 9am near Burgundy and Piety streets in the Bywater area. This fantastical walking club (no floats) is known for its madcap, au courant, and sometimes risqué costumes.

In between the parades, you can see other elaborately costumed Mardi Gras **walking or marching clubs,** such as the Jefferson City Buzzards, the Pete Fountain Half-Fast, and Mondo Kayo (identifiable by their tropical/banana theme). They walk (or stumble), accompanied by marching bands. Catch the "marchers" anywhere along St. Charles Avenue between Poydras Street and Washington Avenue.

Also keep a watch out for homegrown and rogue krewes, and marching clubs like the sci-fi **Krewe of Chewbacchus;** the legume-adorned **Krewe of Red Beans;** or the severely sideburned, many-wheeled **Krewe of Rolling Elvi.** These groups form among friends or neighbors or along any random theme, and are sometimes announced on **WWOZ.org** or in **Gambit** (www.bestofneworleans.com).

By early afternoon, Rex spills into the Central Business District. Nearby, you may be able to find some of the elusive **Mardi Gras Indians,** small communities of African Americans and black Creoles (some of whom have Native American ancestors). The tribes have an established hierarchy and deep-seated traditions, including enormous, elaborate beaded and feathered costumes. They're entirely made by hand and a great source of pride, each attempting to out-outlandish the next. The men work on them all year in preparation for rituals and parades on Mardi Gras and St. Joseph's Day.

The timing is loose, but traditionally tribes converge throughout the day at main intersections along the Claiborne Avenue median (underneath the interstate), and at St. Augustine Church in the Tremé. Crowds of locals mill around to see the spectacle: When two tribes meet, they'll stage a mock confrontation, resettling their territory. After marching in various parades, they reconvene around mid-afternoon on Claiborne, where a party gets going. Play it cool, however—this is not your neighborhood, nor a sideshow act. It is a ritual deserving of respect. Also, Indian suits are copyrighted works of art; photos of them can't be sold without permission. For times and locations, ask locals, check **www.wwoz.org/inthestreet**, or listen for drums. You can also try to catch these confrontations during St. Joseph's Day, at parties, and at Jazz Fest.

As you make your way through the streets, keep your eyes peeled for members of the legendary **Krewe of Comus,** men dressed in tuxes with brooms over their shoulders, holding cowbells. Ask them if they are Comus, and they will deny it, insisting they are Cowbellians. But if they hand you a vintage Comus doubloon, the truth will be out.

The last parade each day (on both weekends) is loosely scheduled to end around 9:30pm but can run way later, and most krewes hold balls or parties after they parade. Some are members only, but those of Bacchus, Endymion, and Orpheus sell tickets to the public (they're more concerts than formal balls). At the end of the day (or the start of Wed), expect exhaustion. If you're in the Quarter at midnight, you'll see another traditional marvel: The police come en masse, on foot and horseback, and efficiently, effectively, shoo the crowds off—officially ending Mardi Gras. If you're tucked in, tune in to WYES (Channel 12) for live coverage of the Rex Ball—it's serious pomp.

Doing Mardi Gras

LODGING   During Mardi Gras, accommodations in the city and the nearby suburbs are booked solid, *so make your plans well ahead and book a room as early as possible*—a year in advance is quite common. Price spikes, minimum-stay requirements, and "no cancellation" policies apply. Some hotels along the parade routes offer popular but pricey packages including bleacher or balcony seats.

CLOTHING   For the parades before Mardi Gras day, dress comfortably and prepare for whatever weather is forecast (which can vary widely). You'll see some wigs and masks, but most don't dress up. Fat Tuesday is a different story. A **costume** and **mask** automatically makes you a participant, which is absolutely the way to go. You needn't do anything fancy; scan the thrift stores for something loud and it's all good. Anything goes, so fly your freak flag if you're so inclined.

If you've come unprepared, see p. 193 for costume shops, or try the secondhand stores along Magazine Street, Decatur Street, and in the Bywater.

DINING Many restaurants close on Mardi Gras day, but are open the weekend prior. Make reservations as early as possible. Some (such as Emeril's, Herbsaint, and Palace Café) are right on the parade routes, which could be fun. Pay attention to those routes (see

Save the Date

Mardi Gras falls exactly 47 days before Easter: That's February 17, 2015; February 9, 2016; and February 28, 2017.

map on p. 46), because if there is one between you and your restaurant, you may not be able to drive or park nearby, or even cross the street, and you can kiss your dinner goodbye. Thus, restaurants often have a high no-show rate during Mardi Gras, so a well-timed drop-in may work to the nonplanner's advantage.

DRIVING & PARKING Don't. Traffic and navigating during Mardi Gras is horrendous. Take a cab, walk, or pedal (call well in advance for a bike reservation). Parking along parade routes is not allowed 2 hours before and after the parade. Parking on the neutral ground (median strip) is illegal (despite what you may see), and you'll likely be towed. *Note:* Taxis are very busy, and streetcar and bus schedules will be radically altered (none run on St. Charles Ave.). Contact the **Regional Transit Authority** (RTA; www.norta.com; ✆ **504/248-3900**) for more information.

FACILITIES Restrooms are notoriously scant along the parade routes. Entrepreneurs rent theirs and the city brings in the ever-popular porta-potties. Bring tissues and take advantage of the facilities when you come across them. The brilliant **airpnp pottylocator app** launched for Mardi Gras 2014 and quickly went global. If it survives into future years it could be a lifesaver, or at least a bladder saver.

THE DAY PLAN It's not necessary to make a plan for the big day, but it might help. Get your hands on the latest edition of *Arthur Hardy's Mardi Gras Guide,* through **www.mardigrasguide.com** or at nearly any store. Download the app, since schedules and routes occasionally change at the last minute. Also download the real-time **parade-tracker app** from WWLTV.com. Resolve that you'll probably adjust the plan, or throw it out altogether—and that you'll chill and go with it. The fun is everywhere—but with limited transportation and facilities available (and until you've done it enough to determine a satisfying routine), you'll have to make some choices about what to do, in advance and on the fly. Read the rest of this section and check the route maps. Then decide if you want to head uptown, downtown, to the Quarter, the Bywater, Claiborne Avenue, or some combination of the above, as your stamina dictates.

SAFETY Many, many cops are out, making the walk from uptown to downtown safer than at other times of year, but pickpockets enjoy Mardi Gras, too. Take precautions.

SEATING A limited number of bleachers are erected along the downtown parade route. Most are reserved for private use, but some are sold to the public—you'll pay dearly for the convenience. Start checking Ticketmaster and **www.neworleans paradetickets.com** in December. Some folks buy cheap folding chairs at local drug stores, which typically don't make it home; others just bring a blanket or tarp. You might find a spot to use them on the Uptown routes; downtown, you'll probably be standing. The longest parades can last 3-plus hours, so plan according to your staying power.

KIDS Though it may seem contrarian, you can bring the kids to Mardi Gras if you stick to the Uptown locales (you'll see hundreds of local kids seated atop customrigged ladders, the better to catch throws). In fact, it's a terrific family event, as any local will tell you. It's a long day, so make sure to bring supplies and diversions for between parades. There may be some schlepping involved, but their delight increases everyone's enjoyment considerably.

WHAT ELSE TO BRING   The usual dilemma applies: You'll want to stay unencumbered, but well supplied. Much depends on whether you plan to stay in one place or make tracks. A starter set of beverages and snacks is called for, or a full picnic if you desire (food carts and trucks, not to mention enterprising homeowners-turned-delis, are usually available along the routes). Toilet tissue and hand sanitizer are good ideas, and don't forget a bag or backpack for those beads.

How to Spend the Big Day

Despite the popular impression of Mardi Gras, the parades don't even go down Bourbon Street. Your Carnival experience will depend on where you go and whom you hang out with. Here are three ways to do it: nice, naughty, and nasty. Us? We prefer the first two, traversed on two wheels.

NICE   Hang out exclusively Uptown with the families. Find a spot on St. Charles Avenue (which is closed that day) between Napoleon Avenue and Lee Circle, and set up camp with a blanket and a picnic lunch for **Rex,** the truck parades, and walking clubs. Dressed-up families are all around. One side of St. Charles is for the parades and the other is open only to foot traffic, so you can wander about, admire the scene, and angle for an invitation to a barbecue or balcony party. New Orleans kids consider Mardi Gras more fun than Halloween, and the reasons are obvious.

Zulu's route starts at Jackson and goes downriver, so those further uptown will miss out. Staking out a spot downtown is another option; the crowds are a bit thicker and rowdier.

For an utterly different experience, head to Claiborne Avenue around 9am-ish and look for the **Mardi Gras Indian** tribes' meeting (p. 43). It's a hit-or-miss proposition; the Indians themselves never know in advance when or where the gatherings occur. But running across them on their own turf is one of the great sights and experiences of Mardi Gras.

NAUGHTY   Around mid-morning, track down the **Krewe of Kosmic Debris** and the **Société of St. Anne:** no floats, just wildly creative, costumed revelers. At noon, try to be near the corner of Burgundy and St. Ann streets for the **Bourbon Street** awards. You may not get close enough to actually see the judging, but the participants are all around so you can gawk at their sometimes R- and X-rated costumes. It's boisterous and enthusiastic, but not (for the most part) obnoxious. Afterward, head to **Frenchmen Street,** where dancing and drum circles celebrate Carnival well into the night.

NASTY   Stay on **Bourbon Street.** Yep, it's every bit as crowded, booze-soaked, and vulgar as you've heard, and there are no fabulous floats. Every square of the street and every overhanging balcony is packed with partiers. Those balcony dwellers pack piles of beads (some with X-rated anatomical features) ready to toss down in exchange for a glimpse of flesh (by the way, flashing is technically illegal). It's anything goes and wildly fun—but it can grow old fast.

Parade Watch

A Mardi Gras parade works a spell on people. There's no other way to explain why thousands of otherwise rational men and women scream, plead, and sometimes expose themselves for a plastic trinket. Nobody goes home empty-handed (even the trees end

Major Mardi Gras Parade Routes

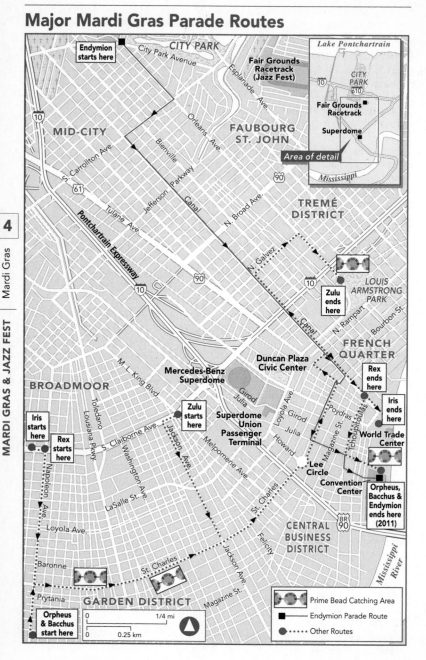

up laden with glittery goods), so don't forget to actually look at the amazing floats. When the nighttime floats are lit by flambeaux torchbearers, it is easy to envision a time when Mardi Gras meant mystery and magic.

These are just a few of the major parades of the last days of Carnival. Also see the route map on p. 46.

- **Muses** (founded 2000): This popular all-gals krewe honors New Orleans's artistic community—and shoes. Their glittery, decorated pumps are highly sought throws. Thursday evening before Mardi Gras.
- **Krewe d'Etat** (founded 1996): Social satire is their specialty. No current event is left unscathed, and their hilarious float designs can fuel water cooler and barstool discussions for weeks. Friday evening before Mardi Gras.
- **Iris** (founded 1917): This women's krewe follows traditional Carnival rules of costume and behavior. Saturday afternoon before Mardi Gras.
- **Endymion** (founded 1967): One of the early 1970s "superkrewes," it features a glut of floats and celebrity guests such as Alice Cooper, Tom Jones, Dolly Parton, and John Goodman. It runs in Mid-City, concluding with a big party in the Superdome. Saturday evening.
- **Bacchus** (founded 1968): The original "superkrewe," it was the first to host international celebrities. Bacchus runs from Uptown to the Convention Center. Sunday before Mardi Gras.
- **Orpheus** (founded 1994): Another youngish krewe, it was founded by a group that includes Harry Connick, Jr., and adheres to classic krewe traditions. Popular for its many stunning floats and generous throws. Follows the Bacchus route on Lundi Gras evening.
- **Zulu** (founded 1916): Lively Zulu's float riders are decked out in woolly wigs and blackface. They carry the most prized Mardi Gras souvenirs: glittery hand-painted coconuts. These status symbols must be placed in your hands, not tossed, so go right up to the float and do your best begging. Zulu parades on Mardi Gras morning.
- **Rex** (founded 1872): Rex follows Zulu and various walking clubs down St. Charles. It features the King of Carnival and some classic floats. Mardi Gras day.

CAJUN MARDI GRAS

For an entirely different experience, take the 2½- to 3-hour drive out to Cajun Country, where Mardi Gras traditions are just as strong but considerably more, er, traditional. **Lafayette** celebrates Carnival in a manner that reflects the Cajun heritage and spirit. The 3-day event is second in size only to New Orleans's celebration with parades and floats and beads a-plenty, but their final pageant and ball are open to the general public. Don your formal wear and join right in!

MASKED MEN & A BIG GUMBO   In towns like Eunice and Mamou in the Cajun countryside, the Courir de Mardi Gras celebration is tied to the traditional French rural lifestyle. Bands of masked men (and women, now) dressed in raggedy patchwork costumes and peaked *capichon* hats set off on Mardi Gras morning on horseback, led by their *capitaine.* They ride from farm to farm, asking at each, *"Voulez-vous reçevoir le Mardi Gras?"* ("Will you receive the Mardi Gras?"). *"Oui,"* comes the invariable reply. Each farmyard then becomes a miniature festival of song, dance, antics, and much beer. As payment for their pageantry, they get "a fat little chicken to make a big gumbo" (or sometimes a bag of rice or other ingredients).

All meet back in town where cooking, dancing, games, storytelling, and general merriment continue into the wee hours, and yes, there is indeed a very big pot of gumbo. Get particulars from the **Lafayette Parish Convention and Visitors Commission** (www.lafayettetravel.com; ℂ **800/346-1958** in the U.S., 800/543-5340 in Canada, or 337/232-3737).

NEW ORLEANS JAZZ & HERITAGE FESTIVAL

What began in 1969 as a small gathering in Congo Square to celebrate the music of New Orleans now ranks as one of the best attended, most respected, and most musically comprehensive festivals in the world. Although people call it Jazz Fest (or just "Fest") the full name is **New Orleans Jazz & Heritage Festival Presented by Shell.** The "Heritage" part is broadly interpreted, and the "Jazz" part hardly represents the scope of the musical fare. Each of the 12 stages showcases a musical genre or three.

Jazz Fest encompasses everything the city has to offer, in terms of music, food, and culture. That, and it's a hell of a party. In 2006, after Shell Oil sponsored Jazz Fest's uncertain return after Katrina, Bruce Springsteen's triumphant, emotionally stunning set sealed its eternal resurrection. Such musical and emotional epiphanies abound at Fest. While headliners like Arcade Fire, Pearl Jam, Stevie Wonder, Van Morrison, Dave Matthews, My Morning Jacket, Maroon 5, The Roots, and Christina Aguillera can draw huge crowds, serious Festers savor the lesser-known acts. They range from the avant-garde to old-time Delta bluesmen, from African artists making rare U.S. appearances to bohemian street folkies, and from the top zydeco players to gospel mass choirs. And, of course, jazz in its many forms.

Filling the infield of the Fair Grounds horse-racing track up near City Park, the festival covers two long weekends, the last in April and the first in May (for 2015, that's Apr 24–26 and April 30–May 3). It's set up about as well as a large event can be. When the crowds get thick, though—especially the popular second Saturday—it can be tough to move around, more so if the grounds are muddy from rain. Lines at the most popular of the several dozen food booths can be frighteningly long, but it's all quite civil and most move quickly (and they're invariably worth the wait).

Attending Jazz Fest means making some tough decisions. Hotels, restaurants, and flights fill up months (if not a year) in advance, but the schedule is not announced until a couple of months before the event. So reserving travel requires a leap of faith in the talent bookings. But truth be told, just about every day at Jazz Fest is a good day regardless of who is playing (avoid the dilemma by going for both weekends). The Thursday before the second weekend traditionally has more locals, on stage and in the audience, and smaller crowds. It's a great time to hit the most popular food booths and check out the crafts areas.

Jazz Fest Pointers

"It's a marathon, not a sprint," as the saying goes. With music in every direction, you can plot out your day or just wander from stage to stage, catching a few songs by various acts—some of the best Jazz Fest experiences come from stumbling across an undiscovered musical gem. Or you can set up camp at one stage—from the big ones with famous headliners to the gospel tent, where musical miracles are pretty much a given. It's akin to sit-down dining versus a buffet: Both have advantages.

At your hotel or as you're walking to Fest, grab a free *Offbeat* magazine (they're dispensed or handed out everywhere). You'll need the schedule "grids" and performer descriptions. Also download the Jazz Fest and Offbeat apps. For $5, the official Fest program also has the schedule, plus food coupons (available on-site).

On a typical Jazz Fest day, you'll arrive sometime after the gates open at 11am and stay until you are pooped or they close at 7pm. The whole thing usually runs as efficiently as a Swiss train. After you leave, get some dinner, and hit the clubs. Every club in the city has top-notch bookings (of note are **Piano Night** at the House of Blues, Tipitina's' **Instruments a Comin'** benefit, and the jam-heavy shows produced by Superfly—check out **www.superflypresents.com**). Alternately, sleep.

The excellent nonmusical aspects of Jazz Fest are plentiful. Local craftspeople and juried artisans fill a sizable area with artwork and products for show, for demonstration, or for purchase. Most vendors will pack and ship goods to your home (and there's a U.S. Post Office on site, too).

And as always in New Orleans, there is food. There are local standbys—not burgers and dogs but red beans and rice, jambalaya, étouffée, and gumbo. More interesting choices include *cochon de lait* (a mouthwatering roast-pig sandwich), a fried soft-shell crab po' boy, quail and pheasant gumbo, and all manner of oyster and crawfish. And that's not even discussing the various ethnic or vegetarian dishes available, or the desserts . . . oooh, the desserts. The terrific kids' area has PB&J, mac and cheese, and other easy-pleasing faves. Try at least one new thing daily, and also share, so you can sample more variety and decide which booths to revisit. *Tip #1:* There's copious cold beer, but the lines can get long. Smaller stages = shorter lines, and it's often worth it to trek there. *Tip #2:* Many hours of sun + many beers = premature crash. Pace thyself, grasshopper.

Experienced Fest-goers also know to duck into the air-conditioned Grandstand for art and folklore exhibits, cooking demonstrations, and **real bathrooms.** The upstairs Heritage Stage features interviews and short performances by some of the top acts in a much more intimate setting. It's highly recommended.

Wear and bring as little as possible; you'll want to be comfy and unencumbered. Do bring sun protection, something that tells time, a poncho if rain is forecast (they sell them there, but at twice what you'll pay at a souvenir store), and moola (cash only for food; credit okay for crafts). Wear comfy, supportive, well-broken-in shoes.

Note: No beverages (apart from 1 liter of water) are allowed. There are seats in the tented stages. Outside, people stand or sit on the ground, a blanket, or a folding chair. When left vacant, these become annoying space hogs. Kind Fest-goers invite others to use their space when they leave temporarily, but don't be shy about asking.

TICKETS Purchase tickets when they go on sale in late fall or early winter, when they are the cheapest. They're available through **Ticketmaster** (www.ticketmaster.com; ✆ 800/745-3000) or at the gate. Daily admission for adults in 2014 was $50 in advance, $70 at the gate, and $10 for children (plus Ticketmaster's ample handling fees). There are also various VIP packages with a range of swanky seating, access, and amenities, topping out at $1,300 for one weekend (and they do sell out). For more information, contact **New Orleans Jazz & Heritage Festival** (www.nojazzfest.com; ✆ 504/410-4100).

PARKING & TRANSPORTATION The only parking at the Fair Grounds is for people with disabilities, at $50 a day, first-come, first-served. Email access@nojazzfest.com or contact ✆ 504/410-6104. Enterprising neighbors provide parking in their driveways or lots at inflated rates. Most people take public transportation or a shuttle. The **Regional Transit Authority** operates bus routes to the Fair Grounds from various pickup points. For schedules, contact ℂ **504/248-3900** (www.norta.com). Taxis, though busy, charge a special-event rate of $5 per person or the meter reading if it's higher (see p. 234). Gray Line's **Jazz Fest Express** (www.graylineneworleans. com; ℂ **800/535-7786** or 504/569-1401) operates shuttles from the steamboat *Natchez* dock in the French Quarter; the Sheraton at 500 Canal Street; and City Park. It's $18 round-trip and you must have a Jazz Fest ticket to ride (purchase shuttle tickets with your Ticketmaster ticket order). *Note:* The **Canal Street streetcar line** will be packed, but it's an option from the Quarter. Take the cars destined for "City Park"—not those to "Cemeteries." Fare is $1.25 or use your multi-day **Jazzy Pass** (p. 235).

PACKAGE DEALS   **Festival Tours International** (www.gumbopages.com/festival tours; ℂ **310/454-4080**) offers a tour that includes accommodations and tickets for Jazz Fest, plus a midweek visit to Cajun Country for unique personal encounters with local musicians. If you're flying to New Orleans specifically for the festival, visit **www.nojazzfest.com** to get a Jazz Fest promotional code from a list of airlines that offer special Fest fares.

WHERE TO STAY IN NEW ORLEANS

Accommodations in New Orleans range from your basic lodger to over-the-top luxurious: like the city itself, there's something for every preference. Prices also vary widely. The **rates shown here don't reflect spikes during high season or discounts during low season, or 14.75% room tax.** Parking rates may not reflect tax or rates for oversized vehicles. Many properties are **entirely nonsmoking,** although most of those provide an outdoor smoking area.

FRENCH QUARTER & FAUBOURG TREMÉ

The Vieux Carré (old square), as it is called, is the picturesque soul of the city that most people envision. The architecture looks much like it did when it was built in the late 17th and early 18th centuries, enabling visitors to walk out of their hotel and feel wholly transported. When you stay in the French Quarter, you are ensconced in the total N.O. experience—from the serene to the sybaritic.

Best for: First-time visitors; short-term visitors; historians; architecture buffs; partiers; everyone.

Drawbacks: During high season it can be bustling with tourists and goings-on. Parking is scarce and expensive.

Very Expensive

Audubon Cottages ★★★   La Liz Taylor stayed here, but it feels like you're staying at *her* place (if she lived in a sublime warren of 18th-century apartments). An unmarked gate and leaf-canopied pathway lead to seven ultra-private one- and two-bedroom cottages with a large courtyard (some private, some shared). Each is gracefully but not overly antiqued amid gorgeous brick walls and gleaming hardwood floors. The cottages surround a brick-lined, heated pool, and it's all attended to by a 24-hour butler. It's easy to imagine naturalist John James Audubon watching birds alight from his studio here (he did), inspiring him to capture their images in his historic paintings. If you have the means, by all means, stay here.

509 Dauphine St., New Orleans, LA 70112. www.auduboncottages.com. ℂ **504/586-1516.** 7 units. $279–$799 room. Rates include welcome beverage, breakfast, bottled water. Valet parking $30. **Amenities:** Butler service, pool, fitness room, free Wi-Fi.

New Orleans Hotels

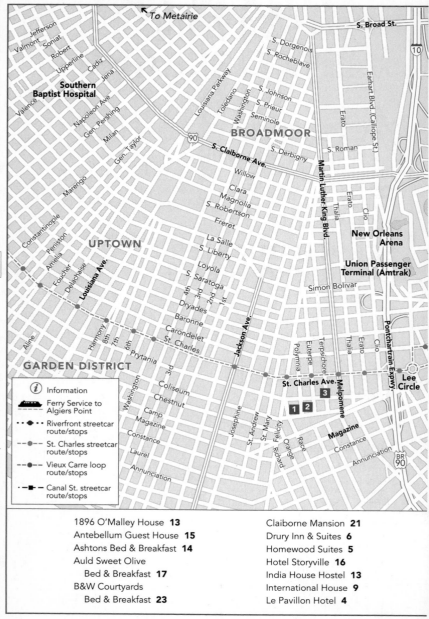

1896 O'Malley House **13**
Antebellum Guest House **15**
Ashtons Bed & Breakfast **14**
Auld Sweet Olive
   Bed & Breakfast **17**
B&W Courtyards
   Bed & Breakfast **23**

Claiborne Mansion **21**
Drury Inn & Suites **6**
Homewood Suites **5**
Hotel Storyville **16**
India House Hostel **13**
International House **9**
Le Pavillon Hotel **4**

Loews New Orleans Hotel **12**
Maison de Macarty **22**
Maison Dubois **19**
Melrose Mansion **18**
Parisian Courtyard Inn **3**
Prytania Park Hotel **2**

Renaissance Arts Hotel **7**
Royal Street Inn & R Bar **20**
St. Charles Guest House **1**
St. James Hotel **10**
The Roosevelt **8**
Windsor Court **11**

Ritz-Carlton New Orleans ★★★   It may not be the ritziest of all Ritz-Carltons, but do expect Ritz-level luxury, service, and amenities, including a stellar spa and the soignée **Davenport Lounge.** It's all quite gracious and stately (as was its previous tenant, legendary department store Maison Blanche), though the hotel is a bit confusing to navigate. Room decor leans very traditional; even the smaller rooms have superb bedding. Try for a larger room on the 12th, 14th, or 15th floor, or better yet, the just-renovated Maison Orleans club level. With its plush lounge, handsome library, 24-hour concierge, and food and bev service, it's the best in town.

921 Canal St., New Orleans, LA 70112. www.ritzcarlton.com/neworleans. ✆ **800/522-8780** or 504/524-1331. 452 units. $199–$329 double, $299–$499 and up executive suites. Valet parking $45. Pets welcome. **Amenities:** Restaurant, bar, concierge, complimentary access to spa and fitness center, room service, shops, Wi-Fi (free in public areas; $13/day in rooms).

Soniat House ★★   Inside these unassuming Creole townhouse exteriors lays an oasis of indulgent calm. The staff spoils guests; Frette linens cradle them; and the sweet courtyards, candlelit at night, soothe them. The handsome rooms differ in size and furnishings. Most in the main house have high ceilings; all have well-selected artwork; some have balconies (a room with both helps justify the rates). Bathrooms are small though some have Jacuzzi tubs. But the experience is gracious, romantic, and adult. It's more about ambience than amenities here (well, except the $13 charge for continental breakfast, even if it is fresh baked and squeezed).

1133 Chartres St., New Orleans, LA 70116. www.soniathouse.com. ✆ **800/544-8808** or 504/522-0570. 30 units. $195–$375 queen or king room, $400–$795 and up suites. Valet parking $35. No children 9 and under. **Amenities:** Concierge, complimentary access to nearby New Orleans Athletic Club, free Wi-Fi.

Expensive

Bourbon Orleans Hotel ★★   Location, location, location. And a big pool. This large property has that, plus good service, and even better history. The formal lobby makes an impressive impression right off the bat, and rooms were fully renovated in 2013, so the decor is fresh (if still standard nouveau hotel) and bathrooms were sexied up in black marble. The smallest rooms are a tad tight; the bi-level loft suites with balcony are ideal for party people (participants *and* spectators) but too noisy for others. Long hallways mean you might be walking your muffuletta off—for some that's a plus (otherwise, request something close to the elevators). Recent improvements to the **Bourbon O** bar are a plus.

717 Orleans St., New Orleans, LA 70116. www.bourbonorleans.com. ✆ **866/513-9744** or 504/523-2222. 218 units. $110–$379 double, $279–$579 suite. Rates include welcome beverage. Valet parking $34. **Amenities:** Restaurant (breakfast and dinner only), bar, concierge, fitness room, outdoor pool, room service (breakfast and dinner only), free Wi-Fi.

Dauphine Orleans Hotel ★★   This labyrinth of vintage rooms, some with private courtyards, others surrounding the popular pool, is quite charming. Avoid those overlooking the dour parking lot. Atmosphere and rooms are both friendly and relaxed—the former welcoming, the latter showing some age. Inclusive breakfast and beverages are a bonus (the bar displays authentication of its history as a former brothel). Easy access to—but a quiet respite from—Bourbon Street.

415 Dauphine St., New Orleans, LA 70112. www.dauphineorleans.com. ✆ **800/521-7111** or 504/586-1800. 111 units. $119–$269 double, $199–$399 suite. Rates include continental breakfast and welcome beverage. Extra person $20. Children 17 and under stay free in parent's room. Valet parking $34. **Amenities:** Bar, coffee lounge, small fitness room, outdoor pool, free Wi-Fi.

French Quarter Hotels

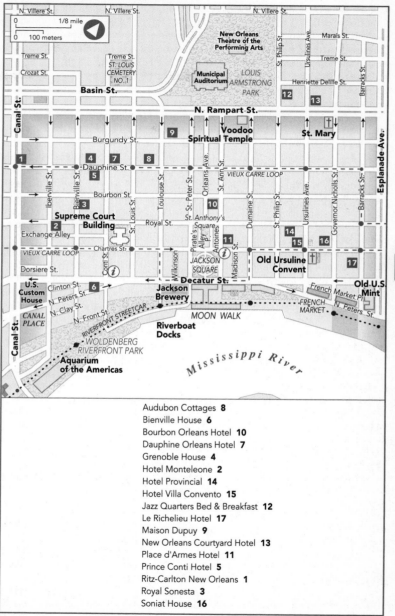

Audubon Cottages **8**
Bienville House **6**
Bourbon Orleans Hotel **10**
Dauphine Orleans Hotel **7**
Grenoble House **4**
Hotel Monteleone **2**
Hotel Provincial **14**
Hotel Villa Convento **15**
Jazz Quarters Bed & Breakfast **12**
Le Richelieu Hotel **17**
Maison Dupuy **9**
New Orleans Courtyard Hotel **13**
Place d'Armes Hotel **11**
Prince Conti Hotel **5**
Ritz-Carlton New Orleans **1**
Royal Sonesta **3**
Soniat House **16**

Hotel Monteleone ★★ There is almost nothing modest about the venerable Monteleone, family-owned since 1886. Not the ornate lobby, not the hallowed literary tradition (Faulkner, Hemingway, Capote, Tennessee Williams, and Eudora Welty slept, drank, and/or wrote here, among others), not the happy hour scene or stellar view at the rooftop pool. And certainly not the fancifully sublime, legendary **Carousel Bar** (p. 179). The larger suites offer roomy, classic gentility, but standard rooms can be, well, on the modest side. Some are quite petite, and those ending in #27 have no windows (though #56 and #59 are bigger and high-ceilinged). The family ownership is reflected in gracious, accommodating service (gentlemen should spring for a proper hot-towel, straight-razor shave in the barbershop here; everyone should spring for something from the pricy but very soothing full-service spa). The fitness equipment is notably good, and **Criollo Restaurant** is a big step up from standard hotel fare.

214 Royal St., New Orleans, LA 70130. www.hotelmonteleone.com. ℂ **800/535-9595** or 504/523-3341. 570 units. $189–$399 double, $579 and up suite. Extra person $25. Children 17 and under stay free in parent's room. Valet parking $40. Pets allowed with fee and deposit. **Amenities:** Restaurant, bar, concierge, fitness center, heated rooftop pool, room service, spa, Wi-Fi (free in lobby; $10 in-room; $15 for hi-speed).

Jazz Quarters Bed & Breakfast ★★★ An unexpected and unassuming enclave of entrancing private cottages (part of the original Tremé plantation) and a languid tropical garden lie hidden behind greenery and gates next to Armstrong Park. The one- and two-room parlor suites are decorated for comfort with smart, contemporary wares, a nod to the birthplace of jazz across the street, and a smattering of antiques (no more is needed—history seeps out from the very brick walls here). The unobtrusive but obliging hosts serve a stellar, Southern-style breakfast (sweet potato bread pudding, oh my) at pretty communal tables, indoors or out. Lots of nice little touches here—a complimentary welcome glass of champagne or wine upon check-in, chilled towels available any time you return from a humid outing—but not many other amenities to speak of. No matter: It's all awfully inviting, especially for small groups, reunions, and romantics, and it's just a block from the French Quarter.

1129 St. Philip St., New Orleans, LA 70116. www.jazzquarters.com. ℂ **800/523-1372** or 504/523-1372. 10 units. $135–$375 cottage. Rates include breakfast. **Amenities:** Free secured parking, free Wi-Fi.

Maison Dupuy ★★ We're quite enamored of this midrange, architecturally picturesque hotel with very good service, set in a quiet part of the Quarter but within walking distance of Bourbon Street. The building surrounds a large courtyard (popular for weddings) with a heated pool. Rooms with courtyard-side balconies are extra pleasant; streetside ones are noisier, but it's a fun view of the action. A mid-2015 renovation promises slightly larger bathrooms and updated decor, and a pleasantly uncluttered mix of antiques and contemporary furnishings. This might mean construction, ergo discounts and/or annoyances, so check the status when you reserve.

1001 Toulouse St., New Orleans, LA 70112. www.maisondupuy.com. ℂ **800/535-9177** or 504/586-8000. 200 units. $169–$369 double, $329–$1,200 suite. Valet parking $36. **Amenities:** Restaurant, bar, exercise room (24 hr.), heated outdoor pool, room service, free Wi-Fi.

Royal Sonesta ★★★ You might forget you're right on Bourbon Street, what with all the graciousness inside. The Sonesta is large, bustling, and classy, with outstanding service for the mix of tourists and business patrons. Rooms, bathrooms, and suites are among the more hand-somely decorated of those that go for French reproductions (get one facing the inside courtyard to avoid the Bourbon Street racket—or facing Bourbon if that's what you're here for). The large courtyard pool is wonderfully welcoming but can get pretty crowded. All the amenity bases are covered; indeed, almost everything you could need is here, including the so-so **Desire Oyster Bar,** the terrific **Restaurant R'evolution** (p. 80), and **Irvin Mayfield's Jazz Playhouse** (p. 171)—which definitely adds to the luster and liveliness.

300 Bourbon St., New Orleans, LA 70130. www.sonesta.com/royalneworleans. ⓒ **800/766-3782** or 504/586-0300. 518 units. $169–$629 double, $400–$2,500 suite. Parking $39. **Amenities:** 3 restaurants, 4 bars, concierge, exercise room, outdoor pool/terrace, room service, free Wi-Fi.

Moderate

Bienville House ★★   This boutique hotel, owned by the Monteleone, injects a touch of class here and there: in the hand-painted murals on the small, classically elegant lobby walls, and in the intimacy of the pool area (you'd never know you're right off a major street, and not in a European mansion). Rooms are showing their age, but have high ceilings and French reproduction furnishings (nothing particularly pizzazzy). Size and brightness vary—a lot—the lowest-priced ones are windowless. Swing one with a balcony if you can—what a difference! The staff here is truly welcoming, even to pets. Take your continental breakfast around the pool rather than in the blah breakfast room. We're crazed with anticipation over the autumn 2014 opening of **Latitude 29 bar and restaurant,** with its pedigreed team and monster promise.

320 Decatur St., New Orleans, LA 70130. www.bienvillehouse.com. ⓒ **800/535-9603** or 504/529-2345. 83 units. $169–$369 double, $499 and up suite. Rates include continental breakfast, afternoon cookies. Parking $32. **Amenities:** Restaurant, outdoor saltwater pool, room service, Wi-Fi (free in lobby; $10 in-room).

Grenoble House ★★   When this mid-range property finally opened in 2013 after a lengthy post-Katrina closure, they did a few things very well, like putting full kitchens in all 17 suites: for those willing to pour their own cereal or re-heat leftovers, the dining out savings add up. A heated pool, spa, and spacious courtyards link 3 historic buildings; newly added columns and moldings riff on their historic bones. Decor is comfy traditional; room sizes and configurations vary (some work well for families or small groups). There's a basic continental breakfast and occasional events at an outdoor bar and BBQ area (that guests can also rent). Street noise can be an issue for the front-facing rooms; in-progress double-window installation should help. Third floor rooms are less expensive for a reason: no elevators. Staff is friendly and helpful though, the property uses a key hold system (guests "check" keys at front desk when leaving).

323 Dauphine St., New Orleans, LA 70112. www.grenoblehouse.com. ⓒ **504/522-1331.** 17 units. $199–$450 suite (advance payment required). Rates include continental breakfast. Valet parking (1 block away) $26. **Amenities:** Pool, spa, free Wi-Fi.

Hotel Provincial ★★　On the whole, this family-run hotel has plenty of charac-ter, from the flickering gas lamps to the rumored ghosts (it's a former Civil War hospital) to the quiet, high-ceilinged rooms (those facing the street still get some noise). The better ones have fireplaces (non-working) or huge windows; the best (on the upper floors) even have a little view of the river—but with no elevators, be willing to climb for that view. We're also fond of those on the first floor that open onto the small courtyard (though they're all a bit of an antiques mish-mosh). Bathrooms, upgraded in 2014, sparkle with white marble. Another courtyard is mostly pool; com-plimentary breakfast is basic but welcome.

1024 Chartres St., New Orleans, LA 70116. www.hotelprovincial.com. ✆ **800/535-7922** or 504/581-4995. 92 units. $99–$349 double. Rates include continental breakfast. Valet parking $26. **Amenities:** Bar, pool, free Wi-Fi.

Hotel Villa Convento ★★　It's not luxurious and the decor is on the fussy side, but the family-owned Creole townhouse boasts balconies with views, guesthouse warmth, and captivating history—all of which infuse it with a slightly sexy vibe. Maybe it's because it's the original House of the Rising Sun, and the spot where a young Jimmy Buffett first, ahem, saw the sun rise as a man (both rumors, but we choose to believe). Free parking (a few blocks away, but still in the FQ) is a big bonus for drive-in visitors; so are the small, hard-to-find single rooms for solo travelers on a budget. Some rooms are pretty dark. Request one with brick walls, the better to feel the history.

616 Ursulines Ave., New Orleans, LA 70116. www.villaconvento.com. ✆ **504/522-1793.** 25 units. $89–$185 double, $125–$205 suite. No children 9 and under. **Amenities:** Computer station, shared fridge and microwave, complimentary coffee in lobby, free Wi-Fi.

Le Richelieu Hotel ★　Nothing here to knock your socks off, but this former row house (and macaroni factory) in the quiet, residential end of the French Quarter has clean, basic rooms and fair prices. The public spaces feel sorta like Daddy-cave additions to a suburban home: a small wood-paneled bar; a glassed-in, poolside cafe; and a dunking pool. It's all oddly cozy and welcoming, and a perfectly okay choice. It was for Sir Paul McCartney and family, who stayed here while he was in town recording *Venus and Mars.*

1234 Chartres St., New Orleans, LA 70116. www.lerichelieuhotel.com. ✆ **800/535-9653** or 504/529-2492. 87 units. $95–$190 double, $200–$550 suite. Extra person, including children $15. Self-parking $20. **Amenities:** Restaurant (breakfast and lunch only), bar, concierge, saltwater pool, room service, free Wi-Fi.

New Orleans Courtyard Hotel ★　This boutique inn on the Tremé side of Rampart Street offers French Quarter proximity at fair rates and pleasantly authentic ambience. They've worked hard to raise their standards over the past few years and it shows, including updating the hotel-generic room furnishings (though there's still work to do—starting with bathroom renovations). Two multi-hued, low-ceilinged buildings are joined by a courtyard and goodly expanse of pool (which the breakfast room overlooks and a sister property—the **French Quarter Suites**—shares). We're partial to the carriage-house rooms, with wood floors, exposed brick, and shutters—though a nearby laundry station means much staff scurrying about. Breakfast is highlighted by the self-serve waffle maker. Rampart brings inevitable street noise (which will worsen when streetcar line construction starts); interior rooms fare best.

1101 N. Rampart St., New Orleans, LA 70116. www.nocourtyard.com. ✆ **504/522-7333.** 21 units. $159–$219 double. Rates include continental breakfast. Onsite parking $25. **Amenities:** Free Wi-Fi.

Place d'Armes Hotel ★　If you're planning to spend a lot of time sightseeing, this is a good choice for French Quarter lodging, especially given the relatively good rates (with basic continental breakfast included). You're a hop-skip from both Jackson Square and Café du Monde, and it's hard to have a care when you're lounging around an amoeba-shaped pool shaded by palm trees. But if your vacation includes much lolling in plush rooms and you live for light-filled mornings, this may not be for you. Several buildings are knitted together by brick hallways and awfully pretty, awfully vieux courtyards. Rooms and decor, while perfectly serviceable, are showing their age a bit (bathrooms, too). Some rooms are dark or windowless, even, but a few splendid ones have terraces with a Jackson Square corner view.

625 St. Ann St., New Orleans, LA 70116. www.placedarmes.com. ⓒ **800/626-5917** or 504/524-4531. 84 units. $99–$459. Rates include continental breakfast. Children 11 and under free. Valet parking $28. **Amenities:** Pool, free Wi-Fi.

Prince Conti Hotel ★   The highlights here are Bourbon Street proximity and the very good **Bombay Club** (p. 179) martini bar/jazz club. Rooms facing Conti may get Bourbon noise; others are set back from the street, which provides a nice sense of seclusion but doesn't help with light (some rooms are windowless or overlook parking). It's got the French Quarter feel, and rooms are clean if a bit shopworn and thin-walled. Nonetheless the small café is convenient for breakfast, the staff is helpful, and given the location and non-Princely rates, it's a good value.

830 Conti St., New Orleans, LA 70112. www.princecontihotel.com. ⓒ **800/626-4319** or 504/529-4172. 76 units. $89–$359 double, $129–$499 suite. Children 11 and under free. Valet parking $28. **Amenities:** Cafe, piano bar, free Wi-Fi.

Inexpensive

Sorry. If you consult former editions of *Frommer's New Orleans,* you'd find options for inexpensive French Quarter hotels. But demand has increased, the recession has recessed, and some formerly acceptable budget properties have upgraded into moderate or high-end hotels. Alas, we regret to say that the days of cheapie French Quarter digs may be gone. Try the Bywater . . . for now.

MARIGNY & BYWATER

A few inns and a slew of B&Bs (many newly minted) dot this gentrified-meets-working-class area. Artists' workshops, galleries, and a fresh crop of darn good restaurants are scattered throughout the area.

Best for: Artists; bohemians; regular folks who prefer staying among the like-minded; LGBTQ; music lovers who want to fall out of bed and onto Frenchmen Street.

Drawbacks: While parts are within walking distance of the French Quarter, others are too far from the action or from public transportation, warranting a car or bike. Expect dicey, rundown shotgun homes commingling with cool renovations.

Expensive

Claiborne Mansion ★★   Secreted a block from the boisterous, tattered hordes of Frenchmen Street is a stately edifice hiding elegance and serenity you'd never expect. What appears to be a private home is a bed and breakfast with two drop-dead stunning suites (and a few other rooms that aren't quite as terrific), and a fairly fabulous swimming pool. Those suites, done up in whites and creams, take full advantage of the original home's original architecture: soaring ceilings, crown moldings, fireplaces (non-working), and huge windows. Continental breakfast is set out in a communal indoor/outdoor kitchen in the expansive backyard (its orange trees provide the juice, when in season), where the saltwater pool might tempt you away from the nearby clubs. Upstairs rooms in the main house are pretty in a lesser way; the carriage-house rooms benefit from location and pool but are otherwise ordinary. Hospitality is more sufficient than solicitous, but architecture buffs will enjoy the owner's insights.

2111 Dauphine St., New Orleans, LA 70116. www.claibornemansion.com. ☎ **504/301-1027.** 7 units. $125–$170 single, $225–$300 suite. Rates include breakfast. Street parking. **Amenities:** Free Wi-Fi.

Moderate

Auld Sweet Olive Bed & Breakfast ★★   Sweet is the operative word for this butter-yellow Creole cottage, from the laziness-inducing wicker porch chairs to the yummy-delish breakfast muffins to the custom-painted, airy rooms. But it's genuine and unfussy, just like hospitable owner Nancy. She's free with the what-to-do tips (it's near the St. Claude Ave. clubs), but hides her Emmy on kitchen shelves of pretty reclaimed wood.

2460 N. Rampart St., New Orleans, LA 70117. www.sweetolive.com. ☎ **877/470-5323** or 504/947-4332. 5 units. $110–$300 double and suite. Rates include full breakfast. Street parking. **Amenities:** Free Wi-Fi.

B&W Courtyards Bed & Breakfast ★★   The simple exterior masks a serene courtyard, a soothing hot tub, and a 6-room B&B—4 blocks and a world away from the madding Frenchmen crowd. They've had some mix-and-match fun here, blending tropical West Indies hues with French antiques and Oriental touches, and each clever room is unique (sometimes even strange—you enter one through the bathroom; saloon-style swinging doors lead from the bathroom to the bedroom); some are more recently updated than others. The hosts are music-lovers who freely share insider club tips and occasionally jam with guests; they also serve a killer hot breakfast (that tasso cheddar frittata, oh baby).

2425 Chartres St., New Orleans, LA 70117. www.bandwcourtyards.com. ☎ **800/585-5731** or 504/267-5007. 6 units. $159–$195 double. Rates include full breakfast. Street parking. **Amenities:** Hot tub, free Wi-Fi.

Maison Dubois ★★   The spacious, raised building dates to the 1920s, so it's decidedly different from the city's 18th-century European and Caribbean influences.

Marigny & Bywater

WHERE TO STAY IN NEW ORLEANS

That's part of its interest, but non-architecture buffs will be more taken by the pretty (if petite) pool and spa, the quiet residential feel, the ever-helpful host, and the proximity to the French Quarter and Frenchmen Street. Nothing's too fancy here: the midsize rooms; the small, clean bathrooms; the continental breakfast. But for location and the comfy indoor and outdoor places to chill, it's a perfectly good choice. The room with a queen and two twin beds is a good family option; the balcony rooms' French doors open to a sweetly scented courtyard.

1419 Dauphine St., New Orleans, LA 70116. www.maisondubois.net. © **866/948-1619.** 5 units. $169–$199 double. Rates include continental breakfast. Limited street parking (free). **Amenities:** Saltwater pool, spa, free Wi-Fi.

Maison de Macarty ★★ Tucked away in the backwaters of the Bywater neighborhood is a Victorian treasure with one of the better backyards we've seen: big pool and deck space complete with cabana bar . . . which seems to have a strong gravitational pull. Six rooms are in the high-ceilinged main house, and two are in separate private cottages; all were smartly decorated (not overly so) with old and new pieces in 2013. Room sizes vary, and bathrooms fluctuate between shower-only style and those with deep Jacuzzi tub. The Storyville room works well with its loft space but is not for the claustrophobic; the others are amply sized, and some open over the courtyard for added airiness. Add plush bedding, a generous sit-down breakfast (crawfish sweet potato Benedict!), and the pet-friendly, inherently neighborly ambience and you're nearly a local. You'll definitely want a car or bike.

3820 Burgundy St., New Orleans, LA 70117. www.maisonmacarty.com. © **504/267-1564.** 8 units. $129–$249. Rates include breakfast. Street parking. **Amenities:** Outdoor mineral water pool, free Wi-Fi.

Royal Street Inn & R Bar ★ The fact that the name of this guesthouse includes the name of the attached bar is not incidental. You're welcomed with complimentary drink tokens, and you should count on participating in the bar action (here or elsewhere) late into the night—lest you become its victim. As long as you're aware that this is part of the experience here (music, cigarette smoke, and all), it's all good—including the actual rooms. They're a hip, clever mix of leather seating, mood lighting, pops of color with the existing wood-and-brick vibe, comfortable but a bit well-worn and ramshackle, like torn jeans. It's the free-spirited Marigny attitude at play—which also describes the service and the clientele. Punk-intellectuals and urban artist/gentrifiers populate the bar, and like-minded visitors stay at the inn. It's decidedly Marigny but also Quarter- and Frenchmen-close; location and atmosphere help you feel a bit like a local (Mondays, dudes can even get a $10 shot and a haircut).

1431 Royal St., New Orleans, LA 70116. www.royalstreetinn.com. © **504/948-7499.** 5 units. $160–$380 double. Rates include bar beverage. Street parking available. **Amenities:** Bar, free Wi-Fi.

MID-CITY/ESPLANADE

This thriving, mostly residential area encompasses diverse socioeconomies and architectural styles amid quiet neighborhood streets and busy commercial corridors. Between City Park and the French Quarter, it includes a number of B&Bs along Esplanade Avenue—grand along some stretches, shabby along others.

Best for: Repeat visitors seeking to experience the city more like a resident; those who prefer B&Bs; Jazz Fest and Voodoo Experience goers; bike riders.

Drawbacks: You'll rely on a car, bikes, taxis, or public transportation. It's a large area with some altogether lovely sections; others not at all.

Expensive

1896 O'Malley House ★★★ A nondescript Mid-City neighborhood unexpectedly houses this grand B&B. It's quite splendid, antiqued but not frilly and steps from the Canal Street streetcar line. Fine art, stunning woodwork, and gorgeous fireplace add architectural interest. Breakfast is served in the formal dining room, or you can take your homemade muffin to an unexceptional outdoor space. The largest rooms are on the second floor; most of the dull bathrooms have Jacuzzi tubs. The smaller, garret-like rooms on the third floor make clever use of their odd shapes and bleached wood. Ghost hunters should request the haunted room. Host Larry and two golden retrievers provide a pleasantly personal, furry touch.

120 S. Pierce St., New Orleans, LA 70119. www.1896omalleyhouse.com. ℂ **866/226-1896** or 504/488-5896. 8 units. $155–$230. Rates include breakfast, snacks, beverages. Limited free off-street parking. **Amenities:** Free Wi-Fi.

Ashtons Bed & Breakfast ★★★ Ashtons stops just short of lavish, remaining comfortable rather than over-the-top. We might even call it homey—if home was a genteel, Esplanade Avenue antebellum mansion—in that once you sink into your comfy bed, you may not want to leave your romantic, pastel-walled, antiques-filled room. But you will, for stellar breakfasts like eggs *cochon de lait.* The main-house rooms are plenty spacious; ceilings are ridiculously high, sheets equally silky. Room #4 has a half-tester bed and an extravagant rain-shower showerhead; #7 has a clawfoot whirlpool tub. It's all light and bright, from the wide front gallery to the huge, oak-shaded backyard, and the on-site hosts are most congenial. Excellence is in the details, and the owners have carefully covered every base here.

2023 Esplanade Ave., New Orleans, LA 70119. www.ashtonsbb.com. ℂ **800/725-4131** or 504/942-7048. 8 units. $189–$229 double. Rates include full breakfast, beverages. **Amenities:** Secure free parking, free Wi-Fi.

Melrose Mansion ★★★ Looks can be deceiving. Enter this grandly columned 1854 Victorian Gothic, and rather than antiques and brocades, you're met with ultra-modern, atonal leather furnishings set against stark white 21-foot-high walls. The architectural bones and original embellishments of the house have been retained, including stunning carved cornices, moldings, and chandelier medallions, now accented with abstract art and a pop of green. The overall effect is a sexy shock to the system. The well-appointed guest rooms in the main house (a former Storyville "party house") and a bungalow range from large to enormous and follow the vibe: low-slung king beds in super-soft sheets, with marble and glass bathrooms (some with Jacuzzi tubs). Similarly chic condo-style suites in a third building have full kitchens and living rooms. Between them is the large pool. There's a generous continental breakfast, evening wine and cheese, and snacks and staff round the clock—the latter are smooth and solicitous, but not at all cold; they'll gladly help with arrangements or share recommendations and anecdotes. Like which perfume the ghost of Miss Kitty wears—it's said to waft through her old room. No worries; it's a (well-scented) storage room now.

937 Esplanade Ave., New Orleans, LA 70116. www.melrosegroup.com. ℂ **800/650-3323** or 504/944-2255. 21 units. $160–$300 double. Rates include continental breakfast and nightly wine and cheese. Street parking or limited off-street parking $26 and up. **Amenities:** Heated outdoor pool, concierge, free Wi-Fi.

Moderate

Antebellum Guest House ★★★ Grandiosity, check. Antiques everywhere. High ceilings. Elaborate breakfast. Check, check, all here. The real difference is in the experience, and the hosts. You could spend your entire visit chatting with them about New Orleans, art, travel, history, and whatever far-flung topics arise. They're interesting and interested, which describes much of New Orleans's population, but now you're at home with them (home being an 1830s Esplanade Avenue glamour gal, the former "party home" to a wealthy plantation family, now tarted up to the nines). Quibblers (Instagram posters of scuffed baseboard shots—who probably shouldn't come to a 300-year-old city) will find things to complain about. The anachronistic, 1970s bathrooms are boring, for starters. But there are loaner bikes to get you to the nearby French Quarter or City Park. And when you step into the dreamy, moss-hung backyard, with its hot tub and a secret garden, magic begins.

1333 Esplanade Ave., New Orleans, LA 70116. www.antebellumguesthouse.com. © **504/943-1900.** 3 units. Around $150 double. Rates include full breakfast. Street parking. **Amenities:** Hot tub, bicycles, free Wi-Fi.

Hotel Storyville ★ Great location (especially for Jazz Fest goers), friendly host, clean and unfussy rooms with kitchenettes: all good. The exterior looks fittingly New Orleanean, with tall columns and wide double galleries, and its mint-green color hints at the hotel's beachy tone (aqua, and laid-back). Rooms vary in size and configuration, from a tiny single to a multi-bedroom. The huge back yard is event-ready, which may or may not work to your benefit (if a crawfish boil is on, you're probably invited; if a wedding is on—which is often—there's a party in your yard). Other amenities and services are scant so don't expect to be doted on, but the price is surely right.

1261 Esplanade Ave., New Orleans, LA 70116. www.hotelstoryville.net. © **504/948-4800.** 9 suites. $99–$299 single and double. Secured off-street parking $5, or limited free off-street parking. **Amenities:** Free Wi-Fi.

Inexpensive

India House Hostel ★ Foreign travelers and students (passport or student ID required) looking for budget lodging and an instant party, welcome home. The four buildings comprising India House have private rooms (some with their own bathrooms) and bunk-bed dorms, a usable kitchen that also serves good cheap meals, aboveground pool, outdoor bar, and a ready-made social scene. There's a den with TV, and frequent events—the stage next to the pool is well used by local and visiting bands. It's close to the Canal Street streetcar and bus lines, and tour companies pick up here regularly. It's funky but not filthy, friendly, and backpacker-ready. Book directly for the best rates.

124 S. Lopez St., New Orleans, LA 70119. www.indiahousehostel.com. © **504/821-1904.** 168 beds. $20–$90. Limited off-street parking; street parking. **Amenities:** Outdoor pool, kitchen privileges, free Wi-Fi.

CENTRAL BUSINESS DISTRICT

The "CBD" abuts the French Quarter along Canal Street and extends west to include the Warehouse District, with loft-conversion hotels, a thriving club scene, and the arts district. As the city's commerce center, modernity and history mix—as do tourists and businesspeople. Some of the city's finest restaurants and hotels are here, as are some good deals (especially on weekends and off-season), and most of it is still walking distance to the French Quarter action.

Best for: Hipsters; foodies; conventioneers; Superdome attendees; museum-goers; the budget-minded; families (lots of suite and chain hotels are here).

Drawbacks: It's New Orleans, not New York, but it *is* a city center. There are office buildings and people who may actually be working. Pricey parking.

Very Expensive

The Roosevelt ★★ This grandiose Waldorf property is fairly regal throughout, but the movie-star glamorous, block-long lobby is positively stunning, and the history and pedigree equally impressive. Sizes and views in the well-appointed, traditional rooms vary: luxury suites are more than ample, but the smallest rooms are simply too small for what you're probably paying, and service sometimes feels stretched (though check for seasonal package deals). Some have tubs (even clawfoots!); some on the upper floors overlook the city or the fourth-floor pool. All have luscious beds. But guest rooms really take a back seat to the exceptional lobby and other common areas: the sumptuous spa, **Domenica** restaurant (p. 104), **Sazerac Bar** (p. 183), and the historic **Blue Room** club. Holiday season here is magical.

123 Baronne St., New Orleans, LA 70112. www.therooseveltneworleans.com. © **877/887-1006** or 504/648-1200. 504 units, including 125 suites. $199–$499 double, $299–$999 suite. Valet parking $42. Pets less than 25 lbs. allowed ($175 fee). **Amenities:** 2 restaurants, coffee shop, bar, Blue Room club, concierge, fitness room, gift shop, Jacuzzi, pool, room service, spa, Wi-Fi (free in lobby and cafe; $15/day in room).

Windsor Court ★★★ There's a kind of hush at this ultra-fine hotel, for decades the center of New Orleans high society. Everything is serene and mannerly, from the proper high tea to mind-blowing hallway galleries of original 17th- to 19th-century art to the restaurant—the highest-end **Grill Room.** A massive recent overhaul refreshed all the fabrics and finery; the city's indisputably best hotel spa was added; service has also improved. The spacious accommodations are traditional if not particularly distinctive; suites are enormous—all are large-windowed and full of light. Those with balconies and river views are exceptional (though some "view" rooms are only partial views), and a ritzy club level adds 24/7 concierge service. The terrific rooftop pool is one of several superb places to enjoy a smart beverage here; the cool **Cocktail Bar** and chichi **Polo Club** are also on that list (p. 183).

300 Gravier St., New Orleans, LA 70130. www.windsorcourthotel.com. © **888/596-0955** or 504/523-6000. 316 units. $195–$495 standard double, $225–$555 suite, $320–$800 club level. Children 17 and under stay free in parent's room. Valet parking $40. **Amenities:** Restaurant, 2 lounges, concierge, fitness center, pool, Jacuzzi, room service, spa, free Wi-Fi.

Expensive

International House ★★ Rooms in this boutique sanctuary are minimalist chic in grays and pale gold tones, with comfy beds and fab bathrooms (request one with a tub if you so desire)—a nice contrast to all the Victoriana around, though the building's beautiful old bones still honor its history—thus rooms are small. Black-and-white photos of local musicians give a nod to the locale. All that cool, including craft cocktail bar **Loa,** make this popular with business types and film crews. But it's more about appearances than amenities, so when rates are at their higher end it may not be merited (conversely, it runs some good online specials). At press time, the new restaurant's opening (and restoration of room service) were pending.

221 Camp St., New Orleans, LA 70130. www.ihhotel.com. ℭ **800/633-5770** or 504/553-9550. 117 units. $119–$379 double, $369–$1,799 suite. Valet parking $35. **Amenities:** Restaurant, bar, fitness room, free Wi-Fi.

Loews New Orleans Hotel ★★★   We're fans of the crisply contemporary Loews, with its judicious sprinkles of New Orleans flavor, and the consistently genteel, professional service. The bright, expansive rooms come with local photography and sophisticated finishes. Rooms and all public spaces underwent a full, decorative renovation in fall 2014, getting a crisp new contemporary look; some have terrif river views (others face surrounding buildings). Even the smallest are on the large size (though the handsome wood and granite bathrooms are not too large). All get access to the steamy indoor pool and well-equipped fitness room, not to mention the persistently fine **Café Adelaide** restaurant (a member of the Commander's Palace family) and the **Swizzle Stick Bar** (p. 183).

300 Poydras St., New Orleans, LA 70130. www.loewshotels.com/neworleans. ℭ **866/211-6511** or 504/595-3300. 285 units. $169–$339 room, $600–$1,800 and up suite. Valet parking $39. Pets allowed ($100 nonrefundable fee, plus $25 daily cleaning fee). **Amenities:** Restaurant, bar, concierge, exercise room, indoor pool, room service, spa, Wi-Fi (free in lobby; $13/day in room).

Renaissance Arts Hotel ★★   A film-crew favorite for its loft-conversion style, the proximity to the **Howlin' Wolf** (p. 176) and other Warehouse area attractions, spacious rooms, and terrific modern art throughout the hotel. Nothing's to die for, but everything is clean-lined and well done—and the staff is particularly efficient. The large rooftop pool adds a lot, with spectacular views and a jumping social scene. Streetside rooms have large, original windows; the interior overlooks the '70s-era atrium and courtyard or neighboring buildings.

700 Tchoupitoulas St., New Orleans, LA 70130. www.renaissanceartshotel.com. ℭ **800/431-8634** or 504/613-2330. 217 units. $229–$299 double. Valet parking $43. **Amenities:** Restaurant, bar, concierge, sundries shop, fitness center, newspaper deliver on request, rooftop pool, room service, Wi-Fi (free in public spaces; $13/day in-room).

Moderate

Drury Inn & Suites ★★★   The looming, generic exterior hides a better-than-expected interior and a ton of amenities—made even better through a major 2014 expansion. Most of the spacious rooms, in monochromes with pops of local art, have high ceilings; avoid the darker ones on the lower floors and shorter ones on floors 4 and 5. Suites, though not luxurious, are downright huge. Free, hot breakfast buffet and evening "kick-back" snacks (not fancy, but a nice touch) add big value. Staff is invariably friendly, and the serviceable fitness room looks onto the good-sized pool and whirlpool spa. All that, a good location, and reasonable rates make this one of the better deals in town.

820 Poydras St., New Orleans, LA 70112. www.druryhotels.com. ℭ **800/378-7946** or 504/529-7800. 214 units. $119–$169 regular room, $229–$279 suite. Rates include full breakfast plus weekday evening snacks. Valet parking $25. **Amenities:** Fitness room, heated rooftop pool and spa, free Wi-Fi.

Homewood Suites ★★   This was already one of our top choices, given all its inclusive fringe bennies. Now, after a top-to-bottom 2014 renovation, it's pretty dazzling in a cookie-cutter (Hilton) sort of way. Speaking of cookies, they're among the freebies here. Add a full hot breakfast buffet; the perfunctory but perfectly good free dinner (think lasagna or fried chicken, salad bar, *and wine or beer!*); no-cost business center; indoor pool and whirlpool—and the savings really add up. On top of that, the XL, all-suite rooms have a living room, microwave, and fridge, so if you'd rather spend on sights than tastes and don't need luxury, you can pretty much decamp here and save a ton on dining out (and on transportation, given the convenient location). The fresh decor is well turned-out and well thought-out, and the exterior has plenty of historical appeal so you don't feel completely ensconced in chains. When rates are at the bottom or mid-range, it's a super value, especially for families and extended stays.

901 Poydras St., New Orleans, LA 70112. www.homewoodsuitesneworleans.com. © **504/581-5599**. 166 units. $149–$259 suite. Rates include full breakfast buffet daily and basic dinner Mon–Thurs. Valet parking $31. **Amenities:** Fitness room, snack shop, indoor pool and whirlpool, kitchenette, coin laundry, business center, free Wi-Fi.

Le Pavillon Hotel ★★ One's chin may rise a centimeter or two when entering Le Pavillon's soaring lobby, with crystal chandeliers overhead, plush Oriental rugs underfoot, enormous marble pillars, and ornate carved ceilings. It's a Historic Hotel of America dating to 1907, and the first in New Orleans to have an elevator. It's also famous for late-night peanut butter and jelly service (silver platter and all), with a hot chocolate nightcap; we're equally amused by the classical statuary around the heated rooftop pool. The heavily draped rooms are fine, but pale in contrast to the lobby's gleaming luxe, though some have painted ceilings and glam black-granite bathrooms with gold fixtures. Suites, with original art and antiques, are a different story—would that a wee bit of their elegance was extended to the standard rooms. Service and amenities are all topnotch: The **Crystal Room restaurant** is a little touch of Versailles; $16 weekday lunch buffet is a steal. Discounted rates do pop up on travel websites.

833 Poydras St., New Orleans, LA 70112. www.lepavillon.com. © **800/535-9095** or 504/581-3111. 226 units. $129–$699 queen, $595–$1,695 suite. Valet parking $35. **Amenities:** Restaurant, bar, concierge, fitness center, whirlpool spa, heated outdoor pool, room service, free Wi-Fi.

St. James Hotel ★ It's not next to anything in particular, but it's close to so many things, which metaphorically describes the property's quality as well as its geography. The old sugar and coffee trading company pays homage to its Caribbean roots with subtle decorative touches of parrots and palm trees. Rooms are on the small side; it's less noticeable in those in the back building with private or shared terrace space or high ceilings. Top-floor rooms still have some original brick or wood and new hardwood floors; and most have marble-floored bathrooms. A courtyard pool is sweet if miniscule, but complimentary morning coffee and fresh-baked croissants, feather beds, in-room fridge and microwave, and good online discounts make up for a lot.

330 Magazine St., New Orleans, LA 70130. www.saintjameshotel.com. © **888/211-3447** or 504/304-4000. 86 units. $109–$299 double. Valet parking $30. **Amenities:** Restaurant, concierge, pool, free local gym passes, free Wi-Fi.

Inexpensive

Nada. Some of our recommended moderate to higher-priced CBD hotels run super specials, especially over summer; and the many chains here might work if convention business is slow that week. But there aren't any year-round inexpensive options in this area that we'd guide you toward, dear reader. Just being honest.

UPTOWN/
THE GARDEN DISTRICT

The residential Garden District offers iconic Old South charm, complete with moss-laden greenery and palatial, columned homes. Not all of Uptown is as grandiose as the name might suggest—there are many more modest, no less charming properties—but the best sections are both spacious and gracious.

Best for: Repeat visitors; romantics; history buffs; claustrophobes; garden lovers; lollers-about; style-seeking shoppers (for nearby Magazine Street).

Drawbacks: Allow extra time and expense to get around—you're not in the thick of the action or the city's top attractions. You'll likely be near public transportation, but some prefer a car or bike.

Expensive

Grand Victorian Bed & Breakfast ★★ This magazine-gorgeous 1893 Victorian home on St. Charles Avenue is what we picture when we think of a sumptuous, antiques-filled Southern B&B. All of the elegantly furnished rooms vary; several have antique beds that are small by today's standards, and some have Jacuzzi tubs or balconies. If you can snag one of those balcony rooms or any room, really, during Carnival season, you've scored: you're right on the parade route (and convenient to the St. Charles streetcar year-round; the rumble might bother some people, but we love it). Friendly owner Bonnie sees to it that feather mattresses are fluffy, coffee and snacks are available round-the-clock, and all your needs are met.

2727 St. Charles Ave., New Orleans, LA 70130. www.gvbb.com. ✆ **800/977-0008** or 504/895-1104. 8 units. $165–$325 double. Rates include continental breakfast. Street parking. **Amenities:** Free Wi-Fi.

Maison Perrier Bed & Breakfast ★★ The impressive exterior of this former house of ill repute is frillier than inside, though there is still plenty to impress here. Antiques abound, but they're not overdone, and a smattering of country touches help create genuine, unstuffy comfort. The beds are deep and piled with soft linens, and room configurations are amenable to couples, families, and friends (two- or four-legged). Nearly all the well-appointed bathrooms have whirlpool tubs—some big enough for two. A full breakfast with Southern specialties like puffed pancakes, an honor bar, ample supply of homemade sweets, and weekend wine and cheese parties round out the very pleasing experience here. Check the website for excellent seasonal deals.

4117 Perrier St., New Orleans, LA 70115. www.maisonperrier.com. ✆ **888/610-1807** or 504/897-1807. 14 units. $145–$275 double. Rates include tax, breakfast, snacks. Parking available on-street; free limited on-site parking as well. **Amenities:** Concierge, free Wi-Fi.

Moderate

The Chimes Bed & Breakfast ★★★ This gem has no grand airs, just pure charm and contentment in a true neighborhood setting. Rooms vary in size, but all are a tasteful, unfussy, unpretentious mix of antiques, creature comforts, and thoughtful amenities. The helpful hosts bring in breakfast pastries daily from the beloved Le Boulangerie bakery—tastier yet in the pretty courtyard. They also bring 25+ years of hospitality experience (they built The Chimes themselves), and it shows in the caring

Uptown Hotels

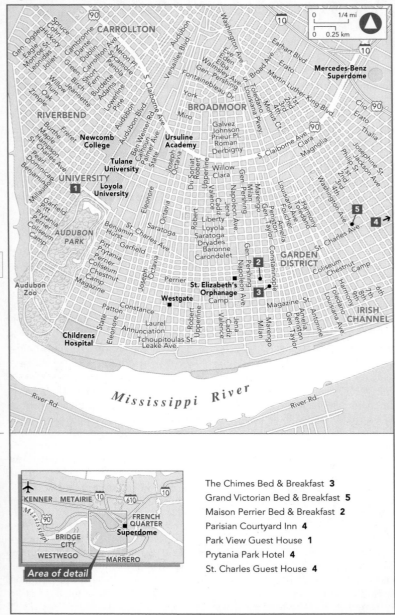

The Chimes Bed & Breakfast **3**

Grand Victorian Bed & Breakfast **5**

Maison Perrier Bed & Breakfast **2**

Parisian Courtyard Inn **4**

Park View Guest House **1**

Prytania Park Hotel **4**

St. Charles Guest House **4**

details. Rooms got a thorough renewal in 2013, with fresh furnishings, pretty linens, and an impressive gallery wall displaying striking black-and-white photographs of local musicians—the work of one of their many repeat guests.

1146 Constantinople St., New Orleans, LA 70115. www.chimesneworleans.com. ℂ **504/899-2621** or 504/453-2183. 5 units. $128–$250 double. Rates include breakfast, tax, parking. **Amenities:** Free Wi-Fi.

Parisian Courtyard Inn ★★★

Hospitality and location are the keywords here, though the accommodations in this converted 1846 mansion are by no means slouchy. The Lower Garden District locale is far enough from the name-brand action to merit slightly lower rates, but close enough to access it all by foot or nearby streetcar. Affable Aussie host Tracey will ably direct you and ply you with afternoon brownies. If a lucky wind blows, her musician husband and friends might entertain you in the soignée parlor with its elaborate ceiling details and porcelain chandeliers (among the many fab light fixtures). All that helps to make up for the bathrooms—if you're one of those vacationers who seek the best in rest(rooms), these teensy tubless ones won't cut it. Rooms have plenty of carved antiques; sizes vary from liberal to slight (we like the 2nd-floor balcony suites; 3rd and 4th floors have angled ceilings). The outdoor courtyards are pleasant enough.

1726 Prytania St., New Orleans, LA 70115. www.theparisiancourtyardinn.com. ℂ **504/581-4540.** 8 units. $135–$225 double. Rates include breakfast, afternoon snacks. Street parking. **Amenities:** Free Wi-Fi.

Park View Guest House ★★

For Tulane and Loyola visitors and others staying far uptown, this late 1800s boardinghouse with St. Charles Avenue frontage (easy streetcar access) is a splendid choice. The park in view is verdant Audubon Park, which brings serenity and spaciousness to the large breakfast room and park-facing guest rooms (some with deep clawfoot tubs). Decor is Victoriana-meets-reproduction; smaller and non-view rooms can be cramped and/or dark. The Wi-Fi signal is stretched in the back, but the wide front porch is stellar for sitting a spell. The ample buffet breakfast also ranks high; daily cookies and afternoon wine add delightful touches.

7004 St. Charles Ave., New Orleans, LA 70115. www.parkviewguesthouse.com. ℂ **888/533-0746** or 504/861-7564. 21 units. $159–$219 double. Rates include breakfast, afternoon wine and snacks. Street parking available. **Amenities:** Free Wi-Fi.

Inexpensive

Prytania Park Hotel ★

Most rooms in this Lower Garden District budget property are decorated in standard motel contemporary; they will get a needed refurnishing in mid-2015 when the property undergoes renovations (inquire about the status). Meanwhile, go for those with hardwood floors and brick walls to feel like you're actually in New Orleans. Part of the hotel dates to the 1840s; other sections are in newer buildings; in between is a small courtyard where breakfast (packaged pastries) is served and smokers hang. Light sleepers should request an off-street room. It's conveniently situated between St. Charles Avenue and Magazine Street, and not too far from the Warehouse District. Amenities are basic, but continental breakfast, parking, and Wi-Fi are free; plus, summer and off-season rates can be downright cheap.

1525 Prytania St. (enter off Terpsichore St.), New Orleans, LA 70115. www.prytaniaparkhotel.com. ℂ **800/862-1984** or 504/524-0427. 62 units. $89–$139 double. Children free in parent's room; extra adult $10. Must be 21 to check in. Rates include continental breakfast. Free off-street parking (except during Mardi Gras). **Amenities:** Fridge, microwave, vending machines, free Wi-Fi.

NOT YOUR MOTHER'S room & board

Wherever you stay in New Orleans, good food is close by. But if that's just not close enough—if you're one of those who selects your accommodations based on its culinary offerings—here are a few hotels with outstanding restaurants:

○ **Café Adelaide** in Loew's New Orleans (CBD)

○ **Domenica** (p. 104) in the Roosevelt Hotel (CBD)

○ **The Grill Room** in the Windsor Court (CBD)

○ **Latitude 29** in the Bienville House (FQ)

○ **Lüke** in the Hilton St. Charles (CBD)

○ **MiLa** (p. 102) in the Renaissance Pere Marquette (CBD)

○ **Restaurant R'evolution** (p. 80) in the Royal Sonesta (FQ)

○ **The Rib Room** in the Omni (FQ)

○ **Vacherie** (p. 87) in the Hotel St. Marie (FQ)

St. Charles Guest House ★   The three 1890s buildings are humble, funky, old, slightly crumbling, and not for everyone. But if you're a non-partying budget traveler and don't demand spick-and-span, you'll appreciate the value, location, pool, and even the offbeat charm (if the owner is around, chat him up for some great tales of yore). Some rooms are downright spartan (no A/C); others are larger and even furnished with antiques; upkeep is imperfect. Keep expectations in check (generally, and specifically regarding the continental breakfast), and don't overpay for accommodations during a festival—that will only leave you bitter.

1748 Prytania St., New Orleans, LA 70130. www.stcharlesguesthouse.com. ℂ **504/523-6556.** 25 units, 22 with private bathroom. $55–$105 double. Rates include continental breakfast. No credit cards; PayPal accepted. No in-room phones. Parking available on street. **Amenities:** Outdoor pool, free Wi-Fi.

WHERE TO DINE IN NEW ORLEANS

N ew Orleans restaurant matriarch Miss Ella Brennan says that whereas in other places, one eats to live, "In New Orleans, we live to eat." It's hard to spoil such a big appetite.

Here, we don't call a friend and ask, "How are you?" Instead, it's either the colloquial "Where y'at?" or, more often, "What're you eatin'?" Here, cuisine is community, cuisine is culture, cuisine is practically church (literally and figuratively— except for the fact that Church is church). Food forms the crucial threads of the city's multicolored fabric: It weaves through the people, the music, the history, the parties, the traditions. A style of gumbo can define a neighborhood. A roux technique can unite (or divide) generations of families.

At last count New Orleans had more than 1,400 restaurants, so there's goodness in every direction and on every level: in centuries-old grande-dame restaurants and the corner po' boy shops; in a gas station with shockingly good steam-table food; and in the sleek bistro of a brash, upstart culinary-school grad fusing Grandma's recipes with unpronounceable techniques and ingredients. And that's not even counting the many bars and nightclubs serving seriously stellar snacks.

There are culinary training grounds like the recently renovated **Café Reconcile** (1631 Oretha Castle Haley Blvd.; www.cafereconcile.org; ⓒ **504/568-1157**) and **Liberty's Kitchen** (422½ S. Broad St.; www.libertys kitchen.org; ⓒ **504/822-4011**), serving sturdy meals while training young men and women for careers in food service. And there are fourth-generation chefs working backstreet dives whose menus and ingredients haven't varied since, well, forever.

You are going to want to eat a lot here. And you are going to want to eat here, a lot. And then you are going to talk about it. You'll probably adopt the local custom of talking about dinner while you're at lunch (and lunch while you're breakfasting). The food here is utterly, unashamedly regional, which isn't to say that (in some cases) it's not also utterly of the moment and sophisticated. But it's ingredient- and chef-driven, which makes it uniquely New Orleanean: It will never be Copenhagen or Bilbao, or New York for that matter, nor does it want (or need) to.

In many restaurants, certainly in the more traditional ones, dishes are based largely on variations of Creole recipes. Others, the innovators, take Creole as a cue and go wildly afield. Creole food was originally based on recipes brought by the French settlers, the herbs and filé (ground sassafras leaves) used by the Native Americans, and saffron and peppers introduced by the Spanish. From the West Indies came new vegetables, spices, and sugar cane, and when slave boats arrived, an African influence was added. Today, the Italian influence runs deep, and even Vietnamese has found its way onto the plate, brought by a newer wave of immigrants. And while nearly all restaurateurs source fresh ingredients from local purveyors, the ban on butter never took hold here (thankfully). Flavor comes first.

So indulge and enjoy. It's what you do here. Try some of everything. We're particularly big on lunching, since many of the best restaurants have terrific prix-fixe lunch deals that include dishes that'd cost twice as much during dinner. Then start planning the next trip, so you can do it again.

Please keep in mind that all prices, hours, and menu items in the following listings are subject to change according to season, availability, or whim. You should call in advance to ensure the accuracy of anything of import to you.

Make sure to check out our "**Best of**" recommendations in chapter 1.

OF BEIGNETS, BOUDIN & DIRTY RICE

Many of the foods in New Orleans are unique to the region and consequently may be unfamiliar. This list that will help you navigate local menus:

Andouille (ahn-doo-*we*)   A spicy Cajun sausage made with pork.

bananas Foster   Bananas sautéed in liqueur, brown sugar, cinnamon, and butter, drenched in rum, set ablaze, served over vanilla ice cream.

barbequed shrimp   Not actually grilled or BBQ-sauced, but a butter-soaked, garlicky, pepper-shot peel-and-eat Gulf specialty.

beignet (bin-*yay*)   A big, puffy, deep-fried, hole-free doughnut, liberally sprinkled with powdered sugar—the more sugar, the better.

boudin (boo-*dan*)   Cajun liver-and-rice sausage of varying spice levels.

café brûlot (cah-*fay* brew-*low*)   Coffee, spices, and liqueurs, served flaming.

crawfish   A tiny, lobsterlike creature common locally and eaten in every conceivable way, including boiled whole with spices and peeled by hand.

debris   The rich, juicy bits of meat that fall off during roasting and carving.

dressed   A "dressed" po' boy comes with lettuce, tomato, mayonnaise, and sometimes pickles.

étouffée (ay-too-*fay*)   A Cajun stew (usually containing crawfish or shrimp) served with rice.

filé (*fee*-lay)   Ground sassafras leaves, frequently used to thicken gumbo.

gumbo   A thick, spicy soup of poultry, seafood, and/or sausage, with okra in a roux base, served with rice. Gumbo z'herbes, a Good Friday tradition, eschews meat for greens.

holy trinity   Onions, bell peppers, and celery: the base of much Creole and Cajun cooking.

Hurricane   A local drink of rum and passion-fruit punch.

jambalaya (jum-ba-*lie*-ya)   A stew of yellow rice, sausage, seafood, poultry, vegetables, and spices.

lagniappe (lan-*yap*)   A little something extra: a bonus freebie.

mirliton (*mur*-li-tone)   A pear-shaped squash also called chayote.

muffuletta (moo-foo-*let*-ta or moo-fuh-*lot*-ta)   A mountainous sandwich made with Italian deli meats, cheese, and olive salad, piled onto a specially made round bread.

oysters Rockefeller Oysters on the half shell in a creamy spinach sauce, so called because Rockefeller was the only name rich enough to match the taste.

po' boy, po-boy, poor boy A sandwich on long French bread, similar to submarines and grinders. Often filled with fried seafood or roast beef, or famously with French fries and gravy, they can include most anything. Originally, free sustenance for striking transit workers, those "poor boys."

pralines (*praw*-leens) A sweet confection of brown sugar and pecans.

rémoulade A spicy sauce, usually over shrimp, concocted of mayonnaise, boiled egg yolks, horseradish, Creole mustard, and lemon juice.

roux A mixture of flour and fat that's slowly cooked over low heat, used to thicken stews, soups, and sauces.

Sazerac The official cocktail of New Orleans, consisting of rye whiskey (or sometimes cognac) with sugar and bitters.

shrimp Creole Shrimp in a tomato sauce seasoned with what's known around town as the "holy trinity:" onions, bell peppers, and celery.

RESTAURANTS BY CUISINE

AMERICAN, NEW AMERICAN & REGIONAL AMERICAN

Emeril's ★★★ ($$$$, p. 99)
Root ★★ ($$$, p. 103)
Square Root ★★ ($$$$, p. 103)
Stanley ★★ ($, p. 90)

ASIAN

Dong Phuong ★★ ($, p. 115)
Yuki Izakaya ★★ ($$, p. 93)

BAKERY (ALSO SEE DESSERTS)

Buttermilk Drop Bakery and Cafe ★★ ($, p. 116)
Café Beignet ★ ($, p. 88)
Café EnVie ★ ($, p. 117)
Cake Café & Bakery ★ ($, p. 93)
Croissant D'Or ★★ ($, p. 117)
District Donuts. Sliders. Brew. ★★★ ($, p. 114)
La Boulangerie ★★★ ($, p. 117)
Mr. Gregory's ★★★ ($, p. 90)
Petite Amelie ★ ($, p. 86)

BARBECUE

The Joint ★★★ ($$, p. 92)
McClure's ★★ ($, p. 92)
Walker's ★★ ($, p. 115)

BARS & CLUBS WITH NOTABLE FOOD

Bacchanal ★★★ ($$, p. 91)
Bombay Club ★ ($$, p. 179)
Cane & Table ★★★ ($, p. 179)
Erin Rose/Killer Po' Boys ★★★ ($, p. 180)
Kukhnya ★★★ ($, p. 94)
Little Gem Saloon ★★★ ($$, p. 177)
Napoleon House ★★ ($, p. 181)
Oxalis ★★★ ($$, p. 183)
Siberia ★★★ ($, p. 177)
Snug Harbor ★★★ ($$, p. 174)

KEY TO ABBREVIATIONS:
$$$$** = Very Expensive **$$$** = Expensive **$$** = Moderate **$ = Inexpensive

SoBou ★★ ($$, p. 181)
Three Muses ★★★ ($$, p. 174)
Tico Tolteca ★★ ($, p. 181)

BISTRO

Café Degas ★★★ ($$, p. 95)
Coquette ★★★ ($$$, p. 108)
Dante's Kitchen ★★ ($$, p. 112)
Dominique's on Magazine ★ ($$$, p. 109)
Herbsaint ★★★ ($$$, p. 101)
La Petite Grocery ★★★ ($$$, p. 110)
Lilette ★★ ($$$, p. 110)
Martinique Bistro ★★ ($$$, p. 110)
Patois ★★★ ($$$, p. 111)
Rue 127 ★★★ ($$, p. 96)
Sylvain ★★★ ($$, p. 87)

CAFES/COFFEEHOUSES

Biscuits & Buns on Banks ★★★ ($, p. 97)
Café Beignet ★ ($, p. 88)
Café du Monde ★★★ ($, p. 116)
Café EnVie ★ ($, p. 117)
Café Maspero ★ ($, p. 89)
Croissant D'Or ★★ ($, p. 117)
DeVille Coffee House & Creperie ★★ ($, p. 89)
District Donuts. Sliders. Brew. ★★★ ($, p. 114)
Hi Volt ★★ ($, p. 118)
Merchant ★★★ ($, p. 118)
Mr. Gregory's ★★★ ($, p. 90)
Morning Call ★★ ($, p. 118)
P.J.'s Coffee & Tea Company ★★ ($, p. 118)
Somethin' Else Café ★★ ($, p. 90)
Spitfire ★★ ($, p. 118)

CAJUN/CONTEMPORARY CAJUN

Brigtsen's ★★★ ($$$, p. 108)
Cochon ★★ ($$, p. 103)
Cochon Butcher ★★★ ($, p. 104)
K-Paul's Louisiana Kitchen ★★ ($$$$, p. 77)
Toup's Meatery ★★ ($$, p. 96)

CREOLE/CONTEMPORARY CREOLE/NEW LOUISIANA

Annunciation ★★★ ($$$, p. 100)
Antoine's ★★ ($$$, p. 82)

Appoline ★★ ($$$, p. 106)
Arnaud's ★★★ ($$$, p. 82)
Brigtsen's ★★★ ($$$, p. 108)
Café Adelaide ★★ ($$$, p. 101)
Clancy's ★★★ ($$$$, p. 105)
Commander's Palace ★★★ ($$$$, p. 106)
Coop's ★ ($, p. 89)
Court of Two Sisters ★ ($$$, p. 83)
Dante's Kitchen ★★ ($$, p. 112)
Dooky Chase ★★ ($$, p. 95)
EAT New Orlean's ★★ ($$, p. 86)
Elizabeth's ★★★ ($$, p. 92)
Emeril's ★★★ ($$$$, p. 99)
Felix's Restaurant & Oyster Bar ★★ ($, p. 89)
Jacques-Imo's ★★ ($$$, p. 109)
Joey K's ★ ($, p. 114)
Killer Po' Boys ★★★ ($, p. 180)
K-Paul's Louisiana Kitchen ★★ ($$$$, p. 77)
Lil' Dizzy's ★★ ($, p. 97)
Liuzza's ★★ ($$, p. 95)
Liuzza's by the Track ★★★ ($, p. 98)
Louisiana Bistro ★★ ($$, p. 84)
Mandina's ★★ ($$, p. 96)
Mr. B's Bistro ★★ ($$$, p. 84)
Mother's ★ ($, p. 105)
Muriel's ★ ($$$, p. 85)
Napoleon House ★★ ($, p. 181)
Palace Café ★ ($$$, p. 85)
Patois ★★★ ($$$, p. 111)
Praline Connection ★ ($$, p. 93)
Ralph's on the Park ★★★ ($$$, p. 94)
Restaurant August ★★★ ($$$$, p. 99)
Restaurant R'evolution ★★ ($$$$, p. 80)
Tableau ★★ ($$$, p. 85)
Tujague's ★ ($$$, p. 86)
Upperline ★★ ($$$, p. 111)
Vacherie ★★ ($$, p. 87)
Ye Olde College Inn ★★★ ($$, p. 97)

DESSERT/ICE CREAM/SNOBALL

Angelo Brocato Ice Cream & Confectionery ★★★ ($, p. 116)

Buttermilk Drop Bakery and Cafe ★★
($, p. 116)
Café du Monde ★★★ ($, p. 116)
Cake Café & Bakery ★ ($, p. 93)
Creole Creamery ★★★ ($, p. 117)
Hansen's Sno-Bliz ★★★ ($, p. 119)
La Divina Gelateria ★★ ($, p. 117)
Meltdown Ice Pops ★★ ($, p. 117)
Morning Call ★★ ($, p. 118)
Pandora's SnoBalls ★★★ ($, p. 119)
Piety St. SnoBalls ★★★ ($, p. 119)
Plum St. SnoBalls ★★★ ($, p. 119)
Sucré ★★★ ($, p. 118)

DINER
Camellia Grill ★★ ($, p. 90 and 113)
Clover Grill ★ ($, p. 89)
The Grill ★★ ($, p. 90)
Joey K's ★ ($, p. 114)
Port of Call ★★ ($$, p. 87)

FRENCH/CLASSIC CREOLE
Antoine's ★★ ($$$, p. 82)
Arnaud's ★★★ ($$$, p. 82)
Café Degas ★★★ ($$, p. 95)
Galatoire's ★★ ($$$$, p. 77)
Martinique Bistro ★★ ($$$, p. 110)
Restaurant August ★★★ ($$$$, p. 99)
Tableau ★★ ($$$, p. 85)
Tujague's ★ ($$$, p. 86)

HAMBURGERS (SEE DINER)

ICE CREAM (SEE DESSERT)

INTERNATIONAL
Bacchanal ★★★ ($$, p. 91)
Bayona ★★★ ($$$, p. 82)
Booty's Street Food ★ ($, p. 118)
Dominique's on Magazine ★
($$$, p. 109)
Green Goddess ★★ ($$, p. 87)
Kukhnya ★★★ ($, p. 94)
Lola's ★★ ($$, p. 96)
Mondo ★★ ($$, p. 115)

ITALIAN
Domenica ★★★ ($$, p. 104)
Irene's Cuisine ★★★ ($$$, p. 84)
Liuzza's ★★ ($$, p. 95)
Mandina's ★★ ($$, p. 96)

Marcello's ★★ ($$$, p. 102)
Mariza ★★ ($$, p. 92)
Mosca's ★★★ ($$$, p. 115)
Napoleon House ★★ ($, p. 181)
Nor-Joe's Importing ★★ ($, p. 91)
Pascal's Manale ★★ ($$, p. 112)
Pizza Domenica ★★ ($, p. 104)

LIGHT FARE
Acme Oyster House ★★★ ($, p. 88)
Biscuits & Buns on Banks ★★★
($, p. 97)
Café Amelie ★★ ($$, p. 86)
Café EnVie ★ ($, p. 117)
Café Maspero ★ ($, p. 89)
Cake Café & Bakery ★ ($, p. 93)
Camellia Grill ★★ ($, p. 90 and
p. 113)
Central Grocery ★★★ ($, p. 91)
Cochon Butcher ★★★ ($, p. 104)
Coop's ★ ($, p. 89)
The Counter ★ ($, p. 84)
Dat Dog ★ ($, p. 114)
DeVille Coffee House & Creperie ★★
($, p. 89)
District Donuts. Sliders. Brew. ★★★
($, p. 114)
EAT ★★ ($$, p. 86)
Frady's ★ ($, p. 88)
Gene's Po' Boys ★★ ($, p. 94)
The Grill ★★ ($, p. 90)
Guy's Po' Boys ★★ ($, p. 114)
Johnny's Po-Boys ★ ($, p. 90)
Liuzza's by the Track ★★★ ($, p. 98)
Mr. Gregory's ★★★ ($, p. 90)
Morning Call ★★ ($, p. 118)
Mother's ★ ($, p. 105)
The Old Coffee Pot ★ ($, p. 90)
Oxalis ★★★ ($$, p. 93)
Parkway Bakery and Tavern ★★★
($, p. 98)
Petite Amelie ★ ($, p. 86)
Quarter Grocery ★ ($, p. 88)
QuarterMaster ★ ($, p. 88)
R&O's ★★ ($$, p. 115)
The Sammich ★★ ($, p. 116)
Sammy's ★★ ($, p. 115)
Somethin' Else Café ★★ ($, p. 90)
Stanley ★★ ($, p. 90)
Sucré ★★★ ($, p. 118)

THE FRENCH QUARTER

Very Expensive

Doris Metropolitan ★★ STEAK   Doris opened to much fanfare in late 2013, audaciously displaying its dry aging beef in the front window like an Amsterdam madam. Besides the distinctive, slightly pungent flavor of dry-aged steaks (theirs are sourced from raised-to-specification cattle), the Israeli-based restaurant brought some Middle-Eastern touches to its menu, like a delectable charred eggplant appetizer with glossy tahini. Servers are warm and knowledgeable to the allowable extent (the "classified cut" is described by flavor and texture, but the actual cut is not betrayed). The room's indisputably handsome presentation—from artsy olive oil forward—is downright beautiful. Locals have embraced the hopping bar with its beguiling wines and view of the open-kitchen view, and a luxe, chill vibe permeates the moneyed air in the comfortable dining rooms. There were serious missteps on our first visit here—an inedibly tough steak (returned to the Chef, who concurred and corrected it), and a serious overcharge on the bill. But we persevered and things notably improved—with some of the non-steak items, oddly enough, faring best. The juicy pan-glazed chicken that knocked us over wouldn't be our logical first choice; silken tuna tartare is superb. But yes, it's about the beef. In due time, we found the carnivorous knowledge we sought in the Butcher's Cut, its crunch of char displaying a perfectly marbled, ultra flavorful, and densely sensuous mouthful. Okay, all is forgiven.

620 Chartres St. www.dorismetropolitan.com. 🕾 **504/267-3500.** Main courses $19–$42. Fri–Sun noon–2:30pm, daily 5:30–10:30pm.

Galatoire's ★★ CLASSIC CREOLE/FRENCH   Considered New Orleans's consummate old-line Creole French restaurant, Galatoire's is a time-honored, fine-dining classic beloved by generations—perhaps because their families are beloved by Galatoire's. Or perhaps because Tennessee Williams supped here, as did his characters Stella and Blanche in *A Streetcar Named Desire.* It oozes tradition: Ceiling fans whir, bentwood chairs strain, mirrored walls reflect the civilized frivolity. But the jovial obsequiousness that the tuxedoed waiters lavish upon their regulars isn't always bestowed upon *moi et toi.* Things are a tad more somber in the (lesser—but perfectly fine) upstairs dining room. Either way, the drinking commences upon arrival, and doesn't (and shouldn't) let up for a few hours.

No one comes here for great gastronomy, but Galatoire's does know fish (it's had 110 years of practice, after all). Go with a classic shrimp rémoulade, crab maison, or the eggplant fingers. Ask the waiter which fish is best today, get it a la meunière and topped with crabmeat; or order the soft-shell crab if available and some creamed spinach. We're not fond of the heavy sauces they ladle on the fine fish, but don't scoff at asparagus with spot-on hollandaise. The puffy soufflé potatoes are legally required. Skip the meh desserts; order a glass of port instead. Reservations accepted for upstairs only; reserve well in advance.

209 Bourbon St. www.galatoires.com. 🕾 **504/525-2021.** Jackets required after 5pm and all day Sun. Main courses $21–$42. Tues–Sat 11:30am–10pm, Sun noon–10pm. Fri lunch: Recommend lining up 45–60 min. before opening.

Galatoire's 33 ★★ STEAK   Galatoire's regulars have known for years that the seafood specialists grill a mean steak. In 2013, venerable Galatoire's, dowager queen of the New Orleans restaurant scene for 100+ years, spawned a steakhouse offshoot. The fun starts with starters. We love the high-styled deviled eggs, the burly bone marrow—generous, filthy rich, and a bargain at $8—and the unskimping lobster maison. Six prime cuts, from a single-source ranch that raises the cattle to G33's exacting specifications, comprise the crux of the menu—and each is done to perfection. The bone-in tenderloin is just a meat marvel. Sauces and sides include many favorites from Big G next door (like Brabant potatoes, with garlic here). It doesn't have the high-society-playground feel of the original Galatoire's (give it a few decades), but that actually makes it more approachable for visitors, and the bar here is a good hang.

215 Bourbon St. www.galatoires33barandsteak.com. 🕾 **504/335-3932.** Appetizers $8–$22, entrees $24–$52. Tues–Sat 11:30am–10pm, Sun noon–10pm. Bar: Mon 5pm–close, Tues–Sat 11am–close, Sun 11:30am–close.

K-Paul's Louisiana Kitchen ★★ CAJUN/CREOLE   Paul Prudhomme started the Cajun cooking craze in the 1980s and is responsible for introducing the term "blackened" to our culinary vocabulary. His sauce-and-spice empire still thrives, and the restaurant remains a standard-bearer for American regional food—but it's difficult to justify the sky-high prices. We're partial to the blackened beef tenders with debris

Angelo Brocato's Ice Cream
  & Confectionery **5**
Annunciation **37**
Bacchanal **51**
Biscuits & Buns on Banks **2**
Booty's Street Food **45**
Borgne **22**
Buttermilk Drop
  Bakery and Cafe **18**
Café Adelaide **32**
Café Degas **14**
Cajun Seafood **28**
Cake Café & Bakery **43**
Cochon **36**
Cochon Butcher **36**
Dat Dog **21, 41**
Domenica **23**
Dooky Chase **20**
Drago's **33**
Elizabeth's **48**
Emeril's **34**
Frady's **45**
Gene's Po'Boys **40**
Herbsaint **26**

Kukhnya **39**
La Boca **36**
Liberty's Kitchen **16**
Lil' Dizzy's **29**
Liuzza's **7**
Liuzza's by the Track **15**
Lola's **13**
Mandina's **6**
Marcello's **26**
Mariza **44**
Maurepas Foods **46**
McHardy's Chicken **17**
Meltdown Ice Pops **49**
Merchant **25**
MiLa **24**
Morning Call **9**
Mother's **31**
Nor Joe's **1**
Oxalis **45**
Pandora's SnoBalls **10**
Parkway Bakery
  and Tavern **12**
Peche **27**
Peity St. SnoBalls **47**

Praline Connection **41**
Ralph's on the Park **8**
Restaurant August **30**
Root **35**
Rue 127 **4**
Sammy's **38**
The Joint **50**
Toup's Meatery **11**
Willie Mae's
  Scotch House **19**
Ye Olde College Inn **3**
Yuki Izakaya **42**

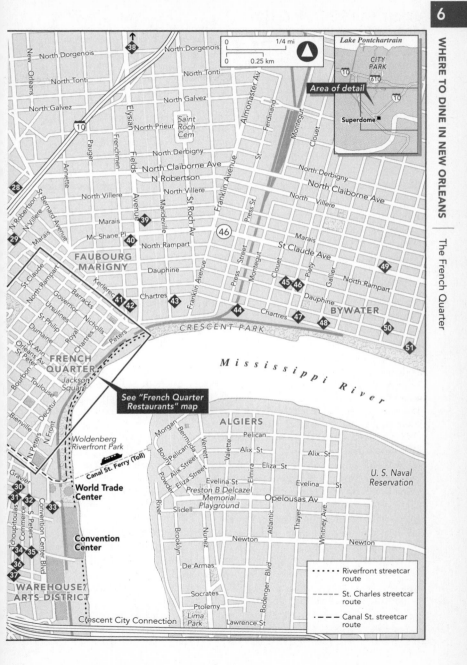

YOU GOT YOUR cajun IN MY CREOLE!

The difference between Cajun and Creole cuisine lies chiefly in distance between city and countryside. Cajun cooking came from the Acadians who settled in the swamps and bayous of rural Louisiana and adapted the recipes of French heritage to their new location. Their cuisine is like their music: robust and full of flavor (and despite the reputation, not necessarily spicy). They used available ingredients like sausage, seafood, poultry, and rice in single-pot stews that fed large families and farms. Creole dishes, on the other hand, were developed by French and Spanish city dwellers and feature fancier sauces and ingredients. Today, the two cuisines have a happy marriage, blurring the distinctions and inviting other influences. Our advice? Disregard the classifications, try it all, and decide what *you* prefer.

from the rotating menu, and now that the classic blackened drum is served (albeit on a po' boy) during the "deli lunch," that's how we roll: with counter service, paper plates, and entrees about $25 less than dinner. Reserve in advance for dinner.

416 Chartres St. www.kpauls.com. 🕐 **504/524-7394.** Business casual; gentlemen are asked to remove hats and caps inside. Main courses $30–$40 dinner, $12–$14 lunch. Thurs–Sun 11am–2pm, Mon–Sat 5:30–10pm.

Restaurant R'evolution ★★ NEW LOUISIANA   Two years (and $6 million) in the making, two food-world icons at the helm (John Folse and Rick Tramonto), two tons of hype, and two years post-debut—it nearly lives up to the brash name claim. Taking Creole cuisine in globe-hopping directions keyed to New Orleans's influences, this is big-league, big-idea, big-ticket dining in a fanciful but refined setting. The most r'evolutionary aspect may be that this restaurant is 2 years old, not 102— this much grandness is rarely launched any more. It's Event Dining, so make it memorable. Tour each elegant but disparate room (ask to see the private rooms if they're available—better yet, book one, or request the stunning Storyville Parlor). Indulge in something marvelous from the wine list, so enormous that only an iPad can contain it (dessert options are also delivered via device). Augment your order with sides, sauces, and toppings—the menu is flush with them. Then, having saved your paychecks for a month or two, hope for the best—experiences here have been inconsistent and service is a bit casual for a restaurant of this caliber and cost. But the plating is unconditionally beautiful. A dark pool of "Death by Gumbo," rich as your surroundings, surrounds a baby quail, and it's terrific. The gently crisped crab beignets, each in a different rémoulade dollop, are also a hit. Terrines, including a lustrous duck liver mousse and a more rugged country pâté, are the best bang. We couldn't justify the pastas, but the shrimp and grits, with its chili-and-ginger Asian kick, were a favorite; the voluminous veal chop was temperature-perfect and bursting with flavor. The jewelry box with tiny cookies tucked into its drawers is a nice dessert lagniappe. Other desserts were almost an afterthought after all this excess, but we fell for the "beignets with coffee," a mocha pot de crème. Reserve well in advance during special events.

777 Bienville St. (in the Royal Sonesta Hotel). www.revolutionnola.com. 🕐 **504/553-2277.** Entrees $19–$62. Reserve well in advance for dinner. Wed–Fri 11:30am–2:30pm, Mon–Thurs 5:30–10pm, Fri–Sat 5:30–11pm, Sun 10:30am–2pm and 5–10pm.

French Quarter Restaurants

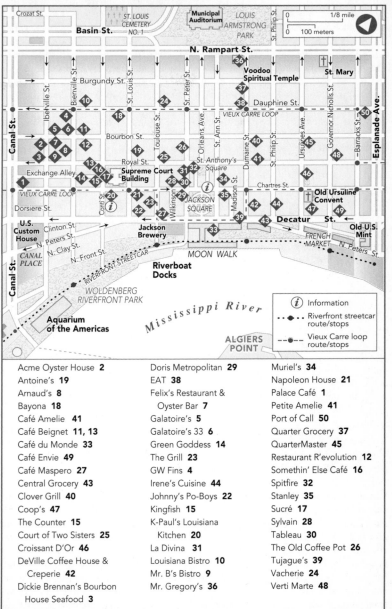

Acme Oyster House **2**	Doris Metropolitan **29**	Muriel's **34**
Antoine's **19**	EAT **38**	Napoleon House **21**
Arnaud's **8**	Felix's Restaurant &	Palace Café **1**
Bayona **18**	Oyster Bar **7**	Petite Amelie **41**
Café Amelie **41**	Galatoire's **5**	Port of Call **50**
Café Beignet **11, 13**	Galatoire's 33 **6**	Quarter Grocery **37**
Café du Monde **33**	Green Goddess **14**	QuarterMaster **45**
Café Envie **49**	The Grill **23**	Restaurant R'evolution **12**
Café Maspero **27**	GW Fins **4**	Somethin' Else Café **16**
Central Grocery **43**	Irene's Cuisine **44**	Spitfire **32**
Clover Grill **40**	Johnny's Po-Boys **22**	Stanley **35**
Coop's **47**	Kingfish **15**	Sucré **17**
The Counter **15**	K-Paul's Louisiana	Sylvain **28**
Court of Two Sisters **25**	Kitchen **20**	Tableau **30**
Croissant D'Or **46**	La Divina **31**	The Old Coffee Pot **26**
DeVille Coffee House &	Louisiana Bistro **10**	Tujague's **39**
Creperie **42**	Mr. B's Bistro **9**	Vacherie **24**
Dickie Brennan's Bourbon	Mr. Gregory's **36**	Verti Marte **48**
House Seafood **3**		

Expensive

Antoine's ★★ CLASSIC CREOLE   We're sentimental about Antoine's, it being one of the first fine-dining restaurants in the New World. It's been owned and operated by the same family (and serving generations of patrons' families) for an astonishing 175 years. It's as classic as New Orleans dining gets, but truth be told, there's better food (and presentation) elsewhere. Still, the experience can be well worth it. The best strategy: Go for conviviality, classics, and drama. Request Johnny or Sterling as your server. Befriend neighboring guests. Order the spinach-soaked baked oysters Rockefeller (invented here); buttery, crab-topped trout Pontchartrain; and a side or two of the hollowed soufflé potato puffs; finish with a *café brûlot* (see "Anythin' Flamin'," p. 108) and the frivolous, football-size (and -shaped) baked Alaska. Get one or two of the daily featured 25¢ cocktails. Then tour some of the 15(!) memorabilia-packed rooms, peek at the astounding wine alley, and catch some good local music in the **Hermes Bar.** The three-course, prix-fixe weekday lunch at $20.15 is worth every penny. Make dinner reservations well in advance during peak periods.

713 St. Louis St. www.antoines.com. ✆ **504/581-4422.** No shorts, sandals, or T-shirts; collared shirts for gentlemen (jackets welcome, not required). Main courses $26–$47. Mon–Sat 11:30am–2pm and 5:30–9pm, Sun 11am–2pm.

Arnaud's ★★★ CLASSIC CREOLE   Arnaud's isn't the best-known of the old New Orleans restaurants, but it tops them in quality, and far exceeds them in the cocktail arena. It's classically atmospheric, with white tile floors and dark wood accents, and the recipes are classics as well. Thus, it's not wildly creative, but the quality and attention to detail are there. Have the signature shrimp Arnaud appetizer (topped with a spicy rémoulade sauce), and the spicy pompano Duarte or the definitive *filet au poivre*. We also love the quail Elzey—petite, elegant fowl stuffed with foie gras mousse, wrapped with bacon, and ensconced in a truffle-wine sauce, and no one should leave without ordering some puffy soufflé potatoes and bananas Foster, flamed tableside (see the "Anythin' Flamin'" counsel, p. 108), although our resident crème brûlée expert rates theirs very high. Allow time to visit the impressive Mardi Gras museum upstairs. A more casual jazz bistro room features nighttime entertainment (a $4 cover goes to the band)—all of which makes Arnaud's a good fine-dining introduction for well-behaved children. Make dinner reservations well in advance during peak periods.

813 Bienville St. www.arnaudsrestaurant.com. ✆ **866/230-8895** or 504/523-5433. Reservations suggested. Business casual. Main courses $27–$40. Dinner nightly 6–10pm, Sun brunch 10am–2:30pm.

Bayona ★★★ INTERNATIONAL   Even while celebrating 25 years in business, chef-owner Susan Spicer's modern classic restaurant still tops many "Best of" lists, with good reason. The food, cocktails, and wine list continue to be thoughtful and inspired. The ambience inside and out is positively lovely, and if service occasionally suffers a tad, that is the exception. Begin with the signature cream of garlic soup; and select among extremes of sweetbreads with lemon caper butter (another signature), any rabbit preparation, or whatever vegetarian dish is on—ever-changing preparations of the latter are consistently superb. At lunch, the famed smoked duck with cashew butter and pepper jelly is a knockout, but the ever-clever specials may sway you. Desserts center on seasonal fruits, like the divine mango cheesecake flan with pistachio crust and blackberries. Deal alert: Wednesday through Saturday's $25 light lunch features three small-plate options. Reservations required for dinner; book early.

430 Dauphine St. www.bayona.com. © **504/525-4455.** Main courses $14–$16 lunch, $28–$38 dinner. Wed–Sat 11:30am–1:30pm, Mon–Thurs 6–10pm, Fri–Sat 5:30pm–close.

Court of Two Sisters ★ CLASSIC CREOLE   No doubt about it, this is one of the prettiest places around, thanks to the huge, wisteria-shaded courtyard and the 200-year-old building, and you should soak up that ambience by enjoying a smart cocktail or two. Then you should go out to eat. Sadly, the food is just mediocre, and let's face it, even supermodels eventually need some personality. The daily jazz brunch buffet is nonetheless popular, and we do get the attraction, so you'd do best to stick with the basics (like simple eggs Benedict) and enjoy the company. Make brunch reservations well in advance.

613 Royal St. www.courtoftwosisters.com. © **504/522-7261.** Main courses $25–$37; brunch buffet $29 adults, $13 children. Daily 9am–3pm jazz brunch buffet and 5:30–10pm.

Dickie Brennan's Bourbon House Seafood ★★ SEAFOOD   Although it looks a bit sprawling and formulaic from the street, this modern version of a classic New Orleans fish house has much to recommend it. Hang out at the super-fresh raw bar, or order the head-turning *fruits du mer* platter. A simple grilled redfish is perfect (top it with fresh lump crabmeat for $12 more, a worthy addition). In a city of good BBQ shrimp dishes (shrimp sautéed in a buttery, garlicky spicy sauce—bread-sopping heaven), we love their bourbon-finished version. Leave room for a frozen bourbon milk punch, a dreamy booze-shake. Naturally they're committed to, and knowledge-able about, all things bourbon. Great happy hour ($5 small plates, $3 Abita Amber on draft, plus a good shucker show) and $26 three-course lunch.

144 Bourbon St. www.bourbonhouse.com. © **504/522-0111.** Main courses $11–$16 breakfast, $12–$32 lunch, $20–$36 dinner. Daily 6:30–10:30am, Sun–Thurs 11am–10pm, Fri–Sat 11am–11pm.

GW Fins ★★★ SEAFOOD   Here's the city's best modern seafood restaurant, and one of its best restaurants, period. It is polished from the top down, with the owner prowling the floor like a tiger mama assuring that no imperfection makes it to the table, or even enters into diners' consciousness. It's clear that GW Fins takes the same care in sourcing its fish, which comes from the Gulf and far beyond, and is just bratty fresh. Preparations are stylish enough but don't dare upstage the star—like the perfectly seared yellowfin tuna or the signature "scalibut" (thin-sliced scallop "scales" atop grilled halibut) on lobster risotto, worthy of its fame. A diverting starter of watermelon and pork belly is also to be savored, as are the lobster dumplings with a light brush of fennel. The wine list thoughtfully complements the cuisine, with a good range of mid-priced bottles and a much-appreciated, extensive array of finer pours by the glass. Order the pretzel-crusted salty malty ice cream pie, even if you only have room for a bite. The large, tiered dining room is handsome and high-ceilinged, while also manag-ing to be conversation conducive. We love those high-backed gangsta booths along the back wall. Check the website for excellent seasonal multicourse deals. Make dinner reservations well in advance.

808 Bienville St. www.gwfins.com. © **504/581-3467.** Collared shirts for men; better jeans; no shorts or flip-flops. Main courses $21–$38. Sun–Thurs 5–10pm, Fri–Sat 5–10:30pm (summer from 5:30pm).

Irene's Cuisine ★★★ ITALIAN   If you detect the scent of simmering garlic from blocks away and aren't lured to its source, Irene's may not interest you. No worry—that leaves more of the French Provincial and Creole-Italian cooking for the rest of us. Irene—herself a Quarter institution—and her friendly crew create delectable house-made pastas and sauces, but the *secondi* are the real standouts. Locals come on Thursdays for the ginormous osso buco flavor bomb, and someone at the table needs to order Duck St. Phillip (with raspberry-pancetta demi-glace) so that everyone can taste it and wish they had ordered it. The seemingly simple *pollo rosemarino*—marinated, par-cooked, re-marinated, and roasted—is nearly perfect. The cramped, low-ceilinged little rooms have a strange, mob-headquarters sort of appeal. Would that the desserts were a little bit better, but the cheesecake will do. Irene's is notorious for long waits, even with reservations, and alas, it can be true. Just figure it into your plans. Limited reservations accepted if space is available; it's worth it to try.

539 St. Philip St. *C* **504/529-8811.** Main courses $18–$38. Mon–Sat 5:30–10pm. Closed major holidays and week of Labor Day.

Kingfish ★★ CONTEMPORARY SOUTHERN   Craft-cocktail guru Chris McMillan (coming out of retirement) and veteran local chef Greg Sonnier opened Kingfish with a high-profile bang in 2013. The ample bar space, surrounded by the elongated, brick and tin-paneled dining room, has the edge over the kitchen: the drinks are stellar; the sophisticated but easygoing Southern food is a step below that. The slightly strange ramen with duck turned out to be a favorite, and while the signature "King" pompano, seared and served on a salt brick, didn't live up to expectations, we do like the creative impulses behind it. They succeeded in the gooey/crunchy oysters thermidor and crab-stuffed, prosciutto-wrapped shrimp salad. Next door, their casual little bro **The Counter** ★ has simple but quality grab-and-go salads and sandwiches (and a convenient make-your-own bloody Mary bar). It's good for a quickie.

337 Chartres St. www.cocktailbarneworleans.com. *C* **504/598-5005.** Main courses $19–$39. Mon–Sun 11am–3:30pm, Sun–Thurs 5:30–10pm, Fri–Sat 5:30–11pm. Bar 5pm–midnight.

Louisiana Bistro ★★ CONTEMPORARY CREOLE   You've seen the movie. On a ramble through Paris, you stumble into *une petite cafe,* just 11 tables, with a nutty chef at the helm. You can hear him shouting at someone from behind the kitchen doors; waiters roll their eyes conspiratorially, and shrug. Then Chef Mars appears at your side, flashing a charming smile, saying "Trust me, you'll like it." So you do, and you do. The a la carte menu here is just a concession to the three-, four-, and five-course "Feed Me" tasting menus, made to order based on market availability and Chef Mars' whim. Call it Louisiana *omakase.* You might get dreamy crawfish beignets in brown beurre, or maybe a cast-iron-bronzed Louisiana swordfish with a shocking drizzle of jalapeño hollandaise. It's good. It's fun. It's good fun. Skip dessert, not wine.

337 Dauphine. www.louisianabistro.net. *C* **504/525-3335.** Entrees $26–$36; "Feed Me" tasting menu, 3 courses $39, 5 courses $59. Wed–Sun 6–10pm.

Mr. B's Bistro ★★ CONTEMPORARY CREOLE   The "B is for Butter." BBQ shrimp is the claim to fame here, and that's what you should get. Not that anything else is bad (the gleaming ginger-glazed pork chop is terrific, for example), but the plump, peppery house special is the standout and indeed the distinguishing feature here. The hunt-club motif draws a businessmen's lunch crowd for the strong drinks and attentive service.

201 Royal St. www.mrbsbistro.com. ℭ **504/523-2078.** Business casual; no shorts or tank tops. Main courses $17–$24 lunch, $25–$38 dinner. Jazz brunch entrees $20–$28. Mon–Sat 11:30am–2pm, bar menu 2–5:30pm, dinner 5:30–9pm; Sun jazz brunch 10:30am–2pm.

Muriel's ★ CONTEMPORARY CREOLE   The dreaded "fine." That's how we feel about perennially popular Muriel's. We want to fall in love with, or at least in, their romantic, red-walled dining rooms, and pose on the elegant balconies overlooking Jackson Square. We want to *ooh* over the crawfish and goat-cheese crêpes, like others seem to do. But except for the admittedly fab atmosphere there's just nothing especially inspired or inspiring here, on the plate or working the floor. So we opt for the safety of the pan-roasted half-chicken or the three-course table d'hôte menu (value priced at $38). Visit the ghost's table, have your palm read in Jackson Square, and the night is still a good one. Lunch here is a waste of atmosphere. Reserve in advance during peak periods.

801 Chartres St. (at St. Ann). www.muriels.com. ℭ **504/568-1885.** Main courses $11–$19 lunch, $17–$23 brunch, $18–$37 dinner. Mon–Sat 11:30am–2:30pm, Mon–Fri 5:30–10pm, Sat–Sun 5–10pm; Sun jazz brunch 11am–2pm.

Palace Café ★ CONTEMPORARY CREOLE   This is a good standby for low-key, non-intimidating Creole dining, and the setting is just right—a historic, two-story building (the former Werlein's music store) with sidewalk seating for good people-watching. It comes with the stamp of New Orleans authenticity that Brennan-family ownership conveys, and its oft-practiced multi-server attention. The crabmeat cheesecake appetizer is what makes people pound the table, and it's truly delish. The Andouille-crusted fish is a winner, and a simple rotisserie chicken with truffle mashed potatoes may be available nationwide, but it's done right here, and more than a few people will be happy to see something familiar. Then there's the white-chocolate bread pudding, which they invented. Pay homage. In fact, weather permitting, we enjoy just desserts at one of those streetside tables (also the "$5 after 5pm" happy-hour small plates, one of their frequent good deals, including summer specials).

605 Canal St. www.palacecafe.com. ℭ **504/523-1661.** Main courses $12–$28 lunch, $18–$35 dinner, $16–$20 brunch. Mon–Sat 11:30am–2:30pm and 5:30–10pm, Sun brunch 10:30am–2:30pm.

Tableau ★★ CLASSIC CREOLE   The pristine white space betrays the fact that Tableau, with its soaring staircase and impressive, high-arched entries, is brand new. But that balcony view overlooking Jackson Square is ageless—and peerless. We relish an afternoon in this scenic spot with a well-balanced classic cocktail, slices of the addictive tart bread, and a "Grand Royal" quartet of seafood starters—including sublime bacon-wrapped, rosemary-skewered oysters. In cooler climes, opt for a hearty red and the heartier, hopped-up onion soup. The airy main dining room looks onto the gleaming open kitchen and brick courtyard; the genteel upstairs room features gold-flocked, vaulted ceilings (in either spot, the $14 two-course lunch deal feels like it should cost double). Like the cuisine, the overall Tableau experience is classic New Orleans, turned up—not to racing speed, but enough to honor gastronomy in 1880 as well as 2015. Things we like: servings in full or demi portions, aiding those who want less *and* those who want more. Chicken Tableau's juicy dark and white portions in a rich Béarnaise sauce. Time-honored poached-egg dishes on the dinner menu. Rare tournedos of steak, with a buttery red-wine reduction and a seared foie-gras souvenir. The logo-branded crème brûlée, served in a shallow, wide bowl (as at other Brennan's restaurants), masterfully maximizes the crispy-crust-to-silken-custard ratio. Service can use a little smoothing out, but overall Tableau is a well-tuned baby grand.

675 St. Peter St. www.tableaufrenchquarter.com. © **504/934-3463.** Dinner main courses $15–$42. Mon–Thurs 11:30am–10pm, Fri–Sat 11:30am–11pm, Sun 10am–10pm; brunch Sat–Sun.

Tujague's ★ CLASSIC CREOLE   Spared the wrecking ball in 2013 (it almost succumbed to a T-shirt-shop takeover), this 1856 landmark is now more precious than ever (and spiffier, after the old-line dining room's revamp last year). Its perfect Sazerac and anti-nouvelle, fork-tender brisket are blessings to be cherished. The threat of closure also kick-started some needed changes to the menu and decor (style-wise, you'd never know, but it's eons fresher). There's an a la carte menu now, but being traditionalists, we still say opt for the six-course prix-fixe menu with a choice of entrées. Choose the veal chop or the soft-shell crab meunière when in season, or go off-menu for the baked garlic chicken Bonne Femme. It's solid if not earth-shattering, authentic Creole cooking, from the sinus-clearing shrimp rémoulade appetizer to the last bread pudding bite, and while the experience is priceless, the menu prices are more than right. Do visit their famous **bar** (p. 182) before or after dinner.

823 Decatur St. www.tujagues.com. © **504/525-8676.** Main courses $14–$22 lunch, $20–$33 dinner; add $23 to entree price for 5-course dinner. Mon–Fri 11am–3pm, Sat–Sun 10am–3pm, daily 5pm–close.

Moderate

Café Amelie ★★ CONTEMPORARY SOUTHERN/LIGHT FARE   The pretty-as-a-chocolate-box courtyard and fresh, straightforward local cuisine are Amelie's calling cards; now it's the place where Beyonce & Jay-Z dined quite publicly days after the scandalous Solange elevator beat-down. Amelie's serves cafe standards with something for everyone to enjoy, like crab cakes or a goat cheese and beet salad, and local faves like a *cochon de lait* pork sandwich or grilled catfish with a kick. It's an awfully nice, relaxing spot, calling loudly for a lemonade or mint julep, which might even entice the ladies (and men) who lunch to indulge in a slice of lemon doberge cake. We concur with that decision. (All that lovely old slate, brick, and greenery make this a popular wedding spot; they're frequently closed for events). Reserve in advance for Sunday brunch. Of note for quick dining: offshoot **Petite Amelie** ★, a few doors down, offers a tasty array of prepared takeaway meals, soups, salads, cheeses, pastries and such via counter-service.

912 Royal St. www.cafeamelie.com. © **504/412-8965.** Main courses $15–$29, brunch $12–$17. Wed–Sun 11am–3pm and 5–9pm (Fri–Sat till 10pm); Sun brunch 11am–3pm. Closed occasionally for special events; call to check. **Petite Amelie:** 900 Royal St. Wed–Sun 8am–8pm.

EAT New Orleans ★★ CONTEMPORARY CREOLE/LIGHT FARE   This charming bi-level corner spot in a tucked-away French Quarter section attracts plenty of locals. The chatty, efficient servers will make you feel like one of them. Trust them when they suggest the hearty, down-to-earth chicken and dumplings or the surf-and-turf stuffed red pepper. At brunch, eggs Dumaine are just what the hangover ordered. *Note:* Proximity to a nearby school means no liquor license, but they will gladly serve whatever you bring from nearby **Matassa's** (1001 Dauphine St.).

900 Dumaine St. www.eatnola.com. © **504/522-7222.** Lunch $10–$18, dinner $13–$24. Tues–Fri 11am–2pm, Tues–Sat 5:30–10pm; brunch Sat–Sun 9am–2pm.

Green Goddess ★★ INTERNATIONAL   The masses of international attention and praise heaped upon Green Goddess when it opened in 2009 were well-deserved. People waited hours for the scarce alleyway tables, to taste the groundbreaking, "globetrotting cuisine" and cocktails inspired by Spanish, Indian, Hawaiian, and Middle Eastern cuisines (for starters). Six years hence, one of the original chefs is gone (the partner remains), the seating has quadrupled, and there's even an indoor dining room. The Bohemia-in-a-bowl concept (tamped down a bit) remains, including a few of the original recipes. The service, never stellar, hasn't changed. But the imaginative, vegetarian-friendly cuisine is still good to very good—ditto for the offbeat atmosphere and very fair prices. Top choices include the shrimp-and-pork-belly *banh mi;* a watermelon and Burrata cheese salad; and Father Pat's grilled cheese, made with Guinness and pear butter. Pair with something from the thoughtful list of (mostly French) wines by the glass. Skip the over-lauded bacon sundae and get the sultan's nest. In fact, if you just come for that dessert and the still-superb cocktails, you'll be in good stead. Reservations not accepted.

307 Exchange Place. www.greengoddessrestaurant.com. ✆ **504/301-3347.** Main courses $13–$22. Wed–Sun 11am–9pm.

Port of Call ★★ HAMBURGERS   For a decade or two before the great national gourmet burger tsunami overtook New Orleans, Port of Call was putting out a product that drew hordes. That hasn't changed. This is not a burger for teeny-patty people. It's a dripping, half-pound monster, served with a loaded baked potato. You're probably going to wait a while for it (get the fruity signature Monsoon cocktail to bide the time), and you probably won't even be able to see it inside the dark den of a dining room. They have steaks, but they're irrelevant. Sometimes you just need a good burger, and even with the serious contenders around town now, Port of Call's still holds up. No reservations.

838 Esplanade Ave. www.portofcallnola.com. ✆ **504/523-0120.** Main courses $10–$27. Sun–Thurs 11am–midnight, Fri–Sat 11am–1am.

Sylvain ★★★ BISTRO   Little-known fact: Not long ago, the French Quarter was a cool-restaurant desert. Sylvain changed that. With its side-alley entrance, speckled flooring reclaimed from an old church, and Civil-War-meets-Soho vibe, it's almost hip overkill (one local calls it So Vain). It even has a resident ghost (with a literary backstory, no less) and requisite craft cocktails. But dang if the service isn't downright friendly and the food straight-up delicious. For the ultimate gastropub, it's shockingly unpretentious. Thus it's often packed to the gills . . . ergo waits, noise, and service slowdowns. No place is perfect. But the absurdly tender beef cheeks are, and the lightly dressed shaved-apple and Brussels sprout salad is awfully close. The lush chicken liver crostini and the "Buffalo" style sweetbreads are worthy starters. At brunch (and after) you'll want the fried chicken and biscuits. The menu doesn't skew light, so you might be forced to share the chocolate pot du crème. On a nice evening, the discreet back-alley tables have their own cool vibe: a quieter one.

625 Chartres St. www.sylvainnola.com. ✆ **504/265-8123.** Main courses $16–$26. Mon–Thurs 5:30–11pm, Fri–Sat 11:30am–2:30pm and 5:30pm–midnight, Sun 10:30am–2:30pm and 5:30–10pm.

Vacherie ★★ CONTEMPORARY CREOLE   What a surprising little find. The new owners have clearly taken some care with both the food and the look of the small, attractive room at this 2013 newbie. Ask about the stunning pastoral oil painting and the intriguing sepia-toned photographs, and their connection to the philosophy of Vacherie's Cajun Louisiana–driven cooking. For breakfast, try the Andouille hash or

BACK-ROOM bites

Long before there were pop-up restaurants, there were back-room deli counters in unassuming corner stores. It's how a lot of French Quarter residents still eat, because it's fast, cheap, diverse, available 'round-the-clock, and often surprisingly good. Take it out or have it delivered, and be sure to ask for utensils. True locals eat while leaning against a wall or seated on someone's front stoop.

- **Frady's** ★ (This one's in the Bywater at 3231 Dauphine St.; ⓒ **504/949-9688;** Mon–Fri 8am–6pm, Sat 9am–3pm). Best choice: Hot sausage or oyster po' boy.
- **Quarter Grocery** ★ (836 Burgundy St.; ⓒ **504/529-2702;** daily 9am–9pm). Best choice: anything fried. Chicken, potatoes, catfish.
- **QuarterMaster** ★ (1110 Bourbon St.; ⓒ **504/529-1416;** 24/7). Best choice: Basic po' boys, especially the French-fry po' boy, and greasy burgers.
- **Verti Marte** ★★ (1201 Royal St.; ⓒ **504/525-4757;** 24/7). Best choice: anything in the deli case or from the mother lode of a menu, especially the day's specials, like Grandma's Boardinghouse Meat Loaf or catfish Bienville. Salads, specialty sandwiches, and loads of veggies.

hearty cornmeal Johnnycakes; they also poach eggs perfectly. At dinner, have some yam chips and the boudin-stuffed fried hen with greens—a delicious, rustic curveball. You don't need to cross town for Vacherie, but if you're in the neighborhood of the Hotel St. Marie (where the restaurant is located), you'll find that it is a huge step up from your average hotel dining room (likewise for the little lobby bar).

827 Toulouse St. www.vacherierestaurant.com. ⓒ **504/207-4532.** Breakfast $8–$17, dinner entrees $14–$30. Mon–Fri 7–11am, Mon–Sat 6–10pm; brunch Sat–Sun 7am–2pm. Closed for lunch.

Inexpensive

Acme Oyster House ★★★ SEAFOOD/LIGHT FARE   Is it worth the wait, you ask, eyeing the block-long line-up? They're Gulf oysters, people, and this is the oldest oyster bar in the French Quarter. In other words, yes (unless you're famished—then just go across the street to **Felix's;** see below). The oysters are tastiest when you're standing at the bar, talking tourist trash with the shucker, piling up shells to be tallied later, knocking back some oyster shooters (chilled vodka, cocktail sauce, erster, gullet). But if you sit at a checked-cloth-covered table, you can also order a dozen or two of the garlicky charbroiled oysters, which may change your life. There are po' boys and other Creole standbys (jambalaya, gumbo, red beans and sausage, and so on), good enough for those who do not partake of the pearlmaker. It's boisterous and there's much scurrying about of waiters, so things do move fast once you're inside. No reservations.

724 Iberville St. www.acmeoyster.com. ⓒ **504/522-5973.** Oysters $12/dozen raw or $19 charbroiled, po' boys $8–$17, entrees $10–$24. Sun–Thurs 11am–10pm, Fri–Sat 11am–11pm.

Café Beignet ★ CAFE/BAKERY   Some swear the beignets here are better than those at Café du Monde, and we can attest that they're usually fresh out of the deep fryer, but we're true to the CdM for just the right chewiness and puffiness of its beignets. Still, you won't find insane lines here, and it also serves waffles, brioche French toast, gumbo, and simple sandwiches and salads. Both locations have nice patios;

there's live jazz Thursday through Sunday afternoons and evenings at the Bourbon Street location.

334B Royal St. www.cafebeignet.com. ℂ **504/524-5530.** Most items under $10. Daily 7am–5pm. Also at 311 Bourbon St. ℂ **504/525-2611.** Daily 8am–midnight.

Café Maspero ★ CAFE/SEAFOOD/LIGHT FARE Why is it always so crowded here? We'll give you five good reasons: It's got a big menu, it's inexpensive, the food is decent, the portions are large, and you can watch the Decatur action go by. It may not merit a Facebook posting, but it's easy enough to duck in here for a burger, club sandwich, onion soup, or muffuletta (regular or veggie).

601 Decatur St. ℂ **504/523-6250.** Main courses $8.50–$10. No separate checks. Sun–Thurs 11am–10pm, Fri–Sat 11am–11pm.

Clover Grill ★ DINER The burger here is just a frozen patty thrown on the grill, but it's cooked under a hubcap (the better to seal in the juices), available at 4am, and served by a sassy queen in a "Clever Girl" T-shirt, making it so very worthwhile. Basic egg breakfasts and standard diner fare are also available. Bonus points for: excellent '80s jukebox; Formica counter; red vinyl stools you can spin around on; pie. But mostly for aforementioned sass, which they have in spades here, 24/7.

900 Bourbon St. www.clovergrill.com. ℂ **504/598-1010.** All items under $9. Daily 24 hr.

Coop's ★ CREOLE/LIGHT FARE This divey, former locals-only hangout has long since been discovered by tourists, too, which may mean a sometimes unjustifiably long wait: It's good, but not OMG! awesome. Except for the well-known rabbit-and-sausage jambalaya, and the fried chicken, both of which really are pretty awesome. Decent food, friendly prices, late hours, and a menu that covers all the bases make this a good fallback if the line isn't crazy prohibitive.

1109 Decatur St. www.coopsplace.net. ℂ **504/525-9053.** Entrees $10–$20. Daily 11am–close (usually at least 10pm, later on weekends). 21 and older only.

DeVille Coffee House & Creperie ★★ LIGHT FARE/COFFEE This charming hole-in-the-wall is just what this end of the Quarter ordered: a barista who works wonders with a coffee bean; plus a quick and hearty bite, savory or sweet. The straightforward crepe menu includes varieties from spinach, egg and cheese, to Nutella banana. They're made while you watch, then plated to eat in the darling, double-story dining room (perhaps delivered upstairs via pulley-driven dumbwaiter) or rolled into a cone for grab-and-go convenience. *Tres Parisian,* and easier on the wallet than actual Paris.

508 Dumaine St. www.facebook.com/devillenola. ℂ **504/309-6015.** Crepes $6–$12. Mon and Thurs 10am–3pm, Fri–Sun 10am–8pm.

Felix's Restaurant & Oyster Bar ★★ SEAFOOD/CREOLE Seventy-year-old Felix's got new owners and a thorough, much-needed housecleaning in 2013, and we're happy to say they left most everything else alone. Like Acme, its across-the-street friendly rival, it's just a down-home, nuthin'-fancy oyster bar, but the dozens come out fresh and bitterly chilled, needing nothing more than a squeeze of lemon. You can also have them in stews, soups, pastas, or omelets broiled, fried, or baked. And if it's crawfish season, order up a spicy pile. It's not nearly as much of a scene as Acme (a big plus), and the shuckers have fast hands and quick wit.

739 Iberville St. www.felixs.com. ℂ **504/522-4440.** Oysters $14/dozen raw, po' boys under $15, main courses $12–$21. Sun–Thurs 11am–10pm, Fri–Sat 11am–11pm.

The Grill ★★ DINER/LIGHT FARE   The French Quarter branch of the Camellia Grill is a near-perfect replica (in style, service, and menu) of the original Uptown diner (p. 113), without the "Camellia."

540 Chartres St. ✆ **504/522-1800.** All entrees under $13. Sun–Thurs 8am–11pm, Fri–Sat 8am–3am.

Johnny's Po-Boys ★ LIGHT FARE   Johnny's is the standard-bearer for po' boys in the French Quarter—in fact it's the only proper po' boy shop in the area. Little known insider fact about the family-owned fave: It's also a good, cheap, quick breakfast spot. Other little known fact: They deliver to French Quarter hotels. They'll put almost anything on that crunchy, fluffy Leidenheimer bread, but they're best known for their roast beef po' boy. We have a soft spot for the fried pork chop version, just 'cause it's hard to find one elsewhere. The line moves fast; don't be discouraged.

511 St. Louis St. www.johnnyspoboys.com. ✆**504/524-8129.** Most items under $10; specials may be more. No credit cards. Daily 8am–4:30pm.

Mr. Gregory's ★★★ CAFE/BAKERY/LIGHT FARE   *Bienvenue!* This welcome addition to the upper Quarter brings much-needed coffee, breakfast, and lunch options to this area, all done with a French accent. Pastries are baked on-site, including the elusive proper croissant and decadent *pain perdu* muffins, so gooey with crème anglaise that they must be et with knife and fork. Soups, salads, quiches, and *croque* sandwiches (with gruyére! and house-cured tuna!) round out the lunch menu. There's simple goodness and brewed-to-order French-press coffee for $2.50. *Mais oui.*

806 N. Rampart St. www.mistergregorys.com. ✆ **504/407-3780.** Everything under $9. Mon–Sun 10am–6pm.

The Old Coffee Pot ★ LIGHT FARE   Known for being one of the few places that serve calas, sweetened fried rice cakes that date to the mid-1800s. The egg dishes are okay, but it's the calas you want (and we can't recommend lunch or dinner entrees). The high-ceilinged room and outdoor courtyard will immerse you in the French Quarter aura, and the service is full of "hons" and "dahlins," though no one's moving too fast.

714 St. Peter St. www.theoldcoffeepot.com. ✆**504/524-3500.** Breakfast $9–$14, dinner $16–$25. Mon, Thurs, Sun 8am–10:30pm; Tues–Wed 8am–2:30pm and 5:30–10:30pm; Fri–Sat 8am–11:30pm.

Somethin' Else Café ★★ CAFE/LIGHT FARE   This is an above-average sidewalk cafe with indoor and outdoor seating, and some well-done nods to local cuisine. It's also a good stop for salads—not that easy to find in these parts—and you can design your own here (or just get the mighty good Popeye, with avocado, crab, and grilled shrimp). But enough about healthy things—let's talk carbs. Biscuits of unusual size, specifically. Large, homemade, and served with pulled pork, or boudin balls, which you should get with a side of sweet potato hash. House-ground burgers and oddly textured but tasty shrimp burgers come on fluffy brioche buns—yummy even if they don't hold up well. It's often a wait on weekend mornings, and service isn't exactly speedy. Open late weekend nights, usually till 2-ish.

620 Conti St. www.somethinelsecafe.com. ✆ **504/373-6439.** Omelets, burgers, sandwiches $7–$16. Sun–Wed 7am–10pm, Thurs 7am–midnight, Fri–Sat 7am–3am.

Stanley ★★ AMERICAN/LIGHT FARE   It's cute and convenient (right on the corner of Jackson Square) and serves well-prepared, "regular" food that kids and

WHOLE LOTTA muffuletta GOIN' ON

Muffulettas are sandwiches of (pardon the expression) heroic proportions, enormous concoctions of round Italian bread, Italian cold cuts, cheeses, and olive salad. One person cannot (or should not) eat a whole one—at least not in one sitting. A half makes a good meal; a quarter is a filling snack. They may not sound like much on paper, but once you try one, you'll be hooked. Vegetarians swear they're delicious done meatless.

Several places in town claim to have invented the muffuletta and also claim to make the best one. You decide: Comparison-shopping can be a rewarding pastime.

The lunchtime line can be daunting but moves fast (and it's part of the aura) at world-famous **Central Grocery ★★★**, 923 Decatur St. (✆ **504/523-1620**). There are a few seats at the back of this crowded, garlic-scented Italian grocery, or you can order to go. Best of all, they ship, so you can satisfy your craving or throw an envy-inducing party. Eat it

across the street on the banks of the Mississippi for an inexpensive, romantic meal ($18 for a whole, with tax). The impersonal staff at Central Grocery starts making and wrapping their sandwiches early in the day, so they're ready for the rush. Don't worry about freshness; it actually helps when the olive flavors soak through the layers.

Are the hot muffulettas at **Napoleon House ★★** better or blasphemy? It's a different taste sensation, and a heated debate. Feeling experimental? Drive to **Nor-Joe's Importing Co. ★★**, 505 Friscoe, in Metairie (✆ **504/833-9240**), where the ginormous, outstanding muffulettas, constructed with iconoclastic ingredients like prosciutto and mortadella, have their own cult following. Then there's **Cochon Butcher ★★★** (p. 104), whose house-cured meats form the basis of what may be our new favorite 'letta. Okay it is. There, we said it.

grown-ups will like (pancakes, good burgers, and an old-fashioned soda fountain serving homemade ice cream). So naturally it's popular as all get-out; try to go during off-peak hours. Their take-out shop next door has coffee, ice cream, and ready-made sandwiches to go, which is awfully convenient. But if you choose the sit-down restaurant, the cornmeal-crusted oyster po' boy is a good way to go. For breakfast (served all day), those oysters come Benedict style, with poached eggs and hollandaise. Yum.

547 St. Ann St. (corner of Jackson Sq. and St. Ann). www.stanleyrestaurant.com. ✆ **504/587-0093.** Everything under $15. Daily 7am–10pm.

THE FAUBOURG MARIGNY & BYWATER

For the restaurants in this section, see the "New Orleans Restaurants" map on p. 78.

Moderate

Bacchanal ★★★ INTERNATIONAL   It's a broken-down, ramshackle old building. It's a wine store. It's a bar. It's a jazz club. And now, it's an actual restaurant. Sorta. Whatever it is, it epitomizes New Orleans, and it's one of our favorite spots anywhere.

The unusual, European-leaning wine selection and funky, twinkle-lit outdoor garden with the corner jazz combo attracts locals kicking back in plastic chairs, steampunk wine snobs in deep discussion, maybe a smattering of out-of-towners enlightening to the "real" New Orleans . . . all tantalized by the romantic ambience and Spanish-inspired small plates. You order at a window and grab your own utensils, and a starter of grilled corn with cotija cheese, crema, and spices (or bacon-wrapped dates with chorizo, or smoked trout crostini with crisp apples) shows up. After the 2013 conversion of an attic to an actual dining room, it's accessible even on rainy days, but ahh, that garden. It won't be the best meal you have in New Orleans, but it's frequently tasty, never boring, perpetually affordable, and ultra atmospheric. It all seems thrown together but it melds into something much greater than the sum of its parts.

600 Poland Ave. www.bacchanalwine.com. ✆ **504/948-9111.** Tapas and small plates $6–$16. Daily 11am–midnight (Sun–Mon kitchen closes at 11pm).

Elizabeth's ★★★ CREOLE It's rightly famous for its brown-sugar-coated praline bacon (they were driving the bacon truck long before the bandwagon hooked on), but the rest of the menu is pretty great, too. Thusly, be warned: Breakfast is often crowded, with waits on weekends. But it's worth it. You just don't see a chicken-liver omelet too often, so get it (add onions and a side of creamy grits), unless you get the indulgent bananas Foster *pain perdu.* Or both—we don't judge. The dinner menu is stacked with solid Southern staples—blackened fish, grilled pork chops (thumbs up); a special of osso bucco with grits cakes was impressive. Dessert? More praline bacon, of course.

601 Gallier St. www.elizabethsrestaurantnola.com. ✆ **504/944-9272.** Breakfast and lunch everything under $15, dinner $15–$26 (specials higher). Mon–Sun 8am–2:30pm, Mon–Sat 6–10pm.

The Joint ★★★ BARBECUE When you think of barbecue, you might think Memphis, St. Louis, Texas . . . now think Bywater (unless you're Uptown, then think **McClure's ★★**, 4800 Magazine St.; www.mccluresbarbecue.com; ✆ **504/301-2367**). When that smoked-meat hankering hits, The Joint stands up to the best of them. Its newish location in an old corner store is less joint-like and more modern roadhouse, with picnic tables inside and out. The luscious baby-backs and smoldering, lean brisket are sublime; for something truly local, try the Cajun sausage, made around these parts. The sides are fine, but save room for the peanut butter pie.

701 Mazant St. www.alwayssmokin.com. ✆ **504/949-3232.** Main courses $7–$27. Mon–Sat 11:30am–10pm.

Mariza ★★ ITALIAN Mariza is modern Italian meets Modern American by way of the Bywater, met with a big pedigree. The owners of Iris, for many years one of the better modern American restaurants in the French Quarter, decamped to hipper, more casual, brick-and-glass digs in the Rice Mill Loft building. It seems to be working well for them, and definitely so for me. Yellowfin carpaccio and snapper crudo start things off brightly; follow it with the lamb meatballs topped with a tantalizing poached duck egg. Pastas haven't failed me yet, and are served in small or large portions (though in truth nothing is too large here—a good reason to try more). So far the puffy gnocchi with eggplant and the husky short ribs with mushrooms and mascarpone over rigatoni rate highest; it's the touch of a deft chef that keeps them lighter than expected. A crispy whole snapper, unadorned but for a bit of citrus and herbs, is a bargain at $20. Communal tables are fine, but they could improve upon both the stiff, bar-height seats and the afterthought desserts (when in doubt, always opt for a chocolate terrine; insert snarky seat-meets-dessert comment now). But those are quibbles. Mariza is a most worthy choice.

2900 Chartres St. www.marizaneworleans.com. ℂ **504/598-5700.** Main courses $15–$20. Tues–Thurs 5–10pm, Fri–Sat 5–11pm.

Maurepas Foods ★★ MODERN SOUTHERN These Bywater brainiacs are having fun with food and drink, and you're the beneficiary. Creative, affordable combinations on the plate and in the glass make for a line out the door. We actually like fashioning a meal of the sides here; the veggie options are abundant and are spot-on. Add a well-mixed cocktail (many citrus- or herb-infused) and a fruity *panna cotta,* and call it a day. Unless you get the signature chicken leg with grits and a poached egg—for the quality, it's one of the best deals around at $14. No reservations.

3200 Burgundy St. www.maurepasfoods.com. ℂ **504/267-0072.** Main courses $9–$17. Mon–Tues and Thurs–Fri 5pm–midnight, Sat–Sun 10am–midnight. Closed Wed.

Oxalis ★★★ LIGHT FARE It's a bar, it's a restaurant, and (like many places) it does both well; categorization is tough and not really relevant . . . except that the review is listed under "Bars" (p. 183).

Praline Connection ★ CREOLE/SOUL FOOD The servers in their cute hats and skinny ties are undeniably adorable, but the food and service aren't as adorable as they used to be. The fried chicken is still dependably juicy, though, and our top choice, with some fried pickles. The rest of the menu is only okay, too much something (sweet, in the yams), not enough of something else (flavor, in the greens). But we've had good luck with the nightly specials; they seem to get more care, and it's conveniently Frenchmen Street–close.

542 Frenchmen St. www.pralineconnection.com. ℂ **504/943-3934.** Main courses $13–$24. Mon–Thurs 11am–10pm, Fri–Sat 11–midnight, Sun 11am–9pm.

Yuki Izakaya ★★ ASIAN You could easily miss this nook in the midst of the Frenchmen frenzy, but don't. Yuki Yamaguchi's traditional Japanese *izakaya* (neighborhood pub/noshery) offers an impressive array of imported sakes, beer, *shochu,* and Japanese bar snacks—many from family recipes. We go for octopus *shumai* dumplings; the carbo-reloading udon soup; crispy, lemony beef tongue; and *karaage*–fried chicken. It's tiny and hip and sometimes smells of fish (there's some sashimi, but it's not a sushi house), which we put up with because it screens vintage Japanese films above the bar while **Norbert Slama** plays mournful Piaf tunes on the accordion (sometimes with guitarist **Raphael Bas**). This earns our enduring love.

525 Frenchmen St. ℂ **504/943-1122.** Small plates $4–$15. Mon–Thurs 6–11:30pm, Fri–Sat 6pm–2am or later, Sun 6–10:30pm.

Inexpensive

Cake Café & Bakery ★ COFFEE/BAKERY/LIGHT FARE About a 10-minute walk from Esplanade is this humble bakery-and-then-some. House-baked pastries, bagels, and biscuits are on tap, as are the requisite cupcakes. Theirs, in standard and exotic flavors (Sazerac!), are particularly delish. The lunch fare fares less well; by the charming looks of it all, you expect it to be better. Egg dishes work better than sandwiches, which skew dry. The corned-beef hash special, if available, is a highlight and a simple poached salmon salad worked well. Best buck you'll spend today: dollar cupcake with lunch. It's not called Cake Café for nothing.

2440 Chartres St. www.nolacakes.com. ℂ **504/943-0010.** Everything under $12. Daily 7am–3pm.

Gene's Po' Boys ★★ LIGHT FARE   Just outside the tourist zone is a serious po' boy for people who are serious about po' boys: Gene's homemade hot sausage patty with American cheese. (And we do mean hot—the building is Pepto-pink for a reason.) No chips, no dessert, no atmosphere, comes with a soda, open 24 hours. That's all she wrote and all you need to know.

1040 Elysian Fields Ave. ✆ **504/943-3861.** Everything under $10. Cash only. Daily 24 hr.

Kukhnya ★★★ INTERNATIONAL   Some of the best cheap eats do in fact operate out of a neon-lit window at the back of a dicey, punk-meets-metal nightclub whose Wi-Fi password is "Satan." Once we got past the bouncer (just explain you're there for the food), we fell hard for this place, starting with the pucker-inducing pickled veggies and a simple $2.50 side of crisp, grilled asparagus. The heartier mushroom-and-spinach blini were a bit greasy, but we made return visits for the locally made kielbasa po' boy with spicy cabbage and searingly hot mustard, and the beet-and-lentil burger topped with goat cheese. You'll probably want to take your order to go unless you don't mind the smoke or the music; in that case, pay the cover and order something from the decent beer list. Don't expect their "Slavic soul food" to be anything like they made in the old country; just expect satisfying, adventurous, affordable bar eats the likes of which you probably haven't seen before.

2227 St. Claude Ave. (inside Siberia nightclub). www.siberianola.com. ✆ **504/265-8855.** Everything under $10, cash only. Daily 5pm–midnight. Closed occasionally due to club capacity. Consider calling ahead; phone orders accepted.

McHardy's Chicken and Fixins ★★★ SOUL FOOD   Popeye's will do when we're far from New Orleans, but if we're in town it's gotta be family-owned McHardy's for take-out fried chicken. It's moist, tender, slightly crispy-skinned, perfectly seasoned, and cheap. Stellar. We never have a party without it, and often *make* a party *just* to have it. The other "fixins" are okay—the mustardy, nearly mashed homemade potato salad is the standout—but the bird is the word here. *Tip:* Cheap, hot, to-go breakfasts, too; cooked fresh from $2 up.

1458 N. Broad St. www.facebook.com/pages/McHardys-Chicken-Fixin/176427879083461. ✆ **504/949-0000.** 5-piece box $6; 500-piece (!) $530. Mon–Fri 6:30–9:30am, Mon–Thurs 11am–6:30pm, Fri–Sat 11am–7:30pm, Sun 11am–3pm. Take-out only.

MID-CITY/ESPLANADE

For the restaurants in this section, see the "New Orleans Restaurants" map on p. 78.

Expensive

Ralph's on the Park ★★★ CONTEMPORARY CREOLE   Huge picture windows look out on Spanish moss–draped oaks in City Park. Music from **Joe Krown**'s stylish stride piano seeps from the lounge and across the cream-upholstered dining room. You're sipping a French 75, eagerly anticipating the turtle soup and brown-butter sweetbread starters you've just ordered, gazing out upon the setting sun, the glistening rain, or into your sweetheart's baby blues. Whatevs—it's dreamy here. The fare, a big step up from its straightforward Creole of a few years ago, now approaches dreaminess as well—it's fresh, creative continental, still with a pinch of Creole. Happy to see an appetizer of *ya ka mein* on the menu, there's a polished version of the local ramen-like hangover cure. Roast cobia comes topped with a light hollandaise, barely redolent of the crawfish fat used deep in the recipe.

Desserts are playful and crowd-pleasing (just say chocolate crème brûlée). The whole experience epitomizes Southern elegance—a vacation within a vacation (the daylight view is best, whether brunch, lunch, or early supper), and it's easily reachable by cab or the City Park streetcar. Check the website for terrific multi-course specials (especially for lunch), and allow time to hear Mr. Krown at happy hour or brunch. Reserve well in advance, especially for brunch.

900 City Park Ave. www.ralphsonthepark.com. © **504/488-1000.** Main courses $14–$22 lunch, $22–$44 dinner, $15–$23 brunch. Sun–Thurs 5:30–9pm, Fri–Sat 5:30–9:30pm, Tues–Fri 11:30am–2pm, Sun 10:30am–2pm.

Moderate

Café Degas ★★★ BISTRO/FRENCH   Every neighborhood in every city should have a charming, casual French bistro that serves a perfect salad Niçoise and has a tree growing in the middle of the indoor/outdoor dining room. But only Faubourg St. John has it. It's darling, perfectly suited to a romantic dinner or a gals' lunch. Traditional favorites like escargot, hanger steak, and rack of lamb are straightforward, flavorful, and generous; a delicate roast quail starter was tempting to double as an entrée. It's a popular spot, particularly for brunch, so reserve ahead. Check **www.restaurant.com** and the cafe website for coupons. Reserve in advance during peak periods.

3127 Esplanade Ave. www.cafedegas.com. © **504/945-5635.** Main courses lunch/brunch $11–$17, dinner $18–$30. Wed–Sat 11am–3pm and 6–10pm, Sun 10:30am–3pm and 6–9:30pm.

Dooky Chase ★★ SOUL FOOD/CREOLE   First, the important Dooky trivia: Ray Charles (among other musicians) hung out here after shows and wrote "Early in the Morning" about it. Leah Chase, the nonagenarian chef and Dooky's wife, (aka the "Queen of Creole Cuisine") has won just about every culinary award in existence, (and was the model for Tiana in Disney's delightful film *The Princess and the Frog*). In the '60s, Dooky Chase was an important meeting place for civil rights leaders. Dooky and Leah are still revered and important civic figures. After Hurricane Katrina, the couple lived in a FEMA trailer across the street for 2 years while they were rebuilding the restaurant. Oh, and Presidents Obama and Bush I both dined at Dooky's (not together). It's not quite what it was in the glory days, but us lesser folk can partake of the weekday lunch buffet with traditional Creole standards in the art-filled dining room. A better choice is the Friday dinner, when the neighbor-saturated atmosphere sizzles like the crisp fried chicken—a serious contender for the city's best. Come for the hallowed history; stay for the fried chicken.

2301 Orleans Ave. www.dookychaserestaurant.com. © **504/821-0600.** Lunch buffet $18, dinner main courses $20–$25. Tues–Fri 11am–3pm, Fri 5–9pm.

Liuzza's ★★ CREOLE/ITALIAN   Actual Liuzza's moment: Crusty waitress hands customer a menu ("Here you go, Bay-bee"), then abruptly closes it. "Bay-bee," she instructs, gesticulating with intent, "Numba One, or Numba Two—but *definitely* Numba One." Naturally, the Number One special was ordered (a seafood lasagna, dripping with a white cream sauce) and promptly devoured, in all its enormity. If you've been wondering what Creole Italian is all about, come here. This is a true, humble neighborhood institution, and we're pretty sure that the same regulars that were there before it took on 8 feet of Katrina waters are still going. So when the waitress talks, you betta listen. There's nothing subtle about the hearty, saucy comfort food and po' boys; it's solid and rib-sticking. Do get a massive frosted mug of Abita Amber and the famous deep-fried dill pickles. "You people will batter and deep-fry anything that isn't nailed down!," said yet another astonished visitor. Good times.

3636 Bienville St. www.liuzzas.com. ℂ **504/482-9120.** Main courses $12–$22. No credit cards. ⋅ Sun–Mon 11am–4pm, Tues–Sat 11am–10pm.

Lola's ★★ INTERNATIONAL/SPANISH For something completely different, that feels very European while being very local, try Spanish fare at teeny Lola's in the Bayou St. John neighborhood. Start with the garlic soup (one of several good vegetarian options; another is refreshing gazpacho). Then get a sizzling platter of paella—we prefer the mussel-loaded combination. If there's a wait, relax with a carafe of red or white sangria; if there isn't, relax with a carafe of red or white sangria. Once you're seated, service is prompt, though cooked-to-order paellas take about 30 minutes. Close with the silky homemade flan. A very good day can be had by ending up here after spending time in City Park or at the New Orleans Museum of Art (p. 135).

3312 Esplanade Ave. www.lolasneworleans.com. ℂ **504/488-6946.** Main courses $16–$28, paellas $12–$52. Sun–Thurs 5:30–9:30pm, Fri–Sat 5:30–10pm.

Mandina's ★★ CREOLE/ITALIAN Dis is da ultimate neighbahood N'Awlins restaurant, owned by the same family since the late 1800s—and largely unchanged—as it should be. Nothing innovative here, just comfort food the way Maw Maw made it, served by someone who looks like her. If the daily specials aren't to your liking, get some butter-soaked garlic bread to share and the right and true seafood gumbo or turtle soup au sherry. Then go for the sweet Italian sausage and spaghetti combo or red beans and rice with Italian sausage. Then again, the brown-buttery trout meunière is hard to pass up. The cocktails are strong here; so is the A/C. Bring a sweater.

3800 Canal St. www.mandinasrestaurant.com. ℂ **504/482-9179.** Main courses $14–$25. No credit cards. Mon–Thurs 11am–9:30pm, Fri–Sat 11am–10pm, Sun noon–9pm.

Rue 127 ★★★ BISTRO It's worth seeking out this neighborhood bistro tucked into a petite, converted shotgun house along a busy stretch of Carrollton Avenue. The Mid-City gem works perfectly for dinner with the folks, a girlfriends lunch, or date night with your sweetheart. Try for one of the bright banquettes along the tasteful taupe walls. Crisply attentive servers deliver farm-fresh food done with a French accent and a delicate hand. A butter lettuce salad with ricotta salata is nothing earthshattering, but deserves mention for being a perfectly dressed, perfectly simple salad. Risotto, infused with saffron on one occasion and dotted with heirloom tomatoes on another, was not going to be shared. Diver scallops came with grilled eggplant and more of those heirloom tomatoes, topped with a smoky tomato butter that underscored the bivalves' sweetness; a massive double-cut pork chop was anything but sweet, in its manly whiskey glaze and topped with too few flash-fried onions. While we're on sweetness, dessert also stands out here: the signature cone of deep-fried mini cupcakes are adorable, but a pineapple-tart tatin with rhubarb ice cream floored me. Wines, mostly Spanish, French, and Californian, are carefully matched and fairly marked up. Reservations strongly suggested.

127 N. Carrollton Ave. www.rue127.com. ℂ **504/483-1571.** Main courses $12–$18 lunch, $20–$34 dinner. Tues–Sat 11:30am–2pm, Mon–Sat 5:30–9:30pm.

Toup's Meatery ★★ CONTEMPORARY CAJUN Just another neighborhood spot with killer food, mostly of the porky variety. Talking our language! As you are being seated, order some crunchy porkalicious cracklins to munch on while you're deciding what to eat. As the name implies, one should order the charcuterie plate here. Another should get the cheese plate, just to even things out. We're actually more a fan of lunch here than dinner, but we'll still eat the short ribs if they're on the oft-changing menu. And despite this red-meat-centric advice, the mussels and the sky-high chicken sandwich are both worthy. Absolutely get whatever variety of multi-layered Debbie Does Doberge cake is available.

845 N. Carrollton Ave. www.toupsmeatery.com. © **504/252-4999.** Lunch $11–$20, dinner large plates $15–$28. Tues–Sat 11am–2pm and 5–9pm, Fri–Sat 11am–10pm.

Ye Olde College Inn ★★★ CREOLE/LIGHT FARE If you're headed to Rock 'n' Bowl (p. 177), your dinner destination is next door. Even if you're not, it's a very worthy choice. It's a high-ceilinged 1930s hangout, smartly renovated with an inviting bar, murals, and store signs reminiscent of ye olde New Orleans. The cuisine is more refined than that implies, particularly in the inventive daily specials, and they take the farm-to-table commitment seriously (their own farm, complete with chickens, is across the street). A succulent, perfectly grilled lamb loin comes topped with sun-dried tomatoes and shiitake mushrooms in a red-wine reduction. Even the old-school throwback options are crafted with a deft touch. The platter-size breaded veal cutlet is so much better than the memory (and robbery at $12); the familiar bleu-cheese-and-pecan salad is elevated with aromatic roast duck. For sheer decadence, the award-winning oyster, Havarti cheese, and bacon po' boy is hard to top; but if that's your goal, order the fried bread pudding po' boy. A tower of onion rings for the table is legally mandated. Ask your server for the deets about the $5 discounted admission to Rock 'n' Bowl (same owners).

3000 S. Carrollton Ave. www.collegeinn1933.com. © **504/866-3683.** Main courses $12–$35. Tues–Sat 4–11pm.

Inexpensive

Biscuits & Buns on Banks ★★★ CAFE/LIGHT FARE You don't want to go here. The converted home is inconveniently far from anything, really. You don't want the fluffy eponymous biscuits, with honey or Steen's cane syrup, or laden with immoral Andouille-chorizo gravy. Nobody wants a crispy waffle sandwiched with brie cheese and blueberry compote, or a mozzarella-and-crabmeat sandwich. Think of the calories! Crisp, Andouille-pecan crusted shrimp, in a taco with tangy avocado mango salsa, nicely sauced and balanced with mirliton slaw? Boooring . . . Seriously, better to stay away, the weekend morning lines can get pretty long anyway. Please. We're begging you. (*Note to the sarcasm-challenged:* Only the part about Biscuits & Buns being inconveniently far is true.)

4337 Banks St. www.biscuitsandbunsonbanks.com. © **504/273-4600.** Breakfast and lunch main courses $9–$14. Mon–Fri 7am–3pm, Sat–Sun 8am–3pm.

Lil' Dizzy's ★★ CREOLE/SOUL FOOD This is another quintessential, family-owned, neighborhood restaurant—this time the family is from the Tremé and the menu has soul food and Creole specialties. It's lively with locals at breakfast (mostly average, the homemade hot sausages slightly above that) and for the lunch buffet. If you're a light eater it might be a bit high-priced, so come hungry and dig into the terrific fried chicken, okay gumbo, and red beans, and a few other soul food standards (also come early, they do run out). Better yet, order a la carte—the aforementioned chicken or our favorite, the standout trout Baquet: a delicate fish filet topped with garlic-butter sauce and sometimes fresh crabmeat.

1500 Esplanade Ave. www.lildizzyscafe.com. © **504/569-8997.** Lunch buffet $16 ($7 kids 8 and under), a la carte lunch items under $15, Sun brunch buffet $18. Mon–Sat 7am–2pm, Sun 8am–2pm, Thurs–Sat 4–8pm.

Liuzza's by the Track ★★★ CREOLE/LIGHT FARE Is it gumbo or is it heroin? Well, heroin doesn't start with a deep, rich roux, so it must be Liuzza's gumbo that we're addicted to. When we fly in from out of town, we stop here on the way home just for a gumbo fix. The BBQ-shrimp po' boy is their signature, overstuffed with peppery, butter-soaked shrimp, but we're partial to the garlic oyster sammie. When we're feeling feisty we switch to the drippy garlic-stuffed roast beef, with its pinch of horseradish in the mayo (we'll often get the cup of gumbo and half po' boy deal; choose any except for that BBQ shrimp). Specials can be pretty special, so check the board. The veggie-deprived should opt for the Portobello salad, and everyone here should strike up a conversation with whoever's nearby. It's that sort of place. Avoid prime weekday lunch hours if you can.

1518 N. Lopez St. www.liuzzasnola.com. © **504/218-7888.** Everything under $17. Mon–Sat 11am–7pm.

Parkway Bakery and Tavern ★★★ LIGHT FARE It's hard to believe that this corner shop began life as a bakery more than 100 years ago. Or that it was shuttered for years in between then and now. Or that it was essentially under water after Katrina. Now, after getting love from umpteen magazines and travel- and food-channel shows and a visit from the Obama family, people literally come by the busload. Try to sit inside or on the original deck, either has more charm than the massive outside picnic area, thrown up to accommodate their popularity surge. But don't be put off—all that matters is that the po' boys still hold up terrifically. Claims to fame are the fried shrimp and juicy roast beef—our favorite in the city, even if (maybe because) it's among the sloppiest. We're fond of the Reuben or lighter caprese, too. The homemade potato salad is killer, and the banana pudding is old skool lip-smacking. Round it all out with a bottled Barq's and a stroll along nearby Bayou St. John. They promise that after a pending kitchen expansion, oysters will be back on the menu full time (Mon and Wed only till then—but now available with bacon! Just say yes). The line can be daunting but moves pretty fast (more so with a beer in hand, so hit up the bar), or try for off-peak hours.

538 Hagan Ave. www.parkwaypoorboys.com. © **504/482-3047.** Everything under $18. Wed–Mon 11am–10pm. Closed Tues.

Willie Mae's Scotch House ★★ SOUL FOOD In 2004, this was a humble chicken shack in a not great neighborhood, known to locals, the budding foodie community, and a few enterprising tourists. In 2005, octogenarian Willie Mae and her secret-recipe fried chicken were designated "American classics" by the James Beard Foundation, and the world came knocking. Weeks later, her home and restaurant were 8 feet under water. The remarkable, volunteer-driven recovery began quickly, with hands-on support from local restaurateurs—a testament to New Orleans's supportive food community. Nowadays, with the matriarch's family helming the fryers, the chicken is still beautifully spiced and crisped—on a good day. Which is much more common than a bad (dry or over-salted) day, but we've had them. For safety, we also order the fried pork chops, and we always get the creamy butterbeans (which don't get near the attention the chicken does, but should). Plan for a wait—first in line, maybe for service, then for the fried-to-order bird. Cab recommended.

2401 St. Ann St. © **504/822-9503.** Everything under $15. Mon–Sat 10am–5pm.

> ### Impressions
>
> *New Orleans is one place you can eat and drink the most, and suffer the least.*
> —William Makepeace Thackeray

CENTRAL BUSINESS DISTRICT & WAREHOUSE DISTRICT

For the restaurants in this section, see the "New Orleans Restaurants" map on p. 78.

Very Expensive

Emeril's ★★★ CREOLE/NEW AMERICAN   Yes, Emeril heads an empire, but he's wisely seen to it that his flagship, namesake restaurant has not flagged in reverse proportion to his empire's expansion. It's still remarkably high quality (and high priced), interesting, and exciting dining. The wine list is intelligent and broad; service is professional and helpful. The room is buoyant with energy, the noise is tolerable. The plate shows clear commitment to first-rate, locally sourced ingredients: A salad of local tomatoes and melon is dotted with tiny, crispy duck hearts, a wisp of herb in the vinaigrette.

The menu builds on tradition in tempered but meaningful ways. Grilled pork chops, done perfectly despite their girth, are artfully glazed with tamarind and tomatillo molé sauces. Delicate quail stay on balance even when taking a Caribbean turn with jerk seasoning and ginger-drenched spinach. Submit your chocolate soufflé request when you order your entrées. Then you won't have to decide what to get at dessert time, because you should also get the banana cream pie (it has its own Facebook page, or at least should). As with so many other fine New Orleans restaurants, the bargain three-course lunch is a serious steal ($23 here). It's also one of many places where the open-kitchen bar seating is perfect for single diners (or anyone). Reserve well in advance.

800 Tchoupitoulas St. www.emerils.com. © **504/528-9393.** 3-course lunch $23; main courses $15–$18 lunch, $25–$44 dinner; degustation by advance arrangement. Mon–Fri 11:30am–2pm, daily 6–10pm.

Restaurant August ★★★ CONTEMPORARY SOUTHERN/FRENCH   If you live under a rock (aka, don't watch cable food shows), you may not know about Chef John Besh's meteoric rise in culinary circles. But he's not just about blue eyes and backlighting: His local-boy-made-good routine is real. He's won a James Beard Best Chef award, and all of his New Orleans area restaurants (7 at last count) range from very good to excellent. August, his fine dining flagship, is a marvel of Creole and Cajun creativity. There is a rare mishit here, when a boundary-pushing dish goes one ingredient over the limit, say, or a molecular gimmick interferes rather than enhances. On the whole your experience will be memorable—decorous, cultured, and stunningly plated—and mostly spectacular.

These are masters of foie gras. It's unfailingly off the charts, done "Three Ways" or in any incarnation. The sweet, tart pork belly with peach mustard met the palate with a quick crunch before introducing a velvet mouthfeel: divine. In braised short ribs, days of simmering produce a soaring orchestra of flavors: apples, wine, root vegeta-bles, and tender, beefy sweetness; it's a triumph of earthy richness. But a calabaza squash ravioli was overpowered by its oxtail-and-bone marrow brew. The sweets themselves are slightly exotic yet urbane. The deconstructed banana pudding has a following; we're more taken with a summery Meyer lemon soufflé tart; pastry chef Kelly Fields works wonders with fruit. The service is professional and unhurried, whether in the sedate main dining room, where chandeliers glint off the tall windows, or in the warm, wood-paneled wine room with the clever overhead cellar. If the $$$$ prices are off-putting, the Friday prix-fixe lunch, 3 courses at $20, makes August indisputably doable. If the degustation is doable for you, do it.

301 Tchoupitoulas St. www.restaurantaugust.com. ℂ **504/299-9777.** Reservations recommended. 3-course lunch $20; main courses $34–$38; 3-hr. degustation menu $97/person, $147 with wine (whole table must participate). Fri 11am–2pm, daily 5–10pm.

Expensive

Annunciation ★★★ CONTEMPORARY CREOLE Chef Steve Manning, co-owner of Annunciation, picked up plenty of lessons learned during his 20 years helm-ing the kitchen at Clancy's, one of New Orleans's most-favored-son restaurants (p. 105). This Warehouse District spot is a bit sleeker and slicker, but mines the classic bentwood chairs and white tablecloths decor. It also shares the "good time was had by all" tone of its ancestor, as well as some of its spotless service and time-honored reci-pes. Fried oysters with spinach and brie, and buttery, crispy chicken bonne femme au jus are two such signature dishes, and both belong on the table. A salad of abundant crab and a creamy herb dressing was delicious; and the tender veal with crawfish and Andouille cornbread dressing is a little bit Southern, a little bit city, and a lot of flavor. A stunning soft-shell crab special was enough for two, but too good to share. Despite the cool brick, jet-black stained floors, and angular black and white abstract artwork, there's a warmth to the room that sets the mood on genial. And if form follows, good moods mean wine and dessert. The wine list is a bit more interesting, but the budino and a tawny Port will lengthen a lovely night of lingering.

1016 Annunciation St. www.annunciationrestaurant.com. ℂ **504/568-0245.** Main courses $17–$27. Mon–Thurs and Sun 5:30–10pm, Fri–Sat 5:30–11pm.

Borgne ★★★ SEAFOOD We like Borgne, the fish-focused John Besh property helmed by Chef Brian Landry, formerly of Galatoire's. We like its easygoing vibe and the well-versed servers who show up when we want them to and don't when we don't. We like most of the items we've tried here, with their interesting Spanish accents. We love that they serve a $10-plate lunch every day, especially Tuesday's ropa vieja. We like the loooong bar and the friendly service there. In fact, we quite like dining in the bar, separated from the main room by a low wall that provides a bit of a sound buffer. Which brings us to the thing we like least about Borgne: The shell-crusted columns and cement floor look cool, but the expansive, slightly sterile, hard-surfaced room incites a cross-table shouting match. Shame that we can't talk about how good the soothing oyster spaghetti is, or ask our friend if she's going to eat that last duck popper—a bacon-jalapeño rillette that we're still thinking about. Whatever's on special is a good bet here, and the server may push the Hummingbird cake on you; stick with the chocolate hazel-nut puddin'. Make dinner reservations in advance during peak periods.

601 Loyola Ave., in the Hyatt Regency. www.borgnerestaurant.com. ℂ **504/613-3860.** Plate lunch $10, entrees $10–$30 lunch, $20–$30 dinner. Sun–Thurs 11am–10pm, Fri–Sat 11am–11pm.

Café Adelaide ★★ CONTEMPORARY CREOLE   This undersung hotel restaurant from the Commander's Palace branch of the Brennan family borrows some of their time-tested aspects, including 25¢ martinis at lunch. They're even cheaper—as in free—if you wear a hat to Sunday brunch, and optional prix-fixe lunch and dinner menus are such good value that they're hard to pass up. The regular menu covers the people-pleaser requisites, then goes off script with some winning, whimsical culinary curveballs—starting with the must-have shrimp-and-tasso corndog starter—sweet, spicy, and addictive. There's a wacky crab po' boy with brie cheese and babaganoush, and if that's not rich deliciousness enough, go for the blue crab gnocchi. Their signature dessert, a white-chocolate biscuit pudding, is worth whatever it does to your thighs. Adelaide also benefitted greatly from a smart redecoration in 2014, good happy hour specials, and especially from being next to the splendid **Swizzle Stick** (p. 183), one of the better bars in town.

300 Poydras St., in the Loews Hotel. www.cafeadelaide.com. ℂ **504/595-3305.** Main courses $16–$18 lunch, $24–$28 dinner; 3-course prix fixe $16–$18 lunch, $25 brunch, $34–$38 dinner. Mon–Fri 6:30–10:30am, Sat–Sun 7am–1:30pm, Mon–Thurs 11:30am–2pm, Fri 11:30am–2:30pm, Sun–Thurs 5:30–9pm, Fri–Sat 5:30–10pm. "Off hours" menu available at bar daily 11:30am–10:30pm.

Herbsaint ★★★ BISTRO   Donald Link may not be a Food Channel staple like Emeril and John Besh, but he's right up there in terms of modern New Orleans restaurant royalty. His sweet, window-lined bistro, rooted in French, Italian, and Creole traditions and helmed by Rebecca Wilcomb, is one of New Orleans's best restaurants. It's usually packed and always lacks elbow room but it's uphill from there. As if to prove his mettle, the James Beard Best Southern Chef winner creates some of the city's best gumbos, including a meatless, herb-based gumbo z'herbes version that we crave. The winning signature starter of homemade spaghetti with a creamy, guanciale-spiked sauce is topped with a batter-fried poached egg (yes, you can—and should—double it as an entrée); a watermelon gazpacho with lump crab is a simple little cup of summer. For heartier fare, a slow-cooked lamb neck is astoundingly sized, equally tender, and rich with flavor and arrives on a well-paired bed of saffron fideo. Desserts here are terrific—try whatever they put in a tart shell. A bistro menu served from 1:30 to 5:30pm features light entrees from both the lunch and dinner menus. Reserve well in advance.

701 St. Charles Ave. www.herbsaint.com. ℂ **504/524-4114.** Main courses $15–$20 lunch, $27–$36 dinner. Mon–Fri 11:30am–5pm, Mon–Sat 5:30–10pm.

La Boca ★★ STEAK   One might not think of New Orleans as a steak town, but it's yet another tradition that runs deep here (one friend calls it the Big Meaty—it's the city that gave us Ruth's Chris, after all). You choose your cut and your knife at this Argentinean steakhouse, and you should get the transcendent 3-day fries regardless of what else you order. But for the best-flavored beefiness we suggest the *entraña fina* skirt steak (which can also be had skin-on, interesting but unnecessary) or the *centro de entraña* hanger steak. Temperatures are proper; the trio of chimichurri sauces add zip. Servers know their meats and are helpful about the (accordingly Argentinian) wines, but aren't particularly sociable. We miss the secretive, cavern-like ambience of their original location, but the commodious, loft-like new room does make it easier to get a table.

870 Tchoupitoulas St. www.labocasteaks.com. ℂ **504/525-8205.** Appetizers $9–$22, steaks $26–$48. Mon–Wed 5:30–10pm, Thurs–Sat 5:30pm–midnight.

Marcello's ★★ ITALIAN   Marcello's bills itself as a "wine bar and bistro," and indeed the back dining room doubles as a well-stocked wine shop (the owners were wine merchants before they were restaurateurs); diners can peruse the racks between courses and choose their next pour; prices too are inviting. Fun idea, but in truth we prefer the smaller, more traditional, white-tile-floored front dining room. There's nothing edgy about the Sicilian-focused menu, heavy on seafood, pastas, and recognizable ingredients—but it's inviting and well executed. The dressings and sauces popped, each distinctive flavor showing spryly on the palate and not overwhelming the just-chewy housemade pastas. A divine, lunchtime lobster panzanella and spinach salad is brightly dressed; traditional parmigiana with eggplant (available as an appetizer or entrée; or with chicken or veal), so often plagued with a heavy hand, let the fresh tomato sauce and aubergine shine through. A comforting, herbacious cioppino was bursting with local seafood, while lamb ragu over silken pappardelle more than satisfied a craving for something robust. The accommodating server extolled their tiramisu; it proved to be a fluffy, superb example of the oft-seen standard.

715 St. Charles Ave. www.marcelloscafe.com. ✆ **504/581-6333.** Main courses $11–$19 lunch, $19–$36 dinner. Mon–Sat 11:30am–10pm (2:30–5pm bar and bar bites only).

MiLa ★★★ NOUVEAU SOUTHERN   We're not sure why MiLa doesn't get more buzz. The married co-chefs (one from Mississippi, one from Louisiana, thus MiLa) are skillful kitchen explorers and source from their own farm. It's refined, ultra-fresh, and dependably delectable (not so for the service—it's been excellent, and it's been disinterested). Both the tempura-fried quash blossom filled with crab and crème fraîche, and sweet-potato pappardelle with shiitake mushrooms in a brown butter sauce sound positively lead-footed, yet they're delightful. The peppery barbeque lobster is balanced with lemon confit and punched up with a hint of thyme—a stunner. At lunch, the fresh fish filet (we've had both trout and salmon) is just crisped; sautéed baby bok choy lends extra lightness. The wine list and desserts show equal consideration; the root beer float even adds a welcome touch of quirk. At lunch, local business people energize the contemporary room, its marine blue ceiling hung with cylindrical lampshades.

817 Common St., in the Renaissance Pere Marquette hotel. www.milaneworleans.com. ✆ **504/412-2580.** Main courses $14–$20 lunch, $19–$38 dinner; seasonal tasting menu $75, $110 with wine pairings. Tues–Fri 10:30am–2:30pm, Tues–Thurs 5:30–9pm, Fri–Sat 5:30–10pm.

Peche ★★★ SEAFOOD   In a shocking departure from his pork-centric reputation and surname, noted chef Donald Link opened Peche in 2013 where chef Ryan Prewitt showcases wood-fired seafood. In 2014, Peche picked up the Beard award for Best New Restaurant, and Prewitt won Best Chef, South. We weren't shocked: We've eaten our way through this menu, and have yet to find a dud. Now that we can hear our dining companions it's become a favorite. So we'll gladly excuse the acoustic panels slapped on the ceiling, which tamped down the intolerable clamor to standard restaurant-loud. No one's looking up anyway given what's on the many small plates—which is what you should order—plus a whole grilled fish (ours was buttery, meaty, fire-crusted redfish with aptly low-profile salsa verde; you debone it). This is seafood not to be missed, especially the beer-battered fish sticks (really) and hearty crawfish gratinée. Okay, you can skip the shrimp toast and Betty Crockery tuna dip (it's good, but we feel like we could make it at home; not so for the onion dip with pepper jelly and freshly fried chips). Make full use of the terrific craft beer, cocktail, and European wine menus. For your dessert, the chocolate peanut butter banana pie (duh). For maximum communicability we still like the booths along the back wall, though the raw bar is a fun spot (did we mention the raw fish is almost as good as the grilled, gilled goods?). Ultimately the point is to just go. And get the shrimp roll. Reserve in advance during peak periods.

800 Magazine St. www.pecherestaurant.com. ⓒ **504/522-1744.** Snacks and small plates $7–$14, grilled entrees $14–$27, whole grilled fish $45–$69. Mon–Thurs 11am–10pm, Fri–Sat 11am–11pm.

Root ★★ NEW AMERICAN   The gleaming wood beams, painted cement floors, and leaf-green molded chairs immediately telegraph the high-hip, downscale tone. But the dining-room-as-chemistry-set trend sends our antenna up. So we were primed for disappointment in this critics' darling. We're still not sycophants, but some appreciation has definitely taken, ahem, root. The Root folks are reaching for new culinary targets, and even if they don't always hit dead center, we're curious, and we admire the wit and ambition (they let the freak flag really fly at **Square Root** ★★, their new $150-a-pop, multi-course tasting-menu locale). Other than sourcing locally, Root's modern American cooking makes no concession to Louisiana. House-cured charcuterie and sausage are front and center. We enjoy the former (and loved the condiments and pickled garni) more than the latter (which tended toward tough). Faves: the lardo, pâté de champagne, rosemary guanciale, and Moroccan pork and duck rillettes. The foie-gras cotton candy is adorable, but we'd rather just have a hunk of the stuff (for the record, we also prefer shaved truffles over anything truffle-oiled). The signature cohiba-smoked scallops, served in a fume-filled cigar box, are quite good despite our scoffing. Ditto the Korean short ribs in their little clay pot. But the pork belly went one flavor over the line (echoes of Tim Gunn: edit, edit, edit), and there's better duck around town. Desserts have fun with gimmicks and florals; the fruit-based ones fared best, including a peach crumble with Middle Eastern undertones. The drinks list is equally out there, but they're quite helpful in pairing beer and wine, much appreciated given the complex food's encyclopedia of ingredients. Reserve in advance.

200 Julia St. www.rootnola.com. ⓒ **504/252-9480.** Entrees $13–$32 lunch, $25–$33 dinner. Mon–Fri 11am–2pm, Sun–Thurs 5–11pm, Fri–Sat 5pm–2am.

Moderate

Cochon ★★ CONTEMPORARY CAJUN   We must admit we're not fully on board with the heaps of praise Cochon gets, and we speak fluent pork. It's good, sometimes very good, and it is one of the few games in town for Cajun food—the rustic, country cousin to big-city Creole cooking (see p. 80). The Cochon version, of course, is amped up several notches: This is Donald Link and Steve Stryjewski Cajun, after all. But others have been bowled further over. Still, the things they do well, they do very well, so we'll point you in that direction, and if you end up with one of the good servers, it can be altogether enjoyable. All visits to Cajun country should kick off with some cracklins and a good local beer, maybe the Lazy Magnolia Pecan Ale. Follow with the boudin balls—crunchy outside, savory and porky inside. For a hog break, the briny bite of wood-fired oysters or the chicken livers with pepper jelly will do. Moving on, the fork-tender pork cheeks are disappointing only in terms of serving size (so get two orders) and the skillet-baked rabbit and dumplings is a soul-warming dish that, if you skip everything else, should not be missed. The ambrosia cake is a potluck-perfect finish (well, not like the potlucks *we* go to)—a creamy, fruity, happy ending. Reserve well in advance.

930 Tchoupitoulas St. www.cochonrestaurant.com. ⓒ **504/588-2123.** Reservations strongly recommended. Small plates $8–$12, main courses $19–$28. Mon–Thurs 11am–10pm, Fri–Sat 11am–11pm.

Domenica ★★★ ITALIAN   Bittersweet chocolate walls, soaring ceilings, great art, glossy surfaces, small bar, large crowd, cacophony. Which all sets the scene for perfectly bubble-edged Neapolitan pizzas, arguably the best salumi in the city, and a man in the kitchen (Chef Alon Shaya) who knows his way around a vegetable. We rarely make it to the *secondi* here because it's so easy, and such a pleasure, to load up on antipasti and *primi* (and a pizza or two). Buttery sautéed chanterelle mushrooms are flavored with marrow and cut through with parsley—decadently rich. A whole roasted cauliflower makes an impressive presentation and is a delicious addition to the table. Fresh tagliatelle is sauced with rabbit and porcini mushrooms, hearty and divine, and we'd never leave home if Mom could make a *stracci* with oxtail and fried chicken livers. All this assumes that you've already enjoyed their notable cocktails, worked through a salumi and cheese board, and selected some pizzas from the broad array of toppings (yes, you can do it all—the wisp of a crust makes for easy eating). The better to end with the satiny chocolate hazelnut *budino*. Did we mention that Domenica, like all of John Besh's restaurants, has a superb happy hour from 2 to 6pm, when select pizzas are half-price? No wonder it's cacophonous. The bar pours well-priced boutique Italian wines and popular homemade cellos. Okay, service is inconsistent, ranging from prompt and knowledgeable to perfunctory to disorderly. And still it's worth it. Reserve in advance. Also consider the casual uptown outpost, **Pizza Domenica** ★★ (www.pizzadomenica.com; ℂ **504/301-4978**).

123 Baronne St., in the Roosevelt Hotel. www.domenicarestaurant.com. ℂ **504/648-6020.** Reservations recommended. Pizza $13–$18, antipasti $14–$24, main courses $24–$30. Daily 11am–11pm.

Drago's ★★ SEAFOOD   The booming Hilton lobby isn't too conducive to an atmospheric experience. Fortunately that's irrelevant, because you're here for one thing and one thing only (okay, two): Drago's buttery, garlicky, Parmesan-y, charbroiled oysters—your new paramour, the one you can't get enough of. Other places do them, but none so well. They're like a home renovation project: However many you think you want to order, double it. The bargain-priced Maine lobsters are also worth your while, but not much else matters. Sports-minded folks can sit at the bar, order oysters, and watch what's on—there are worse ways to take in a game (though there are no tap beers—wassup with that?). Be mindful that the sprawling dining room can fill up, and they don't take reservations, so a wait is possible.

2 Poydras St., in the Hilton Riverside. www.dragosrestaurant.com. ℂ **504/584-3911.** Also 3232 N. Arnoult Rd., Metairie. ℂ **504/888-9254.** Raw oysters $13/dozen, charbroiled $20; dinner appetizers $12–$18; main courses $20–$29; Maine lobster $20–$52. Daily 11am–10pm.

Inexpensive

Cochon Butcher ★★★ CONTEMPORARY CAJUN/LIGHT FARE   This could easily be a three-word review: Just. Eat. Everything. So much meaty goodness here it's hard to know where to start. No longer the punk little sister to Cochon (but if it were, we'd be her bestie), a recent expansion catapults Butcher into a full-blown restaurant, with a bar and garage-style doors opening onto the street. Proudly owning its lifeblood, the butchering stations are now front and center, right behind the registers (whole hogs come in on Tuesdays and Thursdays, FYI; the squeamish can head straight to the new bar and order a delightful Trotter's Punch—which contains gin, not trotters). The excellent house-smoked meats and sausages, in small plates or on a sandwich, will rock your world (the boudin sausage link is the best within the city confines (but not outside them). Their muffuletta rivals (okay, surpasses) Central Grocery's; the pork belly with cucumber and mint is wondrous. Get the vinegary Brussels sprouts and dreamy mac and cheese or rue the day you didn't. A few good local beers and choice wines by the glass are offered. Dessert, like everything else, must be had; try the swoonful caramel doberge cake if it's available.

930 Tchoupitoulas St. www.cochonbutcher.com. ℂ **504/588-7675.** Sandwiches $10–$12, charcuterie plate $16, sides and small plates $3–$6. Mon–Thurs 10am–10pm, Fri–Sat 10am–11pm, Sun 10am–4pm.

Mother's ★ CREOLE/SOUL FOOD/LIGHT FARE   Mother's gets the haters who accuse it of being touristy, but hey, Paris is touristy. And if it's good enough for Beyoncé and Jay-Z (who selfied from here in 2013), it's . . . actually that has no bearing on anything. Mother's worth is in direct proportion to the line of people waiting to get in. If it extends past the second window (say, more than 3 to 4 parties ahead of you), it's not worth waiting. It's good, not great. If you can waltz right in, fine: You'll get solid Creole cooking in an easy-access location, good for an introduction to the cuisine and family-friendly. The traditional Creole hot plates (jambalaya, shrimp Creole) are serviceable; mild or hot homemade sausage elevates the red beans (go hot). Po' boys are the safer bet, especially anything that revolves around Mother's signature baked ham. The Ferdi (ham, roast beef debris) is the top seller, but we think the ham gets lost in all that. We prefer it solo with cheese, or combo'd with turkey, which stands up better. We'll also have the ham with biscuits at the unsurprising breakfast. The bread pudding needs to be experienced, if only to guffaw at the retro use of canned fruit cocktail, maraschinos and all (it's also freakishly good). Make no never mind, Mother's has rules: 1) Get in the cafeteria line to order food and get steam-table items; 2) order and receive drinks; 3) pay; 4) then and only then find a table—don't send a scout to save one; 5) a server delivers the rest of the food. Follow these rules lest you get some hostess lip.

401 Poydras St. www.mothersrestaurant.net. ℂ **504/523-9656.** Menu items $6–$25. Mon–Sun 7am–10pm.

UPTOWN/THE GARDEN DISTRICT

Very Expensive

Clancy's ★★★ CONTEMPORARY CREOLE   Clancy's epitomizes the New Orleans tradition of fine neighborhood dining. Although it's been at this location for 70 years, it's been reenergized and popularized since a late-1900s renaissance, and a favorite ever since. It's got the look: tuxedoes on the waiters, linen on the tables, white beadboard on the walls. It's got the attitude: It's fun, fine dining, aspirational for some; a weekly ritual for others. It's got a menu full of new Creole classics, superbly done: flash-fried oysters topped with brie; creamy, succulent shrimp and grits; a colossal smoked duck leg that stands on its own with the simplest of sides. When softshell crab is in season, it's de rigueur on every menu in town, but here it's smoked—and it's a wonder. We've had great success with veal here, lighter than it sounds despite the Béarnaise and crabmeat. If we were going all in, we'd order several of the pricey starters; the mussels with Andouille in tomato broth and crawfish vol au vent, to name two; the ample wine list is also short on lower-end options. But once you give in to the kind of splendid evening that can be had here, you may choose to give in to all that, too, and commune over conversation and cognac. Reserve in advance.

6100 Annunciation St. www.clancysneworleans.com. ℰ **504/895-1111.** Main courses $26–$35. Mon–Sat 5:30–10:30pm, Thurs–Fri 11:30am–2pm.

Commander's Palace ★★★ CONTEMPORARY CREOLE   The Commander's Palace miracle is that they are meal (and mood) mentalists. It's as if there is a sliding scale of formality, and they have an uncanny ability to serve up just the amount your mood requires (and a room to match it). An elegant, "event" evening? Got it. Rollicking (civilized) good time? Jaded foodie who wants a wow? They're on it. Marriage proposal in the offing? Just tell them when to serve the ring. They understand that in the ultimate New Orleanean experience, stately needn't be stuffy; formal can still be fun; and that sometimes, innovation is the best way to honor tradition—and they immerse you in it. They're also leaders in mentoring and fostering the city's culinary scene: A who's who of New Orleans restaurant owners, chefs, and front-of-house managers resembles a Commander's family tree. Yet regardless of how many "best of" lists and awards Commander's racks up, they never rest on their laurels (we'll just mention the James Beard "Best Chef" award that Tory McPhail picked up in 2013).

The continually changing menu reflects Chef McPhail's commitment to local ingredients and fervent imagination, on best display in the seven-course "Chef's Playground." The a la carte menu mixes their classics (spicy-sweet shrimp and tasso henican, the gateway drug of Commander's Palace dishes; consistently perfect pecan-crusted Gulf fish) with seasonal newbies (a sublime boudin-stuffed quail with a pepper jelly and sugarcane reduction). The gumbo can be a tad salty; opt for the robust turtle soup instead. For enders, the famed bread pudding soufflé is a puff of gladness with whiskey sauce. The wine list is one of the finest in this or any city, with a good selection offered by the glass in half or full pours. Everyone should eat at Commander's, and everyone can. Its unintimidating finery, and multicourse lunch and happy-hour deals start under $20 (less than some po' boys); $38 at dinner. So worth it. Reserve well in advance.

1403 Washington Ave. www.commanderspalace.com. ℰ **504/899-8221.** No shorts or T-shirts; jackets preferred for men at dinner. Main courses $26–$40; tasting menu $95, $146 with wine; 3-course dinner $38–$40. Mon–Fri lunch only 25¢ martinis. Mon–Fri 11:30am–2pm, brunch Sat 11:30am–1pm and Sun 10:30am–1:30pm, daily 6–10pm (June–Aug from 6:30pm).

Expensive

Appoline ★★ NEW LOUISIANA   If you were to take a drive up Magazine Street, you could probably fall out of the cab and into the door of a good bistro or restaurant along any stretch of the street. But some are better than others. Appoline, a relative newcomer, is one of them. The sweet front porch of this converted Creole cottage conceals the creamy tones and bleached hardwood walls of the fully updated interior. We can't help thinking that in other cities (or other times), this room would be full of close conversations and hushed tones. Here it's a bit more casual; jeans mix with suits, and laughter permeates the place. Maybe it's the excellent cocktails and keen, reasonable wine list. Maybe it's the playful watermelon and crabmeat salad starter, with a sprinkling of feta cheese and pistachios. Or the crunchy fried quail, sharing the plate with a chunk of lush pork belly. Probably it's the signature "Hooty Tootie Pie," the exploded adult peanut butter cup with a name too silly to say out loud. So just point to it on the dessert menu, if you must.

4729 Magazine St. www.apollinerestaurant.com. ℰ **504/894-8881.** Main courses $28–$32. Tues–Thurs and Sun 5:30–9:30pm, Fri–Sat 5:30–10:30pm, Sat–Sun brunch 10am–2pm.

Uptown Restaurants

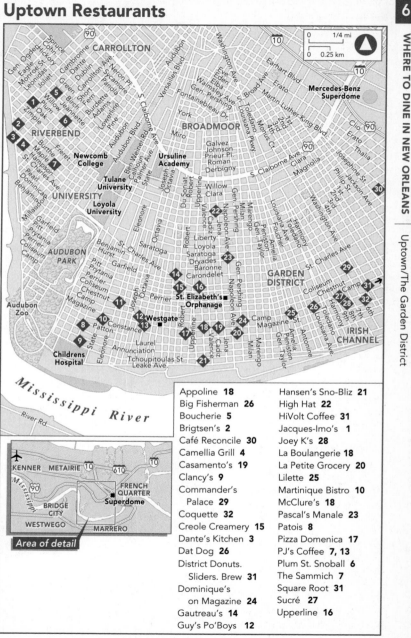

Appoline **18**	Hansen's Sno-Bliz **21**
Big Fisherman **26**	High Hat **22**
Boucherie **5**	HiVolt Coffee **31**
Brigtsen's **2**	Jacques-Imo's **1**
Café Reconcile **30**	Joey K's **28**
Camellia Grill **4**	La Boulangerie **18**
Casamento's **19**	La Petite Grocery **20**
Clancy's **9**	Lilette **25**
Commander's	Martinique Bistro **10**
Palace **29**	McClure's **18**
Coquette **32**	Pascal's Manale **23**
Creole Creamery **15**	Patois **8**
Dante's Kitchen **3**	Pizza Domenica **17**
Dat Dog **26**	PJ's Coffee **7, 13**
District Donuts.	Plum St. Snoball **6**
Sliders. Brew **31**	The Sammich **7**
Dominique's	Square Root **31**
on Magazine **24**	Sucré **27**
Gautreau's **14**	Upperline **16**
Guy's Po'Boys **12**	

Once upon a time, while waiting for Casamento's doors to open and just moments from an oyster loaf, three youngish tourist gals struck up a chat (as happens nearly automatically in New Orleans) with the three Uptown ladies-of-a-certain-age ahead of them. They were St. Charles–born and –bred, dined at Casamento's weekly, and offered us NOLA newbies some well-tested tips. This one still sticks (and sounds best when read with a high-pitched, breathy lilt): "You simply *must* go to any of the fine, old French restaurants, and when you do, why you just order anythin' flamin'." Meaning, go to Antoine's, Arnaud's, Commander's Palace, or Galatoire's, and get bananas Foster, baked Alaska, *café brûlot,* or anything prepared tableside and involving conflagration. Naturally we bought the ladies a round, and to this day we're still following their fine advice and living by the "anythin' flamin'" creed: Indulge a bit, relish fun, and while one needn't embrace drama in all aspects of life, when it comes to dessert, by all means *bring it on.*

Brigtsen's ★★★ CONTEMPORARY CAJUN/CREOLE Brigtsen's was one of the early modern Creole revolutionaries, and one of the first to convert a beautiful, 19th-century house into an upscale neighborhood restaurant way back in 1986. The perennial favorite still maintains a warm, romantic intimacy, with the hostess circulating amiably though the sweet little mural-decorated rooms. The service and cuisine—which shows homey, Cajun country roots—have been polished to consistent excellence. The "Shell Beach Diet," their famously grand seafood platter, changes seasonally but includes five to six sauced, baked, or otherwise unfried seafood items. It's an impressive extravagance for sharing or for a hungry, indecisive diner. Chef Brigtsen has a special touch with game and rabbit. His panéed sesame-crusted version in a tangy Creole mustard sauce, as well as his crispy, moist roast duck are known far and wide; his pecan pie with its perfect, copious crust is also justifiably revered. A modest wine list satisfies, but could be improved. Reserve well in advance during peak periods.

723 Dante St. www.brigtsens.com. ✆ **504/861-7610.** Reservations highly recommended. Main courses $26–$34. Tues–Sat 5:30–10pm.

Coquette ★★★ BISTRO It's hard to believe Coquette is just 6 years old. It feels like it's occupied its tin-ceilinged, chandeliered, bistro-chic space for much longer. We mean this in the best way—it's smart and polished, and altogether comfortable in its skin, even if that skin changes daily. We're sure that somewhere in an attic Chef/Owner Michael Stoltzfus has a menu that's aging—because his well of culinary creativity seems to keep Coquette eternally fresh. That, plus dedication to ingredient perfectionism, and top talent heading the bar and pastry programs, lands Coquette firmly in the upper echelon of New Orleans's restaurants.

Whatever we suggest will be long gone by the time you get there (and really what you should do if at all possible is spring for the five-course tasting menus). Tuna crudo interspersed with compressed cantaloupe and garnished with herb-dusted popcorn had us chuckling with delight. Chicken-fried sweetbreads on a blueberry puree are a miracle in the mouth; baby eggplant paired with ricotta gnocchi over a chilled peach-tomato sauce wasn't a beautiful sight—but was altogether divine on the palate. If any version of cheesecake is on the menu, make that your choice, unless you're a chocolate lover. Then get the pudding and the delicate strawberry vacherin (for balance). If all this sounds a bit daunting, the $23 three-course lunch menu might be one of the best deals in town.

2800 Magazine St. www.coquettenola.com. ✆ **504/265-0421.** Reservations highly recommended. 3-course lunch $23, lunch entrees $11–$18, 5-course blind tasting $70 (wine pairing $30), dinner entrees $26–$32. Wed–Sat 11:30am–3pm, Wed–Mon 5:30–10pm, Sun brunch 10:30am–2pm.

Dominique's on Magazine ★ BISTRO/INTERNATIONAL

Chef Dominique Macquet's cuisine is mature yet adventurous, reflecting his experience in some of the city's finest restaurants; his Mauritian roots explain the French-African influences that seep into the gently unforeseen flavor profiles. His sense of style is evident in this sleek, bleached-out room, with enough accent mirrors to ensure that you don't miss seeing yourself (hearing is a different story). Service, like the room, also tends toward the cool—and occasionally confused—perhaps. Chef Macquet's food aims high and hits the target or just below. Ceviche with gorgeous shrimp was punched up by fresh jalapeños and herbs from the vertical backyard garden. Grilled lamb with basil, mint, and harissa jus is spot-on. But housemade spaghetti with wagyu meatballs in veal jus is anachronistic and avoidable. There's not much bar to speak of—too bad since the drinks are terrific—but the white-on-white courtyard is pleasant and more sedate than the main dining room; a good choice, weather permitting.

4213 Magazine St. www.dominiquesonmag.com. ✆ **504/891-9282.** Main courses $23–$32. Mon–Thurs 5:30–9:30pm, Fri–Sat 5:30–10:30pm.

Gautreau's ★★ CONTEMPORARY SOUTHERN

Tucked away in a residential Uptown neighborhood, with no signage to speak of, is a reclusive spot that pretty much every major food magazine has managed to find. Chef Sue Zemanick has been lavished with their praise, garnered umpteen awards, and by the time you read this may be a Top Chef Masters winner. There's a finery to the food here that hews close to that at classic French treatments, but steps forward by virtue of modernity and perfect ingredients. A dewy foie-gras torchon adds a reduction of stone fruit and huckleberries, with bits of macadamia for crunch. A bright starter marries jicama and watercress with roast pineapple. Moist, sautéed snapper is uncluttered by a bright sauce Americaine and crisp snap peas. The grown-up wine list matches the low-ceilinged room, with its trompe l'oeil linen walls and warm lighting. The talented pair heading Gautreau's is taking us in new directions with **Ivy** and **Marti's,** both new in 2014, but we'll surely return to the original. Reserve in advance.

1728 Soniat St. www.gautreausrestaurant.com. ✆ **504/899-7397.** Appetizers $14–$18, main courses $26–$36. Mon–Sat 6–10pm.

Jacques-Imo's ★★ CREOLE/SOUL FOOD

Speaking of food trucks, the gator-painted pickup in front of Jacques-Imo's actually has a table set up in its bed, where some lucky couple can dine (they'll have way more space than in the crowded dining room). This funky, colorful spot with the long line (longer in proportion to who's playing next door at the **Maple Leaf;** p. 177) is hugely popular for all that jacked-up fun, not to mention the giant portions and Creole soul-food stylings. Fortunately, the drinks are well made, and as soon as you're seated you'll be appeased with righteous cornbread muffins. The signature shrimp and alligator-sausage "cheesecake" (more like a quiche) has fans and detractors (we're on board); the diamond-hard crunchy fried chicken and less-complicated Creole specialties fare best: blackened redfish with a crab-chili hollandaise is a winner, and the lightly batter-fried softshell-crab "Godzilla" worked. The food may ride a bit on the coattails of the rowdy party atmosphere, and you'll feel that you've earned it after the wait.

8324 Oak St. www.jacques-imos.com. ℂ **504/861-0886.** Reservations for 5 or more required; smaller parties are first-come, first-served. Main courses $20–$34. Mon–Thurs 5–10pm, Fri–Sat 5–10:30pm.

La Petite Grocery ★★★ BISTRO   Among the many bistros along Magazine Street, this way-Uptown standard-bearer is more traditionally French than some in terms of decor and wine selections. They've eased into a reliably good, comfortably welcoming groove here, and the food is a distinctive mélange of Creole creativity, relying on local ingredients, keen technique, and the adroit palate of Chef/Owner/*Top Chef* contestant Justin Devillier. We believe deeply in the steak tartare (though it seems to come and go from the menu), and require the blue crab beignets as well as the ricotta dumplings with lobster and fresh peas. But they're also soup geniuses here, so preliminary courses are a tough choice. For entrees, the smoky shrimp and grits with roasted mushrooms is one of the better treatments we've tried; and the beef tenderloin gets a deep, satisfying sear from the pan roasting. A side of fried green beans is good to munch on at the bar, and marvel at superstar pastry chef Bronwen Wyatt's creations. Her floral addition to a simple local strawberry shortcake changed our view of that dessert forever; then she exalted a silky cheesecake with cardamom and candied kumquats. The bar can get pretty lively—good or not so much depending on your goals for the evening—and the usually smart, on-point service might suffer a tad during peak periods.

4238 Magazine St. www.lapetitegrocery.com. ℂ **504/891-3377.** Main courses $15–$31 lunch, $16–$32 dinner. Tues–Sat 11:30am–2:30pm, Sun 10:30am–2:30pm, Sun–Thurs 5:30–9:30pm, Fri–Sat 5:30–10:30pm.

Lilette ★★ BISTRO   Lilette's pedigreed chef-owner brings his training in some of New Orleans's finest kitchens and at Michelin-starred restaurants in France to bear here, resulting in an artistic, serious approach. The NOLA classic space—high-ceilinged, columned, tiles—is made East Village–ready with tobacco-toned walls. Lunch is thick with business people and ladies who lunch; dinner (which gets dear) sees a mixed crowd of tourists, neighbors, and young hipsters, all here for the tasteful, clean lines of the cooking. Start with the truffled Parmigiano toast with wild mushrooms, marrow, and veal glace (you may end with it, too; it's divine) and the sharply flavorful fried sardines (if you stop now, you've done well). A roast chicken breast with Brussels sprouts and balsamic-glazed onions is flawless simplicity; gnocchi with intensely unctuous beef cheeks and chanterelles is immorally rich. Desserts are worth the indulgence, notably the curious signature of goat-cheese crème fraîche rounds, paired with vanilla-poached pears sprinkled with pistachios and lavender honey (baklava is turning in its grave). If you're a wine enthusiast trying to decide between the Uptown bistros, Lilette is your choice.

3637 Magazine St. www.liletterestaurant.com. ℂ **504/895-1636.** Main courses $12–$24 lunch, $25–$45 dinner. Tues–Sat 11:30am–2pm, Mon–Thurs 5:30–9:30pm, Fri–Sat 5:30–10:30pm.

Martinique Bistro ★★ BISTRO/FRENCH   Dining in this sleek but romantic courtyard, surrounded by tall, private greenery, one might expect someone, anyone, to propose at any moment. It's a favorite among locals for that ambience, as well as the French- and Mediterranean-influenced dishes. A Gulf fish stew done Mediterranean style is just right under the stars. Modern Southern specialties are also on hand, the ubiquitous pork belly done deliciously here with peach preserves and a jalapeño-and-goat-cheese corncake. The boneless New Zealand lamb loin with pickles, couscous, and a Meyer lemon-watercress aioli and tomato-sherry vinegar sounds like it would be one ingredient over the line, but that wasn't at all the case. We should mention that there is an indoor space, but request a courtyard table for best effect (doable even in inclement weather thanks to a retractable roof). If no one proposes, it's also a great spot for a girls' lunch or brunch.

5908 Magazine St. www.martiniquebistro.com. ℂ **504/891-8495.** Main courses $28–$32 dinner, $11–$20 brunch. Tues–Sun 5:30–9pm, Sat–Sun 11am–2pm.

Patois ★★★ BISTRO/CONTEMPORARY CREOLE   Can we just cut to the chase and say that this is a near-perfect bistro? The tucked-away restaurant is chic but inviting; the locally sourced ingredients are bright with freshness; service is practiced; and the menu is French meets modern Southern bistro and shakes hands with Spain. Your head won't spin round, but you'll likely enjoy every precisely done option. We sampled an octopus carpaccio made lively with a pepper-and-chorizo citrus vinaigrette, and loved a simple lamb-ribs appetizer—just right with a dollop of marinated eggplant and Creole tomato jam. The grilled hanger steak, in a rich red-wine bone-marrow reduction, is deeply flavored, and local dessert favorites are tweaked in amusing, inviting ways—king-cake bread pudding with Creole cream-cheese ice cream (though the pretzel-crust peanut butter cup gives it a run). All are sweet and worthy. Reserve well in advance during peak periods.

6078 Laurel St. www.patoisnola.com. ℂ **504/895-9441.** Main courses $27–$34 dinner, $12–$18 lunch. Wed–Thurs 5:30–10pm, Fri 11:30am–2pm and 5:30–10:30pm, Sat 5:30–10:30pm, Sun 10:30am–2pm.

Upperline ★★ CONTEMPORARY CREOLE   These past few years, eyebrows were raised by chef turnover here, but it was for naught: Genial owner/host JoAnn Clevenger has maintained the hospitable vibe that has always been a touchstone at this charming residential spot, and the new chef has kept signature items unmolested while adding a few tricks of his own. Standout appetizers include fried green tomatoes with shrimp rémoulade sauce (an oft-copied dish that was invented here) and a gumbo as rich as Bill Gates (and many shades darker). For entrees, the moist roast duck with a spry ginger-peach sauce is crispy perfection on a plate; a mellow, sautéed drum comes with a shock of spicy shrimp. If you're in town in the summer, the all-garlic menu is great fun. Don't leave without having the warm honey-pecan bread pudding, touring the art-filled restaurant, and thanking JoAnn (though she'll probably get to you first to do the same). Reserve well in advance during peak periods.

1413 Upperline St. www.upperline.com. ℂ **504/891-9822.** Reservations suggested. Main courses $20–$30, 3-course prix-fixe menu $40. Wed–Sun 5:30–9:30pm.

Moderate

Boucherie ★★★ CONTEMPORARY SOUTHERN   To tell or not to tell: That was the moral dilemma we faced when we first tried Boucherie. And we don't just mean *you,* we mean our best friends. But with food this good, a diminutive dining room this cute and fun-inducing, and prices this solidly affordable, word gets out. They parlayed food-truck-turned-bricks-and-mortar success into what Chef/Owner (and *Chopped* alumni) Nathaniel Zimet calls "fine dining for the people." There's so much Cajun-inflected goodness (and dashes of global influences) that you could blindly point at the menu and be happy with whatever wine, drinks, and plates small or large are put in front of you. Especially if it's the duck confit with plantains (with butternut squash and duck-and-tasso "baklava" in another treatment); or the pulled pork cake with tangy purple slaw; or the refreshing cauliflower and ramps. Oddly, we think the signature house-smoked *boudin* balls *are* skippable. Super-sweet Krispy Kreme bread pudding is no longer the hilarious curiosity that it once was; get the Thai chili chocolate pie or chocolate terrine instead if they're available. Rumor has it that an expansion may be in the offing for take-out and retail. We'd hit that, too. Reserve well in advance.

8115 Jeannette St. www.boucherie-nola.com. ℭ **504/862-5514.** Dinner small plates $6–$13, large plates $13–$18. Tues–Sat 11am–3pm and 5:30–9:30pm.

Dante's Kitchen ★★ BISTRO/CONTEMPORARY CREOLE   Locals give this low-profile spot steady love, understandably given the shrewd use of seasonal and local products, cheerful "This Old House" interior, and obliging staff. Their lively New Orleans cuisine comes with little surprises, alternately simple and refined. At dinner, hope that the herb-suffused redfish "on the half shell" is on the menu, or go for crispy confit pork steak with braised greens and an apple compote—just like mom never made. Despite these pork-focused suggestions, most everything they do with veggies is wondrous; one could make a meal of just them (a pea soup with crab butter and bacon counts). Brunch is a strong alternative. We like their reworked Benedict, in which tender rosemary-crusted pork replaces Canadian bacon, honey sweetens the hollandaise, and a caramelized biscuit supports it all. It's a ways from the FQ, but just 2 blocks off the St. Charles streetcar line where it makes the big turn onto Carrollton Avenue (Hampson stop). Reserve in advance during peak periods (reservations not accepted for brunch).

736 Dante St. www.danteskitchen.com. ℭ **504/861-3121.** Main courses $10–$14 brunch, $23–$28 dinner. Nightly (except Tues) 6–10pm, Sat–Sun brunch 10:30am–2pm.

High Hat ★★★ CONTEMPORARY SOUTHERN   If you make it here (by cab or car), you'll have the fringe benefit of checking out Freret Street, a booming restaurant street and one of the best post-Katrina success stories. This casual neighborhood spot had nothing to go on but an idea and original tile floors, and what a go they've made of it. It's become one of our solid, go-to spots for no-fuss lunches and dinners made with obvious care. We come for the always interesting drinks, often fashioned with house-made ingredients. We come for the graceful oyster fennel soup, and the upgraded Southern comfort foods, like a mound of fork-tender, slow-roast pork with sublime braised greens. But mostly we come for the crispy, light, piled-high fried catfish with tangy slaw and house-made tartar sauce (everything here save the Delta tamales is made in-house, even the condiments). Then we get whatever freshly made pie is available, and the inane Grillswith—a grilled donut topped with melting ice cream—because it would be equally inane to skip it.

4500 Freret St. www.highhatcafe.com. ℭ **504/754-1336.** Everything under $18. Sun–Thurs 11am–9pm, Fri–Sat 11am–10pm.

Pascal's Manale ★★ ITALIAN/STEAK/SEAFOOD   We adore the old-school neon, and the where-everybody-knows-your-name feel at this definitive, century-old neighborhood joint. But more than anything we love the barbecued shrimp—the bowl of colossal, buttery crustaceans that made Manale (mu-*nah*-lee). Make sure you get them (schedule a long workout tomorrow), some turtle soup, and—trust us—classic spaghetti and meatballs while you're at it, but start the meal at the oyster bar. The bivalves might be frigid (in contrast to their effect, some might say), but if Thomas is shucking, his repartee is hot. Ask him anything, and your party is officially started. When it's crowded it can be boisterous—it's the kind of place where neighboring tables spontaneously converse here, but unlike at a cozy bistro, it's a welcome intrusion (people wear bibs here, fer Pete's sake).

1838 Napoleon Ave. www.pascalsmanale.com. © **504/895-4877.** Main courses $18–$39. Mon–Fri 11:30am–9pm, Sat 5–10pm.

Inexpensive

Big Fisherman ★★ SEAFOOD   This. Is. The. Stuff. If you really want a true local experience, that means eating a sack of boiled seafood—crawfish, shrimp, crab, whatever's in season. Order shellfish by the pound, and potatoes, half cobs of corn, heads of boiled garlic, maybe some sausage by the piece. Make sure to grab a beer or sweet tea to soothe the spice, plenty of paper towels, and a fistful of newspapers by the door. That's to dump your hot seafood onto, often done on a patio table, in a park, or sitting atop a levee watching the river run (there's no seating here). But no reason it can't be done in a hotel room (as long as you're okay with some lingering eau de shellfish). Contrary to logic, go at peak times, even if there's a line. Boiled seafood is best when it's straight out of the pot. They ship or pack for travel, too, so you can have a home boil. If you're on the other end of town, **Cajun Seafood ★★** in the rougher 7th Ward provides a similar experience and quality, with table seating and prepared foods, too.

3301 Magazine St. www.bigfishermanseafood.com. © **504/897-9907.** Boiled seafood $3–$10/lb. (market price). Mon–Fri 11am–6pm, Sat 10am–6pm, Sun 10am–5pm. **Cajun Seafood:** 1479 N. Claiborne St. www.cajunseafoodnola.com. © **504/948-6000.** Daily 10:30am–9pm.

Camellia Grill ★★ DINER/LIGHT FARE   Even though it's *only* been a part of the city's food culture since 1946, the Camellia Grill seems to have always been there. That may change soon: A 2013 lawsuit is threatening to force a change to the name or the iconic white-columned building. We hope not, because there's really nowhere else to go for luncheonette-style counter service with white linens, Southern hospitality, witty banter dished out by white-jacketed servers, and a classic grilled burger. The omelets manage to be simultaneously heavy and fluffy and come in the standard varieties (if it's been a rough night, we go with chili cheese. That'd be American cheese—the square stuff). Late-night hours make both locations popular after-club spots, but any time is good for the chocolate pecan pie (heated on the grill and a la mode, please). Good prices, true character.

Uptown: 626 S. Carrollton Ave. © **504/309-2679.** All items under $10. Sun–Thurs 8am–midnight, Fri–Sat 8am–2am. **French Quarter:** 540 Chartres St. © **504/522-1800.** Sun–Thurs 8am–11pm, Fri–Sat 8am–3am.

Casamento's ★★★ SEAFOOD   Probably the best "erster" joint in the city, Casamento's takes its oysters so seriously that it simply closes down when they're not in peak season (well, Gulf oysters are always in season nowadays, but we're sure they've got their reasons). The all-tile restaurant has been family owned since 1919. The oysters are scrubbed clean and well selected; the shucker is a hoot (if you dare him, he'll shoot a bivalve into your mouth from across the room). You should absolutely take the plunge and order the oyster loaf: a whole loaf of bread fried in butter, filled with oysters (or shrimp), and fried again to seal it. Seriously.

4330 Magazine St. www.casamentosrestaurant.com. © **504/895-9761.** Dozen raw oysters $12, main courses $9–$25, market price on some items. No credit cards. Tues–Sat 11am–2pm, Thurs–Sat 5:30–9pm. Closed early June to early Sept and major holidays.

Dat Dog ★ LIGHT FARE This darling of the gourmet hot-dog boom will pretty much satisfy any dog-related craving, what with 16 types of franks and sausages and umpteen toppings. Success depends on your personal selections, and as dog traditionalists we like the brats and imported German wieners best. Our attempt at "server's choice" left us with lesser base sausages and uninspired toppings, but decent fries. And while you might like the gator, turducken, or crawfish dogs better than us, we admit the duck version with blackberry sauce was pretty darn good, and the fluffy buns held up well. The bright blue buildings at all three locations make for an easy, fun hang with a brew and your crew, and while it's an inexpensive dinner, it's still a $7 to $9 hot dog.

5030 Freret St. www.datdognola.com. *©* **504/899-6883.** All items under $10. Cash only; ATMs on site. Mon–Sat 11am–10pm, Sun 11am–9pm. Also at 3336 Magazine St. *©* **504/324-2226.** Mon–Thurs 11am–10pm, Fri–Sat 11am–11pm, Sun 11am–9pm. And one more at 601 Frenchmen St. *©* **504/309-3362.** Sun–Wed 11am–midnight, Thurs 11am–1am, Fri–Sat 11am–3am.

District Donuts. Sliders. Brew. ★★★ LIGHT FARE/BAKERY The idea of District Donuts. Sliders. Brew sounded so much like it emerged from a 4am brainstorm after a very long frat party that we hesitated to try it. And then we went. Three days in a row. Yes, that happened. The sliders come in cheeseburger, fried chicken, and tofu every day (but it's a far cry from White Castle and Winchell's), and three other rotating varieties. Pork belly and oyster shows up frequently (which is to your benefit). They're invariably carefully topped with house-made dressings, slaws, or a balancing bit of greenery—a spicy avocado goat cheese schmear on soft shell crab. Donuts follow a similar pattern: you can always get a good ol' glazed, chocolate, or cinnamon sugar, and then the donut Heavens open. Fresh fruit jelly filled (pomegranate, muscadine, whatever's at the farmer's market); Nutella drenched; tart lemon ginger; maple bacon sriracha . . . it goes on. Surprisingly, their "Brew" has nothing to do with beer—so much for the misguided frat presumption. (Patrons can grab a beer from the excellent Stein's liquor store next door.) It's actually coffee (pulled from deceptive taps), mostly from 1,000 Faces, an Athens, Georgia, purveyor. Among other options, there's a nitrogen cold-brewed version that is nearly as smooth as advertised. So that 3-day bender has started to make sense, right? Go at off-peak times to avoid the lines.

2209 Magazine St. www.donutsandsliders.com. *©* **504/570-6945.** Donuts $1.25–$2.50, sliders $3.50–$4.75. Sun–Thurs 7am–9pm, Fri–Sat 7am–10pm.

Guy's Po' Boys ★★ LIGHT FARE This is the Uptown choice for a lowdown po' boy. We hate to be repetitive, but as with all good po' boy joints, the bread is Leidenheimer's and the best choices are the fried shrimp or the gravy-soaked roast beef—you can't go wrong with either. This lunch-only spot isn't a slick operation; it takes time to fry and slice, so you may wait a few minutes for your sammie. We promise you, it's worth it, so make friends with the locals, sip on your Barq's, and be patient, grasshopper.

5259 Magazine St. (at Tchoupitoulas St.). *©* **504/891-5025.** All items under $10. Cash only. Mon–Sat 10am–4pm.

Joey K's ★ CREOLE/SEAFOOD/DINER This corner hangout gets locals and a few visitors, who know that the trout Tchoupitoulas—a rocking pan-fried trout topped with grilled veggies and shrimp—is worth a stop if you're out for a shop. Nothing else will blow your hair back here, but the daily blackboard specials such as brisket, lamb

road trip EATS

You can snag plenty of good eats out in the suburbs and parishes in and around New Orleans. If you have a car (or a friend with one), these local favorites are well worth the 10- to 30-minute drives.

Deanie's ★★ This well-respected seafood joint is the very model of a neighborhood restaurant. There's one in the French Quarter now, but we prefer the original.

1713 Lake Ave., Metairie. ✆ **504/831-4141.** $10–$25 or market price. Tues–Sat 11am–10pm, Sun 11am–9pm.

Dong Phuong ★★ *Banh mi, pho,* and other Vietnamese specialties are among the many excellent contributions that New Orleans's huge Vietnamese population has made to the city. Head east for the best.

14207 Chef Menteur Hwy., N.O. East. ✆ **504/254-0214.** $3–$10. Mon and Wed–Sun 8am–4pm (bakery only open till 6pm).

The Galley ★★ The folks who do the softshell crab po' boys at Jazz Fest do other things just as well, and they're nearby in pretty Old Metairie.

2535 Metairie Rd. ✆ **504/832-0955.** $10–$27. Tues–Sat 11am–9pm.

Middendorf's ★★★ A classic on-the-water joint that fries up the crispiest, thinnest, freshest catfish imaginable.

30160 Hwy. 51 South, Akers. ✆ **985/386-6666.** $12–$19. Wed–Sun 10:30am–9pm.

Mondo ★★ Bayona chef Susan Spicer's popular, casual place in the suburb of Lakeview.

900 Harrison Ave., Lakeview. ✆ **504/224-2633.** $9–$15 lunch, $12–$27 dinner. Mon–Fri 11:30am–2:30pm, Mon–Thurs 5:30–10pm, Fri–Sat 5:30–10:30pm, Sun brunch 11am–2pm.

Mosca's ★★★ Generations of New Orleaneans make the drive and wait the wait for killer old-school Italian. (We categorically deny allegations that it's an old mob hangout).

4137 U.S. Hwy. 90 West, Avondale. ✆ **504/436-8950.** $11–$34. No credit cards. Tues–Sat 5:30–9:30pm.

R&O's ★★ Thoroughly unpretentious, old-school neighborhood joint serving the usual classics: po' boys, fried seafood, Italian essentials.

216 Hammond Hwy., Metairie. ✆ **504/831-1248.** Most items under $15, crab $24. Mon–Fri 11am–3pm, Wed–Thurs 5–9pm, Fri 5–9:30pm, Sat 11am–9:30pm, Sun 11am–4pm and 5–9pm.

Sal's Seafood ★★★ Many locals cite the fresh, meaty, spiced-just-right boiled crawfish at this hole-in-the-wall as the best around. Worth the half-hour drive across the river into suburban Marrero.

1512 Barataria Blvd., Marerro. ✆ **504/341-8112.** Boiled seafood $3–$9/lb. (market price). Tues–Sat 9am–9pm, Sun 9am–7:30pm.

Sammy's ★★ Out of the tourist zone but close enough for a cab. The Ray Ray po' boy (fried chicken, grilled ham, Swiss cheese) made one health-conscious skeptic laugh aloud with joy on first bite.

3000 Elysian Fields Ave. ✆ **504/947-0675.** $5–$15. Mon–Thurs 10:45am–5pm, Fri 10:45am–7pm, Sat 10:45am–4pm.

Walker's ★★ Another Fest favorite. The *cochon de lait* po' boy comes from right here, along with really good barbecue.

10828 Hayne Blvd., Lakefront. ✆ **504/241-8227.** $5–$17. Wed–Sat 10:30am till sold out.

shank, and white beans with pork chops are just fine, and somehow we often end up around this stretch of Magazine when hunger strikes.

3001 Magazine St. www.joeyksrestaurant.com. ✆ **504/891-0997.** Main courses $10–$21. Mon–Sat 11am–9pm.

The Sammich ★★ LIGHT FARE   Enter the Sammich—boldly stating its post-po' boy purpose by stepping over the requisite local nomenclature (we do po' boys here, not sammiches). Starters of escargot and foie gras terrine are the next clue. Lest you start thinking they're too big for their britches, it's a paper plate and plastic utensil kind of place, albeit with snappy nautical decor; and their 40-item beer selection includes $2, $3, and $4 options. But we digress. Start with an order of the addictive, perfectly crisped duck fat fries—not for the table but for each of you, lest fisticuffs ensue. The depth of flavor in the smoked tuna dip comes from capers and Kalamata olives. Get some. Other places do shredded roast beef po' boys; here it's a soul-hugging osso buco with marrow mayo; the standard fried oyster is elevated with brie, applewood bacon, and meuniere sauce—crazy good! We're not usually mixed-meat eaters, preferring our surf-and-turf on separate plates, but their fried chicken sandwich with barbecued pulled pork and house-made coleslaw converted us.

7708 Maple St. www.thesammich.com. ✆ **504/726-6424.** Sammiches: $12–$15. Daily 11am–10pm.

COFFEE, BAKERIES & DESSERTS

For other sweet treats, see the section on "**Candies, Pralines & Pastries**" in chapter 9, p. 192.

Angelo Brocato Ice Cream & Confectionery ★★★ ICE CREAM/ DESSERT   Though this sweet, genuine ice cream parlor celebrated its 100th birthday under 5 feet of water, it's long since come back—and ostensibly not a thing has changed. Run by the same family since 1905, the Brocatos make rich Italian ice cream and ices, cookies, and pastries amid a wonderful throwback atmosphere. Standards like chocolate and *stracciatella* (chocolate chip) are capital-P Perfect; hard-to-find Italian specialties like spumoni and casatta are spot-on; and the fresh lemon ice is legendary (don't try to decide between that and seasonal fresh fruit ices, like Ponchatoula strawberry and blood orange; just get both), while the panna cotta custard has brought us to our knees. After that we get a freshly filled cannoli. Heck yeah, we do.

214 N. Carrollton Ave. www.angelobrocatoicecream.com. ✆ **504/486-1465.** Everything under $10. Tues–Thurs 10am–10pm, Fri–Sat 10am–10:30pm, Sun 10am–9pm. Closed Mon.

Buttermilk Drop Bakery and Cafe ★★ BAKERY/DESSERT   Dear Donut People (and you know who you are): After you've done Café du Monde, you need to see Henry the Donut Whisperer for the $20 dozen: around $6 for 12 of the Platonic ideal donuts, the rest for the cab from the Quarter and back. It's less than what you'd pay for a ride to the Maple Leaf, and equally worth it. Have the cab wait, hope the line is short, stick to the drops and classic glazed. *Fun fact:* Dwight Henry starred in the film *Beasts of the Southern Wild*.

1718 N. Dorgenois St., 7th Ward. www.buttermilkdrop.com. ✆ **504/252-04538.** A dozen donuts around $6. Cash only. Daily 6am–6pm.

Café du Monde ★★★ COFFEE/DESSERT   Excuse us while we wax rhapsodic. Since 1862, iconic Café du Monde has been selling café au lait and beignets (and nothing but) on the edge of Jackson Square. A New Orleans landmark, it's a must-stop for fried goodness and people-watching, 24 hours a day. A beignet (ben-*yay*) is a square French doughnut–type object, steaming-hot and covered in powdered sugar. You might be tempted to shake off some of the sugar. Don't. Trust us. Spoon more on, even (just beware not to inhale as you ingest); at three to an order for under $2.50, they're a hell of a deal. Wash them down with chicory café au lait (good with extra powdered sugar) or really good hot chocolate. Feeling guilty? The fresh orange juice is excellent, too, and presumably has vitamins. *Tip:* Don't wait for a clean table. Just sit—only then will the surly servers clear them.

In the French Market, 800 Decatur St. www.cafedumonde.com. © **504/525-4544.** 3 beignets for $2.42. Cash only. Daily 24 hr. Closed Christmas.

Café EnVie ★ COFFEE/BAKERY/LIGHT FARE

This handsome coffeehouse at the gutterpunk end of Decatur has a nice selection of drinks, pastries, bagels—and a full breakfast stuffed into a go-cup. Good for a shot of espresso while waiting for the clubs on Frenchmen to get cranking.

1241 Decatur St. www.cafeenvienola.com. © **504/524-3689.** Everything under $10. Daily 7am–midnight.

Creole Creamery ★★★ ICE CREAM/DESSERT

Shakes and malts and scoops, oh my! Thick, luscious ice cream with a rotating list of standard and exotic flavors, from lavender-honey and absinthe to red velvet cake and tiramisu. Refreshing, maybe even mandatory in summer, and open late enough for a scoop on the way to or from an Uptown club or bar.

4924 Prytania St. www.creolecreamery.com. © **504/894-8680.** Everything under $10 except 8-scoop "Eating Challenge" and whole cakes. No credit cards. Sun–Thurs noon–10pm, Fri–Sat noon–11pm.

Croissant D'Or ★★ COFFEE/BAKERY

A quiet and calm place with the same snacks you might find in a cosmopolitan coffeehouse, and you can almost always find an open table inside or in the pretty courtyard. Are the croissants made of gold? The prices feel like it sometimes, but they are credibly French.

617 Ursulines St. www.croissantdornola.com. © **504/524-4663.** Sandwiches and pastries under $6. Wed–Mon 6am–3pm.

La Boulangerie ★★★ BAKERY

This bakery would be a jewel even if it were in a major bread city. It sells perhaps the only authentic, crusty baguettes in the city (the owners are from France, so they are particular about their bread, as one might presume). Alternately, opt for the heavily studded olive bread, just slightly greasy (in a good way) with olive oil. Heaven. They also do marvelous pastries and croissant variants and savory sandwiches.

4600 Magazine St. (Uptown). © **504/269-3777.** Breads, pastries, sandwiches $3–$8. Mon, Wed–Sat 6am–6pm, Sun 6:30am–4pm. Closed Tues. Holiday hours vary; closed in July (call for dates).

La Divina Gelateria ★★ ICE CREAM/DESSERT

This superb gelato place has a great selection of standard and exotic ice cream flavors made from Louisiana dairy. Look for seasonal fruits and flavors and daily options like dark chocolate with cayenne gelato, sorbets of fruit, herbs, or local Abita Turbo dog beer—and the dairy is from Louisiana cows. They also have nice light lunches and excellent coffee, enjoyable at the tables in the alleyway outside.

621 St. Peter St. (French Quarter). www.ladivinagelateria.com. © **504/302-2692.** Everything under $10. Mon–Wed 11am–10pm, Thurs 8:30am–10pm, Fri–Sat 8:30am–11pm, Sun 8:30am–10pm.

Meltdown Ice Pops ★★ DESSERT/ICE CREAM

If you're exploring the edgier end of the Marigny or Bywater, nearby Meltdown ice pops come in standard and

bean FREAKS

If you're one of those single-source, third-wave, cold-pressed, pour-over-only people— and you know who you are— here are a few joints that might satisfy you. Might. All except purist Spitfire offer some variation on pastries and light savory fare.

- **Booty's ★** (Bywater): 800 Louisa St. (© **504/266-2887.** Daily 9am–11pm.) Not a coffee joint per se, but they serve Stumptown for those who require it.

- **Hi Volt ★★** (Lower Garden District): 1829 Sophie Wright Pl.

(www.hivoltcoffee.com; © **504/ 123-4567;** Mon–Fri 6:30am–7pm, Sat 8am–8pm, Sun 8am–2pm).

- **Merchant ★★★** (CBD): 800 Common St. (www.merchant neworleans.com; © **504/571-9580;** Mon–Fri 7am–5:30pm, Sat–Sun 8am–4:30pm).

- **Spitfire ★★** (French Quarter): 627 St. Peter St. (© **504/384-0655;** Mon–Thurs 8am–7pm, Fri–Sat 8am–8pm).

exotic flavors made from local ingredients (hand-picked berries, even). Daily flavors range from Vietnamese coffee and salted caramel (our personal favorite) to herb-inflected concoctions like pineapple basil and Ponchatoula strawberry basil, some with chunks of fruit. The straightforward fudgsicle, watermelon, or peanut butter are kid-pleasers.

4011 St. Claude St. www.meltdownpops.com. © **504/301-0905.** $3 each. Cash only. Wed–Mon noon–7pm. Meltdown Truck sometimes travels to the French Market or elsewhere; call to make sure shop is open.

Morning Call ★★ COFFEE/DESSERT/LIGHT FARE The original French Quarter Morning Call was a Café du Monde rival back in the 1870s. This new outlet, in the midst of glorious, oak-filled City Park, harkens back to that old style and is a very welcome addition to Mid-City. You're here for café au lait and beignets, 3 for $2, which usually come fresh from the fryer. You self-sprinkle powdered sugar atop them to your liking (which may mean removing the lids of the shaker bottles). They also have a few Creole standbys, jambalaya and red beans and such, which are awfully handy at 4am or if you're famished from a longer-than-expected museum visit.

3325 Severn Ave., in the Casino Building, City Park (east of the Sculpture Garden). www.morning callcoffeestand.com. © **504/885-4068.** $2–$10. Cash only. Daily 24 hr. Closed Christmas.

P.J.'s Coffee & Tea Company ★★ COFFEE P.J.'s is a local institution with many locations. It offers a great variety of teas, coffees, and espressos, and it roasts its own coffee beans. The iced coffee is made with a 12-hour cold-water process. The granita "slushee" is great on those hot, muggy Louisiana days.

5432 Magazine St. www.pjscoffee.com. © **504/355-2202.** Drinks and pastries $1–$6. Daily 6am–9pm (sometimes later on Sat and Sun). About 30 other locations, including Tulane University, © **504/865-5705;** 644 Camp St., © **504/529-3658;** and 7264 Maple St., © **504/861-5335.**

Sucré ★★★ DESSERT/LIGHT FARE See the listing for this high-end confectionery under "Candies, Pralines, & Pastries," on p. 192. A new French Quarter location at

A snoball's CHANCE

Shaved ice clone, let us assure you: It's no such thing. These mouthwatering concoctions are made with custom machines that shave the ice so fine that skiers envy the powder. And the flavors—including exotic ones such as wedding cake (almond, mostly), nectar (think cream soda, only much better), and orchid cream vanilla (bright purple that must be seen to be believed)—are absolutely delectable (the better proprietors make their own flavored syrups). Order them with condensed or evaporated milk if you prefer your refreshing drinks on the more decadently creamy side, or go further—some shops have started spiking them with booze. Or double the decadence with a hot rod—a snoball stuffed with ice cream. At any time on a hot day, lines can be out the door, and like so many other local specialties, loyalties are fierce. You should stop in at any snoball stand you see, but the following are worth seeking out. Hours vary, so call ahead; most open midday till 7 or 8pm and many close for winter. Go with a sweet tooth and get plenty of napkins.

Hansen's Sno-Bliz ★★★ (4801 Tchoupitoulas St.; www.snobliz.com; 🕿 504/891-9788). Hansen's snoballs are a revered city tradition, still served with a smile by third-generation owner Ashley Hansen, who officially took over after her grandparents died in the months following Katrina (and won the 2014 James Beard "American Classic" award). Those grandparents invented the shaved-ice machine in use here and elsewhere, and concocted their own proprietary syrups. Snoballs come in a souvenir cup. Try the bubble-gum-flavored Sno-bliz. **Plum St. Snoballs** ★★★ (1300 Burdette St.; www.plumstreetsnoball.com; 🕿 **504/866-7996**) has been cooling New Orleanians for more than 70 years, serving favorites in Chinese food containers. Fans of **Pandora's** ★★★ (901 S. Carrollton Ave.; 🕿 504/289-0765) say its ice is the softest anywhere, and the flavor list is so long it's taking over the neighborhood. You'll have to fight the hordes of school kids in line, even, it often seems, during school hours. But clearly they've learned where to get a good snoball. Bywater upstart **Piety Street Snoballs** ★★★ (612 Piety St.; [tel **504/782-2569**) is attracting the foodie crowd with their fresh-fruit extracts and novel flavors, like Vietnamese coffee and hibiscus pomegranate.

622 Conti St. (opening in late 2014) will offer all of Sucre's wonderful sweet stuff plus pour-over coffee, made-to-order soufflés, light savory fare, and a full bar in a second-floor salon.

3025 Magazine St. www.shopsucre.com. 🕿 **504/520-8311.** All desserts under $10, except full cakes. Sun–Thurs 8am–10pm, Fri–Sat 8am–midnight. (622 Conti St. hours and prices TBA.)

EXPLORING NEW ORLEANS

We've made no secret of our favorite New Orleans activities: walking, eating, ogling, listening to music, dancing, and eating again. But between those activities, there's much to see, do, and experience. New Orleans is a vibrant, visual, utterly authentic city with a rich history and gobs of culture worthy of your time—some of which is indoors and blessedly air-conditioned, which is ever so welcome when you need to escape the rain or heat.

While the French Quarter certainly is a seductive place, going to New Orleans and never leaving the Quarter is like visiting Soho and believing you've seen New York. Stroll the lush Garden District, marvel at the oaks in City Park, ride the streetcar on St. Charles Avenue and gape at the gorgeous homes, or go visit some gators on a swamp tour. Take a walk along Bayou St. John, tour the remarkable Tremé neighborhood, or ride a bike through the Bywater. We'll guide you to some of the city's amazing museums, diverse neighborhoods, and prettiest parks, with suggestions for action-lovers and armchair adventurers, history buffs, and party animals.

THE FRENCH QUARTER

Those who have been to Disneyland might be forgiven if they experience some déjà vu upon first seeing the French Quarter. It's more worn, of course, and, in spots, a bit smellier. But despite the fact that Walt actually did replicate a French Quarter street in Disneyland's New Orleans Square, there ain't nothing like the real thing baby. This one is nearly 300 years old and one of the most visually interesting neighborhoods in America. The endless eyefuls of florid architecture, the copious cultural oddities, and the stories that seem to emanate from the very streets make it easy to look beyond the ubiquitous souvenir shops and bars. We certainly enjoy the lure of an occasional venture to Bourbon Street in all its tacky, outlandish glory, and absolutely recommend it. But the operative word is "occasional," and the key to this city is getting out and fully exploring it.

A French engineer named Adrien de Pauger designed the Quarter in 1718. Today it's a great anomaly in America, where many other cities have torn down or gutted their historic centers. Thanks to a strict local preservation policy, the area looks much as it always has and is still the heart of town.

Jackson Square bustles with musicians, artists, fortune tellers, jugglers, and those peculiar "living statue" performance artists entertaining for change (we try to always carry some $1 bills, so we're prepared to throw something in the hat of those that catch our eye or ear). Pay attention to that seemingly ad-hoc jazz band that plays right in front of the Cabildo—these talented musicians might be in jeans now but may very well be in tie and tux later, playing high-end clubs. **Royal Street** is home to stellar street musicians, numerous antiques shops, and galleries, with other interesting stores on **Chartres** and **Decatur streets** and the cross streets between.

The closer you get to **Esplanade Avenue** and toward **Rampart Street,** the more residential the Quarter becomes (in the business sections, the ground floors are commercial and the stories above are often apartments). Peep in through any open gate; surprises await in the form of graceful brick- and flagstone-lined courtyards filled with foliage and bubbling fountains. At the same time, be mindful that throughout the Quarter, you are walking by people's homes. Be courteous, quiet, and clean, folks.

The Vieux Carré Commission is ever vigilant about balancing contemporary economic interests in the Quarter with historical preservation. There are few chain stores or restaurants, and no traffic lights in the whole interior of the French Quarter (they're relegated to fringe streets); streetlights are the old gaslight style. Large city buses are banned, and during part of each day Royal and Bourbon streets are pedestrian malls. No vehicles are *ever* allowed around Jackson Square. The Quarter streets are laid out in an almost perfect rectangular grid, so they're easily navigable. It's also well-traveled and thus relatively safe. Again, as you get toward the fringes and as night falls, you should exercise caution; stay in the more bustling parts and try not to walk alone.

The French Quarter **walking tour** in chapter 10 will give you the best overview of the historic structures in the area and its history. Many other attractions that aren't in the walking tour are listed in this chapter (and mapped on p. 124), so make sure to cross-reference as you go along.

As mentioned elsewhere, driving in the French Quarter isn't ideal. But if you must, and you're planning on a full day of sightseeing, you can reserve a parking spot at lots owned by **Premium Parking** (www.premiumparking.com). It's not a bad idea to have a designated parking destination, and it's a very good idea during events and peak seasons.

Major Attractions

Audubon Aquarium of the Americas ★★★
It's been a busy few years at the world-class Audubon Institute's Aquarium of the Americas. Penguin evacuees made a star-studded post-Katrina return via a chartered FedEx flight, waddling home down a (FedEx) purple carpet as news cameras rolled. Then, rescued sea turtles were rehabilitated here after the Gulf oil spill; some made the Aquarium their permanent home. These instances point up just how topical and relevant an aquarium can be, besides being full of cool fishies. This one, which has a strong focus on the Mississippi and the Gulf of Mexico, is highly entertaining and painlessly educational for kids and grown-ups. There's plenty of interactivity including a new "Geaux Fish!" exhibit that follows fish from the waters to the plate. We love the huge interior rain forest complete with birds and piranhas, and being able to peer below the surface of a swamp. Not to be missed are a fine exhibit on frogs, a rare albino gator, and a manta-ray touch tank.

New Orleans Attractions

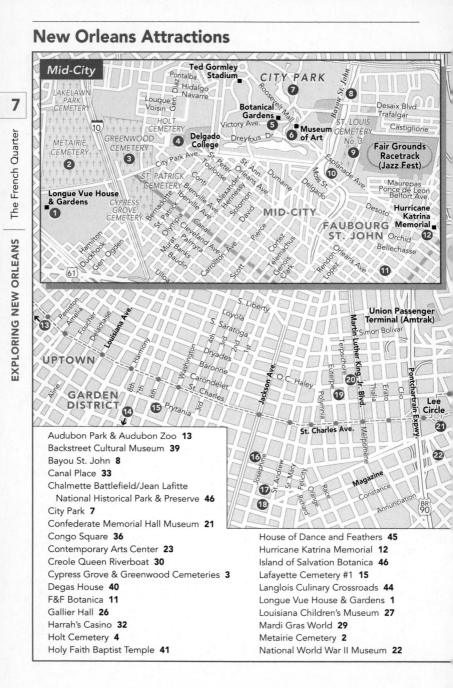

Mid-City

LAKELAWN PARK CEMETERY
Louque Voisin
HOLT CEMETERY
METAIRIE CEMETERY
GREENWOOD CEMETERY
ST. PATRICK CEMETERY
CYPRESS GROVE CEMETERY
Longue Vue House & Gardens

Pontalba
Hidalgo
Navarre
Ted Gormley Stadium
CITY PARK
Roosevelt Mall

Botanical Gardens
Victory Ave.
Museum of Art
Delgado College
Dreyfous Dr.
ST. LOUIS CEMETERY No. 3

Desaix Blvd.
Trafalgar
Castiglione
Fair Grounds Racetrack (Jazz Fest)

Esplanade Ave.
Maurepas
Ponce de Leon
Belfort Ave.
Desoto
Orchid
Bellechasse
MID-CITY
FAUBOURG ST. JOHN
Hurricane Katrina Memorial

Hamilton
Duckhoe
Gen. Ogden
Bernadotte
St. Patrick
Olympia
Murat
Palmyra
Baudin
Ulloa
Carrollton Ave.
Scott
Pierce
Cortez
Telemachus
Gelois
Clark
Orleans Ave.
Rendon
Lopez

UPTOWN
Peniston
Amelia
Foucher
Delachaise
Louisiana Ave.
Harmony
8th
7th
9th
GARDEN DISTRICT
Aline
St. Charles
Prytania
3rd
S. Liberty
Loyola
S. Saratoga
4th
Dryades
Baronne
Carondelet
Washington

Union Passenger Terminal (Amtrak)
Simon Bolivar
Jackson Ave.
O.C. Haley
Martin Luther King, Jr. Blvd.
Terpsichore
Euterpe
Polymnia
Erato
Thalia
Clio
Melpomene
Pontchartrain Expwy.
Lee Circle

St. Charles Ave.
Josephine
St. Andrew
St. Mary
Felicity
Orange
Race
Richard
Constance
Annunciation
Magazine
BR 90

Audubon Park & Audubon Zoo **13**
Backstreet Cultural Museum **39**
Bayou St. John **8**
Canal Place **33**
Chalmette Battlefield/Jean Lafitte
  National Historical Park & Preserve **46**
City Park **7**
Confederate Memorial Hall Museum **21**
Congo Square **36**
Contemporary Arts Center **23**
Creole Queen Riverboat **30**
Cypress Grove & Greenwood Cemeteries **3**
Degas House **40**
F&F Botanica **11**
Gallier Hall **26**
Harrah's Casino **32**
Holt Cemetery **4**
Holy Faith Baptist Temple **41**

House of Dance and Feathers **45**
Hurricane Katrina Memorial **12**
Island of Salvation Botanica **46**
Lafayette Cemetery #1 **15**
Langlois Culinary Crossroads **44**
Longue Vue House & Gardens **1**
Louisiana Children's Museum **27**
Mardi Gras World **29**
Metairie Cemetery **2**
National World War II Museum **22**

Ogden Museum of Southern Art **24**
Old U.S. Mint **43**
Outlet Collection at Riverwalk **31**
Pitot House **10**
Southern Food and Beverage Museum/
  Museum of the American Cocktail **20**
St. Alphonsus Church **18**
St. Augustine Church **42**
St. Louis Cemetery No. 1 **35**
St. Louis Cemetery No. 2 **34**
St. Louis Cemetery No. 3 **9**
St. Mary's Assumption **17**
St. Patrick's Church **25**
St. Roch Cemetery and the Campo Santo **45**
Trinity Episcopal Church **16**
Zion Hill Missionary Baptist Church **37**

New Orleans African American
  Museum of Art, Culture & History **38**
New Orleans Botanical Gardens
  & Train Garden **5**
New Orleans Convention Center **28**
New Orleans Cooking Experience **19**
New Orleans Museum of Art
  & Sculpture Garden **6**
NOLA Brewing **14**

French Quarter Attractions

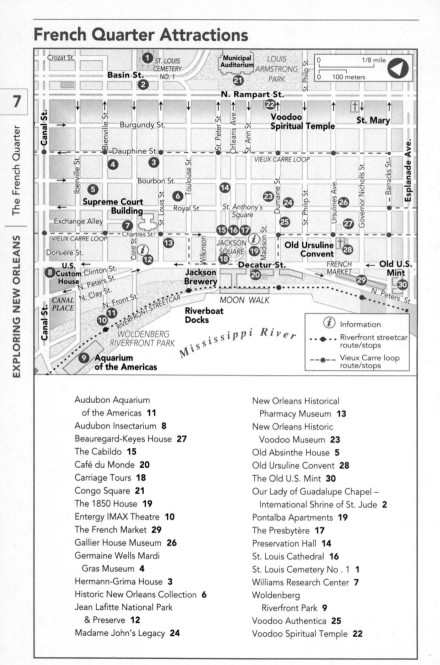

Right on the edge of the Quarter, it's a handy refuge from the heat or rain and part of a complex of Audubon attractions, including an **IMAX theater ★★** next door; the **Insectarium** (see below) a block away; and the **Audubon Zoo** (p. 141) uptown. If you plan to visit more than one, get a combination admission package.

1 Canal St., at the river. www.auduboninstitute.org. ℭ **800/774-7394** or 504/581-4629. Aquarium $23 adults, $17 seniors, $16 children 2–12. IMAX $11 adults, $9.50 seniors, $8 children. Four-attraction combo ticket: $40 adults, $28 seniors and children 2–12. Aquarium and IMAX daily 10am–5pm; after Labor Day–Feb 28 closed Mon. Call for IMAX showtimes. Closed Mardi Gras, Thanksgiving, and Christmas.

Audubon Insectarium ★★   This fascinating museum is dedicated to all things bug and arachnid, specifically 900,000 species of critters that creep, crawl, and flutter. Located in the old U.S. Customs House, it's the largest free-standing museum in the world dedicated to its multilegged, winged subjects.

The journey through ickiness (kidding! Bugs are great!) begins in the Prehistoric hallway with 30-inch insect replicas. A gallery that simulates the experience of being underground exposes the tiny world living in our soil. In the **Tiny Termite Café,** each glass-topped table houses an insect colony (watch silkworms spin their fibers while you dine), and the **Bug Buffet** even serves a few creepy-crawler-based snacks. Finally, the Japanese-inspired **butterfly gallery,** full of fluttering beauty, is a peaceful departure from the hustle outside.

423 Canal St. www.auduboninstitute.org. ℭ **800/774-7394** or 504/581-4629. Admission $17 adults, $13 seniors, $12 children 2–12. Insectarium, Aquarium, and IMAX tickets $40 adults, $28 seniors and children 2–12. Daily 10am–5pm; after Labor Day–Feb 28 closed Mon. Last entry at 4pm. Closed Mardi Gras, Thanksgiving, and Christmas.

The French Market ★★   Legend has it that the site of the French Market was originally used by Native Americans as a bartering market. It grew into an official market in 1812. From around 1840 to 1870, it was part of Gallatin Street, an impossibly rough area full of bars, drunken sailors, and criminals. Today it's a mixed bag, and not nearly as colorful as its past, but a fun amble. The goods at the farmer's market, from fresh produce and seafood to more tourist-oriented items like hot sauces and Cajun spice mixes, are pricier than at local supermarkets—but here they'll pack it for air travel or ship it home. Snacks like gator on a stick will amuse the kids, while the raw bar and food vendors will satisfy the grown-ups (**Meals from the Heart** and **Organic Banana** are standouts). There are all-important clean public bathrooms here, and a stage featuring live music or cooking demonstrations. The famed flea market section is kind of junky, but sprinkled among the T-shirts, caps, and cheap sunglasses are a few original art vendors (original art here is tax-free). It's convenient for souvenir shopping and New Orleans–related jewelry, especially inexpensive silver and all manner of fleur-de-lis. If you've outshopped your luggage, you can pick up a duffle bag or small suitcase.

On Decatur St., toward Esplanade Ave. from Jackson Sq. www.frenchmarket.org. ℭ **504/522-2621.** Daily 9am–6pm (tends to start shutting down about an hour before closing).

St. Louis Cathedral ★   The St. Louis Cathedral prides itself on being the oldest continuously active cathedral in the United States. It's not the prettiest, though—the outside is all right, but the rather grim interior wouldn't give even a minor European church a run for its money. Still, history and spirituality seep from within, so it's worth a look—if you're lucky, you may catch a choir practice. Volunteer docents, available most weekdays, are full of fun facts about the windows and murals and how the building nearly collapsed once from water-table sinkage. Note the sloping floor: Clever architectural design somehow keeps the building upright even as it continues to sink. Outside, a plaque marks the visit by Pope John Paul II in 1987.

The cathedral formed the center of the original settlement, and remains the French Quarter's central landmark. This is the third building to stand on this spot. A hurricane destroyed the first in 1722. On Good Friday 1788, the bells of its replacement were kept silent for religious reasons (or wind, some say) rather than ringing out the alarm for a fire—which eventually burned down the cathedral and 850 other buildings. Rebuilt in 1794 and remodeled and enlarged between 1845 and 1851, the structure's bricks were taken from the original town cemetery and covered with stucco to protect the mortar from dampness. That issue arose again during Katrina, which caused a leaky roof to ruin the $1-million organ (it's been rebuilt and returned). Outside, two magnificent, ancient live oaks fell, narrowly missing a statue of Jesus. His thumbs were amputated, however, and Archbishop Hughes, in his first post-Katrina sermon in the cathedral, vowed not to replace them until all of New Orleans is healed. The dramatically lit statue makes a resplendent, if somewhat eerie, nighttime silhouette. Well, we think so; others call it "Touchdown Jesus"—do make a point to walk by at night to see why.

615 Pere Antoine Alley. www.stlouiscathedral.org. (✆) **504/525-9585.** Free admission. Self-guided tour brochure available ($1 donation); formal tours by advance reservation, Mon–Sat 9am–4pm, Sun 9am–2pm. Cafe and gift shop Mon–Sat 10am–3pm, Sun 1–4pm. Mass Mon–Sat 7:30am, Sun 9am and 11am.

Historic Buildings

Beauregard-Keyes House ★ This "raised cottage," with its Doric columns and handsome twin staircases, was built as a residence by a wealthy New Orleans auctioneer, Joseph LeCarpentier, in 1826. Confederate General P. G. T. Beauregard lived here between 1865 and 1867. From 1944 until 1970 it was the residence of Frances Parkinson Keyes (pronounced *Kize*), who wrote many novels about the region. Her most famous, *Dinner at Antoine's,* was written here, as was *Madame Castel's Lodger,* concerning General Beauregard's stay in this house. Mrs. Keyes left her home to a foundation. The house, gardens, and her collections of dolls and porcelain veilleuse teapots are open to the public.

1113 Chartres St., at Ursuline St. www.bkhouse.org. (✆) **504/523-7257.** Admission $10 adults; $9 seniors, students, and AAA members; $4 children 6–12; free for active military and children 5 and under. Mon–Sat 10am–3pm. Tours on the hour. Closed holidays.

The 1850 House ★★ James Gallier, Sr. and his son designed the historic Pontalba Buildings for the Baroness Micaela Almonester de Pontalba, who had them built in 1849 in an effort to combat the deterioration of the older part of the city (see box below and the French Quarter walking tour on p. 199). The rows of townhouses on either side of Jackson Square were the largest private buildings in the country at the time. Legend has it that the baroness, miffed that her friend Andrew Jackson wouldn't tip his hat to her, had his statue erected in the square where to this day he continues to doff his chapeau toward her top-floor apartment. It's probably not true, but we never stand in the way of a good story.

Here, the **Louisiana State Museum** presents a demonstration of life in 1850, when the buildings opened for residential use. The self-guided tour uses a fact-filled sheet explaining the history of the interior. Period furnishings show how the rooms were typically used. It vividly illustrates the difference between the upstairs portion of the house, where the upper-middle-class family lived in comfort (and the children, largely confined to a nursery, were raised by servants), and the downstairs, where the staff toiled in considerable drudgery to make their bosses comfortable. It's a surprisingly enjoyable look at life in the good, or not so good, old days.

Lower Pontalba Bldg., 523 St. Ann St., Jackson Sq. www.crt.state.la.us/louisiana-state-museum. ℰ **800/568-6968** or 504/568-6968. Admission $3; $2 students, seniors, and active military; free for children 12 and under. Tues–Sun 10am–4:30pm. Closed all legal holidays.

Old Absinthe House ★ The Old Absinthe House was built in 1806 and now houses a bar and restaurant. The drink for which the building and bar were named was once outlawed in this country (certain chemical additives, not the actual wormwood used to flavor the drink, caused blindness and madness). Now you can legally sip the infamous libation in the bar and feel at one with the famous types who came before you, listed on a plaque outside: William Thackeray, Oscar Wilde, Sarah Bernhardt, and Walt Whitman. Andrew Jackson and the Lafitte brothers plotted their desperate defense of New Orleans here in the War of 1812.

The house was a speakeasy during Prohibition, and when federal officers closed it in 1924, the interior was mysteriously stripped of its antique fixtures—including the long marble-topped bar and the old water dripper that was used to infuse water into the absinthe. Just as mysteriously, they reappeared in another bar down the street, and then once again returned to one of the restaurants on this site. The bar is now covered with business cards (and drunks), so don't come looking to recapture some kind of old-timey classy atmosphere. But it's still a genuinely fun, historic hangout.

240 Bourbon St., btw Iberville and Bienville sts. www.ruebourbon.com/oldabsinthehouse. ℰ **504/523-3181.** Free admission. Daily 9am–2am (Fri–Sat till 3am).

Old Ursuline Convent ★★ Forget tales of America being founded by brawny, brave, tough guys in buckskin and beards. The real pioneers—at least, in Louisiana— were well-educated Frenchwomen clad in 40 pounds of black wool robes. That's right; you don't know tough until you know the Ursuline nuns, and this city would have been a very different place without them.

The Sisters of Ursula came to the mudhole that was New Orleans in 1727 after a journey that nearly saw them lost at sea or succumbing to pirates or disease. Here, they provided the first decent medical care (saving countless lives) and later founded the first local school and orphanage for girls. They also helped raise girls shipped over from France as marriage material for local men, teaching them every-thing from languages to homemaking of the most exacting sort (laying the founda-tion of many local families).

The convent dates from 1752 (the sisters themselves moved uptown in 1824, where they remain to this day), and it is the oldest building in the Mississippi River Valley and the only surviving building from the French colonial period in the United States. It also houses Catholic archives dating back to 1718.

The **self-guided tour** of the convent shows rooms typical of the era, as well as religious and artistic icons (the top floor, where the ghost supposedly lives, is off-limits, unfortunately). It includes access to St. Mary's Church, original site of the Ursuline convent and a former archbishop's residence. The whole convent can be viewed in an hour or less.

1100 Chartres St., at Ursuline St. www.oldursulineconvent.org. ℰ **504/529-3040.** Admission $10 adults, $9 seniors, $8 students, children 6 and under free. Mon–Sat 10am–4pm (last admission 3:30pm).

The Old U.S. Mint ★★ This is one of the many places that got pummeled during Katrina, and came out better for it. After renovation, it reopened with a split personality, but both parts are good. It's the only building in America to have served as both a U.S. and a Confederate mint, and the first floor is now a coin museum of interest for numismatists (look! O-minted coins, struck right here!) and regular folk (oooh, so *that's* how they made those, back before computers!). Upstairs is an exhibit celebrating the 50th Anniversary of Preservation Hall, small but worthy, with some very significant artworks, instruments, recordings, and artifacts including Louis Armstrong's first horn. An extensive jazz museum, waylaid since Katrina, will return here once the budget permits. The third floor has a gorgeous new performance space, which has music, lectures, cooking instructions, or something equally interesting most days. They're usually free and definitely worth checking out. This is an easy museum to peruse in 60 to 90 minutes. ***Fun fact:*** Ghost hunters believe William Mumford, who met the noose here in 1862, still hangs around.

400 Esplanade Ave., at N. Peters St. (enter on Esplanade Ave. or Barracks St.). www.crt.state.la.us/louisiana-state-museum and www.musicatthemint.org. ℂ **800/568-6968** or 504/568-6993. Free admission. Tues–Sun 10am–4pm. Closed all legal holidays.

Our Lady of Guadalupe Chapel—International Shrine of St. Jude ★ This "funeral chapel" was erected in 1826 conveniently near St. Louis Cemetery No. 1, specifically for funeral services, so as not to spread disease through the Quarter. We like it for three reasons: the catacomb-like devotional chapel with plaques thanking the Virgin Mary for favors granted; the gift shop full of religious medals including a number of obscure saints; and the statue of St. Expedite. The saint got his name, according to legend, when his crate arrived with no identification other than the word EXPEDITE stamped on the outside. Now he's the "saint" you pray to when you want things in a hurry (we are not making this up). Expedite has his cults in France and Spain and is also popular among the Voodoo folks. He's just inside the door on the right. For those interested in some extra prayer power for lost causes, the St. Jude solemn novena runs the last weeks of January, April, July, and October for 9 days at a time—call for the exact start dates.

411 N. Rampart St., at Conti St. www.judeshrine.org. ℂ **504/525-1551.** Gift shop Mon–Sat 9am–5pm. Masses Mon–Sat starting at 7am, Sun from 7:30am.

Museums

In addition to the destinations listed here, you might be interested in the **Germaine Wells Mardi Gras Museum** at 813 Bienville St., on the second floor of Arnaud's restaurant (p. 82; ℂ **504/523-5433**). It has a collection of Mardi Gras costumes and ball gowns dating from 1910 through 1960. Admission is free, and the museum is open daily during restaurant hours.

The Cabildo ★★ One of two fine museums flanking St. Louis Cathedral in the heart of the French Quarter, the Cabildo houses the premier collection of New Orleans and Louisiana historical artifacts. It starts with the earliest explorers and covers slavery, post–Civil War reconstruction, and statehood. It is well qualified to do so: The Cabildo is the site of the signing of the Louisiana Purchase transfer (this 1795 building was the seat of government at the time; at other times it served as a courthouse and a prison). The detailed history is covered from a multicultural perspective and touches on topics like antebellum music, mourning and burial customs (a big deal during the

lady bountiful: BARONESS DE PONTALBA

New Orleans owes a great debt to Baroness Micaela Almonester de Pontalba and her family. Without them, Jackson Square might still be a soggy mess. Her father, Don Almonester, used his money and influence to have St. Louis Cathedral, Cabildo, and Presbytère built. The baroness was responsible for the two long brick apartment buildings that flank Jackson Square and for the renovation that turned the center of the Quarter into what it is today.

Born in 1795 into the most influential family in New Orleans, the baroness married her cousin, who subsequently stole her inheritance. When she wanted a separation at a time when such things were unheard of, her father-in-law shot her several times and then shot himself. She survived, though some of her fingers did not (nor did he). In subsequent portraits, she would hide the wounded hand in her dress. In the end, she got her money back—she used it for those French Quarter improvements—and also ended up caring for her slightly mad husband for the rest of his life. She died in Paris in 1874; her home there is now the American ambassador's residence. The book *Intimate Enemies*, by Christina Vella (Louisiana State University Press, 1997), details this remarkable woman's life.

yellow fever epidemics), immigration and assimilation, and the role of the Southern woman. Portraits of historical figures and incidents are hung throughout, and then there's Napoleon's death mask. The item and its story (it almost ended up in a trash dump) are quite fascinating. "Unsung Heroes: The Secret History of Rock 'n' Roll" is a cool collection of music doodads, costumes, instruments, records, and posters highlighting Louisianans, famous or unknown, who impacted rock music. In 2015, "From Dirty Shirt to Buccaneers" opens, celebrating the bicentennial of the Battle of New Orleans. It's a dense but terrific museum.

701 Chartres St. www.crt.state.la.us/louisiana-state-museum. ✆ **800/568-6968** or 504/568-6968. Admission $6 adults; $5 students, seniors, and military; free for children 12 and under. Discounts for visiting multiple Louisiana State museums. Tues–Sun 10am–4:30pm.

Gallier House Museum ★★ James Gallier, Jr. (it's pronounced *Gaul*-ee-er, by the way; he was Irish, not French) and his father were the leading architects in New Orleans in the mid-1800s. They designed the French Opera House, Municipality Hall (now Gallier Hall), and the Pontalba Buildings. The Gallier House Museum is the architect's personal home. It's meticulously restored, with the fancy furnishings appearing much as they would have when the Gallier family resided there (some claim Gallier's ghost still does). The home displays some of his innovations—such as early indoor plumbing—and a decided lack thereof in the slave quarters. It's made even more gorgeous for holiday season, with period decor; check the website for other special programs. *Fun fact for Anne Rice fans:* This house was her muse for Louis and Lestat's New Orleans residence in *Interview with the Vampire*. Combination tickets with the Hermann-Grima House are available.

1118 and 1132 Royal St., btw. Gov. Nicholls and Ursuline sts. www.hgghh.org. ✆ **504/525-5661.** Admission $12 adults; $10 seniors, students, AAA members, children. Guided tours Mon, Tues, Thurs, Fri at 10am, noon, 2pm; Sat noon, 1pm, 2pm. Call ahead as hours can change; usually closed 1–2 weeks in Aug for vacation and sprucing.

Hermann-Grima House ★★ This symmetrical Federal-style building (perhaps the first in the Quarter) is very different from its French-style neighbors. The house, which stretches from St. Louis Street to Conti Street, passed through two different families before becoming a boardinghouse in the 1920s. It has been meticulously restored and researched, and a tour of the house is one of the city's more historically accurate offerings. The knowledgeable tour docents make this a satisfactory stop at any time, but keep an eye out for the frequent special tours. At Halloween, for example, the house is draped in typical 1800s mourning cloth, and the docents explain mourning customs. On Tuesdays and Thursdays from October through May, cooking demonstrations take place in the authentic 1830s kitchen, using methods of the era. (Alas, health rules prevent those on the tour from sampling the results.) The house also contains one of the Quarter's last surviving stables, complete with stalls. Combination tickets with the Gallier House are available.

820 St. Louis St. www.hgghh.org. (✆) **504/525-5661.** Admission $12 adults; $10 seniors, students, AAA members, and children 8–18, free children 7 and under. Guided tours Mon, Tues, Thurs, Fri 10am, noon, 2pm; Sat noon, 1pm, 2pm. Call ahead as hours can change; usually closed 1–2 weeks in Aug for vacation and sprucing.

Historic New Orleans Collection—Museum/Research Center ★★ This complex of historic buildings in the middle of the French Quarter is secreted away with little signage or fanfare. But a hidden treasure lies within. All were owned by the collection's founders, General and Mrs. L. Kemper Williams, and remain an excellent look at what once was. One building is a rare survivor of the great fire of 1794. Behind a courtyard lies the elegant former residence of General and Mrs. Williams, open for tours. There are galleries with wonderful artworks, maps, and historic documents, and tours that focus on landscaping, architecture, and Mardi Gras (during Carnival season). It's all of great relevance to anyone interested in architecture or local history, and each building has a centuries-old tale to tell. Another grandly restored, Beaux-Arts–style building belonging to the complex is the **Williams Research Center,** 410 Chartres St., near Conti Street (✆ **504/598-7171**), which houses many of the collection's items. It presents rotating exhibits and serves as a research center for academics and members of the public who can access research documents with librarian assistance: If you're curious about anything regarding New Orleans or Louisiana history, the answer is probably here.

533 Royal St., btw. St. Louis and Toulouse sts. www.hnoc.org. (✆) **504/523-4662.** Free admission; guided tours $5. Tues–Sat 9:30am–4:30pm, Sun 10:30am–4:30pm. Tours Tues–Sat 10am, 11am, 2pm, and 3pm; Sun 11am, 2pm, and 3pm. Closed major holidays and Mardi Gras.

Madame John's Legacy ★ This is the second-oldest building in the Mississippi Valley (after the Ursuline Convent) and a rare example of Creole architecture that miraculously survived the 1794 fire. Built around 1788 on the foundations of an earlier home that was destroyed in the fire of *that* year, the house has had a number of owners and renters (including the son of Governor Claiborne), but none of them were named John (or even Madame!). It acquired its moniker courtesy of author George Washington Cable, who used the house as a setting for his short story '*Tite Poulette*. The protagonist was a quadroon, Madame John, named after the lover who willed this house to her. Of interest mostly for its unusual exterior architecture, the occasional art exhibit, like a recent show of stellar Newcomb pottery, makes a peek inside worth the (free) price.

632 Dumaine St. www.crt.state.la.us/louisiana-state-museum. (✆) **800/568-6968** or 504/568-6968. Free admission. Tues–Sun 10am–4:30pm. Closed state holidays and Mardi Gras.

New Orleans Historical Pharmacy Museum ★★ Leeches. LEEEEECHES. Yeah, they're here. So are many other icky things, and fascinating potions, and instruments-of-torture-looking artifacts (antique surgical devices, in actuality). The first licensed pharmacist in the United States, Louis J. Dufilho, Jr., opened an apothecary shop in this Creole-style townhouse in 1823. This bizarre and beguiling museum opened in 1950 and displays old apothecary bottles, Voodoo potions, opium products of every ilk, suppository molds, and all variant of snake oil—in exquisite wood and glass cases. Also interesting are old makeup and perfume paraphernalia, which were brewed up by pharmacists back in the day. You'll never appreciate a modern doctor's appointment more. Try to go on a Thursday or Friday when the insightful, sometimes shocking guided tour is offered.

514 Chartres St., at St. Louis St. www.pharmacymuseum.org. ℭ **504/565-8027.** Admission $5 adults, $4 students and seniors, children 5 and under free. Tues–Fri 10am–2pm, Sat 10am–5pm. Guided tours noon on Thurs and Fri. Closes early for private events some Saturdays—call ahead.

New Orleans Historic Voodoo Museum ★ This small museum is packed with dusty displays of Voodoo objects from around the world and right here in New Orleans, including some that allegedly belonged to the legendary Voodoo queen, Marie Laveau. While serious practitioners might scoff at the tourist orientation of this place, it really does offer a good introduction to the truth behind the myths of this much-maligned practice. You'll get the most out of your visit if you engage with the museum's founder, usually found manning the front desk. Whoever is there is usually involved in Voodoo, either as a priest, priestess, or educator, and invariably happy to discuss it with those with a sincere interest. They can even arrange a reading or custom gris-gris bag for you, or hook you up with herbs or Voodoo dolls. Why not? (Don't confuse this place with the Marie Laveau House of Voodoo on Bourbon Street.)

724 Dumaine St., at Bourbon St. www.voodoomuseum.com. ℭ **504/680-0128.** Admission $7 adults; $5.50 students, seniors, military; $4.50 high-school students; $3.50 children 11 and under; mention website offer for discount. Cemetery tour $19 adults, $10 children 12 and under. Daily 10am–6pm.

The Presbytère ★★★ The Presbytère, which flanks St. Louis Cathedral to the right, was originally built to house the clergy serving in the cathedral. That never came to pass, and the clergy's loss is our gain. It's now a museum with two excellent permanent exhibits. Upstairs, the Mardi Gras exhibit walks visitors through the holiday's history—which is so much more (and so much more interesting) than cwazy kids doing cwazy kid stuff. It shows ornate Mardi Gras Indian costumes and antique Mardi Gras Queen jewels, and there's even a replica float so you can toss mock beads at mock crowds. (To see the real thing, visit Blaine Kern's **Mardi Gras World;** p. 134.) On the first floor, the multimedia exhibit "Living with Hurricanes: Katrina and Beyond" is an in-depth look at the history and human drama of hurricanes. First-person audio, video, and interactive displays create an educational but wholly accessible experience, and an emotionally evocative one at that (but with enough optimism, humor, and science to keep it from being too downcast). One man's "IN CASE OF EMERGENCY" memo hangs on a wall: his jeans, scrawled with his name, blood type, and next-of-kin. A reproduction of a small attic with a rough hole chopped through its ceiling—and the very axe one woman used to commit a similar act—accompany her voiceover describing the incident. It's powerful stuff.

751 Chartres St., Jackson Sq. www.crt.state.la.us/louisiana-state-museum. ℭ **800/568-6968** or 504/568-6968. Admission $6 adults, $5 seniors and students, free for children 12 and under. Discounts if visiting multiple Louisiana State museums. Tues–Sun 10am–4:30pm.

Woldenberg Riverfront Park ★ This 20-acre park along the river serves as promenade and public art gallery, with numerous works by popular local and internationally-known artists amid green lawns and hundreds of trees. Seek out the kinetic Holocaust memorial sculpture by noted Israeli sculptor Yaacov Agam, and make a slow circle around it to get the full impact of its changing perspectives, which use a rainbow to unexpected symbolic effect.

The nearby **Moonwalk** ★★★ is a paved pedestrian thoroughfare along the river, a wonderful walk on a pretty New Orleans day but really a must-do for any weather other than pouring rain. It has steps that allow you to get right down to Old Muddy—on foggy nights, you feel as if you are floating above the water. There are many benches from which to view the city's busy port—perhaps while enjoying a muffuletta to a street musician's song, or watching the moon rise over the river. To your right, you'll see the Greater New Orleans Bridge and the World Trade Center of New Orleans (formerly the International Trade Mart) skyscraper as well as the Toulouse Street wharf, the departure point for excursion steamboats.

Along the Mississippi from the Moonwalk at the old Governor Nicholls St. wharf to the Aquarium of the Americas at Canal St. ⓒ **504/861-2537.** Daily dawn–dusk.

OUTSIDE THE FRENCH QUARTER
Uptown & the Garden District

If you can see just one thing outside the French Quarter, make it the Garden District. These two neighborhoods are the first places that come to mind when one hears the words "New Orleans." The Garden District has no significant historic buildings or important museums—it's simply beautiful—enough for authors as diverse as Truman Capote and Anne Rice to become enchanted by its spell. Gorgeous homes stand quietly amid lush foliage, elegant but ever so slightly (or more) decayed. You can see why this is the setting for so many novels; it's hard to imagine that anything real actually happens here.

But it does. Like the Quarter, this is a residential neighborhood, so please be courteous as you wander around. To see the sights, you need only mosey around and admire the exteriors and gardens of beautiful houses. We've mapped out a comprehensive **walking tour** (p. 207) to help guide you to the Garden District's treasures and explain a little of its history. Naturally it starts with a ride on the St. Charles streetcar. You might also check out the listings starting on p. 187 to find the best shops, galleries, and bookstores on **Magazine Street,** the eclectic shopping strip that bounds the Garden District.

Meanwhile, a little background: Across Canal Street from the Quarter, "American" New Orleans begins. After the Louisiana Purchase of 1803, an essentially French-Creole city came under the auspices of a government determined to develop it as an American city. Tensions between Creole society and the encroaching American newcomers began to increase. Some historians lay this tension at the feet of Creole snobbery; others blame the naive and uncultured Americans. In any case, Creole society succeeded in maintaining a relatively distinct social world, deflecting American settlement upriver of Canal Street (Uptown). The Americans in turn came to outpace the population with sheer numbers of immigrants. Newcomers bought up land in what had been the old Gravier Plantation (now the Uptown area) and began to build a parallel city. Very soon, Americans came to dominate the local business scene, centered along

Canal Street. In 1833, the American enclave now known as the Garden District was incorporated as Lafayette City, and—thanks in large part to the New Orleans–Carrollton Railroad, which ran the route of today's St. Charles Avenue streetcar—the Americans kept right on expanding until they reached the tiny resort town of Carrollton. It wasn't until 1852 that the various sections came together officially as a united New Orleans.

Bayou St. John, Esplanade & Lake Pontchartrain ★★★ Bayou St. John is one of the key reasons New Orleans exists. This body of water originally extended from the outskirts of New Orleans to Lake Pontchartrain. Jean-Baptiste Le Moyne, Sieur de Bienville, was commissioned to establish a settlement in Louisiana that would both make money and protect French holdings in the New World from British expansion. Bienville chose the spot where New Orleans now sits because he recognized the strategic importance of the Bayou St. John's "back-door" access to Lake Pontchartrain, and ultimately to the Gulf of Mexico. Boats could enter the lake from the Gulf, then follow the Bayou to its conclusion. From there, they were within easy portage distance of the mouth of the Mississippi River. Native Americans had used this route for years.

The early path from the city to the bayou is today's Bayou Road, an extension of Governor Nicholls Street in the French Quarter. Modern-day Gentilly Boulevard, which crosses the bayou, was another Native American trail—it led around the lake and on to settlements as far as Florida.

As New Orleans grew and prospered, the bayou became a suburb as planters moved out along its shores. In the early 1800s, a canal was dug to connect the waterway with the city, reaching a basin at the edge of Congo Square (which begat today's Basin Street). The Bayou became a popular recreation area, lined with fine restaurants and dance halls (and meeting places for Voodoo practitioners, who held secret ceremonies along its shores). Gradually, New Orleans reached beyond the French Quarter and enveloped the whole area—overtaking farmland, plantation homes, and resorts.

The canal was filled in long ago, and the bayou is a meek re-creation of itself (though plans to re-open nearby floodgates, allowing more natural ebb and flow from Lake Pontchartrain, may soon bring its ecosystem closer to its thriving original state). It is no longer navigable (even if it were, bridges were built too low to permit the passage of watercraft other than kayaks), but residents still prize their waterfront sites, and kayaks, rowboats and paddleboards make use of the bayou's smooth surface. This is one of the prettiest areas of New Orleans—full of the old houses tourists love to marvel at without the hustle, bustle, and confusion of more high-profile locations. A stroll along the banks and through the nearby neighborhoods is one of our favorite things to do on a nice afternoon.

GETTING THERE The simplest way to reach St. John's Bayou from the French Quarter is to drive straight up Esplanade Avenue about 20 blocks (or grab the bus that says ESPLANADE at any of the bus stops along the avenue). Right before you reach the Bayou, you'll pass **St. Louis Cemetery No. 3** (just past Leda St.). It's the final resting place of many prominent New Orleanians, among them Father Adrien Rouquette, who lived and worked among the Choctaw; Storyville photographer E. J. Bellocq; and Thomy Lafon, the black philanthropist who bought the old Orleans Ballroom as an orphanage for African-American children and put an end to its infamous "quadroon balls" (p. 15). Walking just past the cemetery, turn left onto Moss Street, which runs along the banks of St. John's Bayou. To see an example of an 18th-century West Indies–style plantation house, stop at the **Pitot House,** 1440 Moss St. (p. 140).

To continue, drive along Wisner Boulevard, on the opposite bank of St. John's Bayou from Moss Street, and you'll pass some of New Orleans's grandest modern homes—a sharp contrast to those on Moss Street. Stay on Wisner to Robert E. Lee Boulevard, turn right, drive to Elysian Fields Avenue, and then turn left. That's the **University of New Orleans campus** on your left. Turn left onto the broad concrete highway, Lake Shore Drive. It runs for 5½ miles along the lake, and normally in the summer the parkway alongside its sea wall is swarming with swimmers and picnickers. On the other side are more luxurious, modern residences. About 2 miles down the road to the west is the fishing-oriented **Bucktown** neighborhood. You may notice some leftover Katrina desolation along this drive. This area, home to commercial fishing since the late 1800s, was totally devastated by the 17th Street Canal breech, including the marina, where the storm piled boats atop each other. But you'll also probably see construction, including a thriving restaurant hub along Harrison Avenue—good to know in case you want a snack after your drive.

As you return, you can pass through the **Lakeview** neighborhood, south of Robert E. Lee, between Canal and City Park—another suburb that is thriving in the post-Katrina comeback.

Lake Pontchartrain is some 40 miles long and 25 miles wide, and is bisected by the 24-mile **Greater New Orleans Causeway,** the longest bridge in the world.

Museums & Galleries

Backstreet Cultural Museum ★★★   This small cultural gem in the heart of the Faubourg Tremé is dedicated to certain wholly unique New Orleans cultural traditions, mostly of the African-American community. The social aid and pleasure clubs, the second-line parades, brass bands, Mardi Gras Indians, and jazz funerals are all well documented and recollected here. We guarantee that the Mardi Gras Indians' ornate beaded costumes are like nothing you've ever seen, and they are best appreciated up close. But the suits are just an entree into the intriguing traditions themselves. Founder Sylvester Francis is often in the house (this scrupulous collection is largely his own). He's a fount of knowledge and a true New Orleanean, so spend a few minutes with him if you can, and say thanks.

1116 Henriette Delille St. www.backstreetmuseum.org. ℂ **504/522-4806.** Admission $8. Tues–Sat 10am–5pm.

Confederate Memorial Hall Museum ★★   This museum's next-door neighbor, the Ogden Museum of Southern Art, attempted a bold takeover of the gorgeous, circa-1891 brick facility, but like a proud, stalwart soldier it stood firm and held off the attack. Among its collection of Confederate memorabilia—the second-largest in the country, including guns, swords, photographs, oil paintings, battle flags, and Confederate uniforms—are many preserved items that came into its possession right after the Civil War, and thus are in excellent condition. Civil War buffs will be in their glory (sorry), but others will also be fascinated by the personal effects of Confederate General P. G. T. Beauregard, Confederate President Jefferson Davis, and Robert E. Lee displayed here.

929 Camp St., at St. Joseph's. www.confederatemuseum.com. ℂ **504/523-4522.** Admission $8 adults, $5 children 7–14, free for children 6 and under. Tues–Sat 10am–4pm.

Mardi Gras World ★★   The scandal-ridden Kerns are the first family of float-making, and this is their headquarters. The Kerns design and build some 75 percent of the floats used by the Mardi Gras krewes during Carnival Season, so you'll see floats from previous years and those in the works for the next season. Sketches, sculptures (and sculptors at work), engineers' drawings, and king cake and coffee are all included on the tour—plus you can try on some of the elaborate, sparkling costumes that float riders wear. It's pretty nifty to see the handiwork up close, and if you can't come for Mardi Gras, at least you can get a taste here—and a better understanding of what goes into it.

1380 Port of New Orleans Place. www.mardigrasworld.com. © **504/361-7821.** Admission $20 adults, $16 students and seniors (65 and over), $13 children 2–11. Daily 9:30am–5:30pm. Last tour at 4:30pm. Closed Mardi Gras, Easter, Thanksgiving, Christmas.

National World War II Museum ★★★ Opened in 2000 on the anniversary of D-Day, this museum has become a New Orleans highlight and a true world-class facility. Its collection of artifacts is beyond abundant, its educational materials are top of the line, and its exhibits, which emphasize personal stories (including audio and video of civilians and soldiers recounting their first-hand experiences), make for an incredibly moving, interactive experience.

Originally the creation of the late historian and best-selling author Stephen Ambrose, with extensive support from Tom Hanks (Ambrose wrote the war film *Saving Private Ryan*, which starred Hanks), the museum has expanded tremendously in size and scope. Its 6 acres span 3 (soon to be 4) buildings, each with a theme. In the newest, the U.S. Freedom Pavilion, seven original warplanes hang from a 10-story ceiling. From the ground up, it's an imposing sight; from eye level, it's an almost intimate perspective. Other exhibits of note are the "What Would You Do?" kiosks, which pose thoughtful moral and technical questions; a short, shocking film about the atomic bomb (not for kids)—appropriately silent except for a few excerpts of classical music; a copy of Eisenhower's backup speech apologizing to the nation in the event that D-Day failed; and the amazing story of the B-17 known as **"My Gal Sal"**—its desolate downing, the daring rescue, and its comeback decades later. **"Final Mission: USS Tang"** enlists visitors into "silent service" within a realistic mock submarine as it undergoes its harrowing, heartbreaking final sea battle ($5 additional). Perhaps most affecting are the intimate stories told through the artifacts and personal items of former soldiers and their loved ones.

The **Stage Door Canteen** lightens the mood with live, 1940s-era USO-style shows. It's good, clean swinging fun for a dinner or brunch show (adults $50–$65; children $45–$57; $30 show only). Showing in the **Solomon Victory Theater,** *Beyond All Boundaries* is a short, widescreen film with "4D" multisensory effects—shaking seats, flashing lights, falling snow ($5 additional). It's moderately successful at interesting kids in war history, but they may not buy the video game.

War veterans and civilians who were involved in the war effort often volunteer at the museum. If you meet any (and you should; they're usually ready to share their recollections—which is the best possible museum experience), say thanks. You could spend days here, but allow at least 3 hours.

945 Magazine St., in the Historic Warehouse District. www.nationalww2museum.org. © **504/528-1944.** Museum admission $22 adults; $19 seniors; $13 active or retired military with ID and children K–12th grade; free WWII veterans, military in uniform, and children 4 and under. Other discounts apply for combination tickets. Daily 9am–5pm. Closed holidays.

New Orleans Museum of Art ★★★ The crown jewel of City Park, and of New Orleans art, NOMA houses a 40,000-piece collection of 16th- through 20th-century European paintings, drawings, sculptures, and prints; early American art;

Asian art; pre-Columbian and Native American ethnographic art; a gallery entirely devoted to Fabergé; and one of the largest decorative glass collections in the country. Not everything is on display, of course, and this very manageable museum does not need to take hours to visit. The visiting exhibits of the last few years have been unfailingly interesting ("King of Arms," Rashaad Newsom's astounding 2013 solo show, for example, and Hale Woodruff's murals in 2014). The building itself is of interest: From the front, the original 1911 neoclassical building is an imposing sight among the greenery of City Park. The contemporary rear portion is all angles and curves, steel and glass; and the handsome interior galleries are well lit and organized. It all works to the visitor's advantage.

Next door is the superb **Besthoff Sculpture Garden ★★★**, which spotlights 60 modern sculptures amid 5 serene, landscaped acres. Artists' works by George Segal, Henry Moore, Elisabeth Frink, Gaston Lachaise, and a version of Robert Indiana's famous pop-art *LOVE* sculpture are here. It's a cultural highlight, and admission is free. We like to grab a **Parkway Bakery** po' boy (p. 98) on the way there and picnic amid the artwork. Alternately, **Ralph Brennan's Cafe NOMA** inside the museum has light lunch fare and wine during museum hours; and **Morning Call** (p. 118) is just a short walk away.

1 Collins Diboll Circle, at City Park and Esplanade. www.noma.org. ℰ **504/658-4100.** Museum admission $10 adults, $8 seniors (65 and over) and students, $6 children 7–17, free for kids 6 and under and local students. Free admission Wed. Tues–Thurs 10am–6pm, Fri 10am–9pm, Sat–Sun 11am–5pm. Closed most major holidays. Sculpture Garden free admission; Mon–Fri 10am–6pm, Sat–Sun 10am–5pm.

The Ogden Museum of Southern Art ★★★   If NOMA is the crown jewel, this is the crown. It's the premier collection of Southern art in the United States. The artists' works are impressive, and the graphics are informative and even clever. We particularly like the permanent exhibit of self-taught and outsider art, including some from the local area. Though the building itself is quite dazzling, anchored around a sky-high atrium, one can't help wondering if that soaring space could be put to better use if it were hung with even more fine Southern art (still, we appreciate the sculptures along Poydras Street in the CBD that the Ogden installed in 2013). If you're able, come on a Thursday for **Ogden After Hours,** when there is music in the atrium. It might be old Delta blues, the New Orleans Philharmonic, 1930s country, or straight-up jazz, but on the list of special New Orleans treats, these evenings are near the top. We're also keen on the well-curated gift shop, which has consistently covetable souvenirs with a local spin.

925 Camp St. www.ogdenmuseum.org. ℰ **504/539-9600.** Admission $10 adults, $8 seniors and students, $5 children 5–17. Wed–Mon 10am–5pm, Thurs 10am–8pm (6–8pm live music).

Southern Food and Beverage Museum & Museum of the American Cocktail ★★   The South's first food-and-beverage museum reopened in a gleamingly brand-new home in late 2014. This informative assemblage of Southern food and drink history, showcasing farmers, cooks, and everything in between, is in an offbeat part of town that is undergoing a major renaissance. The comprehensive collection of alimental artifacts illustrates how different ethnic groups (the usual French, Spanish, and African suspects, but also Germans, Italians, and Irish), geography, and time have contributed to the cuisine of each Southern state. Rotating exhibits go into deep detail on obscure but fascinating food topics, from absinthe drips to Appalachian soups.

The **Museum of the American Cocktail** (MoTAC), a stumble through 200 years of cocktail history and New Orleans's vital role in same, is also here. Founder Dale "King Cocktail" Degroff and curator Ted "Dr. Cocktail" Haigh's mind-blowing collection offers an original and lively glimpse into the colorful history of everyone's favorite poison. Historical artifacts include defunct product packaging and Prohibition-era photos. (We love the bottles of commercially sold gin, rye, and bourbon flavoring that would go into whatever rotgut you made at home to make it palatable.) Exhibits rotate at both SoFAB and MoTAC, and both offer seminars, demonstrations, and tastings. Scholars and researchers will find the extensive cookbook and archival menu library pretty awesome. Onsite restaurant **Purloo,** serving neo-Southern regional fare, caps the foodie fun.

1504 Oretha Castle Haley Blvd. www.southernfood.org and www.museumoftheamericancocktail. org. ✆ **504/569-0405.** Admission to both museums: $10 adults; $8 AAA members; $5 seniors, active military, and students with ID. Unofficial hours at print time Mon–Sat 10am–6pm, Sun noon– 6pm; check for changes.

Historic New Orleans Churches

Church and religion are not likely to be the first things that jump to mind in a city known for its debauchery. But New Orleans remains a very Catholic city—don't forget that Mardi Gras is a pre-Lenten celebration. Religion of one form or another directed much of the city's early history and molded its culture in countless ways. (For a detailed review of the **St. Louis Cathedral,** see p. 125 earlier in this chapter.)

St. Alphonsus Church ★   The interior of this church is probably the most stunning of any church in the city, right up there with some of the lusher Italian splendors. The Irish built St. Alphonsus Church in 1855 because they refused to worship at St. Mary's (see below) with their German-speaking neighbors. The gallery, columns, and sharply curving staircases lead to spooky, atmospheric balconies where the paint and plaster are peeling off in chunks.

The church no longer holds Mass. Ironically, when St. Mary's was restored, St. Alphonsus closed, and the congregation moved across the street. Hopes for similar restoration here are high, but it's no small undertaking. Katrina caused half a million dollars in damage, and the downriver bell tower was blown dramatically across the street.

Currently, the church operates an **Arts and Cultural Center,** which includes a small Irish art and history museum. You can visit the still fabulous-looking museum interior; free tours (donations gratefully accepted and much in need) are conducted on an informal schedule (Tues, Thurs, and Sat 10am–2pm or by advance arrangement; calling ahead to check is recommended).

2030 Constance St., at St. Andrew St. www.stalphonsusno.com. ✆ **504/524-8116** (for additional info call Friends of St. Alphonsus at ✆ **504/482-0008**).

St. Augustine Church ★★   One of the great cultural landmarks of New Orleans's black history, St. Augustine has been a center of community life in the troubled but striving Tremé neighborhood since the mid-1800s. This church was founded by free people of color, who also purchased pews to be used exclusively by slaves (to the frustrating dismay of their white masters). This was a first in the history of slavery in the U.S., and resulted in one of the most integrated churches in the country. In the modern era, under the direction of its visionary and charismatic then-pastor, Father Jerome LeDoux, St. Augustine continued to celebrate its history by integrating

REAL GOSPEL, NO brunch

You could do the slick "Gospel Brunch" at the House of Blues, or you could experience the real thing in a real place of worship. Don't expect fancy robes or masses of choir members, just rooms full of spirit and a seriously joyful noise. Try **Zion Hill Missionary Baptist Church,** 1126 N. Robertson St. (*C* **504/525-0507**). It's humble, right, and true (and Pastor Joshua's preaching can get pretty fiery). You may well be the only non-parishioner there, but the modest congregation is welcoming; show some mutual respect when the collection plate comes 'round. Sunday services are at 10:30am to noonish; communion service on the first Sunday of the month runs longer.

For a different musical religious experience, take in the jazzy Sunday 10am mass at historic **St. Augustine's** (see above). Home church for many a famous local musician, the Sunday mass now incorporates New Orleans–tinged music and cultural color. *Tip:* Right afterward (at noon), the talented **Holy Faith Baptist Temple** band seriously rocks the house of worship just up the street at 1225 Governor Nicholls St. (*C* **504/525-0856**).

And if you must have that brunch, get to nearby **Lil Dizzy's** afterward, p. 97.

---

traditional African and New Orleans elements into its services. Homer Plessy, Sidney Bechet, and Big Chief Tootie Montana all called this their home church. In late 2005 the archdiocese decided to close St. Augustine because of diminished membership, but a major public outcry bought a reprieve, and it's going strong again. Services here are remarkable, especially when the jazzy 10am **Sunday Mass** features a guest performer like James Andrews or John Boutté. Besides the soul-stirring service, this can be one of the best free concerts in town.

Frequent art exhibits celebrating the neighborhood, not to mention the deeply moving Tomb of the Unknown Slave outside, make this worth a stop anytime (though you should call ahead to make sure it's open), and don't forget to leave a donation to help keep St. Aug going.

1210 Governor Nicholls St. www.staugustinecatholicchurch-neworleans.org. *C* **504/525-5934.** Mass: Sun 10am; choir rehearsal: Tues 6pm. Call to arrange a tour.

St. Mary's Assumption ★ Built in 1860 by the German Catholics, this is an even more baroque and grand church than its Irish neighbor across the street (St. Alphonsus Church, above), complete with dozens of life-size saints' statues. The two churches make an interesting contrast to one another. Also inside the church is the national shrine to the hero of the 1867 yellow-fever epidemic, Blessed Father Francis Xavier Seelos, who was beatified (one step away from sainthood) in 2000. You can see his original coffin, some of his personal belongings, a display containing recently discovered locks of his hair, and the centerpiece of the shrine, a reliquary containing his bodily remains. Should Father Seelos become a saint, expect this shrine to be a big deal and place of pilgrimage.

2030 Constance St., at Josephine St. www.stalphonsusno.com. *C* **504/522-6748.** Mass: Mon–Sat 8am, Sat 4pm, Sun 10:30am; otherwise by appointment only.

St. Patrick's Church ★ The original St. Patrick's was a tiny wooden building founded to serve the spiritual needs of Irish Catholics. The elaborate present building, begun in 1838, was constructed around the old one, which was then dismantled. The distinguished architect James Gallier, Sr., designed much of the interior including the altar. It opened in 1840, proudly proclaiming itself as the "American" Catholics' answer to the St. Louis Cathedral in the French Quarter (where, according to the Americans, God spoke only in French).

724 Camp St., at Girod St. www.oldstpatricks.org. ℗ **504/525-4413.** Mass: Mon–Fri 11:30am, noon; Sat 4pm, 5pm; Sun 8am, 9:30am (Latin), 11am, 5:30pm. Adoration: Mon–Fri 11am–1pm, Sun 3–5pm.

St. Roch and the Campo Santo ★★ A local priest prayed to Saint Roch, patron saint of plague victims, to keep his flock safe during an epidemic in 1867. When everyone came through all right, the priest made good on his promise to build Saint Roch a chapel. The Gothic result is fine enough, but what is better yet is the small room just off the altar, where successful supplicants to Saint Roch leave gifts, usually in the form of plaster anatomical parts or medical supplies, to represent what the saint healed for them. The resulting collection of bizarre artifacts (everything from eyeballs and crutches to organs and false limbs) is either deeply moving or among the greatest creepy spontaneous folk-art installations you've ever seen. The chapel, located on the cemetery grounds, isn't always open despite the posted hours, so hope for the best. Go during daylight hours and use caution—this area isn't great.

1725 St. Roch Ave., at N. Derbigny St. Daily 10am–5pm.

Trinity Episcopal Church ★ This is a very pretty church, outside and in: Outside, the Gothic Revival construction dates to 1853; inside, elaborate carved wood panels show off a 5,000-pipe organ. But the big attraction here is that it gets regular play. Weekly pipe organ concerts by the music director, **Albinas Prizgintas,** often accompanied by local singers and musicians, feature traditional repertoire by names you know, like Bach, Pachelbel, Led Zeppelin, and Michael Jackson. On the list of eclectic things to do in New Orleans on a Sunday evening, this is up there.

1329 Jackson Ave. www.trinitynola.com. ℗ **504/522-0276.** Prayer service daily 7:30–9:30am; Sun all day. Free concerts Sun 5pm.

A Few More Interesting New Orleans Buildings

Degas House ★ Legendary French Impressionist Edgar Degas had a tender spot in his heart for New Orleans. His mother and grandmother were born here, and he spent several months in 1872 and 1873 visiting his brother at this house. The trip resulted in a number of paintings, and this is the only residence or studio associated with Degas anywhere in the world that is open to the public. One of the artist's paintings showed the garden of a neighboring house. His brother liked that view, too; he later ran off with the wife of the judge who lived there. The brother's wife and children later took back her maiden name, Musson. The Musson home, as it is formally known, was erected in 1854. It has since been sliced in two, redone in an Italianate manner, and restored as a B&B. It's open to the public daily for tours (you can also combine the tour with a Creole breakfast or painting party here).

2306 Esplanade Ave., north of the Quarter, before N. Broad Ave. www.degashouse.com. ℗ **800/755-6730** or 504/821-5009. Guided tours $29/person; senior, student, military discounts available. Tour plus breakfast and mimosas $50. Breakfast 9am; tours daily 10:30am and 1:45pm. Reservations required.

Gallier Hall ★ This impressive Greek Revival building was the inspiration of James Gallier, Sr. Erected between 1845 and 1853, it served as City Hall for just over a century and has been the site of many important events in the city's history—especially during the Reconstruction and Huey Long eras. Several important figures in Louisiana history lay in state in Gallier Hall, including Jefferson Davis and General Beauregard. Of late, local music legends Ernie K-Doe and Earl King were so honored. Five thousand mourners paid respects to K-Doe, who was laid out in a white costume with a silver crown and scepter before being delivered to his final resting place accompanied by a huge, brassy jazz procession.

545 St. Charles Ave. www.nola.gov/gallier-hall. Not usually open to the public.

The Mercedes-Benz Superdome ★

Completed in 1975, the Superdome is a landmark civic structure that took on a new worldwide image when it was used as a shelter during Katrina. Intended only as a locale of last resort for those who had no other evacuation choice (and with no adequate assistance plans in place), the Superdome quickly turned into hell on earth when tens of thousands of refugees ended up there. It became a symbol of suffering, neglect, and despair, as people were trapped without sufficient food, water, medical care, or, it seemed, hope.

Just months later, the New Orleans Saints reopened the Superdome in 2006 to much hoopla for their first home game (and a halftime show featuring U2), and went on to the playoffs. Three years later they won their first Super Bowl ever (in Miami), to rejoicing far beyond the city boundaries. Atop the team's gleaming success and the Dome's $118-million renovation, the entire building was then "reskinned" in glittery gold tone, a shining beacon of what can arise from the darkest Katrina days. And what arose 2 years later was a lucrative naming-rights deal with Mercedes-Benz and the 2014 Super Bowl—capping a huge symbolic comeback. Do join the locals in a chant of "WHO DAT?!"

The stats: It's the largest fixed-dome structure in the world (680 ft. in diameter, covering 13 acres), a 27-story windowless building with a seating capacity of 76,000 and a computerized climate-control system that uses more than 9,000 tons of equipment. Inside, no posts obstruct the spectators' view of any sporting event while movable partitions and seats allow reconfigurations. Besides sports events, this flying-saucer-like building hosts conventions, balls, concerts, and other productions, as does its sister **Smoothie King Center** next door. **Champions Square,** a new outdoor plaza, has become pre- and post-game central. Official Saints and Pelicans gear is available year-round in the Dome store.

1500 block of Poydras St., near Rampart St. www.superdome.com. ✆ **504/587-3663.**

Pitot House ★★

Set along pretty Bayou St. John, the Pitot House is a typical West Indies–style plantation home, restored and furnished with early-19th-century Louisiana and American antiques. Dating from 1799, it originally stood where the nearby modern Catholic school now stands. In 1810 it became the home of James Pitot, the first mayor of incorporated New Orleans (he served 1804–05). Tours, given by knowledgeable docents or architecture students, are surprisingly interesting and informative.

1440 Moss St., near Esplanade Ave. www.pitothouse.org. ✆ **504/482-0312.** Admission $7 adults, $5 seniors and students, free children 6 and under. Wed–Sat 10am–3pm (last tour at 2:15pm).

PARKS, GARDENS & A ZOO

New Orleans's verdant vegetation and expansive tree canopy is one of its many charms, with greenery bursting from small condo courtyards, lavish mansion landscaping, abundantly overflowing terrace pots—and wonderful public parks and gardens. Glorious live oak trees are a hallmark of the city, seen spreading across streets and over

floating ACROSS THE RIVER TO ALGIERS POINT

Algiers, annexed by New Orleans in 1870, is about a quarter-mile across the Mississippi River from New Orleans. Generally ignored because of its location, it became a sort of God's country after the hurricane because it did not flood at all, and many services, such as mail delivery, were restored quite quickly. It still has the feel of an undisturbed turn-of-the-20th-century suburb, and strolling around here is a delightfully low-key way to spend an hour or two (daytime only). It is easily accessible via the Algiers ferry that runs from the foot of Canal Street. This unfancy ferry is one of New Orleans's best-kept secrets—it's a great way to get out onto the river and see the skyline (and at 30 min. it's perfectly timed for kids' attention spans). See schedule and fare information on p. 235.

roofs everywhere (an amazing 320 million trees were lost to Hurricane Katrina, including many old oaks; thankfully, plenty also survived). The city's parks and gardens can be an inviting respite from pounding the sightseeing pavement.

Audubon Park ★★   Across from Loyola and Tulane universities, Audubon Park and the adjacent Audubon Zoo (see below) sprawl over 340 acres, extending from St. Charles Avenue all the way to the Mississippi River. This tract once belonged to city founder Jean-Baptiste Le Moyne and later was part of the Etienne de Boré plantation, where sugar was first granulated in 1794. Although John James Audubon, the country's best-known ornithologist, lived only briefly in New Orleans (at what is now the **Audubon Cottages** hotel; p. 51), the city has honored him by naming the park, zoo, and even a golf course after him.

The huge trees with black bark are live oaks; some go back to plantation days, and more than 200 were planted to replace the many that did not survive Hurricane Katrina. Other than the trees, it's not the most visually arresting park in the world—it's just pretty and a nice, wide-open place to be. Visitors can enjoy a shaded picnic among statuary, fountains and gazebos, feed ducks in a lagoon, and pretend they're Thoreau. Or they can look with envy at the lovely old houses whose backyards abut the park. The most utilized feature is the 1¾-mile paved, traffic-free walking, running, skating, and biking road that loops around the lagoon and golf course. Along the track are 18 exercise stations. There are tennis courts and horseback-riding facilities, and Audubon Zoo is toward the back of the park across Magazine Street. Behind the zoo, the pavilion and popular green space on the riverbank, called Riverview but nicknamed the **Fly,** has pleasant views of Frisbee players and the Mississippi.

6500 Magazine St., btw. Broadway and Exposition Blvd. www.auduboninstitute.org. © **504/581-4629.** Daily 5am–10pm.

Audubon Zoo ★★★   It's been about 30 years since a total renovation turned Audubon Zoo into one of the best in the country. It's a place of justifiable civic pride that delights even non–zoo fans—small enough to be manageable, but big enough to cover all the important zoo bases including new elephant, leopard, and orangutan exhibits that opened in 2014. Some 1,800 animals (including rare and endangered species) live in natural habitats in a setting of subtropical plants, waterfalls, lagoons, and a Louisiana swamp replica complete with rare white gators.

The funny-looking mound near the river is **Monkey Hill,** constructed so that the children of this flatlands city can see what a hill looks like. There are also some great hot-day diversions for kids: a wading pond for the young ones; the **Cool Zoo** splash park for older kids; and the **Gator Run** lazy river for inner-tube floating. So bring swimsuits and towels if the weather warrants. There are misters and shady oaks for humans of all ages, but hot is hot: For maximum animal action, plan your visit to avoid midday, when the animals are sleeping off the heat. We like taking the St. Charles Avenue streetcar to Audubon Park, where a free shuttle from the park to the zoo departs every 20 to 30 minutes.

6500 Magazine St. www.auduboninstitute.org. © **504/581-4629.** Admission $18 adults, $13 seniors, $12 children 2–12. Cool Zoo $8 additional. Aquarium/IMAX/Zoo combo tickets available. March to Labor Day Mon–Fri 10am–5pm, Sat–Sun 10am–6pm; after Labor Day Zoo closes 1 hour earlier and all day Mon. Last ticket sold 1 hr. before closing. Closed Mardi Gras Day, 1st Fri in May, Thanksgiving, and Christmas.

Chalmette Battlefield/Jean Lafitte National Historical Park & Preserve ★★

These are the grounds where the bloody **Battle of New Orleans** was won on January 8, 1815. Ironically, it should never have been fought: A treaty signed 2 weeks before in Ghent, Belgium, had ended the War of 1812. But word had not yet reached Congress, the commander of the British forces, or Andrew Jackson, who stood with American forces to defend New Orleans and the mouth of the Mississippi River. The battle did, however, succeed in uniting Americans and Creoles, and in making Jackson a hero in this city. Expect rollicking bicentennial celebrations the week of January 4, 2015 and in the weeks leading up to it.

Markers on the battlefield allow you to follow the course of the battle (or you can just watch the film in the visitor center). Inside the park is a national cemetery, established in 1864. It holds only two American veterans from the Battle of New Orleans and some 14,000 Union soldiers who fell in the Civil War. For a terrific view of the Mississippi River, climb the levee in back of the Beauregard House.

8606 W. St. Bernard Hwy. www.nps.gov/jela. © **504/589-3882.** Free admission. Tues–Sat 9am–4pm, Sun–Mon 9:30am–3:30pm. Visitors Center closed Sun–Mon. Park closed Mardi Gras and major holidays (open Veteran's and Memorial Days).

City Park ★★★

Once part of the Louis Allard plantation and named one of America's "Coolest Parks," City Park has seen it all—including that favorite pastime among 18th-century New Orleans gentry: dueling. At the entrance, you'll see a statue of General P. G. T. Beauregard, whose order to fire on Fort Sumter kicked off the Civil War. The 1,300 beautifully landscaped acres provide a charming spot for a jog, bird-watching, or just gazing at the moss-dripping live oaks (the largest collection in the world!). It's also a treasure trove of culture and activity, with botanical gardens, a conservatory, picnic areas, lagoons for boating and fishing, pedal boats (p. 162), and bike paths and rentals (p. 162). But wait, there's more! A brand-spanking-new tennis center, an even newer New Orleans–themed **miniature golf** course (p. 163), a bandstand with summertime concerts, two stadiums, playing fields, and a miniature train you can ride in. That's just a start. **Carousel Gardens** is a kids' amusement area with rides; **Children's Storyland,** inside the Carousel Gardens, has fairy-tale figures for kids to scamper on and over and an antique carousel (see "Especially for Kids," later in this chapter). At Christmastime, the mighty oaks are strung with light displays—quite a magical sight—and during Halloween the park hosts the massive **Voodoo Experience** music festival.

You'll also find the **New Orleans Museum of Art** (p. 135) at Collins Diboll Circle, on Lelong Avenue, in a building that is itself a work of art. Tucked away inside the **Botanical Gardens** is one of the oddest and most charming attractions in this odd and charming city, the **Train Garden.** Imagine a massive train set, the kind every 9-year-old kid (or kid at heart) would kill for. Now imagine that it's located in Dr. Seuss's basement, if Dr. Seuss was obsessed with both New Orleans and organic materials. Along 1,300 feet of track are exacting, ½₂-scale replicas of 1890s streetcars and ornately detailed, bizarrely beautiful representations of actual New Orleans neighborhoods and landmarks—all made from plant matter! In a town of weird and wonderful attractions, this is one more. The Botanical and Train Gardens are open year-round Tuesday to Sunday 10am to 4:30pm; trains run only on Saturday and Sunday 10am to 4pm, weather permitting.

1 Palm Dr. www.neworleanscitypark.com. © **504/482-4888.** Park open daily sunrise–11pm. Each attraction has its own hours and rates that vary by season, so call or check website. Free admission to park. Train Garden Sat–Sun 10am–4:30pm. Admission $6 adults, $3 kids 5–12, free ages 4 and under.

Crescent Park ★   This brand new, river-hugging green space paralleling the Marigny and Bywater neighborhoods is ideal for a picnic, run, or walk, or just to get a different perspective on New Orleans. That starts as you cross the enormous, rust-colored steel arc, aka the Piety Street Bridge, to reach the park. From the freshly planted and paved paths, the French Quarter is a mysterious, distant vision; from the expansive waterfront stage set amid decayed wharves, the area's industrial legacy nips at the heels. Watch for concerts and other events at this substantial, welcome space.

Enter from bridges at Mandeville St. at N. Peters St. (ADA accessible); or Piety St. at Chartres St. (stairs only—lots of 'em). Free admission. Daily 9am–6pm (till 7pm during daylight savings hours).

Longue Vue House & Gardens ★★   Longue Vue mansion is a little pocket of the unexpected. Just 20 minutes from the city center, near the more interesting end of suburban Metairie, is a unique expression of Greek Revival architecture set on an 8-acre estate, constructed from 1939 to 1942 and listed on the National Register of Historic Places. It's like stumbling across a British country-house estate, and while it was never a plantation, it may just satisfy your Tara-esque cravings if you can't get out to River Road (p. 217)—and it's a nice place to ramble on a pretty day.

The mansion was designed to foster a close rapport between indoors and outdoors, with vistas of formal terraces and pastoral woods. The charming gardens were partly inspired by the Generalife, the former summerhouse of the sultans in Granada, Spain; look also for fountains and a colonnaded loggia. Unlike some attractions for garden enthusiasts, kids can actually have fun here in the delightful **Discovery Garden,** clever and amusing exhibits where kids can play (and maybe even learn).

7 Bamboo Rd., near Metairie. www.longuevue.com. © **504/488-5488.** Admission $12 adults, $10 seniors, $8 students, $5 children 3–10. Free for AAA members and active military. Mon–Sat 10am–5pm, Sun 1–5pm. Tours on the hour till 4pm. Closed most major holidays.

NEW ORLEANS CEMETERIES

Along with Spanish moss and lacy iron balconies, the cities of the dead are part of the indelible landscape of New Orleans. Recognized the world over for their elaborate and beautiful aboveground tombs, their ghostly and inscrutable presence enthralls visitors. There are 45 cemeteries in New Orleans—31 are considered historic, and 5 are officially listed in the National Register of Historic Places. Iconic tourist attractions as much as Jackson Square or Bourbon Street, the cemeteries have a fascinating backstory—one that has become twisted over time by mythology. But the truth is so fascinating that it needs little embellishment.

Sometimes called "Cities of the Dead" for their resemblance to urban centers, the cemeteries have of course been a part of New Orleans nearly since its founding. For the earliest settlers, dying wasn't that big of a deal, everyone was doing it, and the dead were buried in common graves or along the riverbanks (except the hoitiest of the toity, who were buried at St. Louis Cathedral). But when the river rose or a major rain caused minor flooding, that didn't work out too well. Old Uncle Etienne had an unpleasant habit of bobbing back to the surface, doubtless no longer looking his best. This practice gave rise to some good stories (though experts debate their veracity) of coffins floating downriver, bodies weighted down with rocks, and holes drilled in caskets to let the water through and prevent them from popping up from the ground like deathly balloons.

Add to that cholera and yellow-fever epidemics, which helped increase the number of bodies and also the possibility of infection. Given that the cemetery of the time was *inside* the Vieux Carré, it's all pretty disgusting to think about.

Around the late 1780s, death was getting to be a bigger deal. Well, death was getting to be more *prevalent,* what with fires and yellow-fever epidemics and such; *honoring* death and the dead was indeed getting to be a bigger, more ceremonial deal. When new cemeteries became necessary, they were plotted on the outskirts of town where illness and odor were less likely to be troublesome. The first, St. Peter, was begun in 1725 by the Catholic Diocese, and rests where a Superdome parking lot now sits. Bodies were buried in the soil there. When St. Peter was full, the famed St. Louis No. 1 came about, in 1789 on what is now Rampart Street. The first major city of the dead, with fancy tombs and a parklike setting, provided a more fitting tribute to departed loved ones. When it filled up, others soon followed, improving on the haphazard layout of St. Louis No. 1 to form designated "streets" in a grid pattern.

Following Old-World Style

It's true that the high water table and muddy soil here influenced the popularity of the aboveground "condo crypt" look—the dead are placed in vaults that look like miniature buildings. But they are actually customary in France and Spain (and elsewhere), so it was just another tradition that the colonists brought with them to New Orleans. Some say St. Louis No. 1 was inspired by the famous Père Lachaise cemetery in Paris. Perhaps it's just because they are such an impressive, prestigious sight.

The aboveground vaults are also often adorned with stunning works of sculptural art, decorations that represent the family name, occupation, or religion (which was invariably Catholic; the first Jewish cemetery was not founded until 1828). Some tombs were not owned by families, but by a group, like the firefighters, police, or a benevolent society. These were decorated thusly: Witness the enormous elk visible from the corner of Canal Street and City Park Avenue. These were helpful for families who could not afford a family tomb. The cemeteries may also have fancy ironwork in the gates and fences—and on the whole are well worth a visit.

Hi Honey, I'm Home

So . . . all that tomb for one dead guy? Not so much. The tombs indeed host multiple bodies. The methodology is actually fairly clever. Inside the tomb are long chambers, one above the other, separated by shelves. When a casket goes in, it rests on the top shelf, and the vault is re-sealed with simple brick and mortar. Heat and humidity act like a slow form of cremation. After a year and a day (by custom and rule—to accommodate the traditional year-long mourning period), another family member may be buried here. Whatever's left of the first one is moved to the bottom level, and the casket bits are removed. In some tombs, that shelf has a gap toward the back, and the remnants just get pushed back, where they fall through the gap to the vault below. Everyone eventually lies jumbled together to continue their quest to a dusty family reunion. And so room is made for a new casket, and the exterior is closed up once again. The result is sometimes dozens of names, going back generations, on a single spot. It's an efficient, space-saving system that gives new meaning to the phrase "all in the family." If a family loses two people within the year, one of them rests in a temporary holding vault until that year-and-a-day period has passed.

Upkeep Issues

By law, families must maintain their tombs. Traditionally, All Saints' Day (Nov 1) is when families gather to honor their dead, and in the days leading up to it you will still see people busily tidying up and washing down the sun-bleached, whitewashed brick buildings. Some are treated with lime, leaving a yellow or green tint. Flowers, candles, photos, and memorabilia are left on and around the tombs of loved ones. To this day, if you go to a cemetery on November 1 (which we recommend), you will likely see a tender graveside party atmosphere.

But many graves have fallen into disrepair, when family members are no longer willing, able, or around to do the maintenance.

There are laws that allow the city to take over and transfer a neglected tomb, but these are largely unenforced (and there's the creepy factor). Other laws and customs around these centuries-old tombs are murky, and responsibility for the expensive upkeep gets shifted or shunted off. So sadly, most cemeteries today face moderate to severe dishevelment. For years, crypts lay open, exposing their pitiful contents—if they weren't robbed of them—bricks, shattered marble tablets, even bones, lay strewn around. Several of the worst eyesores have been cleaned up; others still remain in deplorable shape.

For many years, New Orleans cemeteries were in shambles. Most of the restoration and cleanup efforts have been spearheaded by the nonprofit **Save Our Cemeteries** (www.saveourcemeteries.org; ✆ **504/525-3377**). Consider throwing a few, um, bones

---

A Tomb of One's Own

For a singular souvenir or gift, artist **Michael Clement** sculpts miniature tombs (and shotgun houses) in rough-hewn terra cotta, finished in aged gold, bronze, and gunmetal gray. You're not going to find these in San Francisco. Not in Bali. Only in New Orleans. Prices start around $98 (and remember, no tax is charged on original works of art in many parts of the city) and they're available at the **Historic New Orleans Collection gift shop** (www.hnoc.org; p. 130). It's not everyone who wants a gilt crypt on their coffee table, but we do.

their way, especially since cemetery access is usually free. The website accepts online donations. Save Our Cemeteries also offers tours, events, and lectures.

Survivors

A faux Voodoo practice continues in some of the St. Louis cemeteries, where visitors scrawl *X*s on the tombs. Please don't do this; not only is it a made-up Voodoo ritual, but it destroys the fragile tombs.

Concerns were high for the fate of the iconic cemeteries during the Katrina disaster days, but "the system worked": The tombs survived unscathed, except for some high-water marks much like those borne by any other flooded structure. Shockingly, some unscrupulous visitors and even a terrible tour guide will still revile the tombs with graffiti or other abuse. Call police if you spot this abhorrent, illegal behavior.

For more information, we highly recommend Robert Florence's *New Orleans Cemeteries: Life in the Cities of the Dead* (Batture Press, 1997). It's full of photos, facts, and human-interest stories for those with a deeper interest in this fascinating aspect of New Orleans culture, and is available at bookstores throughout the city.

Three Cemeteries You Should See with a Tour

Lafayette Cemetery No. 1 ★★★   Right across the street from Commander's Palace restaurant, this is the lush uptown cemetery. Once in horrible condition, it's been mostly restored. Anne Rice's Mayfair witches have their family tomb here.
1427 Sixth St.

St. Louis Cemetery No. 1 ★★★   This is the oldest extant cemetery (1789) and the most iconic. Here lie Marie Laveau (p. 149), Bernard Marigny, and (eventually) Nicolas Cage, in the pyramid he had inscribed "Omnia Ab Uno" (Everything From One). It's also recognizable for the acid-dropping scene from *Easy Rider* shot here. See p. 157.
Basin St. btw. Conti and St. Louis sts.

St. Louis Cemetery No. 2 ★   Established in 1823, the city's next-oldest cemetery, unfortunately, is in such a terrible neighborhood that regular cemetery tours don't bother with it and caution is advised. **Save Our Cemeteries** (www.saveour cemeteries.org) offers two tours annually—if one is running when you are in town, go—it's worth it. The Emperor of the Universe, R&B legend Ernie K-Doe, was laid to rest here in 2001; his widow, Empress Antoinette, joined him in 2009.
N. Claiborne Ave. btw. Iberville and St. Louis sts.

Some Cemeteries You Can See on Your Own

Most of these cemeteries (such as St. Louis No. 3 and Metairie) have offices that can provide maps or direct you to a grave location. All have sort-of-regular hours—anytime from 9am to 4pm is a safe bet.

Cypress Grove and Greenwood Cemeteries ★★   Located across the street from one another, both were founded in the mid-1800s by the Firemen's Charitable and Benevolent Association. Each has some highly original tombs; keep your eyes open for the ones made entirely of iron. These two cemeteries are an easy streetcar ride up Canal Street from the Quarter.

120 City Park Ave. and 5242 Canal Blvd. By car, take Esplanade north to City Park Ave., turn left until it becomes Metairie Ave.

Holt Cemetery ★★★   This one is for the more intrepid. It's not so easy to reach or find, but it's worth seeking out. Dating to the mid-1800s, this former burial ground for indigents is the rare New Orleans cemetery with nearly all in-ground graves. They are maintained by the families—or not maintained at all, in many cases—which results in its particular, folk-art appeal, with hand-drawn markers and family memorabilia scattered about. It's incredibly picturesque and poignant in its own way.

635 City Park Ave. (turn down tiny Rosedale Ave., across City Park Ave. from the Burger King and next to Delgado College). Mon–Fri 8am–2:30pm, Sat 8am–noon.

Hurricane Katrina Memorial ★   On the former site of Charity Hospital's paupers' field, this ominous but oddly affecting circle of tombs holds the bodies of 85 unclaimed victims of the 2005 levee failures and the names of others who perished. It's an unfussy place that's easily missed, the better for contemplative solitude, perhaps. Surrounded by a storm-shaped series of pathways, the memorial does its duty in giving one substantial pause.

5056 Canal St. Take the Canal St. streetcar to City Park Ave.

Metairie Cemetery ★   Don't be fooled by the slightly more modern look—some of the most amazing tombs in New Orleans are here. Don't miss the pyramid-and-sphinx Brunswig mausoleum, the "ruined castle" Egan family tomb, and the former resting place of Storyville madam Josie Arlington. Her mortified family had the madam's body moved when her crypt became a tourist attraction, but the tomb remains exactly the same, including the statue of a young woman knocking on the door. Legend has it that the young woman is Josie herself being turned away from her father's house or a virgin being denied entrance to Josie's brothel—she claimed never to despoil anyone. The reality is that it's just a copy of a statue Josie liked. Other famous residents include Confederate General P. G. T. Beauregard, jazz greats Louis Prima and Al Hirt, and Ruth Fertel of Ruth's Chris Steakhouse (in a marble edifice that oddly resembles one of her famous pieces of beef). You'll have to drive or taxi here, but you can also drive the lanes through the cemetery, a good option for a rainy day.

5100 Pontchartrain Blvd. ℭ **504/486-6331.** Daily 8:30am–5pm. By car, take Esplanade north to City Park Ave., turn left until it becomes Metairie Ave.

St. Louis Cemetery No. 3 ★★★   Conveniently located next to the Fair Grounds racetrack (home of the Jazz Fest), St. Louis No. 3 was built on top of a former graveyard for lepers. Storyville photographer E. J. Bellocq lies here. It's a scenic cemetery and neighborhood near **Bayou St. John,** accessible via Esplanade Avenue.

3421 Esplanade Ave. ℭ **504/482-5065.** Mon–Sat 9am–3pm, Sun 9am–noon. Holiday closings vary.

VAMPIRES & VOODOO

Voodoo's mystical presence is one of the most common New Orleans motifs—though it is mostly reduced to a tourist gimmick. With kitschy dolls for sale and exaggerated mythology surrounding Voodoo queen Marie Laveau, a very real, culturally important religion with a serious past gets lost amid all that camp.

Voodoo's roots can be traced in part back to the religion of West Africa's **Yoruba** people, which incorporates the worship of several different spiritual forces that include a supreme being, a pantheon of deities, and the spirits of ancestors. When Africans were kidnapped, enslaved, and brought to Brazil, Haiti, and, ultimately, Louisiana, they brought their religion with them.

Later, other African religions met and melded, and when slaves were forced to convert to Catholicism, they found it easy to merge and practice both religions and rituals. Rites involved dancing and singing to intricate drum rhythms. Some participants might even fall into a trancelike state, during which a *loa* (a spirit and/or lower-level deity intermediary between humans and gods) would take possession of them.

Voodoo was banned in Louisiana until the Louisiana Purchase in 1803. The next year, the Haitian slaves overthrew their government, and new immigrants came to New Orleans, bringing along a fresh infusion of Voodoo.

Napoleonic law (which still holds sway in Louisiana) forced slave owners to give their slaves Sundays off and to provide them with a gathering place: **Congo Square** on Rampart Street, part of what is now Louis Armstrong Park. Voodoo practice there, including dancing and drumming rituals, gave slaves a way to have their own community and a certain amount of freedom. These gatherings naturally attracted white onlookers, as did the rituals held (often by free people of color) along **St. John's Bayou.** The local papers of the 1800s are full of lurid accounts of Voodoo "orgies" and of spirits possessing both whites and blacks. The Congo Square gatherings became more like performance pieces rather than religious rituals, and legend has it that nearby madams would come down to the Sunday gatherings and hire some of the performers to entertain at their houses.

During the 1800s, the famous Voodoo priestesses came to some prominence. Mostly free women of color, they were devout religious practitioners, very good businesswomen with a steady clientele of whites who secretly came to them for help in love or money matters. During the 1900s, Voodoo largely went back underground.

It is estimated that today as much as 15 percent of the population of New Orleans practices Voodoo, though the public perception—casting spells or sticking pins in Voodoo dolls—is largely Hollywood nonsense.

Most of the stores and places in New Orleans that advertise Voodoo are set up strictly for tourism. This is not to say that some facts can't be found there or that you shouldn't buy a mass-produced souvenir. For an introduction to Voodoo, check out the **New Orleans Historic Voodoo Museum** (p. 131) or **Voodoo Authentica** (p. 149). For true Voodoo, however, seek out real Voodoo temples or practitioners. You can find them at the temples listed below or by calling **Ava Kay Jones, © 504/484-6499,** who creates custom gris-gris bags (packets of meaning-infused herbs, stones, and other such bits), potions, candles and dolls by appointment only. If you happen into one of these temples and find no one about, come back or wait quietly; they are probably conducting a reading in a side room. And be sure to check out Robert Tallant's book *Voodoo in New Orleans* (Pelican Pocket, 1983).

Voodoo Temples

The city has three authentic Voodoo temples and *botanicas* selling everything you might need for potions, spells, and ritual implements for altars. The public is welcome, and employees are happy to educate the honestly inquisitive.

The **Island of Salvation Botanica** in the New Orleans Healing Center, 2372 St. Claude Ave. (in the Marigny; ℂ **504/948-9961**) is run by Voodoo priestess **Sallie Ann Glassman.** The botanica is open Wednesday through Saturday 10:30am to 5pm, but call first to make sure they are not closed for readings (or to schedule a reading).

Located right in the French Quarter, the **Voodoo Spiritual Temple,** 828 N. Rampart St. (www.voodoospiritualtemple.org; ℂ **504/522-9627**), is the real McCoy, and interested, respectful tourists are welcome. **Priestess Miriam** belonged to the Spiritual Church in Chicago before setting up this temple and store. Of interest is a haunting CD of Priestess Miriam's Voodoo chants and rituals. The temple is open for rites and readings but keeps irregular hours; call in advance.

Primarily a store, **Voodoo Authentica,** 612 Dumaine St. (ℂ **504/522-2111**), also has working altars and often a practitioner in attendance, reading cards and performing cleansings. For related supplies see p. 197.

Visiting Marie Laveau

Marie Laveau is the most famous New Orleans Voodoo queen. Though she was a real woman, her life has been so mythologized that it is nearly impossible to separate fact from fiction. But who really wants to?

Certainly it's known that she was born a free woman of color in 1794. A hairdresser by trade, Marie became known for her psychic abilities and powerful gris-gris. Her day job allowed her into the best houses, where she heard all the good gossip and could apply it to her other clientele. In one famous story, a young woman about to be forced into a marriage with a much older, wealthy man approached Marie. She wanted to marry her young lover instead. Marie counseled patience. The marriage went forward, and the happy groom died from a heart attack while dancing with his bride at the reception. After a respectable time, the wealthy widow was free to marry her lover.

Marie wholeheartedly believed in Voodoo—and business. Her home at what is now 1020 St. Ann St. was purportedly a gift from a grateful client. A devout Catholic, Marie attended daily Mass and was well known for her charity work.

Her death in 1881 was noted by the *Times-Picayune.* Her look-alike daughter, Marie II, took over her work, leading some to believe (mistakenly) that Marie I lived a very long time, looking quite well indeed—which only added to her legend. But Marie II allegedly worked more for the darker side than her mother. Her eventual reward, the story goes, was death by poison (delivered by whom is unknown). Today, visitors bring Marie tokens (candles, Mardi Gras beads, change) and ask her for favors—she's buried in **St. Louis Cemetery No. 1.**

Anne Rice's New Orleans

Long before Sookie Stackhouse or any Originals, before anyone cared whether you were Team Edward or Team Jacob, there was Lestat—and the originator of the modern vampire era, author Anne Rice. Love her or loathe her, Anne Rice has been one of New Orleans's biggest boosters. Though her popularity may have peaked, visitors still come here because they have read her books, or simply because they're obsessed Twihards mining the eerie ore. Rice writes seductive descriptions of her hometown that are actually quite accurate—minus the vampires, witches, and ghosts, of course—and cites many real locales.

Anne Rice (née O'Brien) was born on October 4, 1941, in New Orleans to Irish parents. When she was 16, her family moved to Texas, where she met her husband, the late poet Stan Rice. They married in 1961 and moved to the San Francisco area, resettling in New Orleans in the 1980s after *Interview with the Vampire* exploded (she now lives in California). Rice remains something of a legendary doyenne of fang fiction. You can find signed copies of her books at the **Garden District Book Shop,** 2727 Prytania St. (p. 192). These landmarks play a role in her books, movies, and inspirations.

Anne Rice in the French Quarter

The romance of the French Quarter seems to attract vampires, who found easy pickins in its dark corners in the days before electricity.

St. Louis Cemetery No. 1, 400 Basin St.: A tomb (empty, of course) with Louis the vampire's name is located here in the Vampire Chronicle books, and Louis occasionally goes to sit on it and brood. Rumor has it that Rice has purchased a tomb here for her eventual use. See p. 146 for more on cemetery tours.

Gallier House, 1132 Royal St.: This famously preserved museum is said by Rice scholars to be the model for the house on Rue Royal that was home to vampires Lestat and Louis in *Interview with the Vampire.* Also see p. 129.

The stretch of 700 to 900 Royal St.: Quite a few of the exteriors for the *Interview with the Vampire* movie were filmed along this stretch—though the set decorators had to labor long to erase all traces of the 20th century, covering the streets in mud. Imagine how folks who live around here must have felt about it.

Madame John's Legacy, 632 Dumaine St.: In the *Interview with the Vampire* movie, this is the house from which the caskets are being carried as Brad Pitt's voiceover describes Lestat and the little vampire Claudia going out on the town: "An infant prodigy with a lust for killing that matched his own. Together, they finished off whole families." Also see p. 130.

Hotel Monteleone, 214 Royal St.: This was Aaron Lightner's house in *The Witching Hour.* Also see p. 56.

Rice's characters spent time dining well at **Café du Monde** (800 Decatur St.; p. 116), **Court of Two Sisters** (613 Royal St.; p. 83), and **Galatoire's** (209 Bourbon St.; p. 77).

Anne Rice in the Garden District

Rice's books have also featured the Garden District and the area around it, where she and her family used to live in and own properties.

Coliseum Theater, 1233 Coliseum St.: In the film version of *Interview with the Vampire,* this is the theater where Louis sees *Tequila Sunrise.*

Pontchartrain Hotel, 2031 St. Charles St.: This upscale hotel and its restaurant, the Caribbean Room (now closed), appear in *The Witching Hour.*

The old Mercedes dealership (now Copeland's Cheesecake Bistro), 2001 St. Charles Ave.: This building was at the center of an amusing local dispute. The vampire Lestat disappeared from this world through an image of himself in the window of this building. Lestat (wink, wink—could it be Copeland himself?) then mysteriously returned to this realm and bought an ad of his own, congratulating Copeland for his "stroke of genius."

St. Alphonsus Church, 2030 Constance St.: This small (now deconsecrated) church with a stunning interior (p. 137) was where Anne's parents married and she was baptized and received communion. She also took Alphonsus as her confirmation name, and it is a setting in *The Witching Hour.*

Commander's Palace, 1403 Washington Ave.: Rice readers will recognize this restaurant as a favorite of the Mayfair family (p. 106).

Lafayette Cemetery No. 1: This centerpiece of the Garden District is also a frequent setting in Rice's work, especially as a roaming ground for Lestat and Claudia in *Interview with the Vampire* and as the graveyard for the Mayfairs in *The Witching Hour.*

ORGANIZED TOURS

There are great advantages to taking tours. Though they're touristy by definition, someone else does the planning, and it's an easy way to get to outlying areas. A good tour guide can entertain, enlighten, and even inspire. We lean toward some of the smaller companies, in hopes that they may have fewer people than the allowable 28 per group. We like to hang close to the guide in case we have questions; they'll often continue to share knowledge while on the way to the next point of interest—and we find that these kinds of serendipitous personal interactions are easier to come by when fewer people are being herded along. We also like that, for tours to the swamps and plantation homes, say, you'll be saving the earth a bit by carpooling (well, buspooling). Finally, we like the fact that New Orleans tour guides must be licensed, which involves actual study and testing. So not just anyone can load you on a bus and take you for a (literal or figurative) ride.

Tours almost always run rain or shine (no refunds), but in some instances you're allowed to move your reservation to another day. Walking tours and large bus tours provide a designated meeting point; smaller van tours usually provide pickup at your hotel. Before booking, check for deals on tickets—they come up pretty regularly on **Groupon** (www.groupon.com) and **Living Social** (www.livingsocial.com).

Be aware: It's fairly common practice for hotel concierges and storefront tour offices to **earn commission on the tours they sell or recommend** (ditto restaurants). Some may have honest opinions about the merits of one over another, and those may be perfectly good options, but for the most part, they're selling you what they get paid to sell. If you're looking for a particular type of tour, do the research yourself and cut out the middleman; no matter how you learned about it, pay the fee directly to the company, not to your concierge or a street-corner booth. And about those **"Free Tours."** It's not that the tours themselves aren't good, per se; it's that they're not really free (and they're always packed to the gills). They usually come with a heavy-hitting request for tips, and by the time you tip the guide, you're not far from the cost of tours from established providers. The business model and the hiring practices are a bit murky, as well. Frankly, we're supportive of legitimate businesses that legitimately support the city we love so much. But that's just us.

Tour Companies

The following companies offer multiple tours (and will often offer discounts if you commit to more than one). Most of them have walking tours of the **French Quarter;** the **Garden District;** and the **cemeteries,** as well as van tours of the **Lower Ninth Ward (Katrina), plantations,** and **swamps** (they provide transportation and tickets to an associated swamp or airboat tour). Other specialty tours are noted, but if you have a particular interest you don't see, contact these companies—customized tours can often be arranged.

G L-f de Villiers Tours ★★★ Multi-degreed, dishy raconteur Glenn de Villiers is a local native who traces his family lineage directly to a key figure in the founding of New Orleans. The city's history, then, is literally in his DNA. The tall, chapeaued bon vivant is worth following around the French Quarter for his laissez-faire saunter and breezy repartee alone, but his insider perspective can't be replicated through a library of books. Glenn describes the customs and culture like he's lived it (he has), and serves up the facts with urbane wit and a generous dollop of gossip. It works best on his Literary and Gay History "Twirl" tours, though his French Quarter, Cemetery, and Louisiana History tours are all worthy. Some might find this personal take tiresome. Not me. Added pluses: He maxes his groups at 12 participants and donates profits to worthy local causes.

www.glfdevilliers.com. ✆ **225/819-7535.** All tours run about 2 hours and are on the pricey side at $30. Check website for schedule and meeting places.

Historic New Orleans Tours ★★★ This is one of our favorite midsize tour companies, mostly because their guides are consistently good. Quite often they have advanced degrees in history or other related disciplines, and they're free to bring their own perspectives and interests to the tour, thereby keeping things fresh. The company emphasizes authenticity over sensationalism, and they're particular experts in cemeteries, with a serious depth of knowledge. The French Quarter and cemetery tours are on foot, as is a terrific "Scandalous Cocktail" tour, which strings together a series of fascinating tales around local bars and cocktails. The tour delves into historic brothels, organized crime, and even the JFK assassination. The colorful bartenders, when not too busy, also tell their own tales (do pace your drinking, though!). They also offer walking and van tours of the Garden District; and a City + Katrina van tour. Other special-interest tours (available by advance arrangement only) include music, literary, Tremé, and Creole Mourning Customs Tours, the latter a particularly novel and fascinating topic.

www.tourneworleans.com. ✆ **800/979-3370** or 504/947-2120. Most tours $20 adults, $15 students, $7 seniors and children 6–12, free for children 5 and under. Scandalous Cocktail and Creole Mourning tours $25 per person. 3-hour City/Hurricane tour $40 adults, $20 children 12 and under. Swamp and Plantation tours vary. Call for times and reservations.

Tours by Isabelle ★ This is a small tour company, and tours are scheduled only when a minimum number of people sign up (so if they don't hit the minimum, there's a chance you'll end up having to switch to a different tour). The upside is you'll get more personalized attention, and van tours are maxed out at 13 people. Isabelle's tours (available in English and French) include: New Orleans overview; plantations; swamps and airboats; and good combination tours—like a 3½-hour City Overview with Katrina Recovery tour, which shows the French Quarter, City Park, and post-Katrina damage and sights. The City and Estate tour adds Longue Vue House and Gardens (p. 143) to a tour of the French Quarter, St. Louis Cemetery No. 3, Bayou St. John, Lake Pontchartrain, and the Uptown and Downtown neighborhoods—a very extensive overview tour with a broad reach. Isabelle also offers swamp and plantation tours, but no Garden District tours.

www.toursbyisabelle.com. ✆ **504/398-0365.** City and Katrina combination tour $75. City and Estate tour $80.

Gray Line ★★ This well-known, well-established national company runs walking and coach tours of the city, swamps, and plantations—in pretty much every combination. Gray Line also manages the **dinner and jazz cruises** aboard the Steamboat *Natchez* (www.steamboatnatchez.com; see p. 159). This is the big kahuna of tour companies, with large groups and full-size buses, so it's a slicker, scripted presentation but also a slicker, glitch-free operation, from the call center to the deep bench of backup tour guides to the very heavy schedule of tours. They pretty much have something going out all the time, so one call can get you set up.

2 Canal St., Ste. 1300. www.graylineneworleans.com. ℂ **800/535-7786** or 504/569-1401. Walking tours start at $26 adults, $15 children. Swamp tour with transportation $49 adults, $24 children. Steamboat *Natchez* dinner and jazz cruise $75 adults, $34 children. Check website for other tour prices and full schedule.

Cajun Encounters ★★ This is also a larger, slicker company, but unlike Gray Line, it is locally owned. That's a point of pride and also a bit of a hallmark, as they like to hire local guides. It's been around for 15 years, and tours are on a 33-seat bus. The City & Cemetery bus tour takes you through the French Quarter, St. Louis No. 1 Cemetery, Marigny and Bywater neighborhoods, Ninth Ward, City Park, and Garden District, with walk-around opportunities at several stops. It also offers transportation and ticketing to a wonderfully eerie nighttime swamp tour.

901 Decatur St. www.cajunencounters.com. ℂ **866/928-6877** or 504/834-1770. City + Cemetery Tour $49 adults, $33 children. Day or nighttime swamp tour (with hotel pickup) $52 adult, $33 children. Check website for other costs, schedules, and discount offers.

French Quarter Intro Walking Tours

Besides the more extensive city tours listed above, these are some good introductory French Quarter walking tours. Needless to say, you can also start with the free, self-guided walking tour that we've developed for you on p. 199.

The nonprofit volunteer group **Friends of the Cabildo ★★** (www.friendsofthe cabildo.org; ℂ **504/524-9118**) offers an excellent 2-hour walking tour of the Quarter. Docents are mostly Quarter residents (ask about their own family histories). It leaves from in front of the 1850 House Museum Store, at 523 St. Ann St., on Jackson Square. The fee is $15 per adult, $10 students, free for children 12 and under. Tours leave Tuesday through Sunday at 10:30am and 1:30pm, except holidays. No reservations—just show up about 15 minutes early.

The **Jean Lafitte National Park and Preserve's Folklife and Visitor Center** is at 419 Decatur St., near Conti Street (www.nps.gov/jela/french-quarter-site.htm; ℂ **504/589-2636**). The super-cool National Park Service rangers there lead an excellent, free **"Riverfront History Stroll."** The walking tour covers about a mile along the riverfront and brings to life the city's history and the ethnic roots of its unique cultural mix. No reservations, and only 25 people are taken in a group. The tour starts at 9:30am Tuesday through Saturday (except for Mardi Gras and Christmas); the office opens at 9am; it's strongly suggested that you get there then to ensure you get a ticket.

Mondays at 10am, the **French Market ★** (www.frenchmarket.org/events/ upcoming; ℂ **504/522-2621**) offers a free, **40-minute walking tour.** It focuses on their properties, and while it's not comprehensive, the excellent guide includes plenty of history and anecdotes about the surrounding areas. The first-come, first-served tour starts at the entrance to the French Market at Ursuline and N. Peters (under the arch) streets, and heads upriver past Café du Monde. It ends at the Upper Pontalba apartments on Jackson Square. Their free **Wednesday tour** focuses on food and music, starting at 1:30pm at the **Jazz National Historical Park** (916 N. Peters, tucked back from the street near Dumaine and Decatur streets, next to Galvez Restaurant). It ends at the U.S. Mint building at Decatur Street and Esplanade Avenue. This one requires in-person registration (at 916 N. Peters), any time after 9am on the tour day.

7 Beyond the Quarter

A walking tour of the Garden District is offered by **Historic New Orleans Tours** (see above) daily at 11am and 1:45pm. It meets at the corner of Washington and Prytania, which is 2 blocks from the St. Charles Streetcar line (Washington stop). Reserve in advance or just show up (cash only for walk-ups; $20 adult, $15 seniors and students, $7 kids 6–12). **Gray Line** (see above) also offers a Garden District walking tour, but theirs transports you via bus from their French Quarter "Lighthouse" depot (Toulouse St. at the Mississippi River), then lets you off in the Garden District where the tour begins; $37 adults, $26 kids. March through October it departs daily at 9:30am; November through December it departs at 9:30am on Monday, Wednesday, Friday, and Saturday only.

Tours of the Lower Ninth Ward focusing on Katrina devastation and restoration are offered by most of the operators listed under "Tour Companies," above. If observed through the right lens, touring the still-recovering areas is witnessing history, and it's important to remember. Still, the residents rebuilding here are understandably tired of being viewed through that very lens. Coming here remains a double-edged decision.

Plantation tours of the **River Road plantation homes** are offered by the operators listed under "Tour Companies," above. See p. 220 for more info.

One of the better and more established **walking tours of the Faubourg Tremé,** focusing on African-American history and the incredible cultural and musical legacy of this historic neighborhood, is offered by **French Quarter Phantoms** (www.french quarterphantoms.com; © **504/666-8300**). It leaves from 834 N. Rampart St. daily at 10am May through October; 1pm November through April. Reservations required; $18 when booked online. The **New Orleans African American Museum,** in the Tremé at 1418 Governor Nicholls St. at N. Villere, an easy walk from the French Quarter (www.noaam.org), also offers an excellent walking tour Saturdays at 10am. However, the museum is closed for renovations through mid-2015, and tours (and tour prices) have been inconsistent during the closure. The guides are mostly Tremé locals, so given their immersion in and personal connection to the area, they are inevitably knowledgeable, making this tour worth seeking out despite the caveats. Reservations are required and it only goes out if at least 5 people reserve. It's $23 adults, $19 students and seniors, $12 children 2 to 12; museum admission is included in the price, so you can expect a discount during the museum's closure. Check website for most current info.

Other Special-Interest Tours

HOP ON, HOP OFF CITY SIGHTSEEING TOURS The big red double-decker buses, seen in London, New York, and gobs of other cities, made it to the Big Easy in 2012. We're not crazy about the sight of these garish eyesores splayed across the city's historic streets, but conceptually it's a good way to see the city at your own pace. The buses stop at 11 locations—from the French Market to the World War II Museum in the Central Business District to Magazine Street in Uptown. Enough buses circulate so that you'll be picked up within 30 minutes at any of the stops. Onboard the enclosed

TREMÉ: true & false

From 2010 to 2014, HBO ran the drama *Tremé* to stellar reviews, intense local curiosity, and a predictable dollop of cynicism. But mostly (given the producers' widely publicized intent to "get it right"), New Orleans collectively tuned in to see itself portrayed to the nation and debate whether the show in fact nailed the authenticity.

Not surprisingly, opinions differed. But all agreed on two things: 1) It did a better job than *The Big Easy*; and 2) the show's location manager had been awfully busy.

Tremé revolves around a collection of musicians and others finding their footing in the gritty months following Katrina. Many of them are from the historic Faubourg Tremé neighborhood. This complex community just north of the French Quarter, considered the oldest African-American neighborhood in America, was the 19th-century home to the city's free people of color and has for generations been a massively productive musical enclave. It remains a leading incubator of talent and a remarkable keeper of cultural flames. The show was filmed in many locations both inside and outside the real Tremé:

TREMÉ, THE NEIGHBORHOOD

o **St. Augustine Church** Considered the first Catholic church to integrate African-Americans and whites, it was and remains the beating heart of the Tremé neighborhood. See p. 137.

o **Backstreet Cultural Museum** A modest but essential collection of the cultural traditions unique to its neighborhood: brass bands, Mardi Gras Indians, jazz funerals, social aid and pleasure clubs, baby dolls. See p. 134.

o **New Orleans African American Museum** Protecting and promoting African-American history,

it's set in a lovely 1820s Creole villa (1418 Governor Nicholls St.; www.noaam.org.) See above.

o **Lil' Dizzy's** This local diner is a gathering place for movers, shakers, neighbors, and nobodies, as much for the neighborhood lowdown as for the divine trout Baquet. See p. 97.

o **Congo Square** Slaves and free people of color gathered here to drum, dance, and practice Voodoo rituals and eventually, many believe, give birth to jazz. See p. 148.

TREMÉ, THE SHOW

o **Bayona** The show's Jeanette Desautel is roughly modeled on Bayona's famed chef/owner Susan Spicer. Restaurant Patois is the actual stand-in for the fictional "Desautel's." See p. 82.

o **Vaughan's** Already a character, Kermit Ruffins plays himself on the series. He played his trumpet at Vaughan's for decades, and now blows at his own Tremé club, the Mother-in-Law Lounge (p. 176).

o **Angelo Brocato's Ice Cream Parlor** Creighton Bernette, played by John Goodman, expresses his longing for the post-storm return of the lemon ice at this beloved 100-year-old institution. See p. 116.

o **Bacchanal** Jeannette's pop-up restaurant at Bacchanal gets rained out, but the scruffy Bywater wine bar with the killer food and lushly unkempt garden lives on, thankfully (p. 91) .

o **Tee-Eva's** The pie-and-praline queen whose shop has been a fixture on Magazine Street for years had a cameo on Tremé as a bus passenger (5201 Magazine St.; www.tee-evapralines.com; ✆ **504/899-8350**).

bus or open-air roof (bring sunscreen), a guide narrates the sights along the way. It's rote but explanatory and helpful. A single day pass is $29 adults and $10 kids; a 7-day pass is $39 adults and $10 kids, and comes with a lagniappe of two free walking tours. You can purchase tickets online, print them, and show up at any stop; or buy a ticket at stops at 700 Decatur St. or 501 Basin St (the Basin St. Station Visitor and Information Center). Buses run continuously from 9:30am to 5pm.

Swamp Tours

A **swamp tour** can be a hoot, particularly if you get a guide who calls alligators to your boat for a little skewered snack (please keep your hands inside the boat—they can look a lot like a snack to a gator). On all the following tours, you're likely to see alligators and waterfowl such as egrets, owls, herons, bald eagles and ospreys. Or less frequently, spot a feral hog, otter, beaver, frog, turtle, raccoon, deer, or nutria. But even during winter hibernation, a morning spent floating on the bayou is mighty pleasant, and learning about how this unique ecosystem contributes to the local culture and economy is quite interesting. Plus, the swamps are simply spookily beautiful.

Most tour operators listed earlier in this chapter under "Tour Companies" (p. 151) provide swamp tours, but they really just coordinate your transportation, narrate the drive, and deliver you to one of the following knowledgeable swamp-tour folks. You can also drive to one of these tours, or contact them directly to arrange your transportation from the city.

Airboat Adventures ★★★ (www.airboatadventures.com; ✆ 888/467-9267). This ain't no cozy roadside junket. It's a slick operation with an expansive gift shop (which also houses a rare albino gator) and a fleet of boats. And you're likely to see and hear those other boats as you ply the waters, rather than disappearing into swampy seclusion (as you might at some other swamp tour outfits). What you might get that you won't find elsewhere (and we've been on *many* a swamp tour) are brothers Paul and Lance, airboat captains who swim with—and *on*—the abundant gators. These fearless, local good ol' boys get shockingly up close and personal, enough to hand-feed and belly-rub the toothy reptiles. They're actual gator wrestlers who grew up with the beasts and know what they're doing. We think. Controversial? Yes. Cool? Um, sorry but yes. There's also the speeding, screeching boats (noise-blocking headphones provided) that intersperse showboating donuts with peaceful stops amid the primordial beauty of Lafitte National Preserve, to observe the flora, fauna, and human-induced petrochemical clear-cutting. Paul and Lance, people—request them by name! $95 per person for a 6- to 8-passenger boat; $75 for a 15- to 27-passenger boat. Includes transportation from New Orleans hotels (about 40 min.). Phone reservations required.

Dr. Wagner's Honey Island Swamp Tours ★★★ (www.honeyislandswamp.com; ✆ 985/641-1769 or 504/242-5877), at 41490 Crawford Landing Rd. in Slidell about 30 miles outside of New Orleans, takes you by boat into the interior of Honey Island Swamp to view wildlife with native professional naturalist guides (captains Charlie and Brian both grew up plying these waters). The guides provide a solid educational experience to go with the purer swamp excitement. Tours last approximately 2 hours. Prices are $23 for adults, $15 for children 11 and under if you drive to the launch site yourself; or $48 for adults and $32 for children with hotel pickup in New Orleans.

Pearl River Eco-Tours ★★, 55050 Hwy. 90, Slidell (www.pearlriverecotours. com; ✆ 866/597-9267, 504/581-3395, or 985/649-4200), is built on Southern hospitality. Captain Neil has been doing tours of Honey Island Swamp for over 10 years, and the other captains also know their stuff. The swamp is beautiful, even during the cooler months when the gators are less frisky. In addition to the regular 18- to 26-passenger boats, these guys also offer a small 6-passenger skiff ($70 per person, $85 with transportation) and **night tours,** which are supremely cool even if they do slightly freak us out ($39 adults, $29 kids 4–12). **Day tours** are $25 adults, $15 children 4 to 12 if you drive; or $49 for adults, $33 for children including transportation. Tours are daily at 10am and 2:30pm.

They're a little farther out and you'll need to provide your own transportation, but we'd be remiss if we didn't add two other excellent guides: **Annie Miller's Son's Swamp and Marsh Tours ★★**, 3718 Southdown Mandalay Rd., Houma (www. annie-miller.com; ℰ **800/341-5441** or 985/868-4758) and **A Cajun Man's Swamp Cruise ★**, 3109 Southdown Mandalay Rd., Houma (www.cajunman.com; ℰ **985/868-4625**). These neighbors are both so utterly authentic you'd swear that swamp water runs in their veins. Jimmy Miller, son of the legendary Alligator Annie, is carrying on in her downhome tradition and knows every inch of these swamps. Self-proclaimed Cajun Man Ron "Black" Guidry is an equally well-informed naturalist and usually brings his guitar and accordion along on the boat. Both require reservations; call for schedules. **Annie Miller's Sons:** $20 adults, $10 children 4 to 12, free 3 and under; tours run 2 to 2½ hours. **A Cajun Man:** $25 adults and $15 children 12 and younger; tours run about 2 hours.

Mystical & Mysterious Tours

Interest in the ghostly, supernatural side of New Orleans has always been part of its appeal. But let's blame author Anne Rice's tales and subsequent stories of sparkly vampires for increasing the interest in tours catering to the vampire set. It has also resulted in some rather humorous infighting as rival tour operators steal each other's guides, shtick, and customers. We enjoy a good nighttime ghost tour of the Quarter as much as anyone, but we also have to admit that what's available is really hit-or-miss in presentation (it depends on who conducts your particular tour) and more miss than hit with regard to facts. Go for the entertainment value, not for the education. All the tours stop outside locations where horrifying things supposedly (or actually) happened, or inexplicable sights have been observed. Allegedly. Just be aware that this isn't a haunted-house tour (you don't enter any buildings other than a bar for a mid-tour break), and no shocking ghouls jump out from around dark corners. If you do see any spectral action, it'll most likely be after that bar stop.

We can send you with a clear conscience on the **Cemetery and Voodoo Tour** offered by **Historic New Orleans Tours ★★★** (www.tourneworleans.com; ℰ **800/979-3370** or 504/947-2120). It is consistently fact-based and not sensation-based, though no less entertaining. The trip goes through St. Louis Cemetery No. 1 and Congo Square and visits an active Voodoo temple. It leaves Monday through Saturday at 10am and 1pm (Sun 10am only) from the courtyard at 334-B Royal St. Rates are $20 adults, $15 students and seniors, $7 children 6 to 12, and free for children 5 and under. They also offer a **nighttime haunted tour,** where knowledgeable guides provide genuine thrills and chills. It leaves nightly at 7:30pm from Pirates Alley Café, 622 Pirates Alley next to Faulkner House Books.

As for those vampire tours . . . let's be perfectly clear: Vampires are not real. But if they were, they'd hang out in the French Quarter. Both are spooky. Both are centuries old. Both are sexy. It makes sense. Personally, we prefer our history with a bit of, well, history—but if tales of bloodsuckery and high drama are what you seek, the current reigning kings are at **French Quarter Phantoms** (www.frenchquarterphantoms.com;

C **504/666-8300**). Costumes, fake blood, Dickensian delivery—the whole magilla (but not all the guides do it). Tours cost $16 to $18 when booked online; free for kids 7 and under. They leave from Flanagan's, 625 St. Phillip, nightly at 6pm and 8pm. The 1½-hour **New Orleans Vampire** tour given by **Haunted History Tours ★**, 97 Fontainebleau Dr. (www.hauntedhistorytours.com; *C* **888/644-6787** or 504/861-2727) is a baby step down on the drama ladder. It departs nightly at 8:30pm from outside St. Louis Cathedral and costs $25 for adults, $18 students and seniors, $14 kids ages 6 to 11, and free for kids 5 and under. Haunted History Tours also offers cemetery and nighttime French Quarter history tours.

Both of these companies are popular, and these tours usually go out with large groups. Try to stay near the front, so you can see and hear your guide. Even the ones with the most booming voices have to regulate their delivery out of respect for the French Quarter residents.

Food & Beverage Tours & Classes

Visitors can take can take their New Orleans culinary experience one tasty step further with a food and beverage tour or class. **Drink and Learn ★★★** (www.drinkandlearn. com; *C* **504/578-8280**) is Elizabeth Pearce's aptly named company. The noted cocktail impresario and author punctuates her walking tour with stops at cocktail-orientated sites, where participants partake of pre-poured smart beverages. Her other "tour," called the **New Orleans Experience**, doesn't leave the gorgeous bar at Broussard's, yet you're transported through several centuries of New Orleans's storied cocktail history. Meanwhile one of the city's premier bartenders is crafting exemplary examples of classic cocktails for your drinking pleasure. Her lively delivery, depth of knowledge, and visual aids make this a far better experience than it sounds, and frankly we prefer this intimate, stationary excursion. Don't mistake these for blotto bar crawls—they're sincere historical tutorials, with the bonus of booze. The Cocktail Tour meets most nights (but not all) at 6 or 6:30pm at Vacherie Restaurant (p. 87), 827 Toulouse St., and costs $50 per person (21 and over only). Reservations required. Book in advance; the small groups fill up fast.

Anyone can quaff a few, but those with an interest in brewing methodology, the history of beer, prohibition, and local beer crafting will appreciate the insider's tasting/tour offered by **NOLA Beer Tours ★★** (www.nolabeertours.com; *C* **504/408-0747**). Besides testing an array of local pours, you'll meet with a pro brewer and get some goodly food tastings (freshly shucked oysters!). Stops vary from a classic, 1850s-era restaurant to a thriving local brewpub to a tap-heavy hipster spot. But the pace is leisurely and the group that drinks together (at one stop, around an antique French table 2 centuries old) grows together, so the vibe is nicely social. Our group had curious couples, a home brewer, and some regular dudes looking for good Louisiana brews. Once you get youthful guide Eric to chat off-script, it's clear that his beer nerdism (and NOLA knowledge) runs deep, and his passion for the pint transfers well. The 2-hour tour is $50; a VIP version with twice the beer and food runs $80.

NOLA Brewing Brewery Tour ★★ isn't a walking tour, but an actual tour through the best local craft brewery in New Orleans. The 35-minute, brewmaster-led look behind the scenes is wildly popular for the free samples, but also because it's interesting and informative. And did we mention free samples? That'll offset the cost of the cab fare to get out here. Tours are offered Fridays at 2pm, but the taproom is also good for a visit anytime. NOLA Brewery is at 3001 Tchoupitoulas St. (www.nolabrewing. com; *C* **504/896-9996**).

Langlois Culinary Crossroads ★★★, 1710 Pauger St. (www.langloisnola.com; ✆ 504/934-1010), has upped the ante for all other cooking classes in the city. Its gorgeous Bywater facility, custom-built and opened in 2013, is spiffy, sleek, and smart, with monitors that allow everyone a view of the action (but all seats are good ones; classes max out at 16 students). The big differences here are that these classes are hands-on and the menus higher-end. A recent menu included fried okra with jalapeño ranch sauce, glazed bacon-wrapped shrimp with pimento cheese grits, and bananas Foster crepes. Participants are invited to help stir, sear, mix, chop . . . and then dig in when the tasty, multicourse meal is served. The menus focus on local ingredients and influences and change often to help keep the instructors as interested as the students. It's a giant step up from the traditional jambalaya and gumbo that some other cooking classes offer (with prices to match—classes range from $89 to $120). Wines by the glass or bottle are available, and Chef Amy and the rest of the crew are fun, funny, and full of useful tips. It's an exceptional experience. Advance reservations required.

Celebrated New Orleans Chef Frank Brigtsen (see p. 108) created the yummy course curriculum at the **New Orleans Cooking Experience** ★★ (www.thenoce. com; ✆ 504/430-5274), which offers half-day cooking courses taught in a beautifully restored Lower Garden District Victorian home near the Southern Food and Beverage Museum (p. 136). Classic but manageable New Orleans Creole dishes are given a gourmet kick in the custom demo kitchen. Brigtsen and other personable, high-profile local chefs cook and teach; then you all dine and wine together. It's fun, informative, and likely to be fattening. *C'est la vie*. Classes are $165 per person and include recipes, a multicourse meal, and vin.

Tastebud Tours ★ (www.tastebudtours.com/tours/new-orleans-tours; ✆ 219/929-6648), a Chicago-based company, uses local guides who do a good job of weaving together culinary traditions and the city's melting-pot history (since the different ethnic groups that have settled here over the years have all influenced the cuisine—among other things). The walking tour doesn't stop at the finest of restaurants, but you'll sample a good cross section of iconic New Orleans dishes: a muffuletta, beignet, po' boy, and a sip of gumbo. The tastes are small- to medium-size (but a small taste of muffuletta alone is pretty filling), so you won't go hungry. The daily 1pm tours are $44 (kids 2 and under are free; others pay full rate) and last 3 to 3½ hours; reservations are required. Vegetarians can be accommodated with advance notice.

Also see the **Confederacy of Cruisers Culinary Bike Tour,** below.

Boat & Kayak Tours

For those interested in doing the Mark Twain thing, a few operators offer ways to get out on the rolling Mississippi. They're touristy but fun if you're in the right mood, and a good family activity. Docks are at the foot of Toulouse and Canal streets, and there's ample parking. Call for reservations (required) and to confirm prices and schedules. We think it best to skip the food—too much time spent at the buffet is time better spent enjoying the river, and besides, you can find better food all over town. Discounts come up often on their websites and **www.groupon.com.**

The steamboat *Natchez*, 2 Canal St., Ste. 1300 (www.steamboatnatchez.com; ✆ 800/233-2628 or 504/569-1401), a marvelous three-deck stern-wheeler docked at the wharf behind the Jackson Brewery, offers at least two 2-hour daytime cruises Monday through Saturday, and a jazz dinner cruise 7 days a week. The narration is by professional guides, and the boat has a cocktail bar, live jazz, an engine room tour, an optional lunch on the first cruise of the day ($11 extra for ages 5 and up, and $8 for kids 4 and under), and a gift shop. Daytime fares are $29 for adults, $12 children. The 6pm evening cruises without dinner are $44 adults and $22 children; kids 6 and under ride free with paid adult. With dinner it's $75 adults, $34 children 6 to 12, and $14 for children 2 to 5. Sunday jazz brunch cruise is $40 and $20 for children ages 2 to 5 ($29/$12 for the cruise only). Times vary seasonally, so call ahead.

The smaller paddle wheeler **Creole Queen,** Riverwalk Dock (www.creolequeen. com; ✆ **800/445-4109** or 504/529-4567), departs from the Poydras Street Wharf adjacent to the Riverwalk every afternoon for a 1½-hour narrated excursion to the port and to the historic site of the Battle of New Orleans. There is also an 8pm jazz dinner cruise. The boat has a covered promenade deck and a snack bar, and its inner lounges are air-conditioned or heated as needed. Daytime fares are $27 for adults and $13 for children 6 to 12 (free for kids 5 and under). The evening cruise is $44 for adults, $20 for children 6 to 12 (free 5 and under). Dinner adds $30 to the adult ticket; $14 to the 6- to 12-year-olds; dinner for kids 3 to 5 is $12.

Kayak-iti-Yat (www.kayakitiyat.com; ✆ **985-778-5034** or 512-964-9499) explains city lore from the unique perspective of a kayak along Bayou St. John. When the weather's right, it's a sublime way to explore some historic neighborhoods. Tours range from 2 to 4 hours, with increasing intensity of upper-body workouts (the better to justify last night's indulgent dinner). It's not difficult even for the inexperienced, and highly recommended. Tours run daily; times vary, and advance reservations are required. Costs range from $40 to $65. Call for reservations, times, and meeting-place directions. All equipment is provided, but there's no bathroom stop so plan ahead. Check **www.groupon.com** for discount coupons.

Bicycle & Other Wheeled Tours

A bike tour is a terrific way to explore some lesser-seen parts of this flat city up close and in depth. Our suggested tours go at an outright leisurely pace, so you needn't be a serious rider, but bike familiarity and a healthy dose of pluck will help you handle the hazards of potholes and traffic (including stretches along some busy avenues). Do opt-in to the optional helmet; bring sunscreen, a hat, rain poncho, and water (though most tours provide a small starter bottle) as conditions dictate. While a restroom stop is included, you'd be wise to take care of that before departure, too. For regular old bike rentals, see p. 234.

Confederacy of Cruisers (www.confederacyofcruisers.com; ✆ **504/400-5468**) offers a bike tour with an itinerary that hits parts of the Marigny, Bywater, 7th Ward, and Tremé on comfortable, well-maintained single-gear cruisers with baskets. The eight-person maximum, guide-led group pulls over about every 10 minutes at such diverse stops as the New Orleans Center for Creative Arts (NOCCA), St. Roch Cemetery, the Mother-in-Law Lounge, and St. Augustine Church, where guides offer up well-informed cultural and architectural insights. The 3-hour tours are $49 and depart twice daily. Their half-day **culinary bike tour** takes different itineraries, but all go to killer, off-the-beaten-track eateries favored by locals. The "tastes" are copious, and guide Cassidy's laid-back delivery belies a serious depth of food knowledge (and history and architecture), which he imparts between bites. It's $89 inclusive, and worth it. Reservations are a must. Depart from Washington Square Park at Elysian Fields and Royal streets, on the outskirts of the French Quarter.

Freewheelin' Bike Tours (www.neworleansbiketour.com; ✆ **504/324-8257**) has a similar itinerary, with stops for snoballs (during the season) and at St. Louis No. 3

Cemetery, where one of the guides' great-grandparents are buried. It goes out at 10am and 2pm every day except Wednesday; a **nighttime French Quarter tour** leaves at 6pm; they also have a quickie (1 hour) **early morning French Quarter tour** that departs at 8am ($20; great for business travelers). It also offers an **Uptown tour** through the Garden District and the Irish Channel that goes along St. Charles Avenue for a bit as well as the Warehouse District. This one departs daily except Wednesday at 9:15am and 1:15pm. We like the sturdy, American-made cruisers, which have been custom constructed for these streets, and that the tours max out at 10 passengers. All depart from 325 Burgundy and cost $49. Reserve in advance.

As for other wheeled ways to see the city, consider the **City Segway,** 214 Decatur St. (http://neworleans.citysegwaytours.com; ✆ **504/619-4162**). There's something disconcerting about seeing these oddball, two-wheeled stand-up vehicles rolling thru the hallowed, centuries-old FQ streets. But the thing is, they're kinda a blast. It gets better after the "How to avoid brain trauma" introductory video, and the in-store training ends when everyone feels comfortable. Still, when you follow the guide onto those potholed streets, it can be intimidating. Till it turns fun. Which happens quickly. The 3-hour ($75) tour beats the 2-hour ($65) one—you get more stops (mostly to French Quarter and Tremé greatest-hits landmarks), more history, and more leg stretches, which you need. And yes, you get a few minutes in an open space to let those horses loose and see what they can really do (about 10 mph). Multiple tour times daily, call or check website for schedule and to book.

Corny it may be, but there is a romantic lure to an old **horse-drawn carriage tour** of the Quarter or beyond. The "horses" are actually mules (they handle the city heat and humidity better), often decked out with ribbons, flowers, and even hats. Drivers seem to be in a fierce competition to win the "most entertaining" award. They share history and rote anecdotes of dubious authenticity; they'll also customize itineraries on request. Carriages wait on Decatur Street in front of Jackson Square from 8:30am to midnight (except in heavy rain). Private carriages are $90 per ½ hour for up to four people; or you can hop into one of the waiting carriages (you may be sharing with other tourists) for $15 per person per ½ hour. A 1½-hour **Garden District tour** runs $270 for one to four people. Contact www.neworleanscarriages.com or ✆ **504/943-8820** for custom tours and hotel pickups.

Antiquing Tours

Antiquing in New Orleans can be an exhilarating if overwhelming experience. For expert guidance, Macon Riddle of **Let's Go Antiquing!** (www.neworleansantiquing.com; ✆ **504/899-3027**) will organize and customize antiques-shopping tours to fit your needs. Hotel pickup is included, and she will even make lunch reservations for you and arrange shipping of any purchases. Prices vary.

ESPECIALLY FOR KIDS

If you plan to give the kids a lifelong complex for confining you to your hotel room when you *know* all that clubbing and fooding is going on outside, then perhaps New Orleans is better done *sans enfants*. But the truth is, despite its reputation, the Big Easy is a terrific family destination, with oodles of conventional and unconventional only-in-New-Orleans activities to entertain them (and you). **Mardi Gras** (p. 40) and **Jazz Fest** (p. 48) are both doable and enjoyable with kids, as are many of the organized tours (p. 151). *Tip:* Those above spooking age love to tour the cemeteries and haunted places, but long walking tours of historic homes and landmarks may be best left to the grown-ups.

The **French Quarter** in and of itself is cool for kids 8 and over. You can while away a pleasant morning on a Quarter walkabout, seeing the architecture and peeking into shops, with a rest stop for powder-sugary beignets at **Café du Monde** (p. 116). If you have kids of museum-going age, the Mardi Gras exhibit at the **Presbytère** (p. 131) or the Hurricane exhibit at the **Cabildo** (p. 128) will hold their attention for a while. Even self-conscious tweens fall for a **horse-and-buggy ride** (see "Bicycle and Other Wheeled Tours," above) around the Quarter (it's text-friendly, after all), and it works for all ages when it's hot and nap time is closing in—it might even rock the little ones to sleep. The **Canal Street Ferry** (p. 235) crosses the Mississippi River and ends just pre-boredom (and makes a great intro to reading *Huckleberry Finn* together). Add a clackety-clacking **streetcar ride** (p. 236), and you've hit the trifecta of ever-fascinating transportation options.

A number of the city's top attractions are obviously family-friendly, including the **Audubon Aquarium of the Americas** (p. 121). Only the most squeamish should skip the **Insectarium** (p. 125), because it's swell.

Outside the Quarter, the highly regarded **Audubon Zoo** (p. 141), complete with a seasonal splash park for the pool-deprived, is both lovely and a great diversion. For more animal action, a **swamp tour** (p. 156) is a sure-fire winner. While you're not guaranteed to see gators, it's a pretty good bet, and even so, hey, you're on a boat in a swamp. Many also offer speedier **airboats** for young adrenaline junkies.

And then there is the wonder known as **City Park.** We've already mentioned some of the all-ages features there (see p. 142, and pay particular attention to the **Train Garden;** even the **Besthoff Sculpture Garden,** p. 136, with its fountains and giant spider sculpture, is suitable for most kids). If you happen to be in New Orleans in December, pay a visit here, when thousands of holiday lights turn the landscape and trees into fairy-tale scenery for the annual **Celebration in the Oaks.**

Here are a few more of the city's offerings for kids and parents to love.

Amusement Park and Children's Storyland ★★ The under-8 set will be delighted with this playground (rated one of the 10 best in the country by *Child* magazine), where well-known children's stories and rhymes inspired the charming decor. It offers plenty of characters to slide down and climb on and generally get juvenile ya-yas out.

Kids and adults will enjoy the carousel, Ferris wheels, bumper cars, miniature trains, Tilt-a-Whirl, lady-bug-shaped roller coaster, and other rides at the **Carousel Gardens,** also in City Park. Delighting local families since 1906, the carousel (or "da flying horses," as real locals call it) is one of only 100 all-wood merry-go-rounds in the country, and the only one in the state.

City Park at Victory Ave. www.neworleanscitypark.com/in-the-park/carousel-gardens. ✆ **504/483-9432.** Admission to Carousel Gardens, Botanical Gardens, and Storyland $3; rides $3 each, unlimited rides $17. Amusement park mid-Mar through mid-Nov Fri–Sun 11am–6pm; extended weekend hours June 3–Aug 3. Storyland Tues–Fri 10am–5pm, Sat–Sun 10am–6pm.

Big Lake Boating and Biking ★★ Big Lake in City Park is a pretty spot for a boat ride, and the kids can scour the shoreline for turtles. There are **pedal boats** and **rowboats** for rent from **Wheel Fun,** which also rents **bicycles, tandems,** and **surreys** for use inside City Park. All that pedaling action can be a workout, which means you can justify a visit to nearby **Angelo Brocato's** ice cream parlor afterward (p. 116). Boats hold three people, at least one of whom must be 21 or older. Life jackets (provided) are required. Check website and www.groupon.com for discounts.

Wheel Fun Rentals, Big Lake Trail in City Park. www.wheelfunrentals.com. ☏ **504/300-1289.** Pedal boat $20–$25/hr.; kayak $12–$19/hr.; fishing boat $25/hr.; stand-up paddle board $18/hr.; surrey $20–$30/hr.; bike $9–$12/hr. (in-park use only). Daily Feb–Dec 22 10am–sunset, Dec 23–Jan 5 10am–5pm, Jan 6–Jan 31 10am–5pm Sat–Sun only. Weather permitting.

City Putt Miniature Golf ★　We're par-tial (see what we did there) to the two 18-hole miniature golf courses opened in 2013, and impressed with the design: On one course, each hole is designed around a New Orleans neighborhood, with iconic statues and signage and stuff; the other course keys off of statewide themes (learning is fun!).

On Victory Drive in City Park, across from the entrance to Storyland and the Botanical Garden. www.neworleanscitypark.com/in-the-park/city-putt. ☏ **504/483-9458.** $8 adults, $6 children 4–12, free for children 3 and under. Second round in same visit $4. Jan to mid-Nov: Sun–Mon and Wed–Thurs 10am–10pm, Fri–Sat 10am–midnight. Hours are slightly different mid-Nov to New Year's Day when Celebration in the Oaks is under way in City Park. Last equipment rental an hour before closing.

French Quartour Kids Tour ★★　Believe it or not, this is the only tour in New Orleans designed specifically for kids (ideally ages 6–13). The good news is that it's super. The company's founder and regular guide is a former schoolteacher, and besides being an excellent kid-wrangler (and conducting the tour in costume), she manages to keep the enthusiasm level going for the full 2 hours. The spiel keeps it relatable, with attention to what life was like for kids in the olden days. There's definitely history being conveyed here and historic sites explored, but the lessons use props (which she totes around in a colorful wheeled cart), storytelling, play-acting, and enough gory details to hold most kids' focus. Emphasis on "most." Ask about seasonally themed specialty tours.

www.frenchquartourkids.com. ☏ **504/975-5355.** $20 per person (includes kids and adults; adult chaperone required for up to 4 kids). Tours daily 9:30am (sometimes adjusted for weather). Reservations required; check for schedule of specialty tours. Tours meet at Riverfront behind Jax Brewery in French Quarter.

Louisiana Children's Museum ★★★　This interactive museum is really a playground in disguise that will keep kids occupied for a good couple of hours. Along with changing exhibits, the museum offers an art shop with regularly scheduled projects, a mini grocery store, a chance to "build" a New Orleans–style home, and lots of activities exploring music, fitness, science, and life itself. If you belong to your local science museum, check for reciprocal entry privileges. *Note:* Children 15 and under must be accompanied by an adult.

420 Julia St., at Tchoupitoulas St. www.lcm.org. ☏ **504/523-1357.** Admission $8.50, children under 1 free. Sept–May Tues–Sat 9:30am–4:30pm, Sun noon–4:30pm; June–Aug Mon–Sat 9:30am–5pm, Sun noon–5pm.

GETTING SPORTY

Big Easy Rollergirls ★　Okay, it's a total goof, but a hoot of a goof. By definition, roller derby is going to be a bit wild (though the athleticism can't be denied). Mix in New Orleans and the resulting outcome is pure whack. The Big Easy babes play it up

get the kids JAZZED

In such a musical town, there is a sorrowful lack of music options for the younger set. Parents who might be trying to indoctrinate their kids into the joys of jazz, brass bands, or zydeco (or who just want to enjoy it themselves) will be hard-pressed to find options. Blame it on the booze—most music venues serve alcohol and are legally prohibited from allowing anyone younger than 21 to enter. So the street performers along **Royal Street** and in **Jackson Square** work well, but fear not, we've got a few other interesting ideas.

o **Frenchmen Street Clubs** Yes—you can make the Frenchmen Street scene with kids in tow. The **Maison** (p. 174) and **Three Muses** (p. 174) allow kids for the early shows, which usually start around 4 or 5pm (parents must be in attendance). Grab a table, order snacks, and let the little ones shake their miniature groove thangs. They'll be asked to leave when the tables break down and the drinking crowd moves in, around 9 or 10pm.

o **Mid-City Lanes Rock 'n' Bowl** Hey, you got cool music in our bowling! Wait, you got bowling in our nightclub! It's two in one, and both work. It's hard to go wrong with this one, although the music usually doesn't get started till 8:30ish, so bedtime might need to be pushed back some. Kids with parents are welcome. See p. 177.

o **Preservation Hall** The historic, inimitable traditional jazz venue is open to all ages. The earliest show starts at 8pm nightly; get there early so the young ones can see (if they're really young, sit by the door in case a boredom-induced quick exit becomes required). See p. 171.

o **Tipitina's** On Sundays at 1pm the torch gets passed at the legendary Tip's. The **Youth Music Workshop** is a jam session/music lesson for aspiring players, where some of the city's best musicians give free lessons to kids (and also show off their chops). It's pretty free-form and largely attended by local kids, but anyone can come. Bring an instrument if you have one. See p. 178.

o **U.S. Mint** The gorgeous performance room upstairs in this museum has some form of free music nearly every day, and all ages are welcome. See p. 128.

for all it's worth, and the crowd action is equally rowdy. More of a hipster scene than a family scene, it's all in fun, and worth the modest ticket price just to check out the ever-changing outfits.

University of New Orleans's Human Performance Center, Elysian Fields and Leon C. Simon Dr. www.bigeasyrollergirls.com. Tickets $15 at door, $10 with advance online purchase.

New Orleans Pelicans ★★ Playing in the renovated **Smoothie King Center** (next door to the Superdome), the Pelicans (formerly the Hornets) now command an exclusive area on the sidelines called "Hollywood" where seats can be had for some serious green. A few years ago that was not a possibility. Then Chris Paul came along to change everything by leading the team to the semis and playoffs. Even after he headed west and the franchise ownership saw some upheaval, the Pelicans put on a good b-ball show and remain a major attraction.

1501 Girod St. Ticket info www.nba.com/pelicans. © **504/525-4667.** Tickets $42 and up.

BET YOU CAN FIND places to gamble

Harrah's Casino is quite like a Vegas casino (115,000 sq. ft., 2,100 slot machines, more than 100 tables, Besh Steakhouse restaurant, and the Masquerade Lounge). It's located on Canal Street at the river (www.harrahs. com; ✆ **504/533-6000**). *Tip:* Locals know the voluminous buffet can satisfy the most serious munchies for not-so-serious cash (it's a good deal for an awful lot of food). There's also riverboat gambling in the area. Outside the city, you can find the

Boomtown Casino (www.boomtown neworleans.com; ✆ **504/366-7711** for information and directions), on the West Bank, and the **Treasure Chest Casino** (www.treasurechest.com; ✆ **504/443-8000**) docked on Lake Pontchartrain in Kenner. **Slot machines** can be found in every imaginable locale in the city, from bars to laundromats to riverboats, separated (by law) from the main room by a door or curtain.

New Orleans Saints ★★★ Who dat won the Super Bowl? The Saints' incredible Super Bowl XLIV victory in 2010 was the culmination of the city's 43-year collective dream (to say nothing of the end of 43 years of frustration), in which the beloved 'Aints finally won the big one, becoming a worldwide phenomenon, a metaphor for the city's own comeback, and a source of frenzied pride. The bounty scandal a few years later barely dampened the enthusiasm for this team, and if you're the least bit of a football fan, try to get yourself inside the Superdome (p. 140) for a Saints game—there's really nothing like it. Your best bet is the **NFL Ticket Exchange** (www. ticketexchangebyticketmaster.com). Otherwise, the pregame party at **Champions Square,** outside the Superdome (or any sports bar, really), is an excellent place to start your game day.

Superdome, 1500 block of Poydras St. Saints home office: 5800 Airline Dr., Metairie. www.new orleanssaints.com. ✆ **504/733-0255**. Ticket info: ✆ **504/731-1700**. Tickets $60–astronomical, depending on the game.

New Orleans Zephyrs ★★ There may be no better entertainment value in pro sports than minor-league baseball. An afternoon or evening at Zephyr Field out near the airport affirms that. Mascots Boudreaux D. and Clotile Nutria do their enthusiastic best to ensure that family fun is foremost, with various promotions and fan-participation activities. There's a pool area behind right field (rentable for groups or parties) and a general-admission grass "levee" behind center field.

Zephyr Field, 6000 Airline Dr., Metairie. www.zephyrsbaseball.com. ✆ **504/734-5155**. Tickets $8–$12; family 4-pack with dawgs and sodas $44.

NEW ORLEANS NIGHTLIFE

ew Orleans works her wily exotic charms most effectively after dark, when the jazz singers and cocktail slingers ply their magic. It is impossible to imagine this city without a soundtrack of jazz, brass bands, R&B, hip hop, Cajun, and zydeco. After all, this is the town that sends you to your grave with music and then dances back from the cemetery. It's the city that lets the good times roll, and lets you take them to go (you can stroll the streets with a drink in hand, as long as it's in a plastic "go cup"—or "geaux" to use the faux-French). Here, some of the world's greatest musicians (no exaggeration) can be seen and heard with relative ease in remarkably intimate surroundings. And when the clubs get too full, no matter: The crowd spills into the street, where the talking, drinking, and dancing continue.

We'll help you wend your way through all the awesomeness, but don't forget that tomorrow beckons, with more of the city's enchantments to explore. First, a few things to know:

o **Club hopping is easy.** The city is relatively compact, so most clubs are within easy walking or taxi distance from your hotel or dinner locale. Many are closely clustered so you can hop from one to another. Club clusters can be found on Bourbon Street in the Quarter; Frenchmen Street in the Marigny; Tchoupitoulas Street in the Warehouse District; and around Willow Street in the Riverbend.

o **Showtimes vary.** Posted start and end times range from strict to strictly a suggestion (and sometimes indicate door times, not show times). Call if your schedule depends on it.

o **Bring your ID.** Some clubs allow 18-year-olds, and a few allow kids to early shows when accompanied by a parent (Three Muses, Maison, Rock 'n' Bowl). Mostly, though, it's 21+ and expect to be carded. Even you, grandpa.

o **No cover doesn't mean free.** It means buy drinks (bottled water counts) and tip the band (and/or buy their CDs, merch, whatever).

o **Early shows rock.** Shows starting anywhere from 4 to 7pm are often no or low cover, mellower music, and a great way to avoid the crowds and the crazy.

o **Cover charges vary widely.** During big events and for big acts, they can be much higher than cited here. Crowd sizes also vary accordingly.

o **Music is everywhere.** A blurry line separates "clubs" from bars, restaurants, hotel lounges, streets, parks, and front stoops. All can showcase music, so don't overlook them.

○ **What's going on:** Check **Offbeat.com** and sign up for "Weekly Beats" e-mails or go to **WWOZ.org/livewire** (you can also tune in to 90.7; club lineups are announced at the top of every odd hour). Both have good apps, worthy of downloading for the duration of your visit (and after).

THE RHYTHMS OF NEW ORLEANS

New Orleans R&B legend Ernie K-Doe was once quoted as saying, "I'm not sure, but I think all music came from New Orleans." What might be a more accurate account—and relatively hyperbole-free—is that all music came *to* New Orleans. Any style you can name, from African field hollers to industrial techno-rock to classical, finds its way to the Crescent City. Trent Reznor recorded here—then bought a house. Pianist James Booker, an eye-patched eccentric even by New Orleans standards, could make a Bach chorale strut like a second-line umbrella twirler. Then it gets blended, shaken, and stirred into a new, distinctive, and frothy concoction that could have come from nowhere else.

That sublime hybrid is what you'll likely find: jazz descended from Louis Armstrong and his Storyville compatriots. Bubbly R&B transmitted via Fats Domino and Professor Longhair. Hip hop incorporating rhythmic Mardi Gras Indian chants. Brass bands of the second lines, infused with funk exuberance. Soak it in.

The Jazz Life of New Orleans

With thanks to jazz historian George Hocutt

Music was of great importance to the Louisiana settlers and their Creole offspring, and early on the city had a fascination with marching bands (records of parades go back to 1787). Bands became required for occasions from baptisms to funerals ad infinitum—as they still are today.

In the early 19th century, slaves were allowed to congregate in the area known as **Congo Square** (now part of Armstrong Park) for dancing and drumming to the rhythms of their African and Caribbean homelands. Eventually these slaves and free men of color became accomplished instrumentalists. When blues, work songs, hollers, and spirituals were melded with their native-based rhythms and syncopations, the precursor to jazz was forming. The music was taking on a certain American and distinctly New Orleanean aura.

By the late 1890s, cornetist **Charles "Buddy" Bolden,** the "First Man of Jazz," and drummer **"Papa" Jack Laine** were taking the sounds to the next level, and to white audiences. Meanwhile, the Storyville brothel zone was flourishing on nearby Basin Street. The entertainment lineup at the better houses included a piano player in the parlor, and the immortal Jelly Roll Morton was among them.

By the Twenties, Storyville was folding. Its players took the new sounds on the road: Kid Ory to California, King Oliver and his protégé Louis Armstrong to Chicago, Papa Jack and his Original Dixieland Jazz Band to New York. Their shows drew hordes and their records sold wildly. After World War II, Sidney Bechet and horn set up shop in France, and jazz consumed the continent. The jazz genie was officially out of the bottle and the craze was on.

New Orleans is still producing jazz greats and pushing the form forward. Start with **Ellis Marsalis,** father to jazz-playing sons **Branford, Jason,** and Pulitzer

Prize–winning trumpeter **Wynton. Nicholas Payton, Irvin Mayfield, Terence Blanchard,** and brothers **Troy "Trombone Shorty" Andrews** and **James "Satchmo of the Ghetto" Andrews** (among many others) blow their horns to ever-adventurous distances. Obviously, the city still abounds with creativity.

Meanwhile, the nouveau traditional jazz movement is mad hot. On any given night in any given club, players from their 20s to their 70s share the bandstand, covering Jelly Roll or Django—or playing originals straight outta their eras. The **Jazz Vipers, Moonshiners, Cottonmouth Kings, Smokin' Time Jazz Band, Palmetto Bug Stompers,** and **Hot Club of New Orleans** start the long list.

Brass Bands

Today, there's way more to New Orleans brass bands than the post-funeral "second line" parade of "When the Saints Go Marching In." Now, brass is imbued with funk, R&B, reggae, and hip hop. Further, brass-band appearances on the HBO TV show *Tremé* engendered a new crop of fans. Classics like the **Tremé** and **Olympia Brass Bands** still hold court, but the revival goes back to the late 1980s, when **Dirty Dozen Brass Band** and **Rebirth Brass Band** started mixing things up. Today this horn-heavy, booty-moving, New Orleans born-and-bred style packs the clubs and the streets. Try to catch the sounds of Louis Armstrong look- and sound-alike (and reigning king) **Kermit Ruffins and his Barbecue Swingers; Hot 8; New Birth;** or the **Stooges.** Or newer arrivals like the blazing **TBC (To Be Continued) Brass Band,** raging **Brass-a-Holics,** or the pumping street-corner Gods, **Young Fellaz.**

Cajun & Zydeco

Cajun and zydeco don't come from New Orleans at all. Both originated in the bayous of southwest Louisiana, a good 3 hours away. Their foundations lie in the arrival of two different French-speaking peoples in the swamp country: the white Acadians (French migrants who were booted out of Nova Scotia by the English in 1755) and the black Creoles (who came from the Caribbean slave trade). Both oppressed groups took to the folksy button accordion, newly introduced from Germany and France, which added a richness and power to their fiddle and guitar music. Later, drums, amplifiers, and steel guitars filled out the sound.

The styles began to separate after WWII, with the Cajuns gravitating toward country-and-western swing and Creole musicians being heavily influenced by the urban blues. **D. L. Menard** (the Cajun Hank Williams) and **Clifton Chenier** (the King of Zydeco) pioneered exciting new strains in their respective directions. During the early 1960s folk-music boom, such figures as the **Balfa Brothers** and fiddler **Dennis McGee** performed at folk festivals. A turning point came when a Cajun group received a standing ovation at the 1964 Newport Festival, energizing the form and Cajun pride, and spawning a new generation of Cajun musicians.

The proud new generation was led by accordion guru Marc Savoy and his talented wife Ann, and fiddler **Michael Doucet** and his band **Beausoleil**—with **Steve Riley** and **Zachary Richard** in quick-step. The next generation of ambassadors, like the pioneering **Red Stick Ramblers,** the Grammy-winning **Pine Leaf Boys, Feaufollet,** and intoxicating hybridists **Lost Bayou Ramblers** are mixing in new styles while venerating old-timey music.

As for zydeco, Clifton Chenier led the way from the 1950s on, with a handful of others (the late **Boozoo Chavis, John Delafose, Rockin' Sidney**) adding their own

19 CAN'T-MISS NEW ORLEANS MUSICAL
experiences

- **Kermit Ruffins,** anywhere he and his rowdy trumpet show up (try Blue Nile, Little Gem, Bullets, or the iconic Mother-in-Law Lounge, which he now owns).

- The **Soul Rebels** brass band's roof-raising Thursday sets at Les Bon Ton Roulé.

- The soul-wrenching, party-starting early set of the sublime **John Boutte** at d.b.a.

- **Meschiya Lake,** whose sultry vocals would lead you to believe she time-traveled here from the 1930s (the tattoos will snap you back to reality).

- The mellow tones and vivid lyrics of folk-leaning **Paul Sanchez** or troubadour **Andrew Duhon.**

- Piano wizards **Tom McDermott** or **Jon Cleary,** solo or not.

- **Swank hotel lounging.** Try the **Davenport Lounge** at the Ritz Carlton, the Monteleone's **Carousel Bar,** or the Windsor Court's **Polo Club.**

- Catching someone huge like Pearl Jam or Bonnie Raitt at **Tipitina's** (give the 'Fess Head statue an extra rub for your good fortune).

- Brilliant singer-songwriter-guitarist and Death Valley dry wit **Alex McMurray** in any of his many guises, like the Tin Men trio (or if you hit the jackpot, doing sea shanties with the Valparaiso Men's Chorus).

- **Rebirth Brass Band** at the Maple Leaf on a Tuesday. Or anywhere, any day.

- Clarinetist **Aurora Nealand** with her Royal Roses or in other forms. Try to keep your toes from tapping. Just. Try.

- Bowling and dancing at **Rock 'n' Bowl,** especially on zydeco night. It's a definite Barney Rubble.

- Excellent modern jazz in a quality room, like **Snug Harbor** or **Irvin Mayfield's Playhouse.**

- Seeing the Stooges, Hot 8, Soul Rebels, TBC, or Rebirth and finally **getting what this brass band thing is all about**—and never wanting it to stop.

- **Dr. Michael White,** whose dulcet clarinet snake-charms even die-hard jazz cynics.

- **DJ Soul Sister,** whose rainbow flow just jams the floor.

- **Don Vappie** on banjo, perhaps the swingingest strumming you'll ever see.

- Catching **Hurray for the Riff Raff, King James & Special Men,** or **Brass-a-Holics** before they get any huger. You can say you knew them when.

- That ____ playing the ___ at ___ club/street corner that blew you away. Fill in your own blanks.

embellishments. **Nathan Williams** and the late, great, stately **Beau Jocque** did the same more recently. It's thriving today thanks to some of their musical progeny, including Chenier's son **C. J.,** Delafose's son **Geno,** and various Dopsie kin (**Dwayne and Rockin' Dopsie, Jr.**), and girl powerhouses like "Zydeco Sweetheart" **Rosie Ledet** and **Amanda Shaw. Terrance Simien** won the first zydeco Grammy in 2008, and the latest crop of players, like **Corey Ledet** and **Jeffrey Broussard,** are blending in the influences du jour. Also see "Cajun Country," p. 224.

Rhythm & Blues (& Hip Hop & Bounce, Oh My)

The Delta isn't far, and the blues' gospel and African-Caribbean bloodlines took deep root in the Crescent City. In the 1950s, **Fats Domino** and his great producer-collaborator **Dave Bartholomew** fused those elements into the seminal hits "Blueberry Hill" and "Walkin' to New Orleans." Simultaneously, the unheralded **Professor Longhair** and **"Champion" Jack Dupree** were developing trailblazing piano sounds, contrasting mournful woe with party-time spirit. More piano genii followed, from **James Booker** to **Dr. John.** Crooners **Johnny Adams** and "Soul Queen" **Irma Thomas** kept it smooth; and the still-amazing **Allen Toussaint** wrote, produced, and arranged his way into immortality.

The keepers of the flame today are the **Neville Brothers,** and the funky offshoot **Meters.** The genre has broadly evolved into funk, jam, and hip hop—with **Juvenile** and the Cash Money label driving that end, not to mention the only-in-New-Orleans, proto-twerking "bounce" trend led by gender-tweaking post-rapper **Big Freedia.** And we gotta include funksters **Galactic** and **Dumpstaphunk** and breakout superstar **Troy "Trombone Shorty" Andrews.**

The bluesy end of the spectrum is well represented by late greats like **Snooks Eaglin** and **Earl King,** and current keepers of the acclaim, axe men **Tab Benoit, Anders Osborne,** and **Sonny Landreth,** to name a few.

CLUB LISTINGS
The French Quarter

The Famous Door ★   Open since 1934, this is the oldest music club on Bourbon Street. Many luminaries have played here (including 13-year-old Harry Connick, Jr.). Great historic value, cheap drinks, and a solid cover band make the Famous Door fratty fun, plus there's no cover. 339 Bourbon St. www.myspace.com/famousdoor. ℭ **504/598-4334.** No cover.

Fritzel's European Jazz Pub ★★   From the open street front, this 1831 building looks sketchy, overlookable even. The door folk will aggressively attempt to hustle you to a seat at the cramped picnic tables and rush to take your drink order. Let them: Some of the best traditional jazz is played on the teensy stage here, and the quasi-hofbrau atmosphere breeds community. 733 Bourbon St. www.fritzelsjazz.net ℭ **504/586-4800.** 1-drink minimum per set.

Funky Pirate ★   The XXL attraction here is bluesman "Big" Al Carson, who holds court Tuesday through Saturday. It's popular, sometimes packed, always pirate-y. *Note:* If "Drink from a plastic weapon" is on your bucket list, get the famously horrid Hand Grenade next door at sister bar **Tropical Isle.** 727 Bourbon St. www.thefunkypirate.com. ℭ **504/523-1960.** 1-drink minimum per set. Big Al plays from 8:30pm on.

House of Blues ★   You can find this chain club elsewhere and you can find authentic (vs. ersatz) folk-art-laden roadhouses within a few miles (hello, Tipitina's). It's lost its domineering booking muscle to other venues *but* when there is something worthy (Gaga and Gary Clark, Jr., have played here recently), the sightlines are good and the regionalized, recently improved food is decent. We quite like the lesser-used non-main rooms: The upstairs Parish feels inviting and real; the courtyard is lovely and actually *is* real. 225 Decatur St. www.houseofblues/neworleans.com. ℭ **504/310-4999.** Cover varies.

Irvin Mayfield's Jazz Playhouse ★★★ The über-talented trumpeter-bandleader's Bourbon Street retreat is the go-to spot for ambitious, established, and on-the-rise local jazz artists. Mondays with Gerald French and Wednesdays featuring the New Orleans Jazz Orchestra are sure bets (and even the Friday midnight Burlesque shows have good music). The draperied, midsize room is swank, and the well-prepared drinks aren't inexpensive (and service can be a bit snooty). But there's rarely a cover for the high-caliber talent and atmosphere. 300 Bourbon St. in the Royal Sonesta Hotel. www.irvinmayfield.com. ✆ **504/553-2299.** Usually no cover except for the NOJO and burlesque shows.

Maison Bourbon ★ Despite its location and the DEDICATED TO THE PRESERVATION OF JAZZ sign (an attempt to confuse tourists into thinking this is Preservation Hall?), Maison Bourbon isn't a tourist trap. The music is authentic, often superb Dixieland and traditional jazz, and the brick-lined room is a respite from the mayhem outside. 641 Bourbon St. www.maisonbourbon.com. ✆ **504/522-8818.** 1-drink minimum per set.

One Eyed Jacks ★★ With its bordello-flavored decor (swag curtains and red-flocked wallpaper), Jack's strikes a funky/retro/hip balance. A busy front bar leads to a tiered main-room floor that wraps around another crowded bar. The cool room full of cool people is booked with cool, alternative-leaning local and touring bands (Surfer Blood, Charles Bradley, White Denim). On busy nights, the door policy can sometimes be off-putting. Their 80s nights are legendary. 615 Toulouse St. www.oneeyedjacks.net. ✆ **504/569-8361.** Cover $10–$20 or more.

Palm Court Jazz Cafe ★★ Though the Palm Court lost its beloved, long-time Saturday night act last year (trumpeter Lionel Ferbos, who gigged here till his 103rd birthday!), this stylish dinner club is still a reliable, comfortable venue for topnotch classic and traditional jazz Wednesday through Sunday. Table seating (make reservations) with a small back bar for non-diners. 1204 Decatur St. www.palmcourtjazzcafe.com. ✆ **504/525-0200.** Wed–Sun 7–11pm. Cover $5 and up; entrees $16–$24.

Preservation Hall ★★★ The decaying, ancient-looking building lends just the right air of consecration to this, an essential spot for traditional jazz fans and, well, everyone (Robert Plant and U2's Edge have sat in here). With little air, terrible sight-lines, no bathrooms (you are warned), and constant crowds, the awesomeness is in the hallowed atmosphere and the superb musicianship. Shows start at 8, 9, and 10pm; the general-admission line starts forming about an hour before. Go early for bench seating or prepare to stand. A few rows of up-front VIP seats are sold online; get them well in advance. 726 St. Peter St. www.preservationhall.com. ✆ **888/946-5299** or 504/522-2841. Cover $15–$20; VIP $30–$40.

Frenchmen Street & the Marigny

Apple Barrel ★ Once upon a time, Frenchmen Street was a quiet little stretch where neighbors shopped, ate, and drank. They did the latter—and still do—right here, especially weeknights when they can fit into the dank shoebox of a room. The Barrel has become almost an afterthought nowadays, given the plethora of the shinier options surrounding it. But for authenticity, divey-ness, and solid, low-key blues acts, it shouldn't be. There's no cover; mid-priced drinks, and **Adolfo's** upstairs serves some of the best Creole Italian food around (put your name on the list about an hour before you get hungry). 609 Frenchmen St. ✆ **504/949-9399.**

Bamboula's ★ Built from scratch in '13 with no retro material left behind, the spacious wood-copper-tin-tile-brick–laden Bamboula does a decent job of fitting in

New Orleans Nightlife

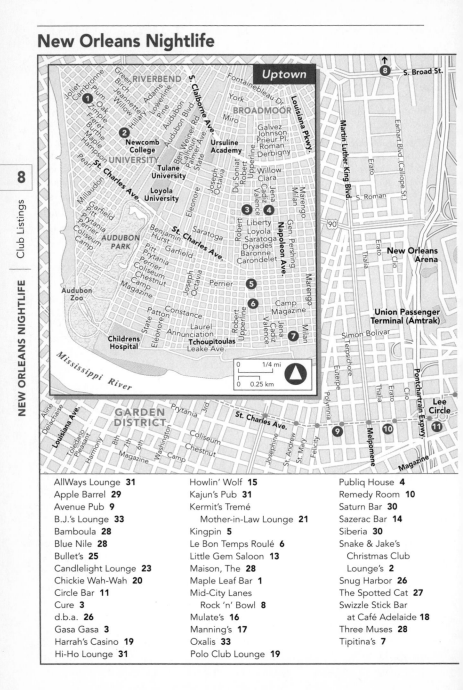

Performing Arts, Theaters, Cruises
Creole Queen **22**
Café Istanbul **31**
Civic Theatre **12**
Mahalia Jackson Theater
  for the Performing Arts **24**
Marigny Opera House **33**

Gay Nightlife
Marigny Art and Books **26**
Phoenix **32**
Country Club **33**

with the street's much-older vibe, but still needs to find its footing. The food bears little mention and the music acts playing the small front stage aren't yet of any particular theme or consistent caliber. There's a much larger stage area in back and a party-ready upstairs lounge. Still, it's fine for a round if the sounds entice you—no cover means no harm, no foul. It's trying (maybe too hard?), so let's watch where it goes and hope it fills its potential. 514 Frenchmen St. www.bamboulasnola.com. ℂ **504/944-8461.** Cover free to $20.

Blue Nile ★★   This midsize club added a killer sound system and removed the view-obscuring pillars in 2013, the better to see and hear the variety of locals, reggae, and jam bands. Late-night DJs upstairs. 532 Frenchmen St. www.bluenilelive.com. ℂ **504/948-2583.** Cover free–$15.

d.b.a. ★★★   Among the best New Orleans bar/nightclubs (best beer and spirits selections, too). Its live bookings feature an occasional, on-the-cusp national or Louisiana act and a wide variety of excellent local acts like magnificent crooner John Boutte, the tight blues of Walter Washington, or breakout bluesy rockers Honey Island Swamp Band. It's nonsmoking, and shows start on time. Mostly standing-room only, and the low stage doesn't help those in the back. *Tip:* Boutte's early Saturday shows now command a small cover charge, but most other nights this well-booked slot is free. 618 Frenchmen St. www.dbaneworleans.com. ℂ **504/942-3731.** Cover $5–$15, occasionally higher.

The Maison ★★   A brick-walled Frenchmen mainstay with always solid local musicians—there's jazz early, but later on the scene gets funkier, danceable, and well . . . it just gets down. The second-level wraparound balcony is a good hang when the main floor gets too packed. Drinks are average, food less so, but the scene is stellar. Kids okay early in eve. 508 Frenchmen St. www.maisonfrenchman.com. ℂ **504/371-5543.** Rarely a cover.

Snug Harbor ★★★   This sit-down, concert-style club and early Frenchmen Street settler is the city's premier showcase for contemporary jazz. Two levels provide mostly good viewing (beware the pillars upstairs—try to sit along the rail). The adjoining restaurant has great burgers, and shows screen on monitors in the low-ceilinged bar: for the budget-minded, it's the next best thing to live. Advance ticket purchase is wise. 628 Frenchmen St. www.snugjazz.com. ℂ **504/949-0696.** Cover $15–$40.

The Spotted Cat Music Club ★★★   Our aesthetic leans toward cramped rooms, little amplification, and scrappy bands with a fresh take on big-band, gypsy, hot—well, any type of swinging jazz. So we adore the oft-crowded Cat. The scarce seats are hardly comfy, but the 100-percent reliably fine music is the real deal; the frenetic-footed jitterbuggers squeezed in front of the minute stage might be the instructors at Wednesday's free 5pm dance lessons. We love the uncrowded early hours (4pm weekdays; 3pm weekends) and local artworks. Cash only. 623 Frenchmen St. www.spottedcatmusicclub.com. No phone. No cover except special events. 1 drink per set. Tip the band!

Three Muses ★★★   Sophisticated modern lounge meets classic 1920s saloon, and we likey. It serves up beautifully balanced, new-timey cocktails and mouthwatering (quite) small plates to old-timey tunes, with no cover (but the food and drinks can add up; feta fries are best for value and sharing). The scant tables and stools go fast; expect a line when the street is hopping. Don't miss Luke Winslow-King, Debbie Davies, or muse Miss Sophie Lee if they're here. Closed Tuesdays, otherwise open 4pm; kids okay till 9-ish. 536 Frenchmen St. www.thethreemuses.com. ℂ **504/252-4801.** A second location on Freret St. is in the works. No cover. Tip the band!

French Quarter Nightlife

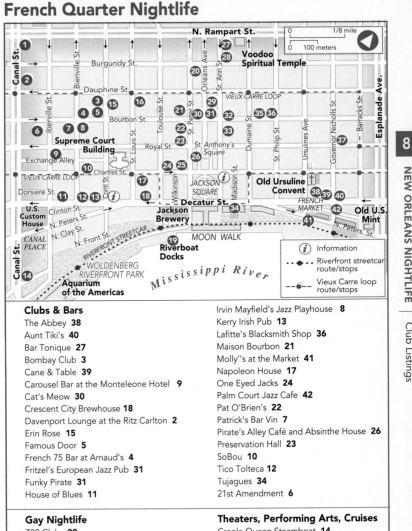

Clubs & Bars

The Abbey **38**
Aunt Tiki's **40**
Bar Tonique **27**
Bombay Club **3**
Cane & Table **39**
Carousel Bar at the Monteleone Hotel **9**
Cat's Meow **30**
Crescent City Brewhouse **18**
Davenport Lounge at the Ritz Carlton **2**
Erin Rose **15**
Famous Door **5**
French 75 Bar at Arnaud's **4**
Fritzel's European Jazz Pub **31**
Funky Pirate **31**
House of Blues **11**

Irvin Mayfield's Jazz Playhouse **8**
Kerry Irish Pub **13**
Lafitte's Blacksmith Shop **36**
Maison Bourbon **21**
Molly''s at the Market **41**
Napoleon House **17**
One Eyed Jacks **24**
Palm Court Jazz Cafe **42**
Pat O'Brien's **22**
Patrick's Bar Vin **7**
Pirate's Alley Café and Absinthe House **26**
Preservation Hall **23**
SoBou **10**
Tico Tolteca **12**
Tujagues **34**
21st Amendment **6**

Gay Nightlife

700 Club **20**
Bourbon Pub—Parade Disco **32**
Café Lafitte in Exile **35**
Golden Lantern **37**
Good Friends Bar & Queens Head Pub **29**
LeRoundup **16**
Oz **33**
Rawhide 2010 **28**

Theaters, Performing Arts, Cruises

Creole Queen Steamboat **14**
Le Petit Théâtre du Vieux Carré **25**
Saenger Theatre **1**
Steamboat Natchez **19**

Elsewhere Around the City

Candlelight Lounge ★ One of the last operating clubs in the Faubourg Tremé, the big event happens Wednesdays around 10pm when the incomparable Tremé Brass Band takes the small stage. Think free red beans and rice, cheap fast-flowing beer, super-friendly staff, and communal tables (some far from the stage). No one in the mixed crowd leaves the streamer-strewn room without smiling or sweating. Cab it here. 925 N. Robertson. ℂ **504/525-4746.** Cover $15–$20.

Chickie Wah-Wah ★★★ We're ever so fond of this Mid-City club, where the best of the local roots, rock, blues, and singer-songwriter acts draw reverent crowds. Cool old tin signs lend ambience to the clean, midsize, shotgun-style room, which is smoke-free save for darn good BBQ served through a small window. It's off the Canal Street streetcar at N. White Street, just past Broad. Try to catch Paul Sanchez, Tom McDermott, John Cleary, or the rollicking, testifying Mercy Brothers. 2828 Canal St. www.chickiewahwah.com. ℂ **504/304-4714.** Cover $8–$20.

Circle Bar ★★ A 2012 renovation of the 1883 building maintained the quirky, elegant decay suitable to the laid-back, Marlboro-loving clientele in this tiny dive. The jukebox feeds the idiosyncratic vibe with mood-enhancing selections from the Velvet Underground, Dusty Springfield, and Curtis Mayfield. There's an alcove where up-and-comers play at happy hour, and good local musicians start thinking about playing at 10pm nightly. 1032 St. Charles Ave., in the CBD at Lee Circle. www.circlebarneworleans.com. ℂ **504/588-2616.** Cover $5–$12.

Gasa Gasa ★ New in 2013, Gasa fills the eclectic, indie rock niche that draw a Tulane-to-20-something crowd to the single room. Occasional readings, arts exhibits, the hopping Freret Street scene, and the mind-blowing exterior mural by Berlin-based street artist MTO add to the allure. 4920 Freret St. www.gasagasa.com. ℂ **504/304-7110.** Cover free–$15.

The Howlin' Wolf ★★ The big (10,000 sq. ft.), not-at-all-bad Wolf brings in leading local and occasional midlevel national acts focusing on rock, funk, and jam (Leftover Salmon, of Montreal; Sharon Jones & the Dap Kings; local faves like Galactic, Anders Osborne, and Dumpstaphunk often do). Good sound, good sightlines, good times—especially Sundays when the Hot 8 brass band plays the smaller "Den." Other nights the Den gets eclectic indie locals, comedy, and acoustic stuff. *Fun fact:* The bar came from Al Capone's hotel in Chicago. Doors open at 9pm; shows start at 10pm. 907 S. Peters St., in the Warehouse District. www.thehowlinwolf.com. ℂ **504/529-5844.** Cover varies.

Kermit's Tremé Mother-in-Law Lounge ★ All aboard! Trumpeter and unofficial NOLA mayor Kermit Ruffins took over this brightly muraled, historic spot in

---

Bender Mender

If the aftermath of clubbing leaves you with a morning-after case of the liquid flu, consider the **Remedy Room.** An actual M.D. hooks you up to an actual I.V. packed with vitamins and various other restoratives, to get you upright and sharp for that 1pm swamp tour or conference call. But next time, how about just trying a glass of water with each cocktail? 1224 St. Charles Ave. ℂ **504/301-1670.** From about $120.

THE ST. CLAUDE scene

The scruffy local alternative types have carved out a pulsing, punk-infused scene (well, with just about every other genre thrown in for good measure) along a stretch of St. Claude Avenue in the Bywater. **Siberia**'s sundry bookings span the punk/funk/death metal/trivia/whatev realms (2227 St. Claude Ave.; www.siberianola.com; ✆ **504/265-8855**). At the spacious, comfortable **Hi-Ho Lounge,** we dig Monday night's BYOBanjo bluegrass jam and Saturdays when DJ Soul Sister's Hustle brings out her massive, multi-culti harem (2239 St. Claude Ave.; www.hiholounge.net; ✆ **504/945-4446**). The **Saturn Bar** falls somewhere between art project and junque-house, but the dive vibe is unfakeable, punk, surf, DJs, and metal rotate (3067 St. Claude Ave.; ✆ **504/949-7532**). The loose, welcoming Karaoke at **Kajun's Pub** (2256 St. Claude Ave.; www.kajunpub.com; ✆ **504/947-3735** or 504/267-6108) and the **AllWays Lounge** (2240 St. Claude Ave.; www.theallwayslounge.com; ✆ **504/218-5778**) round out the tatty, happening street scene. If this sounds like your thing, do take a cab and don't wander in this transitional area. Hungry? Hit **Kukhnya** in **Siberia** for genius-level, crazy-affordable "Slavic soul food."

2014. The former headquarters of dearly beloved Ernie K-Doe (his illustrious manikin is gone) draws 7th Ward locals mostly, but all adventurous souls are welcome. When Kermit fires up the BBQ in the big yard—or his trumpet (Thursdays, if he's in town)—it's worth the trip (and it *is* a trip). Kid Merv (Wednesdays) can also blow and the Tremé Brass Band whoops things up Sundays. Otherwise, it's a lotta cold beer and over-amplified beats. 1500 S. Claiborne Ave. ✆ **504/975-3955.** Cover varies.

Little Gem Saloon ★★★ For those who appreciate jazz history, this is the motherland. The record books may be sketchy, but most agree that jazz began on this block, and perhaps in this building. The first greats—including Buddy Bolden and Jelly Roll Morton—played the 1906 Little Gem, and they'd love the thoroughly restored 2013 iteration. It books top local and visiting jazz acts in the brick-walled, velvet-curtained Ramp Room, and more casual acts at happy hour and brunch in the white tile-floored, first-level saloon. The modern Southern menu reflects similar quality and fun-meets-sophistication, with the chicken 'n' biscuits, monster smoked pork chop, and simple but refined house salad standing out. 445 S. Rampart St. www.littlegemsaloon.com. ✆ **504/267-4863.** Cover free–$30.

Maple Leaf Bar ★★★ This classic New Orleans club is a locals bar by day and a medium-size, tin-ceilinged, twinkle-light-strung club at night (that feels smaller when the crowds pack in, usually by 11). Personal space can become just a wistful memory and the drunk frat crowd can be maddening; seek temporary refuge on the back patio, at the back bar's junky pool table, or on the sidewalk where the overflow party goes. But it's got a vibe you can't manufacture, and when Rebirth rips it up on Tuesdays it's pretty much a must-do (but if you're only around on Thurs, see the Trio). 8316 Oak St. www.mapleleafbar.com. ✆ **504/866-9359.** Cover $10–$20.

Mid City Lanes Rock 'n' Bowl ★★★ Bowling. Bands. Beer. If you can't have fun here, we give up. There's swing on Wednesdays, zydeco on Thursdays, and local blues, rockabilly, rock, who cares on other nights. It's an utter hoot and an unbeatable experience that draws all ages and types to the spacious, well air-conditioned dance

Besides its pedigree as one of the city's premier live-music venues, **Tipitina's foundation** also actively supports and enhances the local scene. At its all-ages Sunday-afternoon music workshops (1–3:30pm), music students can play and study with such leading names as Stanton Moore, Johnny Vidacovich, Kirk Joseph, and Theresa Andersson. This low-key, free scene offers a pretty cool opportunity to participate, watch, and listen as traditions are passed on.

floor. The custom-embroidered bowling shirts make splendid souvenirs. *Fun fact:* The picnic tables are built from the lanes in the old (pre-Katrina) location. *Tip:* Dine next door at **Ye Olde College Inn** (p. 97) and take $5 off admission. 3000 S. Carrollton Ave. www.rocknbowl.com. ℭ **504/861-1700.** Private parties sometimes take over, so call ahead. Bowling $24/hr. per lane and a $1 shoe-rental fee; show admission $5–$25. Mon–Thurs 11:30am–midnight, Fri–Sat 11:30am–2am, Sun check calendar.

Publiq House ★★ The Willy's jeep converted into a sound booth and the second-hand chandeliers hovering above the bar stools indicate something beyond sophomoric self-trashing is afoot at this Freret Street bar, despite its proximity to Tulane. Not that such a thing won't happen here, given the wall of slushy daiquiris (they're actually a step up from the Bourbon Street variety—they're spiked with classier booze). But there's also a decent craft cocktail list, and a round copper-paneled wall houses a dozen well-selected beer taps. All that sets the foundation for the more striking distinction of this clean, spacious room: the people in it, especially the refreshingly diverse crowd that packs the room on Thursday nights for the Brass-a-Holics' residency, when the crowd of all ages (well, 21+), colors, orientations, sizes, and species (there was a black lab out there) morphs into a grooving mass of humanity (and dogmanity). 4528 Freret St. www.publiqhouse.com. ℭ **504/826-9912.** Cover $5–$25.

Tipitina's ★★★ Dedicated to the late piano master Professor Longhair (that's him in bronze just inside the entrance; rub his head for luck), Tip's is, if not *the* New Orleans club, a major musical touchstone and a reliable place for top local and out-of-town roots, brass, jam, and rock bands from Wilco to Willie Nelson. If you can catch locals like Troy "Trombone Shorty" Andrews, Galactic, the Meters, the Nevilles, or especially Dr. John here, do not waver for a sec.

It's nothing fancy: four walls, buncha bars, wraparound balcony (often reserved for VIPs), and a stage (which, if you're under 6 feet, isn't easy to see from the back on busy nights). This uptown institution (location, not atmosphere) has good (loud) sound and air-con, and there's usually some food truck action. Get advance tix for festival bookings (sure sell-outs) and other big-name acts, and plan on cabbing. 501 Napoleon Ave. www.tipitinas.com. ℭ **504/895-8477.** Cover varies.

THE BAR SCENE

You won't have any trouble finding a place to drink in New Orleans. Heck, thanks to "go cups," you won't have to spend a minute without a drink in your hand. But there's more to this town than bars (much), and more to bars than Bourbon Street (ditto), so as with all things, let moderation preside. There, that's our sermon. Now read on for

cajun & zydeco JOINTS

There are surprisingly few of these here in the big city (they're plentiful in Lafayette or beyond—see p. 224). You might catch the world-renowned Beausoleil, raucous Pine Leaf Boys, or Lost Bayou Ramblers at **d.b.a.** (p. 174) or **Tipitina's** (p. 178) while they're "in town." Tip's hosts a Fais do-do Sundays at 5pm, with live Cajun music and dancing. Thursday Zydeco Nights at **Rock 'n' Bowl** (p. 177), where the bands and dancers vie for "hottest" title, are a sure thing. **Mulate's** (201 Julia St., at Convention Center Blvd. in the CBD; www.mulates.com; (Ⓒ) **800/854-9149** or 504/522-1492) is a tourist-friendly dinner-dancehall with patient instructors to help you become one of those dancing hotties (well, we can all aspire). The food is ordinary, but the dancing is folksy, all-ages fun. Open 7pm nightly; call to make sure it's not closed for a private event.

some of the most convivial, quaint, or downright eccentric spots in which to spend your precious cocktail budget. Also keep in mind that many restaurants also have excellent bars; see chapter 6.

The French Quarter & the Faubourg Marigny

Bar Tonique ★★ If we lived in this Quarter's-edge neighborhood, this would be our bar. Except we wouldn't be anti-hip service industry locals, and we'd chat up the tourists more. Mostly we'd glow in the candlelight bouncing off the original brick walls, or cozy up with our honey in the smoochy booths in the offshoot alcove. We'd sip one of the prodigious punches like the Blanche Dubois, or a superbly poured cocktail from another era. You know they're serious about the drinks, because there is nothing—nothing—to eat. 820 N. Rampart St. www.bartonique.com. (Ⓒ) **504/324-6045.**

The Bombay Club ★ This grown-up, wood-paneled jazz-and-martini bar bills itself as casually elegant (which politely means don't wear shorts), but it's not at all snooty. It's also a restaurant, and though the food is okay, the romantic, curtained booths in the back are awfully fetching. 830 Conti St., in the Prince Conti Hotel. www.the bombayclub.com. (Ⓒ) **800/699-7711** or 504/586-0972.

Cane & Table ★★★ Opened in 2013 and quickly added to many "Best Bar" lists, C&T's "sophisticated faded" decor is marked by distressed plaster and brick walls, sparkly chandeliers, and a gleaming white marble bar top. There's also a slim, sexy patio. But rum is the star, constructed by some of New Orleans's most revered craft cocktail revivalists with house-made ingredients and squeezed-to-order juice. They call it proto-tiki; we call it high-culture colonialism. The complex flavors may not be for everyone, so start with the Boss Colada. Small plates follow the Caribbean tide: Share the *chicharones,* but bogart the rum-drenched ribs. 1113 Decatur St. www.caneand tablenola.com. (Ⓒ) **504/581-1112.**

Carousel Bar at the Monteleone Hotel ★★★ No, you're not drunk (or maybe you are). The bar *is* spinning (one drink per rotation is the purported ratio—don't worry, its slo-o-o-w). A 2012 expansion added much-needed elbow room, couch seating, grand windows, and another (stationary) bar. It's a grown-up room with grown-up music and prices to match, but a classic. Try the Vieux Carré Cocktail, invented here some 70 years ago. 214 Royal St. www.hotelmonteleone.com. (Ⓒ) **504/523-3341.**

Pat O'Brien's, 718 St. Peter St. (www.patobriens.com; *(C)* **504/525-4823**), is world-famous for the hefty, vivid red drink with the big-wind name. The bar's owners created the Hurricane's rum-heavy formula during a 1940s whiskey shortage. It's served in signature hurricane-lamp–style glasses, or a 3-gallon magnum that's taller than many small children, served with long straws, and takes a group to finish (one profoundly hopes)—all of whom must drink standing up. Naturally, this attracts tourists and collegians in droves. The line can stretch down the street, despite the plethora of nearby drinking options . . . and the fact that the Hurricane is kinda sickly sweet.

Pat O's is nonetheless worth a stop as a reliable, rowdy, friendly introduction to New Orleans. The large, dueling-pianos lounge is fun (music starts at 7pm) and locals populate the main bar up front, but when weather permits, the rambling, often boisterous tropical patio is the place to be. Your Hurricane automatically comes with a $3 charge for the 28-oz. glass, refunded if you return before leaving. If you're keeping it, ask for the packing materials.

Cat's Meow ★   The drinks and drink specials flow aplenty—the better to loosen the larynx at this foremost karaoke mecca. Whether or not you take the mic, the scene is entertaining and the crowds get thick. The action starts at 4pm Monday through Thursday, and 2pm Friday through Sunday. 701 Bourbon St. www.catskaraoke.com. *(C)* **504/523-2788.**

Crescent City Brewhouse ★★   When it was opened by a world-renowned master brewer in 1991, CCB was the first new brewery in New Orleans in more than 70 years. Its German-style beers still hold up in the current microbrewery heyday, and come with a full menu, excellent balcony view, and live jazz. 527 Decatur St. www.crescentcitybrewhouse.com. *(C)* **888/819-9330** or 504/522-0571.

Erin Rose ★★★   Triple threat: unassuming Irish Pub, craft cocktail bar, and **Killer Po' Boys** in the back room. That's the name *and* the bold-but-accurate description of the enterprise. Try the rum-marinated pork-belly po' boy with citrus lime slaw. Killer, indeed. Good drinks, too. 811 Conti St. www.erinrosebar.com. *(C)* **504/523-8619.**

French 75 Bar at Arnaud's ★★★   A beautiful, intimate bar space in one of the Quarter's most venerable restaurants (p. 82). It feels like drinking in New Orleans should: classic and classy (and cigar-smoky later in the eve). Acclaimed bartender Chris Hannah and others are equally adept at vintage cocktails and original concoctions, including a perfect Ramos Gin Fizz and the namesake French 75 champagne cocktail. Order a side of Arnaud's dreamy soufflé potatoes to munch on. 813 Bienville St. www.french75.com. *(C)* **504/523-5433.**

Kerry Irish Pub ★   This pub has darts, pool, a proper pint of Guinness, and Beth Patterson, who mashes traditional Celtic folk, honeyed originals, metal-to-acoustic conversions, and hilariously filthy knockoffs. The Kerry specializes in very-late-night drinking. Nightcap, anyone? 331 Decatur St. www.kerryirishpub.com. *(C)* **504/527-5954.**

Lafitte's Blacksmith Shop ★★   Even if it wasn't the oldest bar (and maybe building) in the Quarter or a legendary pirate's lair, Lafitte's would merit a visit. It's ancient and ultra-atmospheric, so even amid the crowd chatter and blaring jukebox, sipping an ale in the crumbling, cavernlike, candlelit interior is nearly akin to time traveling. Stick with beer and ambience; the mixed drinks are mediocre. 941 Bourbon St. www.lafittesblacksmithshop.com. © **504/593-9761.**

Molly's at the Market ★ *The* hangout for bohos and literary locals, who chew over the state of their world and their city in this casual, comfortable, East Village–feeling bar. A kind of Platonic ideal bar, it's perpetually popular. Hopefully that teeny kitchen in the back reopens soon with something tasty. 1107 Decatur St. www.mollysatthe market.net. © **504/525-5169.**

Napoleon House ★★★ Set in a landmark building, the cave-dark barroom and romantically faded courtyard seem almost too perfectly aged. No plastic surgery here. Even locals come for the toasty muffuletta and signature Pimm's Cup, a cucumber-infused glass of summer. 500 Chartres St. www.napoleonhouse.com. © **504/524-9752.**

Patrick's Bar Vin ★★ Half a block and a million miles from Bourbon Street, Patrick Van Voorhees, one of the city's premier sommeliers, serves conviviality and an excellent selection of wines by the glass (and other spirits). The bar feels like your great uncle's decorous but restful library (if his had rich wood paneling and ample club chairs); the sweet outdoor courtyard screams for something bubbly. 730 Bienville St., in the Hotel Mazarin. www.patricksbarvin.com. © **504/200-3180.**

Pirates Alley Café and Absinthe House ★ Its tucked-away locale behind St. Louis Cathedral has European-style outdoor alleyway tables. Purists will balk at its absinthe service, but it's fun for others—flaming sugar cube and all. The food's nothing much, but it may come in handy. 622 Pirate's Alley. www.piratesalleycafe.com. © **504/524-9332.**

SoBou ★★ At a self-service gastropub, do you tip yourself? The fun here includes tables with their own beer taps and machines dispensing wine (think soda fountains, but grapier). It's less kitschy and more full-service than this sounds—it's by the Commander's Palace folks, after all. A second room is highlighted (literally—and strikingly) by a wall of white LED-lit bottles, and the pedigreed drinks are skillfully composed. The food is hit-or-miss; skip the lauded yet disjointed tuna cones, but not the shrimp *pinchos* or crispy chicken legs. Good happy hour deals. 310 Chartres St., in the W Hotel. www.sobounola.com. © **504/522-4095.**

Tico Tolteca ★★ Welcome (back) to Bali Ha'i, circa 1961. At this tiki temple, there's bamboo, flaming bowls of booze, and a DJ spinning Esquivel. But it's a sincere homage, and these are not your mother's rum sugarbombs: They're deftly made

---

Game On

Pretty much every bar and club in town, no matter how unsporty, becomes a **sports bar** on Saints game days. So if you're looking for a place to watch the game, try anywhere. We'll single out **Mannings** for its wall-size screen and fully reclining leather lounge chairs. Reserve them well in advance and expect to pay a hefty bounty (pardon the poor choice of words), from $25 in food and drink for an average Red Wings game to $100 for a Saints games—chair and beer bucket only (519 Fulton St.; www.facebook.com/ ManningsNOLA; © **504/593-8118**).

If you'd rather drink with Tom Waits than Tom Cruise, you'll appreciate New Orleans's fine dive bars—and by fine, we mean down-and-dirty, neighborhood holes-in-the-wall with regulars straight out of a Jim Jarmusch casting call. **Snake & Jake's Christmas Club Lounge**'s only illumination comes from dwindling Christmas lights, which doesn't make it easier to find this crowded, sweat-soaked, off-the-beaten-path shack. It's BYOD (dog), so you know it's friendly (7612 Oak St., Uptown; ✆ **504/861-2802**). Smoke-filled **Aunt Tiki's** in the depths of Decatur Street is laden with Halloween dreck and affable, slouching degenerates.

As if that's not good enough, the drinks are strong and cheap (1207 Decatur St., French Quarter; ✆ **504/680-8454**). At the Elvis-themed **Kingpin**, 20-somethings in CBGB tees come for shuffleboard and cheap drink specials (1307 Lyons St., Uptown; www.kingpinbar.com; ✆ **504/891-2373**). **The Abbey** has a few motley stained-glass windows, but everything else is the antithesis of church. Yet the David Lynchian clientele pray at their bar 24/7, and a jukebox with classic country *and* the Cramps is worthy of worship (1123 Decatur St., French Quarter; ✆ **504/523-7177**).

cocktails from original recipes and homemade ingredients, done up old- and new-school style by and for deft bar chefs. Ditto for the tapas menu: We're hep to the wee pork *tostones* and the savory braised oxtails. 301 N. Peters St. inside Felipe's, up the back stairs. www.facebook.com/tikitolteca. ✆ **504/267-4406**.

Tujague's ★★   The attraction here is the centuries-old bar with the wall-size mirror, which was hand-carried—whole—from France to New Orleans (well, with some sailing). The bartenders will tell the tale while pouring one of the better Sazeracs in town. There are few seats but usually some colorful characters worth sidling up to. After a recent scare that Tujagues could become a T-shirt shop, we're happier than ever to sidle. 823 Decatur St. www.tujaguesrestaurant.com. ✆ **504/525-8676**.

Elsewhere Around the City

Avenue Pub ★★   This is beer geek heaven, what with 40+ options on tap and many more in bottles. Proper glassware and weekly cask ales show they're serious about their suds, but even the PBR crowd enjoys the upstairs balcony overlooking St. Charles Boulevard (and the jalapeño, cream cheese, and bacon poppers). 1732 St. Charles Ave. www.theavenuepub.com. ✆ **504/586-9243**.

BJ's Lounge ★★   All Bywater roads lead to junked-up corner bar BJ's on Mondays, when the local denizens, pool shooters, and High Life drinkers all groove to the soul-searing blues and raucous rhythms of **King James and the Special Men.** Little Freddie King hits it occasionally, and some guy named Robert Plant played a surprise set in 2013. Cab it. 4301 Burgundy St. www.facebook.com/bjs.bywater. ✆ **504/945-9256**.

Cure ★★★   This mixologist mecca helped instigate the resurgence of both craft cocktails in New Orleans and now-booming Freret Street. The oasis of sleek boasts great small plates and some of the most knowledgeable bar chefs in town, who blend exceptional ingredients with personable chat. Beat the late crowds and go at happy hour. 4905 Freret St. www.curenola.com. ✆ **504/302-2357**.

Le Bon Temps Roulé ★ Another way-uptown, rundown shack with a smoky, cramped bar and decent beer list. So? So schedule your visit to be in town on a Thursday, when the Soul Rebels brass band blows this here roof off. The archetypal local characters are quite welcoming the other 6 nights of the week, too. 4801 Magazine St. ℭ **504/895-8117.**

Oxalis ★★★ Oh, Oxalis, you're like a gastropub boyfriend. You're smart and well-dressed; eclectic but not weird; and yeeeah, you've got that bad boy thing going on . . . you with your mysterious warren of rooms and pumped-up shelves of whiskey. In your main room with its dark wood and long picnic table, you're in worn Levis and a perfectly broken-in, vintage leather jacket: comfortable and classically cool. In the intimate picture room, it's a slim-cut, charcoal gray suit. You get sultry in the big green courtyard, and freaky in the surprising, taxidermy-laden back lounge. That back patio? Sweet dreams, babe. TMI? We'll admit we fell pretty hard for this stylish Bywater bar with its carefully crafted drinks and vibe. Prices are sane and options range from tippy-top shelf to "plastic cap." Food is anything but an afterthought, showing global-inflections in a sweet potato poutine, mussels in tangy coconut milk, and crispy, sticky, Korean-style wings—go on and get messy! 3162 Dauphine St. www.oxalisbywater.com. ℭ **504/267-4776.**

Polo Club Lounge ★★★ Upstairs in the Windsor Court Hotel (p. 64), the well-heeled Sazerac-and-cigar crowd lounge on velvet sofas and leather armchairs to a cool piano combo, as big money deals and serious romances discreetly work themselves out. Or there's the columned lobby's **Cocktail Bar,** where guests and local professionals who prefer a refined hipness enjoy the updated cocktail program and mellow swing. 300 Gravier St. www.windsorcourthotel.com. ℭ **504/523-6000.**

Sazerac Bar at the Roosevelt ★★ If the New Orleans bar scene were a monarchy, the historic Sazerac Bar in the glamorous Roosevelt Hotel might be queen. The sinuous wood walls and Deco-era murals here have borne witness to movie stars, political scandals, and we don't want to know what (check the bullet hole above the back kitchen door). You're here for all that panache as much as the namesake cocktail. 123 Baronne St. www.therooseveltneworleans.com. ℭ **504/529-4733.**

Swizzle Stick Bar ★★ Lu Brow, high goddess and doyenne of New Orleans's craft cocktail revival, started it here. There are cooler bars now, but for those who like some sass with their class, this art-filled spot still serves inventive, finely honed beverages and pre-Prohibition classics (and stellar bar food from adjoining Café Adelaide). 300 Poydras St., in the Loews Hotel. www.cafeadelaide.com. ℭ **504/595-3305.**

21st Amendment ★ New in 2014 but harkening to the prohibition era, the former mob den (for reals) is a bit too spiffy for a proper speakeasy, with its copper-topped bar and, matching Tommy guns, and carefully hung gangster photos. But the small, tucked-away room and well-crafted hooch make for a clean getaway from nearby Bourbon. The big draw is up against the wall: an ancient, gorgeous upright piano. When Tom McDermott plays era-appropriate jazz, the joint's appeal soars. 725 Iberville St., in the Loews Hotel. www.21stamendmentnola.com. ℭ **504/378-7330.**

GAY NIGHTLIFE

Most of these bars catering to New Orleans' thriving LBGTQ community are along the French Quarter's illustrious 4-block "fruit loop." Expect late hours, friendly folk, and *insane* crowds during Southern Decadence (p. 26), Mardi Gras, Halloween,

Easter (yes)—basically at the drop of any quasi-celebratory hat. Also see the resources on p. 238.

Bars & Clubs

In addition to those listed below, you might try the long-running **Golden Lantern,** 1239 Royal St. (© **504/529-2860**), the Cheers of NOLA, described as "half of Noah's Ark, with one of everything—one drag queen, one leather boy, one guy in a suit." For Levi's and leather, check **Rawhide 2010,** 740 Burgundy St. (www.rawhide2010.com; © **504/525-8106**), or the anything-goes **Phoenix,** 941 Elysian Fields Ave. (www. neworleansphoenix.com; © **504/945-9264**).

The Bourbon Pub—Parade Disco ★★ Of the two hyper-popular bars, the downstairs pub is a bit calmer for most of its 24 hours. Upstairs, Parade Disco's high-tech dance setup comes alive on weekends. It gets going around 9pm and early Sundays, when the cover includes free well drinks from 6 to 8pm. 801 Bourbon St. www. bourbonpub.com. © **504/529-2107.** Downstairs is 24/7; upstairs closed Mon and Wed.

Café Lafitte in Exile ★★ This is one of the oldest gay bars in the U.S., established in 1953 and claiming Tennessee Williams as a former patron (believe what you will). There's a theme-night cruise bar downstairs (not so much for teeny-boppers or twinks); a friendly, publike atmosphere upstairs. We don't really get the famous Sunday-night "Love is in the Air" napkin toss, but we love it. 901 Bourbon St. www.lafittes. com. © **504/522-8397.** Downstairs is 24/7; upstairs Thurs–Sun 1pm–till close.

Country Club ★★ It's a bar, a pool, a restaurant, a club, and a nude beach. Sorta. Everyone's welcome at this converted Creole cottage in the Bywater, with its pretty veranda and dining room. You can sip a cocktail while soaking in a Jacuzzi or lounging by the pool without having a fancy hotel room or fancy friends. It's clothing-optional, but no one looks. Okay maybe, but the zero-tolerance policy for hassling keeps it very civil. 634 Louisa St. www.thecountryclubneworleans.com. © **504/945-0742.** Pool access $8–$15; more for events.

Good Friends Bar & Queens Head Pub ★★ This truly is a friendly spot, drawing mixed genders, types, and ages. We like that the decor and music aren't generically techno'ed out—it at least tries to maintain some NOLA feel—and that the straight-welcoming local denizens will gladly chat you up. The upstairs Queens Head Pub is most entertaining during the Sunday 3pm singalong. 740 Dauphine St. www.good friendsbar.com. © **504/566-7191.** Open 24 hr. on weekends; till 2am weekdays; upstairs Thurs–Sun only.

LeRoundup ★ LeRoundup attracts the most diverse crowd around, 24 hours a day: drag queens, the trans community, working boys—even well-groomed men in khakis (now this just sounds like SNL's Stefon). 819 St. Louis St. © **504/561-8340.**

Oz ★★ This world-renowned, bass-heavy dance club might be overrated, but it still has an incredible light show, go-go boys atop the bar (usually), and drag on Wednesdays. It's a see-and-be-seen spot for a mostly young crowd including plenty of straights. The dance-floor view from the upstairs balcony is worth it alone. 800 Bourbon St. www.oznewrleans.com. © **504/593-9491.** Cover varies.

700 Club ★ No, not *that* 700 Club. Just a simple, chill bar where you can wander in and get a decent drink and something from the kitchen. The scene here is *no* scene. Sometimes that's perfect. 700 Burgundy St. www.700ClubNewOrleans.com. © **504/561-1095.**

PERFORMING ARTS, THEATERS & CONCERT HALLS

In addition to the resources below, culture vultures may want to see what's on tap at **Loyola** (www.loyno.edu/calendar) or **Tulane University** (http://tulane.edu/calendar), and at several eclectic performance spaces: **Zeitgeist** (1618 Oretha Castle Haley Blvd.; www.zeitgeistinc.net; ℂ **504/352-1150**); **Marigny Opera House** (725 St. Ferdinand St.; www.marignyoperahouse.org; ℂ **504/948-9998**); and **Café Istanbul** (2372 St. Claude Ave.; www.cafeistanbulnola.com; ℂ **504/975-0286**).

Civic Theatre ★★   A couple of years ago there was nothing in here but the exquisite Deco chandelier and a flock of pigeons. But we're thrilled that this 1906 midsize theater is back. Nothing was spared on sound, lighting, or restoring the graceful, original plasterwork. The 2013 reopening lineup stretched from Russell Brand to John Prine to cult darlings Neutral Milk Hotel (a coup); the bar program is by the folks from Cure (coup #2). 510 O'Keefe St. www.civicnola.com. ℂ **504/272-0865.** Ticket prices vary according to event.

Le Petit Théâtre du Vieux Carré ★★★   One of the oldest community theaters in the U.S., Le Petit has occupied this building since 1923—save for a scary, 2011 shutdown. Fortunately, a new restaurant on the grounds (Tableau; p. 85) enabled the 350-seat Le Petit to reopen and patrons to enjoy a dinner-and-a-play night out. Local productions of classic dramas, musicals, and comedies vary from very good to stellar. 616 St. Peter St. www.lepetittheatre.com. ℂ **504/522-2081.** Tickets $30–$50.

Mahalia Jackson Theater for the Performing Arts ★   This cultural hub (located in Armstrong Park bordering the French Quarter) is home to the Louisiana Philharmonic Orchestra, the New Orleans Opera Association, and the New Orleans Ballet Association. The handsome, midcentury theater is spacious but not big, so every seat is decent. It also hosts theater, dance troupes, rock concerts, and other live acts. 1419 Basin St. www.mahaliajacksontheater.com. ℂ **504/287-0351.** Ticket prices vary according to event.

Saenger Theatre ★★★   Following an extensive, gajillion-dollar, post-Katrina renovation, this magnificent 1927 stunner from the glory movie-house days was reopened in 2013 to much fanfare. Now technologically state of the art, the Saenger hosts concerts, comedy shows, theater, and other performances. 1111 Canal St. www.saengernola.com. ℂ **504/287-0351.** Ticket prices vary according to event.

Southern Repertory Theatre ★   Focusing (mostly) on Southern playwrights and themes, Southern Rep's productions are consistently high quality, if not always high budget. Anything written by, starring, or otherwise mentioning the hyper-talented Ricky Graham is probably worth catching. Location varies. www.southernrep.com. ℂ **504/522-6545.** Ticket prices vary by production, but usually $20–$40.

CRUISING THE MISSISSIPPI

The *Creole Queen* and the slightly smaller steamboat *Natchez* both host pleasant (if a bit touristy) river cruises with mediocre Creole buffets, but much better live jazz and dancing against a backdrop of the city's sparkling skyline. For more on this nightlife option, see p. 159.

SHOPPING NEW ORLEANS

Shopping in New Orleans is a highly evolved leisure activity, with a shop for every strategy and a fix for every shopaholic—at every budget. Think of the endless souvenir shops on Bourbon Street and swanky antiques stores on Royal Street as the bookends for all the shopping New Orleans has to offer. There's a high-end mall, quaint boutiques filled with strange items gathered from all parts of the globe, a brand spanking new outlet mall, and shops featuring enticing hand-crafted objects produced by local, somewhat twisted, folk artists.

There are sweet deals to be had, or lavish riches to be spent, artworks to be admired, new outfits to wear home. But as all shoppers know, the fun is in the hunt. And New Orleans has some smashing hunting grounds.

MAJOR HUNTING GROUNDS

ART MARKETS If you're in town on the last Saturday of any month, consider a trip to the **Palmer Park Arts Market** (S. Carrollton and S. Claiborne Aves., last stop on the St. Charles streetcar line; www.artscouncil ofneworleans.org; © **504/523-1465**). From 10am to 4pm you'll find paintings, pottery, glass, mosaics, jewelry, handmade frames, and more from quality, juried artists. At the Marigny's hip **Frenchmen Art Market** we like the cool leather jewelry and music photography, and couldn't resist a snap-front shirt embroidered with Big Foot for $35. It's open Thursday to Saturday 7pm to 1am, and Sunday 6pm to midnight (619 Frenchmen St.; www.frenchmenartmarket.com). Admission to both markets is free and all goods are original, local, and surprisingly affordable.

CANAL PLACE At the foot of Canal Street (365 Canal St.) near the Mississippi River, this sophisticated shopping mall holds more than 30 shops, many of them elegant retail chains like Brooks Brothers, Saks Fifth Avenue, Coach, Armani, and a sparkling new Tiffany & Co. There's also a two-story Anthropologie, a recently expanded branch of local jeweler **Mignon Faget** (p. 196), and the RHINO gallery of gorgeous, locally made goods (Right Here in New Orleans). Open Monday to Saturday 10am to 7pm, Sunday noon to 6pm. www.theshopsatcanalplace.com.

THE FRENCH MARKET These historic, open-air shops begin on Decatur Street across from Jackson Square; offerings include candy, housewares, fashion, crafts, toys, New Orleans memorabilia, and jewelry. Recent renovations added a stage for live music or cooking demos, and much-improved food booths include an oyster bar, a terrific fresh juice bar, and the tasty **Meals from the Heart.** The farmers' market section has pretty fruit and veggies, and the stalls with foodstuffs—including local seafood, meats, and spices—can pack your purchases for travel or shipping; the flea market section (near Esplanade) has lots of low-end souvenirs (good buys, if not good quality) and a smattering of actual art and handmade goods. It's a fun stroll. Open daily 10am to 6pm; www.frenchmarket. org. See also p. 125.

JAX BREWERY   Just across from Jackson Square at 600–620 Decatur St., the old brewery building has been transformed into a jumble of shops and cafes (and good bathrooms). It's a good stop for clothing and souvenirs, particularly the crawfish logo'd polo shirts and other preppie wear at **Perlis.** Open daily 10am to 7pm. www. jacksonbrewery.com.

JULIA STREET   Many of the city's best contemporary art galleries (many listed below under "Art Galleries") line Julia Street from Camp Street to the river. The quality of local talent exhibited here—among both creators and curators—is quite astounding.

MAGAZINE STREET   The Garden District's premier shopping drag, 6 miles of antiques, boutiques, galleries, and all manner of restaurants in 19th-century brick storefronts and quaint cottage-like buildings, from Washington Street to Audubon Park. Prime sections are, roughly, the 3700 to 4300 blocks (with the odd block or so of nothing); 1900 to 2100; and 5400 to 5700 blocks. Download or pick up a copy of "Magazine Street Shoppers' Guide" for a free store list and map. www.magazinestreet. com. A car or JazzyPass (p. 235) will help you traverse the avenue.

THE OUTLET COLLECTION AT RIVERWALK   Brand spanking new in 2014, **Neiman Marcus Last Call, Coach,** and 75 other outlet stores fill the 3-story, $80 million mall. Bargains? That's a bonus when you can walk from the French Quarter, shop with a daiquiri in hand, and enjoy the best view from a mall food court in existence at tables overlooking the Mississippi. It's located behind the Hilton at 500 Port of New Orleans Pl. (www.riverwalkneworleans.com; ⓒ **504/522-1555**).

RIVERBEND, MAPLE & OAK STREET   To reach these fetching Carrollton area shops, ride the St. Charles Avenue streetcar to stop no. 44, then walk a block down Maple Street. There, **Maple Street Book Shop** (p. 192), upscale boutique **Angelique,** and delectable po' boy shop **The Sammich** inhabit several renovated old buildings. Four blocks up Dublin Street is the happening Oak Street shopping and dining district. Check out the excellent **Blue Cypress Books,** local goods from **Detour,** and weird and wacky **Rabbit Ears** gallery. For refreshments, try famed restaurant **Jacque-Imo's** (p. 109), and the **Plum Street Snoball** stand a block away.

SHOPPING A TO Z

Antiques

Bush Antiques ★   There is serious stuff here, mostly of the European variety, and some not so serious. But the warren of rooms, some cunningly arranged according to theme, are giddy fun to browse whether or not you're in the market for a 19th-century French Empire settee or an elaborately embroidered priest's garment. Open Monday to Saturday 11am to 5pm. 2109 Magazine St. www.bushantiques.com. Ⓒ **504/581-3518.**

Cohen & Sons ★★ Specializing in antique weapons, coins, and currency from points near and far, dating back to B.C. They're not the friendliest folk (unless you're a serious collector), but it's well worth a look (and a locally minted antique coin or doubloon from actual sunken treasure make splendid souvenirs). Open Monday to Saturday 9:30am to 5pm. 437 Royal St. www.cohenantiques.com. Ⓒ **504/522-3305.**

Collectible Antiques ★★ One of our favorites of the dusty, jumbled, and eclectic antiques/junk stores on the Esplanade end of Decatur. Its stock runs from Art Deco to 1960s collectibles. Open daily noon to 6pm. 1232 Decatur St. Ⓒ **504/566-0399.**

Greg's Antiques ★ A funky mixed bag of serious antiques, junky used furniture, salvaged windows and ironwork, and original local art on consignment—not necessarily pedigreed but at pretty decent prices—make this a personal favorite. Frequent shipments and sales mean goods move fast. **Upcycle,** Greg's most welcome baby sister shop across the street, turns clarinets into lamps and jet engines into coffee tables. Daily 10am to 8pm. 1209 and 1221 Decatur St. www.gregsantiques.net. Ⓒ **504/202-8577.**

Keil's Antiques ★★ Established in 1899 and currently run by the fourth generation of the founding family, Keil's has a considerable collection of 18th- and 19th-century French and English furniture, chandeliers, jewelry, and decorative items spanning three crowded floors and most budgets. Try to talk to one of the members of the family for tales of the doorman who worked his spot for 78 years and whatever other stories you can coax out of them. Pop in Monday to Saturday 9am to 5pm. 325 Royal St. www.keilsantiques.com. Ⓒ **504/522-4552.**

Lucullus ★★★ A wonderful collection of culinary antiques as well as 17th-through 19th-century furnishings to "complement the grand pursuits of cooking, dining, and imbibing." You'll find all manner of china, Art Deco silverware, oyster plates, and even absinthe accoutrements here. They're open Monday to Saturday 9am to 5pm (closed Mon late spring to summer). 610 Chartres St. www.lucullusantiques.com. Ⓒ **504/528-9620.**

Magazine Antique Mall ★ Diggers will dig the superb browsing and many good deals found among the 50-plus variegated stalls here. Daily 10:30am to 5:30pm (Sun from noon). 3017 Magazine St. www.facebook.com/magazineantiquemall. Ⓒ **504/896-9994.**

M.S. Rau ★★★ The sheer scale and absurdity of the inventory makes century-old Rau a must-see for everyone and a destination for serious buyers. Every opulent item that could possibly be crafted from fine metals, gems, crystal, wood, china, and marble, plus articles made by every name known to the antique world, is here for the ogling or the investing, filling room after jaw-dropping room. We particularly like the selection of walking canes and the cave bear skeleton poised in attack-mode. Most every item has a story to tell, and the knowledgeable sales reps pleasantly indulge your curiosity (even if you're just a looky-loo). Monday to Saturday 9am to 5:15pm. 630 Royal St. www.rauantiques.com. Ⓒ **866/349-0705** or 504/523-5660.

Art Galleries

Galleries share the **Royal** and **Magazine Street** landscapes with the aforementioned antiques shops, while in the Warehouse District, the blocks numbered 300 to 700 on **Julia Street** house some 20 contemporary fine-arts galleries, anchored by the **Contemporary Arts Center** and **Ogden Museum of Southern Art** (p. 136). For the more intrepid, explore the burgeoning lowbrow and outsider art movement around **St. Claude Avenue** (www.scadnola.com).

Angela King Gallery ★★★ One of the oldest and still best contemporary art galleries in the city, Angela King shows works by significant artists such as Peter Max, Andrew Baird, Richard Currier, Steve Taylor, Raymond Douillet, Patterson & Barnes, and Michelle Gagliano . . . *and* has a lagniappe mini-gallery dedicated to the art of Dr. Seuss. The gallery is open 10am to 5pm (Sun from 11am). 241 Royal St. www.angelakinggallery.com. ℂ **504/524-8211.**

Antieau Gallery ★★★ We adore the supremely clever Chris Roberts-Antieau's whimsical side: sewn works that riff on current events and social mores; and her dark side: macabre snow globes and a dollhouse recreation of the *In Cold Blood* crime scene. Monday to Saturday 10am to 5pm, Sunday 11am to 8pm. 927 Royal St. www.antieaugallery.com. ℂ **504/304-0849.**

Arthur Roger Gallery ★★ Arthur Roger helped develop the city's fine-art scene when he opened in New Orleans more than 30 years ago, tying the local community to the New York art world and pioneering the Warehouse District. Still blazing trails, Roger schedules shows that range from strongly regional to far-flung work. The gallery represents Francis Pavy, Ida Kohlmeyer, Dawn DeDeaux, Dale Chihuly, Gene Koss, and the stunning, brazen figurative photographs of recently departed local George Dureau. Open Monday to Saturday 10am to 5pm. 432-434 Julia St. www.arthurrogergallery.com. ℂ **504/522-1999.**

Carol Robinson Gallery ★★ The grande dame of the local contemporary Southern arts scene, Robinson still shows accessible but surprisingly affordable works, including the stunning pastels of Sandra Burshell, Jere Allen's mysterious figures wafting in white, James King's haunting oils, and Christina Goodman's exquisite, minute tableaus. Tuesday and Thursday through Saturday 10am to 5pm. 840 Napoleon Ave. www.carolrobinsongallery.com. ℂ **504/895-6130.**

Christopher Porche-West ★★★ Porche-West's stunning portrait photographs are themselves works of art, but when he sculpts and frames them within magnificent assemblages of architectural remnants, mechanical parts, natural materials, and found oddities, he creates highly collectible, singular statement pieces. They keep irregular hours here, so call for an appointment or just take your chances and drop by. 3201 Burgundy St. www.porche-west.com. ℂ **504/947-3880.**

Cole Pratt Gallery ★ A showcase for Southern artists whose creations include abstract and realist paintings, sculptures, and ceramics. The art is of the highest quality, prices are surprisingly reasonable, and the staff is welcoming. Open Tuesday through Saturday 10am to 5pm. 3800 Magazine St. www.coleprattgallery.com. ℰ **504/891-6789.**

Derby Pottery ★★   One of Mark Derby's hand-pressed tiles, glazed in gleaming single hues, makes for a lovely keepsake (particularly the New Orleans street-name tile reproductions). One hundred make for a stunning backsplash or fireplace surround. Ceramic mugs and water meter clocks make excellent, handmade souvenirs. Open Monday to Saturday 10am to 5pm. 2029 Magazine St. www.derbypottery.com. ℰ **504/586-9003.**

Dr. Bob ★★★   He of the now-iconic "BE NICE OR LEAVE" folk-art signs. See p. 5.

A Gallery for Fine Photography ★★★   Do not skip this incredibly well-stocked photography gallery, even if you aren't in the market. It emphasizes New Orleans and Southern history, as well as contemporary culture, including music and black culture. You can buy Ernest Bellocq's legendary Storyville photos, Herman Leonard's jazz images, or something from just about every period, style, or noted photographer. Thursday through Monday 10:30am to 5:30pm or by appointment. 241 Chartres St. www.agallery.com. ℰ **504/568-1313.**

Hemmerling Gallery ★   Bill Hemmerling's paintings of spirituals, jazz musicians, and his muse, "Sweet Olive," have charmed collectors and curators alike with their dignified naïveté. His second career as a painter spanned just 7 years, following his retirement from Sears and until his death in 2009. The gallery features giclees and a few rare originals, as well as works by several protégés. Daily 11am to 6pm (Sun to 5pm). 733 Royal St. www.hemmerlingart.com. ℰ **504/524-0909.**

Jonathan Ferrara Gallery ★★★   Since 1998, Ferrara has been showing emerging cross-media artists. Exhibitions are typically accessible yet thought-provoking, with an eye toward playfulness and irony. Skylar Fein's pop pundit pieces are both hilarious and horrifying in their truth; the G.A.S. Caravaggio photobombs are equally stunning and silly. The gallery is open Monday to Saturday 11am to 5pm. 400a Julia St. www.jonathanferraragallery.com. ℰ **504/522-5471.**

Kurt E. Schon, Ltd. ★★   Behold the country's largest inventory of 19th-century European paintings. The stunning collection, rivaling or exceeding many museums, includes French and British Impressionist and post-Impressionist paintings as well as art from the Royal Academy and the French Salon. You can visit them Monday to Friday 10am to 5pm, Saturday 10am to 3pm. 510 St. Louis St. www.kurteschonltd.com. ℰ **504/524-5462.**

Martine Chaisson Gallery ★★   The stark, sweeping space screams for high-impact, highly saturated imagery, and so far Martine delivers, particularly with Herman Mhire's manipulated portraiture, J. T. Blatty's striking photography of nudes with fossils, and Norman Mooney's frisson-inducing carbon-on-paper imagery. Wednesday to Saturday 11am to 5pm or by appointment. 727 Camp St. www.martine chaissongallery.com. ℰ **504/302-7942.**

New Orleans School of GlassWorks & Printmaking Studio ★★★
This institution, with 25,000 square feet of studio space, houses a 550-pound tank of hot molten glass and a pre–Civil War press. At this sister school to the Louvre Museum

of Decorative Arts, established glasswork artists, bookbinders, and master printmakers display their work, demonstrate glass-blowing, and teach classes, including the popular "Wine & Design" gatherings. Open Monday to Saturday 10am to 5pm. 727 Magazine St. www.neworleansglassworks.com. ℭ **504/529-7279.**

OMG! ★ Well-curated religious art, new and reclaimed, anchored by wonderful statuary and Jan Keels' stirring gossamer, oil-on-wood angels. They also carry the fab Virgins Saints & Angels jewelry. Daily 10am to 6pm. 912B Decatur St. www.omg-nola.com. ℭ **504/522-8443.**

Photo Works ★★ Photographer Louis Sahuc's family has been in New Orleans "since day one," and his life's work has been photo-documenting iconic New Orleans imagery, such as Jackson Square swathed in fog, or fragments of ironwork. Open every day except Wednesday from 10am to 5:30pm. 521 St. Ann St. www.photoworks neworleans.com. ℭ **504/593-9090.**

Red Truck Gallery★★ Noah Antieau's mad, sharp sensibility has resulted in a collection of conceptual art that is sometimes bizarre, often brilliant, and utterly covetous. We'd take any of Jason D'Aquino's minute masterpieces on matchbooks; Bryan Cunningham's whack folk assemblages; or Adam Wallacavage's sea-creature chandeliers. Daily 10am to 9pm (Fri–Sat till 10pm). 938 Royal St. www.redtruckgallery.com. ℭ **504/522-3630.**

Rodrigue Studio New Orleans ★ Cajun artist George Rodrigue's 2013 death may have softened some attitudes toward his ubiquitous Blue Dog, but it's still the Freddy Krueger of New Orleans art: the glaring, bordering-on-kitsch canine, shown in every imaginable pose and setting, invades your consciousness and torments your life. The gallery also displays Rodrigue's considerable classical talents. The studio is open daily 10am to 6pm (Sun till 5pm). 730 Royal St. www.george rodrigue.com. ℭ **504/581-4244.**

Tresor ★ New to the city, this outpost of a Florida gallery leans a little too heavily on pop surrealism tropes, but it's positively worth a visit for Lisa Brawn's celebrity portraits in woodcut and Dave Hind's remarkable piecemealed metalwork amalgamations. Monday and Thursday 11am to 6pm, Friday and Saturday 11am to 8pm, Sunday noon to 6pm. 811 Royal St. www.tresorgallery.com. ℭ **504/309-3991.**

Books

Arcadian Books ★★ Bibliophiles will bask in these wondrous, dusty stacks, especially lovers of the classics (in English and Latin); the history (local and far beyond) inquisitive; and seekers of literature in French, German, or Russian. Proprietor Russell Desmond is ridiculously knowledgeable and nearly as personable, and knows every item in this gloriously decrepit grotto. Monday 10:30am to 5:30pm, Tuesday to Saturday 9:30am to 5:30pm, Sunday 11am to 4pm. 714 Orleans Ave. ℭ **504/523-4138.**

Beckham's Bookshop ★★ Sixty thousand volumes carefully collected by the store's owners jam the two floors at beloved Beckham's—a pillar of the Quarter's thriving indie bookshop scene for nearly 50 years. Used books for all interests (browse the glass cases for rare gems) and a fine, small selection of new, locally focused titles. Daily 10am to 5pm. 228 Decatur St. www.beckhamsbookshop.com. ℭ **504/522-9875.**

Books a Million ★ Hand it to the chains that are still committed to bookselling, and this one stocks a good selection of local titles. If you're passing through, this is a good place to pick up New Orleans–related books on your way to or from the city. Open Monday to Saturday 10am to 9pm, Sunday noon to 6pm. 150 Northshore Blvd. in North Shore Sq., Slidell. www.booksamillion.com. ✆ **985/641-4813.**

Crescent City Books ★★ These two floors of dusty treasures hold serious literature for the seriously literate. The emphasis is on rare history, local interest, literary criticism, philosophy, and art. It's also a general hub of info about literary events. Daily 10am to 8pm (Sun until 5pm). 230 Chartres St. www.crescentcitybooks.com. ✆ **800/524-4997.**

Faulkner House Books ★★★ That Nobel prize–winner William Faulkner lived here while writing his early works is but one literary morsel in this winning recipe for a perfect small bookshop. Shelf after high shelf is occupied by decidedly desirable titles, from stunning first editions to Southern authors and current best-sellers. Just one room and a hallway, Faulkner House feels like somebody's private home (it is)—but the gracious advice and judicious selection make manifest the art of bookselling. Daily 10am to 5:30pm. 624 Pirate's Alley. www.faulknerhouse.net. ✆ **504/524-2940.**

Garden District Book Shop ★★★ This sweet, medium-size shop is stocked with just about every New Orleans– or Louisiana-themed book you can think of, no matter what the focus: interiors, exteriors, food, Creoles, fiction, poetry, you name it—including many signed copies. Best sellers, too. Daily 10am to 6pm (Sun until 5pm). 2727 Prytania St. (in the Rink). www.gardendistrictbookshop.com. ✆ **504/895-2266.**

Kitchen Witch ★★★ In a town of foodies, chefs, cooks, and eaters of all inter-ests and proficiencies, this quirky used cookbook store is the rainbow's end. It stocks nearly 10,000 volumes, from the ultra-rare to the just-released—and if they don't have it, they'll find it. Set the egg timer or you could spend way too much time browsing and chatting here. Monday to Friday 10am to 5pm, Saturday to Sunday 10am to 6pm (closed occasional Tuesdays; call to confirm). 631 Toulouse St. www.kwcookbooks.com. ✆ **504/528-8382.**

Maple Street Book Shop ★★ This beloved uptown destination just celebrated its 50th anniversary. Maple Street satisfies bookworms seeking new, used, or chil-dren's books. Monday to Saturday 10am to 6pm, Sunday 11am to 5pm. 7523 Maple St. www.maplestreetbookshop.com. ✆ **504/866-4916.**

Octavia Books ★★★ For those who adore independent bookstores, this far-uptown beauty with its sweet, tiny patio (complete with waterfall) is worth the detour. There is much more to savor here, in the extensive, well-selected stock and in the frequent signings and readings. Open Monday to Saturday 10am to 6pm, Sunday noon to 5pm. 513 Octavia St. (at Laurel St.). www.octaviabooks.com. ✆ **504/899-7323.**

Candies, Pralines & Pastries

Blue Frog Chocolates ★★ Perhaps the finest chocolate and candy collection in the city. Just for starters, it carries Nancy's truffles, Norman Love chocolates, Michel Cluizel fresh butter creams from France, and Jordan almonds (good ones are difficult to find). Hop on over Monday to Friday 10am to 6pm, Saturday 10am to 5pm, and Sunday noon to 5pm. 5707 Magazine St. www.bluefrogchocolates.com. ✆ **504/269-5707.**

Laura's Candies ★ Charming Laura's is said to be the city's oldest candy store, established in 1913. The pralines are fabulous but the rich, delectable (if pricey) golf ball–size truffles are a personal favorite indulgence. Get your fix daily 10am to 9pm. 331 Chartres St. www.laurascandies.com. *C* **504/525-3880.**

Southern Candymakers ★★★ The pralines here include the usual suspects and the nontraditional (coconut and sweet potato!), but they're all creamylicious. They're made fresh right in front of you (if the display doesn't reel you in, the aroma will). We swoon for the pecan-laden *tortues*, and the boxed chocolate crawfish and gator pops make fine gifts. Open daily 10am to 7pm (1010 Decatur St. only until 6pm). 334 Decatur St. (factory) www.southerncandymakers.com. *C* **504/523-5544.** 1010 Decatur St. *C* **504/525-6170.**

Sucré ★★★ *Ultimate Cake Off* winner Tariq Hanna's high-end confections and gorgeous chocolates are ideal for gifts, or for an afternoon indulgence at this stylish cafe. They're not overly sweet, so opinions vary from bland to brilliant. The sherbet-hued macarons are more than just good-looking, and the boozy "Big Kid Shakes" are great fun. But we're partial to the minicakes, like the luscious "Tiffany." A gorgeous new French Quarter location adds small plates, made-to-order soufflés, and afternoon high tea. Sunday to Thursday 8am to 10pm, Friday and Saturday 8am to midnight (hours may vary, so call ahead). 3025 Magazine St.; 622 Conti St. www.shopsucre.com. *C* **504/520-8311.**

Costumes & Masks

Costumery is big business in New Orleans, and not just for Mardi Gras. Playing dress-up needs no event, and nothing is too elaborate. In addition to these shops, try thrift stores where slightly used outfits can sometimes be found at a fraction of their original cost. Troll lower Decatur and Dauphine in the Bywater (especially **Le Garage,** 1234 Decatur St.; *C* **504/522-6639**). Also check **Uptown Costume & Dance Company** (4326 Magazine St.; www.uptowncostume.com; *C* **504/895-7969;** Mon–Tues 11am–6pm, Wed–Fri 11am–7pm, Sat 10am–6pm).

Carl Mack Presents ★★ The doyen of Mardi Gras entertainment now has a French Quarter shop that rents or creates ornate costumes for Fat Tuesday or any day. This is high-production-value stuff—no naughty nurses here. Monday to Friday 11am to 5pm or by appointment. 223 Dauphine St. www.carlmack.com. *C* **504/949-4009.**

Fifi Mahony's ★★ Wig wackiness, why not? Cutesy or crazy, have the hair you've always wanted (even if just for the day). Worth visiting just to see (or get) their outrageous custom pieces. Salon and makeup services, too. Sunday to Wednesday noon to 6pm, Thursday to Saturday 11am to 7pm. 934 Royal St. www.fifimahonys.com. *C* **504/525-4343.**

Fashion, Vintage Clothing, Hats & Accessories

Dollz & Dames ★★ If the Frenchmen Street jitterbugging scene has released your inner pin-up gal, this is your store. The vintage-y frocks make for darling datewear but we'd wear them any time. Tops cost $60 to $130, and dresses are under $200. Cute accessories, custom T-strap dance shoes, and helpful help, too. Open daily noon to 6pm. 216 Decatur St. www.dollzanddames.com. *C* **504/522-5472.**

Fleur de Paris ★★★ The 1920s and 1930s elegance on display here brings us to our knees with covetousness. Their hand-blocked, stylishly trimmed hats are expensive, but these are works of art. They also have luscious stockings and scarves, an ever-changing collection of vintage gowns, and custom design services. Open daily 10am to 6pm. 523 Royal St. www.fleurdeparis.net. ✆ **504/525-1899.**

Love It ★★   It's easy to pass by this tiny jewel box of a shop, where Danna Lea crafts exquisite purses and accessories from found leather and adornments; and restyles vintage clothes. Not inexpensive, but one-of-a-kind and worth the splurge. Feel the love Wednesday to Sunday 10am to 6pm. 713 Bienville St. www.loveitnola.com. ✆ **504/523-7888.**

Meyer the Hatter ★★★   Family-owned for more than 100 years, this haberdashery has one of the largest selections of fine hats and caps in the South. Men will find distinguished international labels such as Bailey, Stetson, Kangol, Dobbs, and Borsalino (the women's collection is smaller). Let them fuss over you and pick out the proper feather for your new chapeau—these hat whisperers know just how to top every head. Open Monday to Saturday 10am to 5:45pm. 120 St. Charles Ave. www.meyerthehatter.com. ✆ **504/525-1048.**

Muse ★★   Gentlemen, should the city and the spirit move you so that only the emergency infusion of a metallic paisley, madras plaid, seersucker sport jacket will suffice, Muse will fix you right up (seasonally, and for only about $250). Monday to Saturday 10am to 5:45pm. 532 St. Peter St. (on Jackson Sq.). www.museinspiredfashion.com. ✆ **504/522-8738.**

Oh! ★★   Whether or not you need a cocktail dress or ball gown, Sandy Thigpen's collection of vintage new and gently used finery is nonetheless an utter scream—from Halston disco pants to last year's perfect Chanel suit to an authentic fringed flapper get-up to, well, you get the idea. Exquisite, high-end lingerie as well. Buy now and figure out the occasion later. Daily 10:30am to 5:30pm (closed Tues–Wed). 829 Royal St. www.ohfinelingerie.com. ✆ **504/524-8807.**

Rubenstein's ★★   Many a proper young New Orleans man learned the art of attire here. For 90 years the hallowed haberdasher has outfitted gents in custom suits, fine menswear, and perfect prepwear. Their pros will dress you to the nines and fit you to a T. Quick-turnaround tailoring gets you Galatoire's-ready. Daily 10am to 5:45pm (Fri–Sat until 6pm). 102 St. Charles Ave. www.rubensteinsneworleans.com. ✆ **504/581-6666.**

Trashy Diva ★★★   There's actually nothing trashy about the 1940s and '50s vintage-inspired clothes here. The flirty, curve-flattering numbers in silks and velvets appeal to both Bettys and Goths, as do the similar-era shoes and va-va-voom corsets and lingerie. Check the sales racks for good bargains. All shops open daily but hours vary, so give a ring. 537 Royal St. ✆ **504/581-4555.** Shoes and lingerie at 829-831 Chartres St. Another location at 2048 Magazine St. ✆ **504/299-8777.** www.trashydiva.com.

UAL ★   Destination One for local and visiting fashionistas, UAL offers incredible deals on discontinued and leftover designer goods (Chloe, Alaia, Stella McCartney, Jason Wu, Lanvin, Chanel, Sanctuary). The ridiculous markdowns and sparse stock can lead to fiercely competitive (but utterly satisfying) hit-or-miss guerilla shopping. Daily 10am to 8pm. 518 Chartres St. ✆ **504/301-4437.**

Violet's ★   This is a great temptation among French Quarter shops, given our adoration of romantic, Edwardian, and '20s-inspired clothes in lush velvets and satins. The dazzling creations here come with appropriate accessories (jewelry, hats, scarves). Contemporary wear as well, with an emphasis on bling. Monday to

Thursday 11am to 7pm, Friday and Saturday 10am to 8pm, Sunday 10am to 7pm. 808 Chartres St. ☏ **504/569-0088.**

Food, Wine & Liquor

Every souvenir shop in town stocks spices, hot sauce, coffee, and beignet mix. The French Market vendors do too, along with meats and seafoods, and they're set up to ship it home or pack it for travel. If you get a hankering from home, try www.cajun grocer.com.

Keife & Co ★★ If you just can't get out the door, Keife & Co. will deliver a basket with gourmet meats, cheeses, and wine to your Central Business District hotel room. If you *can* get out, stop in to grab a bottle on your way to the restaurant or to take home. Tuesday to Saturday 10am to 8pm. 801 Howard Ave. www.keifeandco.com. ☏ **504/523-7272.**

Martin Wine Cellar ★★ Martin carries an eye-popping selection of wines, beers, and spirits for the connoisseur, the casual imbiber, or the BYOWer, many at surprisingly reasonable prices. Good selection of imported teas, cookies, cheeses, and such for in-room picnicking. At press time, construction of a new store and bistro on the site of their original 1946 Central City location was nearing completion. Open Tuesday to Saturday 10am to 7pm. 3500 Magazine St. and 3837 Barronne St. www.martinwine.com. ☏ **504/894-7420.**

Vieux Carré Wine and Spirits ★★ If you're looking for Herbsaint, absinthe, or Sazerac rye, are a serious wine buyer, or just want a bottle for your hotel room or dinner, this densely packed French Quarter shop will fit the bill. Monday to Saturday 9am to 9pm. 422 Chartres St. ☏ **504/568-9463.**

W.I.N.O. ★ Try before you buy with the Wine Institute of New Orleans's enomatic system. Top up a debit card (do this first; it's easy to run up a jolt of a tab) and set to dispensing 1-, 2-, or 3-ounce pours of some 120 wines, covering many regions and varietals. Order some cheese or tapas, and grab a bottle or 3 for tomorrow's dinner. Or lunch. They're late risers here—open Monday and Tuesday 1pm to 10pm, Wednesday and Thursday 1pm to midnight, Friday and Saturday 1pm to 2am, and Sunday 2pm to 10pm. 610 Tchoupitoulas St. www.winoschool.com. ☏ **504/324-8000.**

Gifts, Home Decor & Bath

Aidan Gill for Men ★★★ Sharp-dressed men and gentlemen gift givers start here for fine accessories and old-fashioned men's grooming implements brought thoroughly up to date. Look for old-fashioned shaving brushes and hand-held razors, fine colognes, and top-shelf skin- and hair-care products. Their superb grooming services start with a hot towel and a whiskey: no less authority than *Playboy* called their straight-razor shave best in America ($40 plus tip). Sunday to Friday 10am to 6pm, Saturday 9am to 5pm (Fulton St. hours differ, so call first). 2026 Magazine St. www.aidangillformen.com. ☏ **504/587-9090.** 550 Fulton St. ☏ **504/566-4903.**

Hazelnut ★ Most of the housewares and gifts here are cute but unremarkable, with one notable exception: the line of toile items with a customized pattern of iconic New Orleans scenes—the St. Charles streetcar, a live oak tree, St. Louis Cathedral, and such. It's desperately darling and we want it all—the bedding, tote bag, and picture frame. Sigh. *Fun fact: Mad Men*'s Bryan Batt is part owner. Monday to Saturday 10am to 6pm (till 5pm in summer). 5515 Magazine St. www.hazelnutneworleans.com. ☏ **504/891-2424.**

Hové ★★★ The oldest perfumery in the city, Hové features a fabulous selection of all-natural scents for men and women. Original creations ("Kiss in the Dark") and Southern smells such as vetiver and tea olive, available in many forms, make lovely presents, even for you. Literature buffs will appreciate the letter from author Tom Robbins confirming that his *Jitterbug Perfume* shop was roughly based on Hové. Daily 10am to 6pm (Sun from 11am). 434 Chartres St. www.hoveparfumeur.com. ℂ **504/525-7827.**

Queork ★★ All-cork merchandise seems a strange concept, till you spy that want-want-want $59 iPad cover. Then it's a slippery slope to a cork belt and cork-upholstered furniture. Great for gifts (and they say it's all surprisingly durable). Open Thursday to Monday 10am to 6pm. 838 Chartres St. www.queork.com. ℂ **504/481-4910.**

Simon of New Orleans/Antiques on Jackson ★★ Folk artist Simon, whose brightly painted signs are seen throughout New Orleans in homes and businesses, will paint to order your own personal sign and ship it to you. There's also a particularly good collection of primitive furniture, antiques, and hodgepodgery. Daily 10am to 5pm (Sun 11am–4pm; Mon by appt. only). 1028 Jackson Ave. ℂ **504/524-8201.**

Jewelry

Marion Cage ★★★ Cage's ultrafine, exquisitely wrought work is popular with collectors in Paris and New York, where she worked before opening this gallery in her native New Orleans. Clean lines of matte rose and yellow gold, rhodium, and hardwoods start around $90, like the tiny, perfectly detailed Chinese zodiac charms. Tuesday to Saturday 10am to 5pm. 3719 Magazine St. www.marioncage.com. ℂ **504/891-8848.**

Mignon Faget, Ltd. ★★ Faget, a New Orleans native, lends her signature style to New Orleans–specific designs in gold, silver, and bronze d'oré (and housewares)—all superb souvenirs or gifts. Monday to Saturday 10am to 7pm, Sunday noon to 6pm (Magazine St. open Mon–Sat 10am–6pm). Canal Place, Level 1. www.mignonfaget.com. ℂ **504/524-2973.** 3801 Magazine St. ℂ **504/891-2005.**

Thomas Mann Designs/Gallery I/O ★ Local jewelry designer Thomas Mann is known for his "techno-romantic" work with metal and found objects, creating curious pieces of highly original jewelry and housewares that straddle a line between classic and contemporary. Monday to Saturday 11am to 5pm. 1810 Magazine St. www.thomasmann.com. ℂ **800/875-2113** or 504/581-2111.

Music

Domino Sound Records ★ A one-room beats shop off the beaten track. Stellar old ska/rock steady and R&B collections, world music from countries you've never heard of, local weirdness, and pretty much everything Sun Ra ever put out. All vinyl except for about 37 cassettes. Bonus points for proximity to McHardy's Chicken (p. 94). You can bop in noon to 6pm any day but Tuesday. 2557 Bayou Rd. www.dominosoundrecords.com. ℂ **504/309-0871.**

Euclid Records ★★ If you love the smell of vinyl in the morning, or any time, Euclid will fire your pheromones. This younger-than-it-feels Bywater record store (sistah of the iconic St. Louis shop) stocks vintage platters from every era and gobs of local goods. There are nominal CDs and occasional in-store performances. Check them out daily 11am to 7pm (Sun till 5pm). 3301 Chartres St. www.euclidnola.com. ℰ **504/947-4348.**

Jim Russell Records ★ A classic, packed-to-the-rafters, musty, messy record shop. Vinyl-digger crack. Monday to Saturday 11am to 5pm. 1837 Magazine St. www.jim russellrecords.com. ℰ **504/522-2602.**

Louisiana Music Factory ★★★ *The* place to get yourself informed about and stocked with New Orleans music, with helpful staff and a large selection of regional music—including Cajun, zydeco, R&B, jazz, blues, and gospel—plus books, posters, and T-shirts. Open late weekends; live performances Saturdays (and beer coupons for a nearby bar). Drop by any day 11am to 8pm (Fri–Sat till 10pm). 421 Frenchmen St. www.louisianamusicfactory.com. ℰ **504/586-1094.**

Peaches Records ★ Peaches' first store (circa 1975) was a stop-off for R&B royalty (Stevie Wonder!) and helped launch local hip-hop artists like Juvenile and Lil Wayne. Still family-owned, the French Quarter store stocks a broad swath of locally focused CDs, vinyl, books, DVDs, T-shirts, and art. Monday to Thursday 9am to 8pm, Friday and Saturday 9am to 9pm, Sunday 10am to 8pm. 408 N. Peters St. www.peaches recordsneworleans.com. ℰ **504/282-3322.**

The Occult

Besides the shops listed here, see p. 149 for Voodoo temples and practitioners.

Bottom of the Cup Tearoom ★ This place has been open since 1929 and bills itself as the "oldest tearoom in the United States." You can have a psychic consultation and also purchase teas, books, jewelry, crystal balls, tarot cards, crystals, and healing wands. Daily 10am to 6pm. 327 Chartres St. www.bottomofthecup.com. ℰ **800/729-7148** or 504/524-1997.

F&F Botanica ★★ This unassuming, jam-packed Mid-City shop is among the largest suppliers anywhere of candles, herbs, icons and elixirs for the serious practitioner (and that's who shops here). Mr. Felix (Figueroa) and son will kindly assist new or non-believers. By taxi only. Daily 8am to 5pm (closed Wed and Sun). 5801 N. Broad St. www.fandfbotanica.com. ℰ **504/482-5400.**

Marie Laveau's House of Voodoo ★ This is tourist Voodoo, to be sure, but the Voodoo dolls and gris-gris bags make great souvenirs for the right friends, and it's a fun store to poke around in. Hours tend to vary, but normally 10am to 11:30pm (Fri–Sat till 1:30am). 739 Bourbon St. www.voodooneworleans.com. ℰ **504/581-3751.**

Voodoo Authentica ★★ The two big rooms of Voodoo paraphernalia feels like a real retail establishment, not a dusty shack, and the merchandise does have a certain authentic feel. The locally made Voodoo dolls, potions, spell candles, and daubs range from cheap to costly, and there are simple souvenirs as well as serious works of art. Daily 11am to 7pm. 612 Dumaine St. www.voodooshop.com. ℰ **504/522-2111.**

T-Shirts & More

If crass suits your style, by all means buy up the Bourbon Street goods. But for a garment with local flavor that's also clever and maybe even has a decent design aesthetic, there are a plethora of superior options. Shirts (and hats, hoodies, and so forth) in these shops will probably run $5 to $10 more than your average show-me-your-whatever tops, but they're softer. And smarter.

Dirty Coast ★★ It's waaay uptown, but their eye-catching and original T-shirt designs (painted in the city) are utterly witty, like the "Crawfish Pi," with the Greek symbol composed of a tasty pile of mudbugs, and "504Ever." Daily 10am to 6pm. 5631 Magazine St. www.dirtycoast.com. © **504/324-3745.** Also 329 Julia St.

Fleurty Girl ★★ It's hard to leave here without one (or more) of its pithy and near-perfect NOLA-centric T-shirts, even if some need a NOLA-to-English translation. Dig the cocktail-related tees, like "Call Me Old-Fashioned" and "Keep Calm and Carry a Go-Cup." Good jewelry, accessories, and $5 NOLA-themed tea towels—a fave gift. Open daily 10am to 6pm (Fri–Sat till 7pm). 632 St. Peter St. www.fleurtygirl.net. © **504/304-5529.** Also 3117 Magazine St. © **504/301-2557.**

Storyville ★★ You've heard it, now wear it: plenty of water-meter, "Who Dat," and other good Saints designs ("Believe"), and perhaps the all-time classic New Orleans tee—the four seasons V-neck: carnival, crawfish, snoball, football. Daily 10am to 8pm. 3029 Magazine St. www.storyvilleapparel.com. © **504/304-6209.**

WALKING TOURS OF NEW ORLEANS

We've said it before, and we'll keep saying it: This town was made for walking. Even at the height of the humid summer months, when everyone's main motivation is to laze in the shade and sip cool drinks, you can still flit between air-conditioned restaurant and air-conditioned museum.

With every step in undeniably unique New Orleans, there is something extraordinary to marvel at and commit to memory, in your mind's eye or on your SD card: a gorgeous building more interesting than the last, a "colorful" character, a tuba-lugging musician in formal wear.

Stroll along Bayou St. John, turning at any corner that strikes your fancy. You might have a street to yourself—or share it with a fleeting ghost? Imagine it 100 years ago; without the cars and wires, it would have looked almost as it does now.

The French Quarter, Garden District, and Bayou St. John each have their own distinct appearances, and all are easily manageable on foot. So put on some good walking shoes, breathe in that tropical breeze, and mosey. Go slow. Take it (big) easy. Admire the lacy ironwork. Peek through French Quarter gateways, where simple facades hide exquisite courtyards with elaborate fountains and thick foliage. Gawk at the mighty oaks, some dripping with swaying Spanish moss.

These walking tours provide a solid introduction to what is simply one of the most beautiful cities anywhere, and answer some "That looks interesting—what the heck *is* it?" queries. For professional, guided tours, see p. 151.

WALKING TOUR 1: THE FRENCH QUARTER

START:	**The intersection of Royal and Bienville streets.**
FINISH:	**Jackson Square.**
TIME:	**Allow approximately 2 hours, not including time spent in shops or historic homes.**
BEST TIMES:	**Any day between 8am and 10am (the quiet hours).**
WORST TIME:	**At night. Some attractions won't be open, and you won't be able to get a good look at the architecture.**

If you only spend a few hours in New Orleans, do it in the exquisitely picturesque French Quarter. In these 80 city blocks, the colonial empires of France, Spain, and to a lesser extent, Britain, intersected with the emerging American nation. It's called the Vieux Carré or "old square," but somehow

Walking Tour 1: The French Quarter

1 Rillieux-Waldhorn House

2 Bank of Louisiana
   (Police Station)

3 Latrobe's

4 Brennan's Restaurant

5 Peychaud's Drug Store

6 New Orleans Court Building

7 The Brulatour Court

8 The Merieult House

9 The Court of Two Sisters

10 Horizon Gallery

11 Le Monnier Mansion

12 The LaBranche House

13 Lacoul House

14 Pat O'Brien's

15 Preservation Hall

16 Lindy Boggs Home

17 Bourbon Orleans Hotel

18 Le Pretre Mansion

19 Spanish Colonial Cottage

20 Madame John's Legacy

21 Lafitte's Blacksmith Shop

22 The Lalaurie Home

23 Gallier House Museum

24 Croissant D'Or

25 Beauregard-Keyes House

26 The Old U.S. Mint

27 The Historic French Market

28 Central Grocery

29 The Pontalba Buildings

30 The Presbytère

31 St. Louis Cathedral

32 The Cabildo

33 Faulkner House Books

34 Tennessee Williams House

35 Café du Monde

it's timeless—venerable yet vibrantly alive. Today's residents and merchants are stewards of a rich tradition of individuality and creativity. This tour will introduce you to its style, history, and landmarks.

Start at the corner of Royal and Bienville streets, heading into the Quarter (away from Canal St.). That streetcar named Desire rattled along Royal Street until 1948 (then came the bus named Desire. Really). Imagine how noisy these narrow streets were when the streetcars ran here. Your first stop is:

1 339–343 Royal St., Rillieux-Waldhorn House

Now the home of Waldhorn and Adler Antiques (est. 1881), the place was built between 1795 and 1800 for Vincent Rillieux, the great-grandfather of the French Impressionist artist Edgar Degas. The wrought-iron balconies are an example of excellent Spanish colonial workmanship.

2 333 Royal St., Bank of Louisiana (Police Station)

Across the street, this old bank was erected in 1826, and its Greek Revival edifice followed in the early 1860s. The building suffered fires in 1840, 1861, and 1931, and has served as the Louisiana State Capitol, an auction exchange, a criminal court, a juvenile court, and an American Legion social hall. It now houses the Vieux Carré police station.

Cross Conti Street to:

3 403 Royal St., Latrobe's

Benjamin H. B. Latrobe died of yellow fever shortly after completing designs for the Louisiana State Bank, which opened here in 1821. He was one of the nation's most eminent architects, having contributed to the design of the U.S. Capitol and White House. Note the monogram "LSB" on the Creole-style railing. It's now an elegant banquet hall named for the architect.

4 417 Royal St., Brennan's Restaurant

The famed, bright-pink Brennan's opened in this building in 1955 and was crowned restaurant royalty almost immediately, which it remained until 2013. At press time, it was close to re-opening following a sad financial, legal, and family squabble during which it was shuttered and changed hands. One of 200 buildings destroyed in the 1794 fire and rebuilt (also by Vincent Rillieux) in 1855, it has been home to the Banque de la Louisiane, the world-famous chess champion Paul Charles Morphy, and the parents of Edgar Degas.

5 437 Royal St., Peychaud's Drug Store

When Masons held lodge meetings here in the early 1800s, proprietor and druggist Antoine A. Peychaud served after-meeting drinks of bitters and cognac to lodge members in small egg cups, called *coquetier*—later Americanized to "cocktails." And so it began (the cocktail and the much-debated legend).

6 400 Royal St., Louisiana Supreme Court

Built in 1909, this was and still is a courthouse, covering the length of the block. The ostentatious baroque edifice laden with Georgia marble seems out of scale here—and many original Spanish-era structures were demolished to pave its way. Granted, those original buildings were indeed run down, and the new construction was positioned as slum-clearing. All this was well before the Vieux Carré Commission formed in the early 1930s to protect the historic French Quarter buildings. Ironically, rulings in this very courthouse upheld the preservation regulations fueled by the Vieux Carré Commission.

Cross St. Louis Street to:

7 520 Royal St., The Brulatour Court

This 1816 structure was home to François Seignouret, a furniture maker and wine importer from Bordeaux. His furniture, with a signature "S" carved into each piece, is still collected. Ask to walk into the exotic courtyard—it's one of the few four-walled courtyards in the French Quarter. From the street, notice the *garde de fries,* an elaborate, fan-shaped guard screen on the right end of the third-floor balcony, with Seignouret's "S" carved into it.

8 533 Royal St., The Merieult House

Built for the merchant Jean François Merieult in 1792, this house was the only building in the area left standing after the 1794 fire. Legend has it that Napoleon offered Madame Merieult great riches in exchange for her hair, to create a wig to present to a Turkish sultan (she refused). Nowadays, it's home to the excellent **Historic New Orleans Collection** museum and research center. (See p. 130).

Cross Toulouse Street to:

9 613 Royal St., The Court of Two Sisters

This structure was built in 1832 for a local bank president on the site of the 18th-century home of a French governor. The two sisters were Emma and Bertha Camors, whose father owned the building; from 1886 to 1906, they ran a curio store here.

10 627 Royal St., Horizon Gallery

Walk through to the magnificent courtyard in back. Seventeen-year-old opera singer Adelina Patti visited and later lived in this 1777 building after becoming a local heroine in 1860. As a last-minute stand-in lead soprano, she saved the local opera company from financial ruin.

11 640 Royal St., Le Monnier Mansion

No one thought the 1811 building would survive a fourth-floor addition in 1876, creating the city's first "skyscraper." 'Sieur George, fictional hero of George W. Cable's scandalous *Old Creole Days,* "lived" here.

Cross St. Peter Street to:

12 700 Royal St., The LaBranche House

The lacy cast-iron grillwork, with its delicate oak leaf and acorn design, makes this one of the most photographed buildings in the Quarter. This is one of 11 three-story brick row houses built from 1835 to 1840 for the widow of wealthy sugar planter Jean Baptiste LaBranche.

Turn left at St. Peter Street and continue to:

13 714 St. Peter St., Lacoul House

Built in 1829 by prominent physician Dr. Yves LeMonnier, this was a boarding-house run by Antoine Alciatore during the 1860s. His cooking became so popular with the locals that he eventually gave up catering to open the famous Antoine's restaurant (p. 82), still operated today by his descendants.

14 718 St. Peter St., Pat O'Brien's

Now the de facto home to the famed Hurricane cocktail (p. 180), this building was completed in 1790. Later, Louis Tabary put on popular plays here including, purportedly, the first grand opera in America. The pretty, popular courtyard is well worth a look, maybe even a refreshment.

15 726 St. Peter St., Preservation Hall

Scores of people descend here nightly for traditional New Orleans jazz (p. 171). A daytime stop affords a glimpse, through the ornate iron gate, of a lush tropical courtyard in back. Author Erle Stanley Gardner, of Perry Mason fame, lived upstairs.

Continue up St. Peter Street until you reach Bourbon Street, and turn left:

16 623 Bourbon St., Lindy Boggs Home

Tennessee Williams and Truman Capote stayed in this house (no, not together), home until recently to Lindy Boggs—much-beloved local politician, ambassador, philanthropist, and mother of journalist Cokie Roberts—who took over husband Hale Boggs' congressional seat after his death in a plane crash. She passed away in 2013.

Turn around and head the other way down Bourbon Street. At the corner of Bourbon and Orleans streets, look down Orleans Street, toward the river, at:

17 717 Orleans St., Bourbon Orleans Hotel

Site of the famous quadroon balls, where wealthy white men were introduced to potential mistresses: free women (and girls) of color who were one-fourth black (quadroon) or one-eighth (octoroon). During these balls, the men and the young women's mothers would carefully negotiate *placage* arrangements, which often included financial, educational, housing, and child support for the mistresses. Imagine the discussions on those balconies . . . . The building later became a convent for the Sisters of the Holy Family, the second-oldest order of black nuns in the country. Their founder (whose mother was a quadroon mistress!), Henriette DeLille, has been presented to the Vatican for consideration for sainthood.

Turn left onto Orleans and follow it a block to Dauphine (pronounced Daw-*feen*) Street. On the corner is:

18 716 Dauphine St., Le Pretre Mansion

In 1839, Jean Baptiste Le Pretre bought this 1836 Greek Revival house and added the romantic cast-iron galleries. The house is the subject of a real-life horror story: In the 19th century, a conspicuously wealthy Turk, supposedly the brother of a sultan, rented the house. He brought an entourage of servants and beautiful young girls—all thought to have been stolen from the sultan—and threw lavish high-society parties. One night screams came from inside; the next morning, neighbors found the tenant and the young beauties lying dead in a pool of blood. The mystery remains unsolved. Local ghost experts say you can sometimes hear exotic music and piercing shrieks.

Turn right on Dauphine Street and go 2 blocks to Dumaine Street and then turn right. You'll find an interesting little cottage at:

19 707 Dumaine St., Spanish Colonial Cottage

After the 1794 fire, all houses in the French Quarter were required by law to have flat tile roofs. Most have since been covered with conventional roofs, but this Spanish colonial cottage is still in compliance with the flat-roof rule.

20 632 Dumaine St., Madame John's Legacy

This structure was once thought to be the oldest building on the Mississippi River, originally erected in 1726, 8 years after the founding of New Orleans. Recent research suggests, however, that only a few parts of the original building survived the 1788 fire. Its first owner was a ship captain who died in the 1729 *Natchez* Massacre; upon his death, the house passed to the captain of a Lafitte-era smuggling ship—and 21 subsequent owners. The structure is a rare example of the original French "raised cottage." The above-ground basement is of brick-between-posts construction (locally made bricks were too soft to be the primary building material). The hipped, dormered roof extends out over the veranda. Its name comes from George W. Cable's fictional character who was bequeathed the house in the short story *'Tite Poulette.* Now part of the Louisiana State Museum complex, it's open to visitors Tuesday through Sunday 10am to 4:30pm; admission is free.

21 941 Bourbon St., Lafitte's Blacksmith Shop

This National Historic Landmark claims to be the oldest continually operating bar in the country (see p. 180), and legend is that it was the headquarters of Jean Lafitte and his pirates, who posed as blacksmiths and used it to fence goods they'd plundered on the high seas. It still reflects the architectural influence of late-1700s French colonists. It may also be the oldest building in the Mississippi Valley, but that has not been documented. An unfortunate exterior renovation trying to replicate the original brick and plaster makes it look fake (it's actually not), but the dim interior is still an excellent place to imagine 19th-century Quarter life and swill some grog.

Turn right onto Bourbon Street and follow it 2 blocks to Governor Nicholls Street. Turn right and go 1 block to the corner of Royal Street:

22 1140 Royal St., The Lalaurie Home

Two-time widow Madame Delphine Macarty de Lopez Blanque wed Dr. Louis Lalaurie, moved into this residence in 1832, and the two were soon impressing the city with extravagant parties. One night in 1834 fire broke out. Neighbors crashed through a locked door to find seven starving slaves chained in painful positions. The sight, combined with Delphine's stories of past slaves having "committed suicide" and rumors of hideous live-subject medical experiments conducted within, enraged her neighbors. Madame Lalaurie and her family escaped a mob's wrath and fled to Paris. After her death, her body was returned to New Orleans—and even then she had to be buried in secrecy. Tales of hauntings persist, especially that of a slave child who fell from the roof trying to escape Delphine's cruelties. The building was a Union headquarters during the Civil War, a gambling house, and home to actor Nicolas Cage. Haunted by financial difficulties, Cage returned the house to the bank in 2009, which converted it to condos.

23 1132 Royal St., Gallier House Museum

James Gallier, Jr., built this house in 1857 as his residence. He and his father were two of the city's leading architects (p. 129). Novelist Anne Rice based Lestat and Louis's home in *Interview with the Vampire* on this house.

Turn left onto Ursulines Street, toward the river.

617 Ursulines Ave., Croissant D'Or 🍵

For a little rest or sustenance, stop in the popular Croissant D'Or, 617 Ursulines St. (www.croissantdornola.com; 𝄢 504/524-4663; p. 117). The pastries here are very good, as is the ambience—inside or out.

At the corner of Ursulines and Chartres streets is the:

24 1113 Chartres St., Beauregard-Keyes House

This raised cottage was built as a residence in 1826 by Joseph Le Carpentier, though it has other important claims to fame (detailed on p. 126). Notice the Doric columns and handsome twin staircases.

Turn left onto Chartres Street until you get to Esplanade Avenue, one of the city's most picturesque historic thoroughfares. Some of the grandest townhouses built in the late 1800s grace this wide, tree-lined avenue, once the parade ground for troops quartered on Barracks Street. The entire 400 block of Esplanade is occupied by:

25 The Old U.S. Mint

This was once the site of Fort St. Charles, built to protect New Orleans in 1792. Andrew Jackson reviewed the "troops" here—pirates, ragtag volunteers, and a nucleus of actual trained soldiers—whom he later led in the Battle of New Orleans. It's now a Louisiana State Museum housing coin and jazz collections (p. 128).

Follow Esplanade toward the river and turn right at the corner of North Peters Street. Follow North Peters until it intersects with Decatur Street. This is the back end of:

26 The Historic French Market

This European-style market (p. 125) has been here for well over 200 years, and today it has a farmers' market, food booths, arty-crafty goods, and flea market stalls with souvenirs. Do stop to shop.

When you leave the French Market, exit on the side away from the river onto Decatur Street toward St. Ann Street. You'll pass 923 and 919 Decatur St., where the Café de Refugies and Hôtel de la Marine stood. In the 1700s and early 1800s these were gathering places for pirates, smugglers, European refugees, and outlaws.

923 Decatur St., Central Grocery 🍵

If it's around lunchtime, pop into Central Grocery (𝄢 504/523-1620; p. 91), and pick up a famed muffuletta sandwich. Eat inside at the little tables, or take it with you and dine al fresco in Jackson Square, near your next stop.

Decatur Street will take you to Jackson Square. Turn right onto St. Ann Street; the twin four-story, redbrick buildings here and on the St. Peter Street side of the square are:

27 The Pontalba Buildings

These highly coveted buildings sport some of the most impressive cast-iron balcony railings in the French Quarter. They also represent early French Quarter urban revitalization—and early girl power. In the mid-1800s, Baroness Micaela Almonester de Pontalba inherited rows of buildings along both sides of the Place d'Armes from her father, the wealthy Spanish nobleman-turned-magnate Don Almonester (who rebuilt St. Louis Cathedral, p. 125, among other developments). In an effort to counteract the emerging American sector across Canal Street, she razed the structures and built high-end apartments in the traditional Creole-European style, with commercial space at street level, housing above, and courtyards in the rear.

The Pontalba Buildings were begun in 1849 under her direct supervision; you can see her mark today in the entwined initials "A.P." in the ironwork. The Baroness also had Jackson Square built, including the cast-iron fence and the equestrian statue of Andrew Jackson. Her scandalous personal story (see p. 129) is equally fascinating.

At the corner of St. Ann and Chartres streets, turn left and continue around Jackson Square; you will see:

28 751 Chartres St., The Presbytère

This, the Cabildo, and the St. Louis Cathedral—all designed by Gilberto Guillemard—were the first major public buildings in the Louisiana Territory. The Presbytère was originally designed as the cathedral's rectory. Baroness Pontalba's father financed the building's beginnings, but he died in 1798, leaving only the first floor done. It was finally completed in 1813. Never used as a rectory, it became a city courthouse and now houses the excellent Louisiana State Museum (p. 126).

Next you'll come to:

29 St. Louis Cathedral

Although it is the oldest Catholic cathedral in the U.S., this is actually the third building erected on this spot—the first was destroyed by a hurricane in 1722, the second by fire in 1788. The cathedral was rebuilt in 1794; the central tower was later designed by Henry S. Boneval Latrobe, again remodeled and enlarged between 1845 and 1851 under Baroness Pontalba. The bell and stately clock (note the nonstandard Roman numeral four), were imported from France (p. 125).

The building on the Cathedral's right is:

30 The Cabildo

In the 1750s, this was the site of a French police station and guardhouse. Part of that building was incorporated into the Spanish government statehouse (known as the "Very Illustrious Cabildo"). It was still under reconstruction when the transfer papers for the Louisiana Purchase were signed in a room on the second floor in 1803. Since then, it has served as New Orleans's City Hall, the Louisiana State Supreme Court, and, since 1911, a Louisiana State Museum (p. 128).

Think those old Civil War cannons out front look pitifully obsolete? Think again. In 1921, in a near-deadly prank, one was loaded and fired. That missile traveled across the wide expanse of the Mississippi and 6 blocks inland, landing in a house in Algiers and narrowly missing its occupants.

Walk down the narrow alley between the Cabildo and the Cathedral. You'll come to Pirate's Alley:

The French Quarter

WALKING TOURS OF NEW ORLEANS

31 624 Pirate's Alley, Faulkner House Books

In 1925, William Faulkner lived here. He contributed to the *Times-Picayune* and worked on his first novels, *Mosquitoes* and *Soldiers' Pay*, making this lovely store a requisite stop for literature lovers and book buyers of any persuasion (p. 192).

To the left of the bookstore is a small alley that takes you to St. Peter Street, which is behind and parallel to Pirate's Alley.

32 632 St. Peter St., Tennessee Williams House

Have a sudden urge to scream "Stella!!!" at that second-story wrought-iron balcony? No wonder. This is where Tennessee Williams wrote *A Streetcar Named Desire*, one of the greatest pieces of American theater. He remarked that he could hear "that rattle-trap streetcar named Desire running along Royal and the one named Cemeteries running along Canal and it seemed the perfect metaphor for the human condition."

Return to Jackson Square. On the left side of the cathedral on the corner of Chartres and St. Peter streets (with your back to the Mississippi River and Jackson Square) is:

813 Decatur St., Café du Monde 🏁

You've finished! Now go back across Jackson Square and Decatur Street to Café du Monde (ⓒ 504/525-4544; p. 116) for beignets and coffee. Do climb the stairs up to the levee and relax on a bench, and watch the river roll.

WALKING TOUR 2: **THE GARDEN DISTRICT**

START:	**Prytania Street and Washington Avenue.**
FINISH:	**Lafayette Cemetery.**
TIME:	**45 minutes to 2 hours.**
BEST TIME:	**Daylight.**
WORST TIME:	**Night, when you won't be able to get a good look at the architecture.**

Walking through the architecturally astounding Garden District, you could get the impression that you've entered an entirely separate city—or time period—from the French Quarter. Although the Garden District was indeed once a separate city (Lafayette) from the Vieux Carré and was established later, their development by two different groups is what most profoundly distinguishes the two.

The French Quarter was settled by Creoles during the French and Spanish colonial periods, and the Garden District was created by Americans after the 1803 Louisiana Purchase. The lucrative combination of Mississippi River commerce, abundant slave trade, and national banks fueled the local economy, resulting in the remarkable antebellum building boom still seen here.

Thousands of Americans moved here after the Louisiana Purchase. Friction arose between these new residents and the Creoles around language barriers, religious division, competition over burgeoning commerce, and mutual snobbery. With inferior business experience, education, and organizational skills, the Creoles worried that *les Americains* would drive them out of business. Americans were thus barred from the already overcrowded French Quarter. The snubbed Americans moved upriver and created a residential district of astounding, in-your-face opulence: the Garden District.

Walking Tour 2: The Garden District

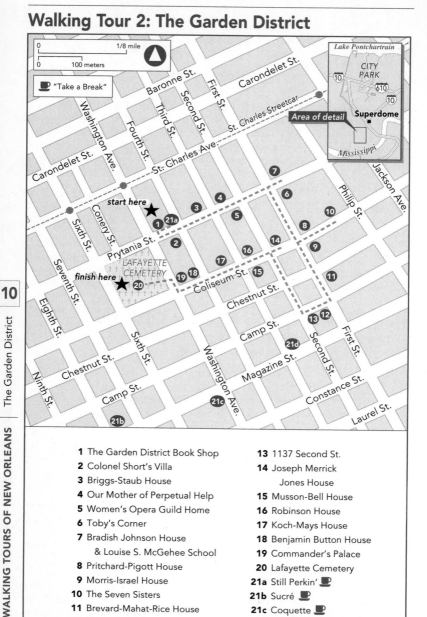

1 The Garden District Book Shop
2 Colonel Short's Villa
3 Briggs-Staub House
4 Our Mother of Perpetual Help
5 Women's Opera Guild Home
6 Toby's Corner
7 Bradish Johnson House
   & Louise S. McGehee School
8 Pritchard-Pigott House
9 Morris-Israel House
10 The Seven Sisters
11 Brevard-Mahat-Rice House
12 Payne-Strachan House

13 1137 Second St.
14 Joseph Merrick
   Jones House
15 Musson-Bell House
16 Robinson House
17 Koch-Mays House
18 Benjamin Button House
19 Commander's Palace
20 Lafayette Cemetery
21a Still Perkin'
21b Sucré
21c Coquette
21d Tracey's

It is, therefore, a culture clash reflected through architecture, with Americans creating an identity by introducing bold, new styles.

Note: With few exceptions, houses on this tour are occupied, private homes and are not open to the public. Several are owned by celebrities (names are omitted for privacy). Please be respectful of the residents.

To reach the Garden District, take the St. Charles streetcar to Washington Avenue (stop no. 16) and walk 1 block toward the river to:

1 2727 Prytania St., The Garden District Book Shop

A stellar collection of national and regional titles, with many signed editions, makes this bookshop (p. 192) an appropriate kickoff for a Garden District tour. The historic property was built in 1884 as the Crescent City Skating Rink, and subsequently acted as a livery stable, mortuary, grocery store, and gas station. Today "the Rink" also offers a coffee shop, restrooms, and air-conditioning (crucial in the summer).

Across Prytania Street, you'll find:

2 1448 Fourth St., Colonel Short's Villa

This house was built by architect Henry Howard for Kentucky Colonel Robert Short. The story goes that Short's wife missed the cornfields in her native Iowa, so he bought her the cornstalk fence. But a revised explanation has the wife requesting it because it was the most expensive, showy fence in the building catalog. Second Civil War occupational governor Nathaniel Banks was quartered here.

Continuing down Prytania, you'll find:

3 2605 Prytania St., Briggs-Staub House

This is the Garden District's only example of Gothic Revival architecture (unpopular among Protestant Americans because it reminded them of their Roman Catholic Creole antagonists). Original owner Charles Briggs built the relatively large adjacent servant quarters for his Irish slaves. Irish immigrants were starting to create the nearby Irish Channel neighborhood across Magazine Street from the Garden District.

4 2523 Prytania St., Our Mother of Perpetual Help

Once an active Catholic chapel, this site was one of several in the area owned by Anne Rice and the setting for her novel *Violin*. The author's childhood home is down the street at 2301 St. Charles Ave.

5 2504 Prytania St., Women's Opera Guild Home

Some of the Garden District's most memorable homes incorporate more than one style. Designed by William Freret in 1858, this one combines Greek Revival and Queen Anne styles. It's now owned by the Women's Opera Guild. Tours are offered on Mondays from 10am to 12pm and 1 to 4pm; $7. (℡ **504/899-1945**).

6 2340 Prytania St., Toby's Corner

The Garden District's oldest known home was built in 1838 for Philadelphia wheelwright Thomas Toby in the then-popular Greek Revival style. The "non-Creole" style still followed Creole building techniques, such as raising the house up on brick piers to combat flooding and encourage air circulation.

7 2343 Prytania St., Bradish Johnson House & Louise S. McGehee School

Paris-trained architect James Freret (cousin of William, see stop #5 above) designed this French Second Empire–style mansion for sugar factor Bradish Johnson in 1872 at a cost of $100,000 ($1.6-plus million today). Contrast the house's awesome detail with the stark classical simplicity of Toby's Corner across the street—it illustrates the effect that one generation of outrageous fortune had on Garden District architecture. Since 1929 it has been the private Louise S. McGehee School for girls.

Turn down First Street (away from St. Charles) and it's a short block to:

8 1407 First St., Pritchard-Pigott House

This grand, Greek Revival double-galleried townhouse shows how, as fortunes grew, so did Garden District home sizes.

9 1331 First St., Morris-Israel House

As time passed, the trend toward the formal Greek Revival style took a playful turn. By the 1860s, Italianate was popular, as seen in this (reputedly haunted) double-galleried townhouse. Architect Samuel Jamison designed this house and the **Carroll-Crawford House** on the next corner (1315 First St.); note the identical ornate cast-iron galleries.

Follow Coliseum Street to the left, less than half a block to:

10 2329–2305 Coliseum St., The Seven Sisters

This row of "shotgun" houses gets its nickname from a (false) story that a 19th-century Garden District resident built these homes as wedding gifts for his seven daughters. Actually, there are eight "Seven Sisters," and they were built on speculation. "Shotgun"-style homes are so named because, theoretically, if one fired a gun through the front door, the bullet would pass unhindered out the back. (Also, a West African word for this native African house form sounds like "shotgun.") The shotgun house effectively circulates air and is common in hot climates. The relatively small shotguns are popular throughout much of Orleans, but rare along the imposing Garden District streets.

Now turn around and go back to First Street and turn left. At the corner of First and Chestnut, you'll see:

11 1239 First St., Brevard-Mahat-Rice House

This 1857 Greek Revival townhouse was later augmented with an Italianate bay, in a fine example of "transitional" architecture. The fence's rosettes begat the house's name, "Rosegate," and its woven diamond pattern is said to be the precursor to the chain-link fence. This was novelist Anne Rice's home and a setting in her *Witching Hour* novels.

12 1134 First St., Payne-Strachan House

As the stone marker out front notes, Jefferson Davis, president of the Confederate States of America, died in this classic Greek Revival antebellum home, that of his friend Judge Charles Fenner. The sky-blue ceiling of the gallery is believed to keep winged insects from nesting there and to ward off evil spirits. Many local homes adhere to this tradition (now that you're aware of it, you'll notice it everywhere).

Turn right on Camp and go less than a block to:

13 1137 Second St.

This house exemplifies the Victorian architecture popularized in uptown New Orleans toward the end of the 19th century. Many who built such homes were from the Northeast and left New Orleans in the summer; otherwise, it would be odd to see this claustrophobic, "cool climate"–style house. Note the exquisite stained glass and rounded railing on the gallery.

Turn right onto Second Street and go 2 blocks to the corner of Coliseum:

14 2425 Coliseum St., Joseph Merrick Jones House

When previous owner Trent Reznor of the band Nine Inch Nails moved in, new anti-noise ordinances were introduced at city council. His next-door neighbor was Councilwoman Peggy Wilson. Coincidence?

Turn left onto Coliseum Street and go 1 block to Third Street. Turn left to get to:

15 1331 Third St., Musson-Bell House

This is the 1853 home of Michel Musson, one of the few French Creoles then living in the Garden District and the uncle of artist Edgar Degas, who lived with Musson on Esplanade Avenue during a visit to New Orleans. On the Coliseum Street side of the house is the foundation of a cistern. These once-common water tanks (Mark Twain once commented that it looked as if everybody in the neighborhood had a private brewery) were mostly destroyed at the turn of the 20th century when mosquitoes, which breed in standing water, were found to be carriers of yellow fever. Yellow-fever epidemics infamously killed 41,000 New Orleaneans between 1817 and 1905.

Turn around and cross Coliseum to see:

16 1415 Third St., Robinson House

This striking home was built between 1859 and 1865 by architect Henry Howard for tobacco grower and merchant Walter Robinson. Walk past the house to appreciate its scale—the outbuildings, visible from the front, are actually connected to the side of the main house. The entire roof is a large vat that once collected water. Add gravity and water pressure: thus begat the Garden District's earliest indoor plumbing.

Continue down Coliseum Street 2 blocks to the corner of Washington Avenue:

17 2627 Coliseum St., Koch-Mays House

This picturesque chalet-style dollhouse (well, for a large family of dolls) was built in 1876 by noted architect William Freret for James Eustis, a U.S. senator and ambassador to France (perhaps justifying the full-size ballroom). It and four other spec homes he built on the block were referred to as Freret's Folly. No detail was left unfrilled, from the ironwork to the gables and finials.

18 2707 Coliseum St., Benjamin Button House

This 8,000 square-footer is best known as the title character's home in the film, *The Curious Case of Benjamin Button*. Ergo Brad Pitt slept here, fictionally (he bought his own French Quarter home soon after filming). The house was owned by the same family from 1870 until its 2009 sale. Thus when the "Button" location scouts came calling they dealt with the family's 90-year-old matriarch, who had raised seven kids under this roof. Or roofs, perhaps, since it's actually two houses combined: the original 1832 cottage sits atop a columned, 1908 Colonial number.

19 1403 Washington Ave., Commander's Palace

Established in 1883 by Emile Commander, this turreted Victorian structure (a bordello back in the 1920s) is now the pride of the Brennan family, the most respected and successful restaurateurs in New Orleans. Commander's Palace has long reigned as one of the city's—nay, the country's—top restaurants (p. 106).

20 1400 Washington Ave., Lafayette Cemetery

Established in 1833, this "city of the dead" is one of New Orleans's oldest cemeteries. It has examples of all the classic above-ground, multiple-burial techniques. These tombs typically house numerous corpses from an extended family—one here lists 37 entrants; others are designated for members of specific fire departments or fraternal organizations. More on p. 146.

Walk to St. Charles Avenue to pick up the streetcar (there is a stop right there) or flag down a cab to return to the French Quarter.

Wind Down at Still Perkin', Tracey's, Coquette, or Sucré ☕

Now go back to your first stop, the Rink, where you can enjoy a cup of coffee and some light refreshments at Still Perkin'. Or head south on Washington to Magazine Street, where a po' boy at Tracey's, lunch at Coquette, or a sweet from Sucré (p. 118) will satisfy other appetites.

WALKING TOUR 3: ESPLANADE RIDGE & BAYOU ST. JOHN

START:	Esplanade Avenue and Johnson Street.
FINISH:	City Park.
TIME:	Allow approximately 2 hours, not including museum, cemetery, and lunch stops.
BEST TIMES:	Monday through Saturday, early or late morning.
WORST TIMES:	Sunday, when attractions are closed, or after dark. If you decide to stay in City Park or in the upper Esplanade area until early evening, plan to return on the bus or by taxi.

If you're heading to City Park, the New Orleans Museum of Art, or the Jazz & Heritage Festival, consider some sightseeing in this overlooked region. We particularly enjoy the quiet, meandering stretch along St. John's Bayou. Historically, the Esplanade

Walking Tour 3: The Esplanade Ridge

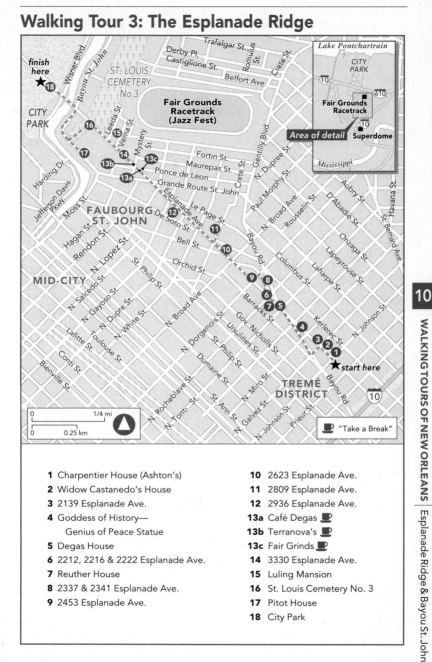

1. Charpentier House (Ashton's)
2. Widow Castanedo's House
3. 2139 Esplanade Ave.
4. Goddess of History—
   Genius of Peace Statue
5. Degas House
6. 2212, 2216 & 2222 Esplanade Ave.
7. Reuther House
8. 2337 & 2341 Esplanade Ave.
9. 2453 Esplanade Ave.
10. 2623 Esplanade Ave.
11. 2809 Esplanade Ave.
12. 2936 Esplanade Ave.
13a. Café Degas
13b. Terranova's
13c. Fair Grinds
14. 3330 Esplanade Ave.
15. Luling Mansion
16. St. Louis Cemetery No. 3
17. Pitot House
18. City Park

Ridge area was Creole society's answer to St. Charles Avenue—it's an equally lush boulevard with stately homes and seemingly ancient trees stretching overhead. The lots are not quite as expansive as along St. Charles, so the grand front lawns are not in evidence. Originally home to the descendants of the earliest settlers, the avenue had its finest days toward the end of the 19th century, and some of the neighborhoods along its path have seen better days. Still, it's closer to the soul of the city than St. Charles Avenue (read: regular people live here, whereas St. Charles always was and still is for the well-heeled).

You can catch a bus on Esplanade Avenue at the French Quarter, headed toward the park and your starting point. Otherwise, stroll (about 15 min.) up Esplanade Avenue to:

1 2023 Esplanade Ave., Charpentier House

Originally a plantation home, this house was designed in 1861 for A. B. Charpentier and now operates as Ashton's Bed & Breakfast (p. 62).

2 2033–2035 Esplanade Ave., Widow Castanedo's House

Juan Rodriguez purchased this land in the 1780s, and his granddaughter, Widow Castanedo, lived here until her death in 1861 (when it was a smaller, Spanish colonial–style plantation home). Before Esplanade Avenue extended this far from the river, the house was located in what is now the middle of the street. The widow tried and failed to block the extension of the street. The late-Italianate house was moved to its present site and enlarged sometime around the 1890s. It's been split down the middle and is inhabited today by two sisters.

3 2139 Esplanade Ave.

A great example of the typical Esplanade Ridge style. Note the Ionic columns on the upper level.

After you cross North Miro Street, Esplanade Avenue crosses the diagonal Bayou Road, which was the route to the French-Canadian settlements at St. John's Bayou in the late 17th century. Veer left at the fork to stay on Esplanade Avenue and look for:

4 Goddess of History—Genius of Peace Statue

In 1886, this triangular plot, called Gayarre Place, was given to the city by Charles Gayarre. George H. Dunbar donated the terra-cotta statue, a victory monument. It was destroyed in 1938 and replaced with the present cement and marble model.

5 2306 Esplanade Ave., Degas House

The Musson family rented this house for many years. Estelle Musson married René Degas, brother of Edgar Degas, the French Impressionist artist. (She and her descendants dropped his last name after he ran off with a neighbor's wife.) Degas is said to have painted the portrait of Estelle, now in the New Orleans Museum of Art, during his brief time living here. The house was built in 1854, and the Italianate decorations were added later when it was split into two buildings. It's a B&B now.

6 2212, 2216, 2222 Esplanade Ave.

Originally built as spec townhomes in 1883, these three Candy Crush–colored Italianate houses now comprise Le Belle Esplanade B&B inn. Although they look like triplets now, they each have their own architectural identities, and their intricate millwork and detailing surely stood on their own stead long before the eye-catching paint job was applied.

7 2326 Esplanade Ave., Reuther House

Check out the collection of metal and cinder-block sculptures in this front yard. The current resident of this house is a founder of the Contemporary Arts Center and a major figure in the city's arts community.

In passing, take a look at nos. 2325, 2329, and 2331—all are interesting examples of Creole cottages. Then, continue to:

8 2337 & 2341 Esplanade Ave.

These houses were identical structures when they were built in 1862 for John Budd Slawson, owner of a horse-drawn-streetcar company that operated along Bayou Road in the 19th century. Back then, they were both single-story shotgun-style houses. Notice the unusual ironwork underneath the front roof overhang.

Cross North Dorgenois Street to:

9 2453 Esplanade Ave.

This house was one of a pair of matching homes at the corner of Dorgenois Street; the other was demolished. Though its architecture has been changed extensively, it's one of the few remaining mansard-roofed homes on Esplanade Ridge.

Cross North Broad Street to:

10 2623 Esplanade Ave.

The Corinthian columns denote the home's classical revival style. Built in 1896 by Louis A. Jung, the Jungs donated the triangular piece of land at Esplanade Avenue, Broad Street, and Crete Street to the city on the condition that it remain public property. Now called DeSoto Park, it is graced by an Art Nouveau fence.

11 2809 Esplanade Ave.

This is one of the more decorative Queen Anne–style center-hall Victorian houses on Esplanade Ridge.

12 2936 Esplanade Ave.

A nice example of what's known as a Gothic villa.

Take a Break at Café Degas, Terranova's, or Fair Grinds 🍵

The shops and restaurants at the intersection of Mystery Street and Esplanade Avenue offer fine lunchtime options. If the weather is nice, the semi-outdoor setting is exceedingly pleasant at Café Degas (p. 95). For snacks or picnic food for City Park, try the family-run Terranova's Italian Grocery, 3308 Esplanade Ave. (📞 504/482-4131), across the street. Or opt for the quirky Fair Grinds coffeehouse behind Café Degas at 3133 Ponce De Leon St. (📞 504/913-9072).

Continue to:

13 3330 Esplanade Ave.

A galleried frame home built in the Creole-cottage style. Also note the orientation of this stretch (and many of the houses along Esplanade Avenue). The lots are on a diagonal, so houses face Esplanade at a slight angle.

Continue along Esplanade until Leda Street, and turn right for a ½-block detour off Esplanade to:

14 Luling Mansion, 1438 Leda St.

Florence Luling, a German sugar and cotton baron, purchased 80 acres and commissioned famed architect James Gallier, Jr., to build this elaborate, three-story Italianate mansion in 1865. Built with a full moat, its ornate formal gardens once stretched all the way to Esplanade Avenue. Later it served as the Louisiana Jockey Club (it backs up to the Fair Grounds Race Track). Although unfortunate modern adjustments have taken a toll, its original magnificence is still apparent.

Return to Esplanade Ave. and turn right. On your right is:

15 3421 Esplanade Ave., St. Louis Cemetery No. 3

The public Bayou Cemetery, established in 1835, was purchased and expanded by the St. Louis diocese in 1856. It contains the burial monuments of many of the diocese's priests and religious orders. It might be called "Restaurateurs' Rest": the tombs for the Galatoire, Tujague, and Prudhomme families are here. If you've been squeamish about going into the cemeteries because of safety concerns, you can explore this one on your own—though as always, you should still be alert.

From the cemetery, head back out to Esplanade Avenue and continue walking toward City Park. When you get to the bridge, go left, following the signs, along Bayou St. John (one of the nicest and least touristy areas of the city), to:

16 1440 Moss St., Pitot House

This Creole country house overlooking the historic Bayou was home to the city's first mayor. Open to the public (p. 140), knowledgeable docents offer a window onto life in the day when Bayou St. John was the city's main trade route.

Head back to Esplanade Avenue, turn left, cross the bridge, and walk straight into:

17 Esplanade & City Park Aves., City Park

Explore the sculpture garden, amphitheater, museum, botanical gardens, lakes, and much more in this glorious, expansive park (p. 142).

SIDE TRIPS: PLANTATION HOMES & CAJUN COUNTRY

I f you have time (say, 3 days), you should strongly consider a sojourn into the countryside outlying New Orleans. It makes for an interesting cultural and visual contrast to the big city. This chapter starts off by following the River Road along the banks of the Mississippi, and the plantation homes that line it, heading upriver from New Orleans. The second part takes you 150 miles west of New Orleans to the heart of Cajun Country.

The River Road trip can be done in a day trip, or one could keep rambling north to visit the plantation homes in the St. Francisville area and stay overnight. The Cajun Country trip requires a one- or two-night stay, more if you can. A GPS will be your friend for either jaunt.

PLANTATIONS ALONG THE GREAT RIVER ROAD

If your image of plantation homes comes strictly from Tara in *Gone With the Wind,* you can see something reasonably close to that Hollywood creation by touring these parts. You'll also see far humbler but realistic plantation homes, and get an idea of plantation life as it was—for better and worse.

THE EARLY PLANTERS Creole plantation houses are low-slung, simple affairs; the showier American style is closer to Hollywood's antebellum grandeur (they got grander after 1850, which most of these predate). They're smaller than you might expect, even cramped compared with the lavish mansions of the Gatsby-era oil barons and today's nouveau riche. If your fantasies would be dashed without pillars and porticos, stick to Destrehan, San Francisco, Oak Alley, and Madewood.

The early planters of Louisiana were rugged frontier people. As they spread out along the Mississippi from New Orleans, they cleared vast swamplands to create unhindered waterways for transporting indigo and other crops. Rough flatboats moving produce to market could be capsized by rapids, sandbars, and floating debris, or captured by river pirates. If they made it to New Orleans, these farming men (and a few extraordinary women) collected their pay and went on wild drinking, gambling, and brawling sprees—earning them a reputation as barbarians among the French Quarter Creoles.

By the 1800s, Louisiana planters (and their slaves) had introduced large-scale farming and brought more acreage under cultivation. King cotton, rice, and sugarcane were popularized around this time, bringing huge monetary returns. But natural dangers, a hurricane, or a swift change in the course of the capricious Mississippi could wipe out entire plantations and fortunes.

THE RIVERBOATS After 1812, the planters turned to speedier and ostensibly safer new steamboats to transport their crops. When the first steamboat (the *New Orleans,* built in Pittsburgh) chugged downriver belching sooty smoke, it was so dirty and potentially explosive that it was dubbed a "floating volcano."

As vast improvements were made, the steamboats became more than a means to move goods to market. Families and slaves could now travel in lavish staterooms amid ornate "grand salons" in these floating pleasure palaces. Some set up dual residences, spending the social season and winters in elegant New Orleans townhouses. They fashioned more elegant lifestyles back in their upriver homes as well, where they shipped fine furnishings and luxury goods.

On the darker side, the boats were the realm of riverboat gamblers and confidence or "con" men. Huge fortunes and no doubt a few deeds to plantations were lost to (and perhaps won back from) these silver-tongued professional gamers and crooks.

BUILDING THE PLANTATION HOUSES During this prosperous period from the 1820s until the beginning of the Civil War, most of the impressive plantation homes were built, as were grand New Orleans townhouses.

Generally located near the riverfront, the plantation home was the focal point of a self-sustaining community. Most were modest, but some had wide, oak-lined avenues leading from its entrance to a wharf. On either side of the avenue would frequently be *garçonnières* (small guesthouses, sometimes used by adolescent sons and their friends). The kitchen was separated from the house because of fire danger. Close by was the overseer's office. Some plantations had pigeon houses or dovecotes—and all had the inevitable slave quarters lining the lane to the crops or across the fields and out of sight. The first houses were simple "raised cottages," with long, sloping roofs, cement-covered brick walls on the ground floor, and wood-and-brick (brick between posts) construction in the living quarters on the second floor. Influenced by West Indian styles, these colonial structures suited the sultry Louisiana climate and swampy building sites, and made use of native materials.

In the 1820s, they began to add Greek Revival and Georgian influences—creating a style dubbed Louisiana Classic. Large, rounded columns and wide galleries surrounded the main body of the house, and the roof was dormered. Inside, rooms flanked an expansive central hall. They had few imported details like fireplace mantels, and were constructed of native materials, like cypress and bricks of cement-sealed river clay.

GRAND & GRANDER By the 1850s, homes grew in tandem with prosperity and became more grandiose. Many embraced the styles of extravagant Victorian architecture, northern Italian villas, or Gothic lines (notably the fantastic San Francisco plantation, sometimes called "steamboat Gothic"; p. 221). Planters and their families brought back ornate furnishings and skilled artisans from their European travels. Glittering crystal chandeliers and *faux marbre* (false marble) mantels appeared.

Social lives, families, and egos also grew. The **Madewood house** on Bayou Lafourche was built explicitly to outshine Woodlawn, the beautiful home of the builder's brother (not open to the public, unfortunately).

Plantations Along the Great River Road

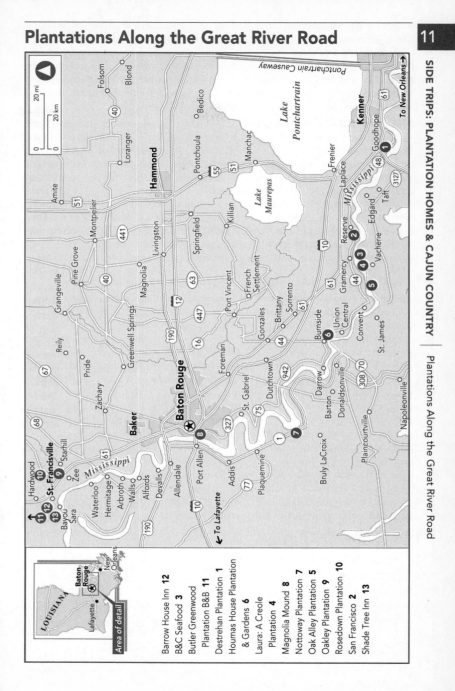

Barrow House Inn **12**
B&C Seafood **3**
Butler Greenwood
Plantation B&B **11**
Destrehan Plantation **1**
Houmas House Plantation
& Gardens **6**
Laura: A Creole
Plantation **4**
Magnolia Mound **8**
Nottoway Plantation **7**
Oak Alley Plantation **5**
Oakley Plantation **9**
Rosedown Plantation **10**
San Francisco **2**
Shade Tree Inn **13**

But the enormous wealth stemmed from an economy based on human servitude. The injustice and cruelty of slavery became the seeds of its own demise. After the Civil War, large-scale farming became impossible without that labor base. During Reconstruction, lands were confiscated and turned over to people who proved unable to run them; many were subdivided. Increasing international competition began to erode the cotton and sugar markets. The culture represented by the plantation houses you'll see emerged and died in a span of less than 100 years.

THE PLANTATION HOUSES TODAY Where scores of grand homes once dotted the riverfront, few remain. Several that survived the Civil War fell victim to fires, floods, or industrial development. Others, too costly to be maintained, were left to the ravages of dampness and decay. But a few have been saved, preserved, and upgraded with electricity and plumbing. Most are private residences, but some are open to visitors, the admission fees supplementing upkeep.

Tours of plantations are hit-or-miss—much depends on your guide. We've listed our favorite choices here. After you visit several, you'll begin to hear many of the same facts about plantation life, sometimes as infill for missing or boring history. It can also be easy to romanticize the era, while giving short shrift to the fact that they would not exist were it not for unthinkably savage, yet unimaginably real, human cruelty.

Planning Your Trip

All the plantation homes shown on the map on p. 219 are within easy driving distance of New Orleans. How many you can tour in a day will depend on your endurance (in the car and on your feet) and time allotment. If returning late, the small highways can be a little intimidating after dark. Don't expect broad river views along the Great River Road (the roadway's name on *both* sides of the Mississippi); it's obscured by tall levees. You'll see sugarcane fields and plenty of evidence of Louisiana's petrochemical industry. But spontaneous detours through little, centuries-old towns might result in finding a choice resale shop or good road food.

If you have minimal time, tour **Laura** and **Oak Alley.** They are a mile apart, and each offers a different perspective on plantation life and the tourism industry. Laura is classic understated Creole and has a low-key but superb presentation. Tara-esque Oak Alley represents the showy Americans and is slicker and glitzier (one could even do an Oak Alley drive-by). Both are approximately an hour from New Orleans. Alternately, a day at **Houmas House,** with its magnificent grounds, is definitely a day well spent.

If you're in town on **Christmas Eve,** consider driving along the River Road to see the huge bonfires residents build on the levees to light the way for the Christ child and Papa Noël (who rides in a sleigh drawn by—what else?—eight alligators!).

Organized Tours

Touring plantation houses via a bus tour is a comfortable, planning-free option and you get some bonus narration along the route. Almost every New Orleans tour company operates a tour to one or two plantations; most offer pickup at hotels or a central French Quarter locale. Costs include transportation and admission.

The reliable 4½-hour tours offered by **Gray Line** (www.graylineneworleans.com; ✆ **800/535-7786** or 504/569-1401) visit Oak Alley or Laura Plantation. Daily tours depart Gray Line's Toulouse Street station; exact times vary during the year, so call ahead (adults $61, children 6–12 $30). Mainstay tour company **Cajun Encounters** has twice-daily combo tours of both plantations ($80 adults, $59 children), as well as a very full day outing that adds a swamp tour ($124 adults, $85 children) (www.

cajunencounters.com; © **866-928-6877** or 504/834-1770). For smaller groups, we like **Tours by Isabelle** (www.toursbyisabelle.com; © **877/665-8687** or 504/398-0365). Isabelle Cossart takes groups of 6 to 13 people in a comfortable van on a half-day expedition to Oak Alley and Laura (others by arrangement) or Houmas House and St. Joseph plantation ($100).

Plantations Between New Orleans & Baton Rouge

The plantations below are listed in the order in which they appear on the map, running north along the Mississippi from New Orleans. Tours range from 1½ to 2½ hours; most people do one or two in a day (and may drive past others). Depending on your choices, you may have to cross the Mississippi River by bridge a few times. The winding river makes distances deceiving; give yourself more time than you think you'll need. The plantations discussed here are roughly 1 hour from New Orleans (the most accessible for visitors to the city) and 15 minutes apart.

Destrehan Plantation ★★   Its proximity (just 30 min. from New Orleans), in-character docents (better than it sounds), and role in *Interview with the Vampire* have made Destrehan Manor a popular plantation jaunt. It's the oldest intact plantation home in the lower Mississippi Valley open to the public. Built in 1787 by a free person of color for a wealthy Frenchman, it was modified from its "dated" French colonial style to Greek Revival in the 1830s. Its warmly colored, graceful lines are aesthetically pleasing, and some original furnishings remain. One room has been left un-renovated, to show the humble rawness beneath the usual public grandeur. Unlike most plantation homes, Destrehan has ramps and an elevator.

13034 River Rd., La. 48, Destrehan, LA 70047. www.destrehanplantation.org © **877/453-2095** or 985/764-9315. Admission $18 adults, $7 children 6–16, free for children 5 and under. Daily 9am–4pm. Closed New Year's Day, Mardi Gras, Easter, Thanksgiving, and Dec 24–25.

San Francisco ★★   This brightly colored "steamboat Gothic" mansion was completed in 1856 by Edmond B. Marmillion, who died before he could occupy the home. He willed it to his two sons, one of whom married in 1855 while on a grand tour of Europe. The new wife undertook elaborate redecorations, leaving the son *sans fruscin*, or "without a cent." Thus its first name, St. Frusquin . . . later changed to San Francisco.

The fanciful, three-story house, which underwent a $1.3 million freshening in 2014, has wide galleries resembling a ship's double decks, and twin stairs leading to a broad main portal. Inside, there is beautiful carved woodwork, cypress ceilings, and walls gloriously painted with flowers, birds, nymphs, and cherubs.

2646 Hwy. 44, Garyville, LA 70051. www.sanfranciscoplantation.org. © **888/509-1756** or 985/535-2341. Admission $17 adults, $16 military with ID and AAA members, $10 children 7–17, free for children 6 and under. Daily Apr–Oct 9:40am–4:40pm, Nov–Mar 9:40am–4pm. Closed New Year's Day, Mardi Gras, Easter, Thanksgiving Day, and Dec 24–25.

River Road Pit Stop

Restaurants are in short supply along the River Road. Houmas House and a new cafe at Oak Alley are the best of the mostly so-so eateries at the plantations. Instead, stop at down-home **B&C Seafood,** just east of Laura Plantation. Join the locals digging into steaming trays of boiled seafood and Cajun standards. (2155 Hwy. 18, Vacherie; © **225/265-8356;** all items $5–$24; Mon–Sat 11am–4:30pm.)

Laura: A Creole Plantation ★★★ If you see only one plantation, make it Laura, simple on the outside but utterly absorbing within. It has no hoop-skirted guides, offering instead a thorough view of daily life on an 18th- and 19th-century sugar plantation, a cultural history of Louisiana's Creole population, and a mesmerizing, in-depth examination of one Creole family. Much is known about this house and its residents thanks to extensive records (more than 5,000 documents researched in France), including the detailed memoirs of its namesake, proto-feminist head-of-household Laura Locoul. Many of the original artifacts on display—from cookware to jewelry—were saved by employees in a devastating 2004 fire, after which the main house and a slave cabin were accurately restored to the 1805 period. *Fun fact #1:* The beloved B'rer Rabbit stories were first collected here by a folklorist in the 1870s. *Fun fact #2:* Fats Domino's parents lived on this plantation.

2247 La. 18, Vacherie, LA 70090. www.lauraplantation.com. © **888/799-7690** or 225/265-7690. Admission $20 adults, $18 for military and AAA members, $6 children 6–17, free for children 5 and under. Tours run every 40 minutes. Daily 10am–4pm; last tour begins at 4pm. Tours in French available Tues and Sat; special-interest tours on Creole architecture, Creole women, children, or slavery available with advance notice. Closed New Year's Day, Mardi Gras, Easter, Thanksgiving, and Dec 25.

Oak Alley Plantation ★★★ This is precisely what comes to mind when most people think "plantation." A splendid white house, its porch lined with giant columns, approached by a magnificent quarter-mile drive lined with stately oak trees (the 1839 house has 28 fluted Doric columns to match the 28 trees)—yep, it's all here. Consequently, this Hollywood honey is the most famous plantation house in Louisiana. It's also the slickest operation, with hoop-skirted guides and golf carts traversing the blacktopped property.

Oak Alley lay disintegrating until 1914; new owners and restorers were responsible for its National Historic Landmark designation. The tour provides fewer details about the families who lived here than about general plantation life. New in 2013, a row of re-created slave quarters needs a few years (or centuries) to feel authentic but their well-researched displays do a good job of illuminating the life of the slaves, and the means by which this plantation survived. Our favorite OA feature (besides the truly impressive row of mighty oaks) may just be the scholarly "Confederate soldier" in the rustic tent out back, who converses with visitors in full character as he polishes his boots or goes about other business of being a soldier (he's not always there, call ahead to check). There's a sit-down restaurant and casual cafe on-site, and you can also stay in one of five pretty, century-old Creole cottages, now bed-and-breakfast rooms.

3645 La. 18, Vacherie, LA 70090. www.oakalleyplantation.com. © **800/442-5539** or 225/265-2151. Admission $20 adults, $7.50 students 13–18, $4.50 children 6–12, free for children 5 and under. Discounts for 65 and over, AAA members, and active military. Grounds open daily at 9am; tours begin every half hour at 10am; Mon–Fri last tour at 4pm; Sat–Sun tours till 5pm. Restaurant hours 8:30am–3pm; casual cafe 9am–5pm. Closed New Year's Day, Thanksgiving, and Dec 25.

Houmas House Plantation & Gardens ★★★ Houmas is actually two houses joined together under one roof: the original, 1775 four-room structure and the larger, Greek Revival–style house, completed in 1828 after 17 years of construction. The former sugar plantation has been restored several times since then, including by the current owner, who invested millions in turning it into a fabulous showcase inside and out, a popular event venue, and his home. It's filled with stunning art and antiques and surrounded by elegant formal gardens. He also installed a lovely cafe, a pleasant bar, and a fine-dining restaurant amid these splendid environs, so one can make a day of it (or 2 days, if one stays in the fetching, new cottages, thoroughly modern in nearly

ST. FRANCISVILLE & SURROUNDING
plantations

St. Francisville doesn't look like much on approach, but by the time you get to the town center, you are utterly charmed. This is not Cajun Country—this area has American plantations only and no French history, but if you're interested in plantations from an architectural, historical, or cultural perspective, you can do well by planting yourself here for an overnighter. It's 30 miles northwest of Baton Rouge and 2 hours by car from New Orleans. Contact the **St. Francisville tourism information office** for details (www.st francisville.us; ℂ **800/789-4221** or 225/635-4224; Mon–Sat 9am–5pm, Sun 9:30am–5pm). Recommended places to stay include the **Barrow House Inn,** at 9779 Royal St. (www.topteninn.com; ℂ **225/635-4791;** $115–$160), with beautifully restored antiques-laden rooms; **Butler Greenwood Plantation B&B,** at 8345 U.S. 61 (www.butlergreenwood.com; ℂ **225/635-6312;** doubles $135), with modest but sweet guest cottages, some with Jacuzzis or fireplaces, set on oak-laden plantation grounds; and **Shade Tree,** 9704 Royal St. (www.shadetreeinn. com; ℂ **225/635-6116;** $145–$195), a peaceful, romantic aerie with a slight hippie bent. Area attractions include:

○ **Magnolia Mound ★** This late-1700s, single-story plantation home was built as a small settler's house and vastly enlarged later. Costumed guides take you through the slave cabins and authentically furnished house, one of the oldest wooden structures in the state (2161

Nicholson Dr., Baton Rouge; www.friendsofmagnoliamound.org; ℂ **225/343-4955;** $10 adults, $8 seniors and students 18–22, $4 children 5–17, free ages 4 and under; Mon–Sat 10am–4pm, Sun 1–4pm; tours begin on the hour with last tour at 3pm).

○ **Oakley Plantation at Audubon State Historic Site ★** This simple home is where John James Audubon painted 32 of his "Birds of America" series. A walk through the gardens and nature trails clearly illustrates why Audubon was so taken with this area; it's part of a 100-acre wildlife sanctuary (La. 965, St. Francisville; www.crt.state.la.us/louisiana-state-parks/historic-sites; ℂ **225/635-3739;** $8 adults, $6 seniors 62 and over, $4 children 6–17, free ages 5 and under; daily 9am–5pm; guided tours of the house hourly 10am–4pm).

○ **Rosedown Plantation ★★** Rosedown is by far the most impressive and historic of the more far-flung plantations, starting with its wide avenue of ancient oaks and dramatic gardens (12501 Hwy. 10, at La. 10 and U.S. 61, St. Francisville; www.lastateparks.com; ℂ **888/376-1867** or 225/635-3332; house tour and historic gardens $10 adults, $8 seniors, $4 students 6–17, free ages 5 and under; daily 9am–5pm; tours begin at 10am).

every way save decor). Note that the upscale restaurant is "event" dining, requiring reservations and proper dress (and a thick wallet).

40136 La. 942, Darrow, LA 70725. www.houmashouse.com. ℂ **888/323-8314** or 225/473-9830. Admission (including guided tour) $24 adults, $15 children 13–18, $10 children 6–12, free for children 5 and under; gardens and grounds only $10. Mon–Tues 9am–5pm, Wed–Sun 9am–8pm. Closed Dec 25 and New Year's Day. Take I-10 from New Orleans or Baton Rouge; exit on La. 44 to Burnside; turn right on La. 942.

Nottoway Plantation ★★ Nottoway is everything you want in a dazzling Old South mansion. Dating from 1858, it's the largest existing plantation house in the South, a mammoth structure with 64 rooms (covering 53,000 sq. ft.) and pillars to rival the White House's. Saved from Civil War destruction by a Northern gunboat officer who had once been a guest here, the still-handsome interiors feature marvelous curlicue plasterwork, hand-carved Corinthian columns of cypress wood in the ballroom, beautiful archways, and original crystal chandeliers. You can also stay here, in rooms with period furnishings and luxurious bathrooms ($240–$320 per night including breakfast; check website for online deals).

31025 La. 1, White Castle, LA 70788. www.nottoway.com. © **866/527-6884** or 225/545-2730. Admission $20 adults, $6 children 6–12, free for children 5 and under. Daily 9am–4pm; tours begin on the hour. Closed Dec 25. From New Orleans, follow I-10 west to La. 22 exit, then turn left on La. 70 across Sunshine Bridge; exit onto La. 1 and drive 14 miles north through Donaldsonville. From Baton Rouge, take I-10 west to Plaquemine exit and then La. 1 south for 18 miles.

CAJUN COUNTRY

This area, also called Acadiana (though you won't find that on the maps) has a history and culture unique in America. It consists of a rough triangle of Louisiana made up of 22 parishes (counties), from St. Landry at the top of the triangle to the Gulf of Mexico at its base. Lafayette is the unofficial "capital" of Acadiana.

Meet the Cajuns

The Cajun's history is a sad one, but it produced a people and a culture well worth knowing. In the early 1600s, colonists from France began settling the southeastern coast of Canada in a region of Nova Scotia they named Acadia. They developed a peaceful agricultural society based on the values of a strong Catholic faith, deep love of family, and respect for their relatively small landholdings.

This pastoral existence was isolated from Europe for nearly 150 years, until Acadia became the property of the British. The king's representatives tried to force the Acadians to pledge allegiance to the British Crown, renounce Catholicism, and embrace the king's Protestantism, but for decades they steadfastly refused. Finally, the British governor of the region sent in troops. Villages were burned and families separated as ships were loaded to deport them. A 10-year diaspora began, scattering them to France, England, America's East Coast, and the West Indies. Hundreds of lives were lost to the terrible conditions onboard.

In 1765, Bernard Andry brought 231 men, women, and children to reestablish a permanent home in Louisiana, a natural destination due to its strong French background. These industrious settlers worked the swampy, wildlife-infested lands, building levees, draining fields, and planting many of the farms you still see here.

Cajun Language

Much of this essay was provided by author, historian, and two-time Grammy nominee Ann Allen Savoy, who, along with her husband, Marc (an acclaimed accordion maker) are members of the Savoy-Doucet Cajun Band and several other groups. The Savoys are celebrated keepers of the culture, not least for having spawned a musical dynasty. All four of their talented children are carrying the cultural torch through their own music and art.

Our standard soundtrack for the drive from New Orleans to Cajun Country begins with the excellent **WWOZ 90.7 FM** (to which we're assiduously tuned while in the city). After an hour on the road, static takes over, signaling the unwrapping of whatever new music we've recently purchased from **Louisiana Music Factory** (p. 197). In about half a CD's time, we can usually pull in **KBON 101.1 FM** for some rollickin' Cajun and zydeco tunes. At that point we know we've arrived, as much in geography as mood.

The French influence in Louisiana is one of the things that sets the state apart from the rest of the United States. Although French is spoken by many of the older Cajuns (ages 60 and up), most middle-aged Louisianans don't speak the language. This is partially because knowledge of the French language, from the 1930s on, became associated with a lack of business success or education. Cajun music was considered hokey, and Cajun culture on the whole was denigrated and stigmatized.

Today, Cajun culture has experienced a resurgence of popularity and respect. The young people are emphatically adopting their ancestors' language, music, recipes, and other traditions and proudly speak with the sharp, bright Cajun accent.

Cajun French is peppered with beautiful old words dating from Louis XIV, unused in France and historically intriguing. It is not a dialect of French, however; many words have been localized (a mosquito can be called a *marougouin* in one area, a *moustique* in another, a *cousin* elsewhere), and "Franglish" is common (*"On va revenir right back"*—"We'll be right back").

Additionally, the fascinating Creole language is still spoken by many black Louisianans. A compilation of French and African dialects, it is quite different from standard French, though Cajuns and black Creoles can speak and understand both languages.

Cajun Music

It's hard to decide which is more important to a Cajun: food or music. In the early days when instruments were scarce, Cajuns held dances to a cappella voices. With roots probably found in medieval France, the strains came in the form of a brisk two-step or a waltz. Traditional groups still play mostly acoustic instruments—a fiddle, an accordion, a triangle, maybe a guitar, and the traditional high, loud wail.

The best place to hear real Cajun music is on someone's back porch, the time-honored spot for eating some gumbo and listening to several generations of players jamming. If you can't wrangle an invitation, the local dance halls on any weekend will do just fine. It's quite the social scene, and there are usually willing dance coaches for newbies (don't be shy—everyone will be watching the really good dancers; you should, too). The following 3-day Cajun weekend takes you on a well-rounded musical introduction to this region. For Cajun music clubs in New Orleans, see p. 170.

Planning Your Trip

You'll see and do a lot during this 3-day weekend, which includes options to customize the trip based on your own interests. A bit of adventurous meandering on your own will most definitely reward you with more finds.

Boudin (boo-*dan*) is a Cajun sausage link made of pork, rice, onions, and spices and stuffed inside a chewy casing. If it's done right, it's spicy and sublime. In these parts, you can get this inexpensive (about $3 per lb.) snack at just about any grocery store or gas station. Disputes rage about whose reigns supreme (**www.boudinlink.com** has digitized the argument). It's best eaten while leaning against a car, chased with a Barq's root beer. Conducting a comparison test is great fun, but the singular choice in these parts is the **Best Stop** (615 Hwy. 93 N., Scott, exit 97 off the I-10; www.beststopinscott.com; ℂ **337/233-5805**). It's always busy, so the links and crunchy pig-fat cracklins (aka *chicharones*) are always fresh. Did we mention that they ship? Send us some *now*, please. Best Stop is open Monday to Saturday 6am to 8pm, Sunday 6am to 6pm.

It's awfully fun to visit Acadiana during **Cajun Mardi Gras** (p. 47), **Festival International de Louisiane** (p. 25), **Festivals Acadiens et Creoles** (p. 26), or the **Breaux Bridge Crawfish Festival**—but any weekend will do. There's plenty of music throughout the year and often a small festival somewhere in the area. If you find one, you simply have to go: they're almost guaranteed to be a memorable social, cultural, and musical experience. (We'll never forget our first Yambilee.)

For tons of good detailed information, contact the **Lafayette Convention and Visitors Commission** (www.lafayettetravel.com; ℂ **800/346-1958** in the U.S., 800/543-5340 in Canada, or 337/232-3737).

Organized Tours

If you only have one day, **Tours by Isabelle** (www.toursbyisabelle.com; ℂ **888/223-2093** or 504/391-3544) offers round-trip van tours that will introduce you to the area ($81 and up). Plan in advance, because they may not be offered every day. Each year, **Festival Tours International** (p. 50) offers a stellar music-focused tour of the area during the 3 days between Jazz Fest weekends. Also see "Organized Tours," p. 151.

A CAJUN 3-DAY WEEKEND

The suggested itinerary for a 3-day side trip from New Orleans to Cajun Country is designed to introduce you to this marvelous, singular culture. The drive from New Orleans is about 2½ to 3 hours, mostly via I-10 (140 miles from New Orleans). If you opt to drive back via U.S. 90, it's about 170 miles. You'll be based in Lafayette and going to the smaller towns of Eunice, Mamou, and St. Martinville for a thorough immersion in real Cajun culture. We've provided main highway directions; a GPS will help get you to the recommended in-town destinations.

Friday, Day 1: Lafayette ★★★

Leave New Orleans early in the day and head for the River Road (Hwy. 18) plantations to tour a plantation (p. 217). Or head directly to Lafayette. *Tip:* Try to avoid going through Baton Rouge at afternoon rush hour.

Cajun Country

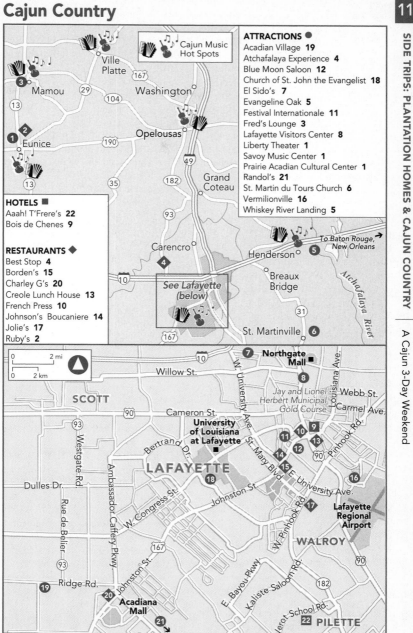

Cajun Music Hot Spots

Ville Platte

Washington

Mamou

Eunice

Opelousas

Grand Coteau

Carencro

Henderson

To Baton Rouge, New Orleans

Breaux Bridge

See Lafayette (below)

St. Martinville

ATTRACTIONS ●
Acadian Village **19**
Atchafalaya Experience **4**
Blue Moon Saloon **12**
Church of St. John the Evangelist **18**
El Sido's **7**
Evangeline Oak **5**
Festival Internationale **11**
Fred's Lounge **3**
Lafayette Visitors Center **8**
Liberty Theater **1**
Savoy Music Center **1**
Prairie Acadian Cultural Center **1**
Randol's **21**
St. Martin du Tours Church **6**
Vermilionville **16**
Whiskey River Landing **5**

HOTELS ■
Aaah! T'Frere's **22**
Bois de Chenes **9**

RESTAURANTS ◆
Best Stop **4**
Borden's **15**
Charley G's **20**
Creole Lunch House **13**
French Press **10**
Johnson's Boucaniere **14**
Jolie's **17**
Ruby's **2**

Northgate Mall

Willow St.

SCOTT

Jay and Lionel Herbert Municipal Gold Course

Webb St.

Carmel Ave.

Cameron St.

University of Louisiana at Lafayette

Bertrand Dr.

LAFAYETTE

Dulles Dr.

Johnston St.

E. University Ave.

Lafayette Regional Airport

WALROY

Ridge Rd.

Acadiana Mall

PILETTE

227

Lafayette is a midsize city of 120,000, with a university (LSU) and plenty of hotel options. But we recommend you opt for an atmospheric B&B instead. Check in at **Aaah! T'Frere's Bed & Breakfast** (1905 Verot School Rd., Lafayette; www.tfreres.com; ℂ **800/984-9347** or 337/984-9347; doubles $135) or **Bois de Chenes Bed & Breakfast** (338 N. Sterling St., Lafayette; www.boisdechenes. com; ℂ **337/233-7816;** doubles $110–$150).

Plan to arrive in time for lunch and go directly to **Creole Lunch House** (713 12th St., Lafayette; www.facebook.com/creolesstuffedbread; ℂ **337/232-9929**). Get a couple of stuffed breads and whatever's been smothered that day (chicken thighs, pork chop, shoe, it's all gonna be ridiculously good).

Relax or take a drive around town. Visit the **Church of St. John the Evangelist** (515 Cathedral St., Lafayette; www.saintjohncathedral.org; ℂ **337/232-1322**), a splendid Dutch Romanesque edifice done in red and white brick, with fine stained glass dating to 1916.

For dinner, try **Charley G's** (3809 Ambassador Caffery Pkwy., Lafayette; www.charleygs.com; ℂ **337/981-0108**), one of Lafayette's better seafood houses. If you have room, squeeze in a sundae from **Borden's** (1103 Jefferson St., Lafayette; www.bordensicecreamshoppe.com; ℂ **337/235-9291**), an ice cream parlor that's hardly changed since it scooped its first cone of creamy goodness back in 1940. Otherwise, head back and hit your relaxing veranda and cushy bed— Saturday is a full day.

Saturday, Day 2: Eunice & Mamou ★★

Make the 35-minute drive to the **Savoy Music Center,** 3 miles east of Eunice (Hwy. 190 E.; www.savoymusiccenter.com; ℂ **337/457-9563;** Tues–Fri 9am– 5pm, closed for lunch noon–1:30pm; Sat jam 9am–noon). On weekdays this working music store sells instruments, equipment, and Marc Savoy's exquisite, world-renowned, hand-crafted accordions (check out the folk-art aphorisms scrawled on his workshop cabinets, if you can). At the Saturday-morning jam sessions, this nondescript, faded-green building becomes the spiritual center of Cajun music, and an experience not to be missed. Local and visiting musicians young and old gather to savor this unpretentious, unparalleled music and culture. It's probably the closest thing to that back-porch experience you'll find. Bring some boudin, an instrument, or just an interest.

Stay and savor this utter authenticity, or cut out (no later than 11:30) to head for the alternate universe known as **Fred's Lounge** in Mamou, about 20 minutes north (west on U.S. 190, then right on LA 13; 420 6th St.; ℂ **337/468-5411;** Sat 8am–2pm; music starts at 9am). This is the other end of the Cajun music spectrum, a small-town bar that for half a century has hosted Saturday daytime dances starting in the early morn. Couples waltz and two-step around the mid-floor bandstand, while 80-something matriarch Tante Sue drinks shots and otherwise presides. It's pure dance-hall stuff (leaning toward the country-western side of Cajun, but much of it in French), where hardworking locals let loose. And we do mean loose (remember, they started with Coors while you were still on coffee).

Back to Eunice, sample a down-home lunch at **Ruby's** (221 W. Walnut Ave., Eunice; ℂ **337/550-7665**). Get the thick, crisp-fried pork chops if they're on the day's menu, and some stewed okra. Revise all that if the crawfish étouffée is on (or just get both; it's a long break before dinner).

Take in some mellow museum time at the **Prairie Acadian Cultural Center** (250 W. Park Ave.; www.nps.gov/jela/prairie-acadian-cultural-center-eunice.htm; ℂ 337/457-8499; free admission, donations accepted; Wed–Fri 9:30am–4:30pm, Sat 9:30am–6pm), a terrific small collection. Most objects on display were acquired from local families who had owned them for generations, and craft demonstrations, cooking demos, or dance lessons may be in the offing. The most worthy attraction may help dispel the myths and patronizing stereotypes perpetuated by the recent rash of Louisiana-based reality shows.

Each Saturday, when the Cultural Center shuts down, visitors—well, the entire town—migrate next door to the 1924 **Liberty Theater** (2nd St. and Park Ave.; www.eunice-la.com; ℂ 337/457-7389; $5; doors open at 4pm, show 6–7:30pm), where the all-French show "Rendez-vous des Cajuns" kicks off with live music, dancing, and jokey storytelling. Even if you speak *non* French, you'll get it. *Note:* Tickets go on sale at 4pm, so you may need to take a break from the Cultural Center to buy them lest they sell out. If you can't make it (big mistake), tune in to 1490 on your AM channel (locally) or krvs.org for the stream.

Your dinner bell is probably ringing loudly, and porky delights await you back in Lafayette at **Johnson's Boucaniere** (1111 St. John St., Lafayette; www. johnsonsboucaniere.com; ℂ 337/269-8878; Tues–Thurs 10am–6pm, Fri 10am–9pm, Sat 7am–9pm). The Johnson family has been smoking meats since 1937, and their brisket (and that crazy grilled cheese and boudin ball sandwich) should not be missed. There are only a few tables, so if you're weary, call in your order from the road and take it to enjoy back at your B&B.

Still up for more? Check out what's on at the **Blue Moon Saloon** (215 E. Convent St., Lafayette; www.bluemoonpresents.com; ℂ 337/234-2422; cover $10–$20; Wed–Sat 8pm–close), the city's premier live music venue. Cajun, zydeco, and all forms of modern alternative roots music brings in the LSU student body and others. For more traditional Cajun music and dancing, two-step to **Randol's** (2320 Kaliste Saloom Rd.; www.randols.com; ℂ 337/981-7080; Sun–Thurs 5–9:30pm, Fri–Sat 5–10:30pm). You may be joined by fellow tourists on the dance floor, but on Saturday nights you'll certainly find an easygoing, accessible scene (you can dine here as well, but the dance scene trumps the cuisine). For the adventurous night owl, find your way to the outskirts of town and **El Sido's** (1523 N. St. Antoine St., Lafayette; www.facebook.com/pages/El-Sidos-Zydeco-Blues-Club.; ℂ 337/235-0647; cover $7–$15; Fri–Sat 9pm–2am, occasionally Sun–Mon during festival weekends). It's not always easy to find out what's on at the gritty, long-standing roadhouse, but on Saturday night it's a good bet it's zydeco, often with a bluesy or urban edge, and some astoundingly good dancing. It gets going around 10pm.

Sunday, Day 3: Lafayette & St. Martinville ★★

After a relaxing breakfast at your B&B, visit **Vermilionville ★★** (300 Fisher Rd., off Surrey St.; www.vermilionville.org; ℂ 337/233-4077; $10 adults, $8 seniors, $6 students, free for children 5 and under; Tues–Sun 10am–4pm; admission desk closes at 3pm), a Cajun-Creole settlement reconstructed on the bayou's banks, where costumed staff and craftspeople demonstrate activities of 18th- to 19th-century daily life and musicians jam. While it sounds like a kitschy "Cajunland" theme park, it's actually quite a good introduction to the culture.

Or take the **Atchafalaya Experience,** Lafayette (www.theatchafalaya experience.com; © **337/277-4726** or 337/233-7816; $50 ages 13 and up, $25 children 8–12, free for 7 and under [1 per family]; call for times and reservations), an outstanding swamp, bird, and wildlife tour led by virtuoso naturalists who were raised on these bayous (if you're staying at Bois des Chenes B&B, it's the men of the house). If you have not yet taken to the waters of the Louisiana swamps, seeing this stunning, primeval, vital ecosystem is a must-do, and these guides are as good as it gets. Bring a hat, sunscreen, water, and insect repellent.

Lunch returns you to downtown Lafayette to the **French Press** (214 E. Vermilion St.; www.thefrenchpresslafayette.com; © **337/233-9449;** Mon–Fri 7am–2pm, Sat–Sun 9am–2pm, Fri–Sat 5:30–9pm), a casual but refined spot on the higher end of the hipness scale. The biscuit sliders with boudin balls and sugarcane syrup are to kill for; the chicken and waffles aren't far behind. If you're ready for lighter fare, the winning shrimp salad boasts a kicking rémoulade.

To further experience the history, legend, and romance of this region, take a leisurely drive to the lovely, historic burg of **St. Martinville.** Get there by taking Pinhook Road to the small country route, LA 96, and driving 16 miles to reach the peaceful town square. St. Martinville dates from 1765, when it was a military station. It was once known as "la Petite Paris" for the many French aristocrats who settled here after fleeing the French Revolution.

The town centers around **St. Martin du Tours Church,** constructed in 1836—the fourth-oldest Roman Catholic church in Louisiana—and poetry. Besides its natural and historic charm, the town is the home of Evangeline Emmeline, the (debatably) fictional heroine of Longfellow's tragic poem. A statue of her next to the church was donated to the town in 1929 by a movie company that filmed the epic here; star Dolores del Rio supposedly posed for the sculptor. At Port Street and Bayou Teche is the ancient **Evangeline Oak** and commemorative mural, where self-proclaimed descendants claim Emmeline's boat landed after her arduous journey from Nova Scotia.

From St. Martinville, return to New Orleans via I-10 again, or alternately, via U.S. 90 for a different view. It's slightly longer and moderately more interesting.

PLANNING YOUR TRIP TO NEW ORLEANS

N o matter what your idea of the perfect New Orleans trip is, this chapter will give you the information to make informed plans about getting here, getting around, and the essentials for an easy Big Easy vacation. We'll also point you toward additional resources, so you can let the *bons temps* begin even before you arrive.

GETTING THERE

By Plane

Most major domestic airlines serve the city's **Louis Armstrong New Orleans International Airport (MSY).** All international flights connect through other cities. The airport is 15 miles west of the city in Kenner. Information booths are scattered around the airport and in the baggage claim area, as is a branch of the **Travelers Aid Society.**

Southern Airways Express (www.iflysouthern.com) operates regional flights from Memphis, Birmingham, Destin, and other midsize Southern cities to **Lakefront Airport (NEW).** The Art Deco airport is 9 miles from downtown New Orleans.

GETTING INTO TOWN FROM THE AIRPORT

For $20 per person (one-way), the official **Airport Shuttle New Orleans** (www.airportshuttleneworleans.com; ✆ **866/596-2699** or 504/522-3500) van will take you directly from the airport to your hotel in the French Quarter, Garden District, Central Business District, or Faubourg Marigny. There are Airport Shuttle information desks (staffed 24 hr.) in the airport. *Note:* If you plan to take the Airport Shuttle *to* the airport when you depart, you must call a day in advance to arrange a pickup time. You can also book and pay for a round-trip ($38) in advance, via phone, or online. It's free for kids 5 and under.

A **taxi** from the airport to most hotels will cost $33 for 1 to 2 people; for 3 or more passengers it's $14 per person. Taxi stands are outside the baggage-claim area.

To ride in style from the airport to your hotel, try **Bonomolo Limousine Service** (www.bonolimo.com; ✆ **800/451-9258** or 504/522-0892). Airport transfer service in a Lincoln MKS starts at $75 plus 20% gratuity.

From the airport, you can reach the **Central Business District** by **Jefferson Transit public bus No. E-2** for $2. The bus goes to Tulane

Heads-Up on Airport Rental Car Facility

The gleaming new airport rental car facility can be easy peazy or nightmarish. If you arrive in New Orleans on a nice day at Concourse D (Delta, United), you and your little roll-aboard can expect a pleasant jaunt to pick up your rental car. If, however, you arrive at Concourse B (Southwest/Air Tran, USAirways), have multiple bags, a weary family, are traveling solo, or if it's humid or raining sideways, the looong, open-air walk to the rental facility can be utterly miserable. There are no regular shuttles, but you can call **MVI Field**

Services to request golf-cart assistance (✆ **615/318-3108**); however, it only goes part of the way. Alternately, if you have a travel companion, leave them with the bags, do the hike, pick up your car, then swing back to retrieve companion and cargo (on the return trip drop [']em all off at the curb first). Otherwise, rent a luggage cart, take deep breaths, and make the trek. Allow ample extra time for the extra hassle. Hopefully this will be fixed when the new terminal opens in 2018—or sooner.

Avenue and Carrollton Avenue daily, or Tulane and Loyola Monday to Friday, where riders can transfer to the Regional Transit Authority lines for an additional $1.25. Buses run from 5:20am, departing from the upper level of the airport about every 25 minutes. The Tulane/Carrollton line runs until 9pm daily; the line to Loyola runs until 6:30pm Monday to Friday only. For more information, call **Jefferson Transit** (www. jeffersontransit.org; ✆ **504/818-1077**) or the **Regional Transit Authority** (www.norta. com; ✆ **504/248-3900**).

By Car

You can drive to New Orleans via **I-10, I-55, U.S. 90, U.S. 61,** or across the Lake Pontchartrain Causeway on **La. 25.** If possible, drive in during daylight and allow time to enjoy the distinctive, swampy scenery. U.S. 61 or La. 25 offer the best views, but the larger roads are considerably faster.

Approximate drive time to New Orleans from Atlanta is 8 hours; from Houston it's 6 hours; Chicago, 15 hours; Baton Rouge is an hour and a half away.

Driving in New Orleans can be a hassle, and parking is a nightmare. It's a great city for walking, and cabs are plentiful and reasonable, so you really don't need a car unless you're planning several day trips. Nevertheless, most major national car-rental companies are represented at the airport.

International visitors should note that insurance and taxes are almost never included in quoted rental-car rates in the U.S., and they can be significant. See "Getting Around," later in this chapter, for more on rental-car age and payment requirements.

By Train

Passenger rail lines pass through some beautiful scenery. **Amtrak** (www.amtrak.com; ✆ **800/872-7245** or 504/528-1612) trains serve the city's **Union Passenger Terminal,** 1001 Loyola Ave. in the Central Business District. The station is on the recently completed Loyola streetcar line, and plenty of taxis wait outside the passenger terminal. Hotels in the French Quarter and the Central Business District are a short ride or a healthy walk away.

By Ship

It's not usually considered "transportation," but several major cruise lines do embark from the Port of New Orleans. Many passengers add a visit to the Crescent City before or after their Caribbean cruise—a right fine vacation. Contact **Royal Caribbean** (www.royalcaribbean.com; ℂ **866/562-7625**), **Carnival Cruises** (www.carnival.com; ℂ **888/227-6482**), or **Norwegian Cruise Line** (www.ncl.com; ℂ **866/234-7350**) for information. **American River Cruises** (www.americancruiselines.com; ℂ **800/460-4618**) and the **American Queen Steamboat Company** (www.americanqueen steamboatcompany.com; ℂ **888/749-5280**) both ply the Mississippi River to New Orleans, while **Blount Small Ship Adventures'** cruise hugs the Gulf Shore (www. blountsmallshipadventures.com; ℂ **800/556-7450**).

Taxi fare from the cruise terminal to most hotels is $10 for the first person and $7 for each additional person.

GETTING AROUND

By Car

Unless you're planning extensive or far-flung explorations outside the major tourist zones, you really don't need to rent a car during your stay in New Orleans. The town is flat, ultra-picturesque, and made for walking; there are plenty of taxis and good public transportation. Indeed, a streetcar ride is as much entertainment as a practical means of getting around. Meanwhile, driving and parking in the French Quarter bring grief. Many streets are narrow, potholed, crowded, and one-way. Outside the gridded Quarter, streets angle in logic-defying directions in attempt to align around the curvy Mississippi River. Street parking is minimal and lots are fiendishly expensive (hotel lots can be criminally high). That said, this book still recommends a few outlying destinations for those who can access them.

You'll pay a premium to pick up a rental at the airport (see the "Heads-up" box above), but it may be worth the convenience. If you're stay is lengthy, weigh the difference between renting from a lower-cost, in-town location, and paying transportation costs to and from that cheaper locale.

If you're visiting from abroad and plan to rent a car in the United States, foreign driver's licenses are usually recognized, but you should get an international one if your home license is not in English.

All the major **car-rental agencies** have a presence in New Orleans and as usual, rates vary widely according to company, demand, and when you book your reservation. Plan in advance, and shop around.

To rent a car in the United States, you need a valid driver's license and a major credit card (and a passport for foreign visitors). Some will accept a debit card with a cash deposit. The minimum age is usually 25, but Enterprise and Budget will rent to younger people for an added surcharge; they may also require proof of ability to pay (such as paycheck stubs and utility bills). It's a good idea to buy insurance coverage unless you're certain your own auto or credit card insurance is sufficient.

At press time in New Orleans, the **cost of gasoline** (also called gas, but never petrol), is about $3.50 a gallon including tax, but we all know how that can fluctuate. Generally, gas costs in New Orleans tends to be at or slightly below the U.S. average. Gas stations are readily available on major streets, but none are located within the

French Quarter. Most accept credit or debit cards right at the pump or via prepayment to the clerk (clerks will also accept cash, of course). Change is given inside if your tank fills up before you reach your prepaid amount.

When driving in New Orleans, **right turns on a red light** are legal except where NO RIGHT TURN ON RED signs are posted, so keep your eyes open for those. Similarly, many major intersections restrict left turns. Drive past the intersection, make a U-turn at the next allowable place, then double back and turn right (a maneuver sometimes called the "Louisiana left").

Streetcars run down the center of Canal Street and St. Charles, Carrollton, and Loyola avenues, requiring motorists to cross their paths frequently. **Look** *both* **ways for streetcars,** yield the right of way to them, and allow ample time to complete track crossings. They'll brake between stops if you're in their way, of course, but it's best not to get stuck on the tracks and impede their progress.

It is illegal to have an open container of alcohol, including "go cups," in a moving car, and, of course, driving while under the influence of alcohol is a serious offense.

Keep doors locked and never leave belongings, packages, or gadgets (GPS, iPods, and the like) visible in parked cars.

By Taxi

Taxis are plentiful in New Orleans, and except during the busiest times (looking at you, Mardi Gras and Jazz Fest) they can be hailed easily on the street in the French Quarter and in some parts of the Central Business District. They also usually line up at taxi stands at larger hotels. Otherwise, call and expect a cab to appear in about 15 minutes; much longer during peak times, events, and in residential areas. The rate is $3.50 when you enter the taxi and $2.40 per mile thereafter. During special events, the rate is $5 per person (or the meter rate if it's greater) to the event site. From the French Quarter to an uptown restaurant or club, expect to spend $15 to $22; cash or credit cards accepted. The fee for transfers between hotels is $10 no matter how short the ride.

The cab behemoth is **United Cabs** (www.unitedcabs.com; ✆ **504/524-9606**). **Nawlins Cab** (a family breakaway from United) operates by smartphone app (www.nawlinscab.com; ✆ **504/522-9059**) as does **Carriage Cab,** the slightly upscale sister to Checker and Yellow Cabs (www.neworleanscarriagecab.com; ✆ **504/207-7777**). No Uber or Lyft options (yet).

You can also hire a taxi for a few hours or day at negotiable hourly rates (usually in the mid-$30/hour rate), a hassle-free way to tour far-flung areas of the city.

On Foot

We can't stress this enough: Walking is by far the best way to see New Orleans (besides, you need to walk off all those calories!). You'll miss the many unique and sometimes glorious sights if you whiz past them. Slow down, stroll, and take it in. If it's just too hot, humid, or rainy, there's always a cab or bus nearby.

By Bike

One of the best ways to see the city is by bike. The terrain is flat, the breeze feels good, there are new bike paths and improved driver awareness, and you can cover ground pretty swiftly on two wheels. But the busy streets can be bumpy and potholed, so experience and comfort with city riding is helpful. **Bicycle Michael's,** 622 Frenchmen St. (www.bicyclemichaels.com; ✆ **504/945-9505**), is the oldest shop and still has good-quality, multigear hybrids and mountain bikes starting at $25 for a half-day (4 hr.), $35 a day. At the other end of the French Quarter, **American Bicycle Rentals,** 317 Burgundy St. (www.bikerentalneworleans.com; ℭ **866/293-4037**) has super-sturdy, well-maintained, cushy-seated single-speed bikes with coaster brakes for $10 an hour; $25 for a half-day, $36 full day. At 1818 Magazine Street in the Lower Garden District, **A Musing Bicycles** (amusingbikes.com; ℭ **504/208-9779**) rents single-speed cruisers by the hour ($8) or day ($30). **Joy Ride Bicycles** (www.joyridebikerentals.com; ℭ **504/982-1617**) delivers lightweight, single-speed cruiser bikes to hotels; full-day rentals only (or longer) start at $35 a day. All include tools; baskets and helmets (recommended, but not required) may be additional. Credit-card deposits and waiver signatures are required, and longer-term rentals are available. Also see "Bicycle & Other Wheeled Tours," p. 160.

By Pedicab

Relatively new to the city, these rickshaw-like tricycles will get two people from A to B via pedal power (a driver's, not yours). They're easy to hail in the French Quarter and occasionally seen in other tourist parts, or you can call to request one—try **Bike Taxi Unlimited** (ℭ **504/891-3441**) or **NOLA Pedicabs** (ℭ **504/274-1300**). Rates are $5 for the first 5 blocks, $1 per block per person after that. It's a great option for fatigued feet or short hops; longer jaunts can add up fast so ask for the rate when you board.

By Ferry

The **Canal Street/Algiers Ferry** is one of the city's great assets, not just for transportation to the old Algiers Point neighborhood, but to get a view of the city from the Mississippi River. It's a working ferry, but it's more than that at night, when the city's glowing skyline reflects on the water. The 25-minute ride from the foot of Canal Street costs $2 each way. The ferry leaves New Orleans at 15 and 45 minutes past the hour Monday to Thursday 7:30am to 6pm, Friday 7:30am to 7:30pm, Saturday 11am to 7:30pm, and Sunday 11am to 5:30pm. Hours are currently in flux; verify them online. (1 Canal St., across the tracks and up the big stairs; www.nolaferries.com; ℭ **504/376-8233.**)

By Bus

New Orleans has a good public bus system that many locals rely on, so chances are there's a bus that runs exactly where you want to go. The fare is $1.25; transfers are an extra 25¢. You must have exact change in bills or coins, or you can use a **JazzyPass;**

Discounted Rides with the JazzyPass

If you don't have a car in New Orleans, invest in a **JazzyPass,** which allows unlimited rides on all streetcar and bus lines. It's a bargain and a convenience at $3 for 1 day or $9 for 3 days. One-day passes can be purchased when boarding. Get multiday passes at area Walgreens drugstores, vending machines at key streetcar stops, some hotel concierge desks, or online (but allow a week, as a physical card is mailed to you). More info at **Regional Transit Authority (RTA;** www.norta.com; ℭ **504/248-3900**).

see box). For route information, contact the **RTA** (www.norta.com; ℂ **504/248-3900**) or pick up one of the excellent city maps at the **Visitor Information Center,** 529 St. Ann St., in the French Quarter.

By Streetcar

Besides being a National Historic Landmark, the **St. Charles Avenue streetcar** is also a convenient, scenic, and fun way to get from downtown to Uptown and back. The iconic green cars click and clack for 6½ miles 24 hours a day at frequent intervals and get crowded at school and business rush hours. Board at Canal and Carondelet streets (directly across Canal from Bourbon St. in the French Quarter) or anywhere along the line.

The tracks wind beyond the point where St. Charles Avenue bends into Carrollton Avenue, ending at Palmer Park (Claiborne Avenue). The original cars run on the St. Charles line, so it's not air-conditioned or wheelchair accessible (and it's a big step up). All other lines have A/C and lifts.

The **Riverfront streetcar** line runs the length of the French Quarter, from the Old Mint at Esplanade past the Convention Center to the Pontchartrain Expressway, with stops along the way. It runs daily 7:30am to 10:30pm, and is a great foot saver as you explore the riverfront. The spiffy, bright-red cars on the **Canal Street** line service two destinations. Check the sign on the front of the car: "Cemeteries" goes to several of the older cemeteries and runs daily 5am to 3am; "City Park" goes through Mid-City, to City Park/the New Orleans Museum of Art and Jazz Fest (expect jammed streetcars during Jazz Fest). The City Park route runs between 7am and 1:15am.

The new **Loyola line** runs along Loyola Street, connecting the Union Passenger Terminal (and Amtrak and Greyhound passengers) with the Canal Street line, and continues to the French Market on weekends (Sat–Sun 6:30am–9:30pm).

The **fare** for any streetcar line is $1.25 each way. Add 25¢ to transfer to or from a city bus. All streetcars take exact change in bills or coins only, or **JazzyPasses**.

FAST FACTS: NEW ORLEANS

African-American Travelers   New Orleans's African-American history is rich with important milestones, from the joyous nascence of jazz to the horrors of the slave trade to crucial civil rights achievements (to say nothing of the essential contributions to the city's culture, cuisine, politics, and literature). The **historic Tremé neighborhood** is a touchstone in itself, with a number of worthy sights within its bounds (see box, p. 155). The statewide **African American Heritage Trail** is an excellent network of cultural and historic points; information and maps are available at www.astorylikenoother.com. A tour of the **9th Ward** may be of interest (see "Organized Tours," p. 151). The **House of Dance and Feathers** (1317 Tupelo St.; www.houseofdanceand feathers.org; ℂ **504/957-2678**) is essential for anyone interested in the Mardi Gras Indian tradition, though it's open by appointment only. The **Essence Festival** is a huge draw (p. 25), and the restaurant and music options relevant to black heritage could fill a weeklong vacation.

Area Codes   The area code for New Orleans is 504.

Business Hours   They vary, but most stores are open from at least 10am to 5pm; bars can stay open until the wee hours, and restaurants' hours vary depending on the types of meals they serve. Expect

African-American Travelers | PLANNING YOUR TRIP TO NEW ORLEANS breakfast to start around 8am, lunch around 11am, and dinner at 6pm.

Car Rental See "By Car" under "Getting There," earlier in this chapter.

Cellphones See "Mobile Phones," later in this section.

Crime See "Safety," later in this section.

Customs For U.S. Customs details and information on what you're allowed to bring home, consult your home country's customs services agency. In the U.S., consult **U.S. Customs** at **U.S. Customs & Border Protection (CBP),** 1300 Pennsylvania Ave. NW, Washington, DC 20229 (www.cbp.gov or www.ct.gov/dcp; 📞 **877/ 227-5511**).

Doctors See "Health."

Drinking Laws The legal age for purchase and consumption of alcoholic beverages is 21; proof of age is required and often requested at bars, nightclubs, and restaurants, so bring ID when you go out. Due to recent crackdowns, nowadays pretty much everyone—even senior citizens—can get carded. Alcoholic beverages are available round-the-clock, 7 days a week. Bars can stay open all night in New Orleans, and liquor is sold in grocery and liquor stores. You're allowed to drink in public, but not from a glass or bottle. Bars will provide a plastic "go cup" into which

you can transfer your drink as you leave (and some have walk-up windows for quick and easy refills).

Warning: Although New Orleans has a reputation for tolerance, make no mistake: Public intoxication and "drunk and disorderly" are most definitely illegal, as many a jailed tourist can testify. Practice moderation and make smart decisions. And don't even think about driving (car, motorcycle, *or* bicycle) while intoxicated: This is a zero-tolerance crime. Further, do not carry open containers of alcohol in your car or any public area that isn't zoned for alcohol consumption. The police can fine you on the spot.

Driving Rules See "Getting Around," p. 233.

Electricity Like Canada, the United States uses 110 to 120 volts AC (60 cycles), compared to 220 to 240 volts AC (50 cycles) in most of Europe, Australia, and New Zealand. Downward converters that change 220–240 volts to 110–120 volts are difficult to find in the United States, so bring one with you.

Embassies & Consulates All embassies are in the nation's capital, Washington, D.C. Some have consulate offices in major U.S. cities, including a few in New Orleans. To find a consulate for your home country, call for directory information in Washington, D.C. (📞 **202/555-1212**), or check www.embassy.org/

embassies. It's always a good idea to enter this information in your contacts before you leave your home country.

Emergencies For fire, ambulance, and police, dial 📞 **911** from any phone (it is a free call). Calls from landlines (hard-wired phones) will route to the local emergency dispatch center. From mobile phones, immediately tell the operator your location and the nature of the emergency.

Family Travel New Orleans doesn't spring to mind as the first place to take a child, but it offers plenty of activities and sights appropriate for children, who often get a real kick out of the city (and love Mardi Gras!). Summer months bring the heat but also the bargains, so weigh your family's tolerance levels for a visit during school vacation. See p. 161.

Gasoline Please see "By Car" under "Getting Around," earlier in this chapter.

Health The widespread mold and floodwater-related illnesses that were feared after Katrina never materialized, and there have been no ill effects on air or water supply from the Deepwater oil spill. Booze and butter pose greater dangers.

If you have a medical condition that may require care, make appropriate arrangements before traveling to New Orleans. See "Hospitals," below, for **hospitals** and an **emergency**

number. If you need a doctor for less urgent health concerns, try **Ochsner On Call** (www.ochsner.org; ℂ **504/842-3155** or 800/231-5257) or visit **New Orleans Urgent Care,** 900 Magazine St. (www.new orleansurgentcare.com; ℂ **504/552-2433;** Mon–Sat 10am–7pm, Sun 9am–1pm) and 201 Decatur St. (ℂ **504/609-3833;** Mon–Sat 10am–5:30pm). Also see "Pharmacies" in this section.

Pollen, sun, uneven sidewalks, overindulgence, and mosquitoes (especially near the swamps and bayous) are the most common medical annoyances. Packing insect repellent, sunscreen, protective clothing, digestive aids, and antihistamines may help prevent minor health annoyances.

Hospitals In an emergency, dial ℂ **911** from any phone to summon paramedics. For nonemergency injuries or illnesses, call or go to the emergency room at **Ochsner Baptist Medical Center,** 2700 Napoleon Ave. (ℂ **504/899-9311**), or the **Tulane University Medical Center,** 1415 Tulane Ave. (ℂ **504/588-5800**).

Insurance Travel insurance is a good "safety net" idea if you think for some reason you may need to cancel or postpone your trip (or even if you don't). Most medical insurance policies cover you if you are on vacation, but check with

your policy before you depart.

Internet, Wi-Fi & Computer Rentals Nearly all major hotels have free Wi-Fi in their lobbies, as do many cafes, bars, and all Starbucks (there's one in the French Quarter in the Canal Place Mall, 365 Canal St.; ℂ **504/566-1223**). The vast majority of hotels also offer some form of in-room Internet access, usually high-speed, often wireless. Many now include the cost in the room charge; some add a daily surcharge of $10 to $20. Barring that, the easiest option is simply to boot up and see what signals you get; or walk down any commercial street and look for "Free Wi-Fi" signs. It's a pretty well-wired city. Alternately, a concierge or front desk attendant should be able to direct you to nearby public Wi-Fi locations.

Most larger hotels have business centers with computers for rent. **FedEx Offices** with fully loaded rental computer stations with Internet access can be found at 555 Canal St. (ℂ **504/654-1057**); 762 St. Charles Ave. (ℂ **504/581-2541**); and several other locations. **Louis Armstrong Airport** has free, so-so Wi-Fi coverage in all passenger areas.

Language English is spoken everywhere, while French, Cajun, and Spanish are heard occasionally in New Orleans.

Legal Aid If you are pulled over by the police for

a minor infraction (such as speeding), never attempt to pay the fine directly to an officer; this could be construed as attempted bribery, a much more serious crime. Pay fines by mail, or directly into the hands of the clerk of the court. If accused of a more serious offense, say and do nothing before consulting a lawyer. Here in the U.S., the burden is on the state to prove a person's guilt beyond a reasonable doubt, and everyone has the right to remain silent, whether he or she is suspected of a crime or actually arrested. Once arrested, a person can make one telephone call to a party of his or her choice. The international visitor should call his or her embassy or consulate.

LGBTQ Travelers New Orleans is a very welcoming town with an extensive and active LGBTQ community. For resources, start with **Ambush Magazine,** 828-A Bourbon St. (www.ambush mag.com). The **Big Easy Metropolitan Community Church,** 6200 St. Charles Ave. (www.MCCNew Orleans.org; ℂ **504/270-1622**), serves a primarily gay and lesbian congregation. The website **www. gayneworleans.com** provides information on hotels, restaurants, arts, and nightlife. The local **Lesbian and Gay Community Center** (www.facebook.com/lgbt ccno; www.lgbtccnew orleans.org) doesn't currently have a drop-in location, but its websites have good info. **Faubourg Marigny Art and Books (FAB)** (600 Frenchmen St.; www.fabonfrenchmen.com; ✆ **504/947-3700**) also serves as an unofficial info source. "The Twirl," a gay-history walking tour of the French Quarter from **G L-f de Villiers Tours** (p. 152), is highly recommended. Also see p. 183 for suggested night (and day) clubbing.

Mail & Shipping   At press time, domestic postage rates were 34¢ for a postcard and 49¢ for a letter up to 1 ounce. For international mail, a first-class postcard or letter stamp costs $1.15. For more information, go to **www.usps.com**. Always include ZIP codes when mailing items in the U.S. Use the lookup tool at www.usps.com/zip4.

If you aren't sure what your address will be in the United States, mail can be sent to you, in your name, c/o General Delivery at the main post office of the city or region where you expect to be. (Call ✆ **800/275-8777** for information on the nearest post office.) The addressee must pick up mail in person and produce proof of identity (driver's license, passport, and so on). Most post offices will hold mail for up to 1 month and are open weekdays

8am to 4pm, Saturdays 9am to noon. New Orleans's main post office (701 Loyola Ave. in the Central Business District) has longer hours.

Medical Care   See "Health."

Medical Requirements Unless you're arriving from an area known to be suffering from an epidemic (particularly cholera or yellow fever), inoculations or vaccinations are not required for short-term visitors to the United States.

Mobile Phones   Mobile (cell) phone and texting service in New Orleans is generally good, with the larger carriers all getting excellent coverage. Some dead zones still exist around the city and inside old brick buildings. International mobile phone service can be hit-or-miss (despite what you may have been told before you began your trip). If you plan to use your phone a lot while in New Orleans, it may be worthwhile to purchase an inexpensive, no-contract phone locally. You can get hooked up at **Radio Shack,** 717 Canal St. (✆ **504/523-4827**) or 6045 Magazine St. (✆ **504/895-4765**); or the **Office Depot,** 1429 St. Charles Ave. (✆ **504/561-8846**). Carefully compare the plans' sign-on offers, roaming and

data use charges, usage requirements, and limitations to make sure you're not purchasing more extensive or longer-term services than you need.

If you have a computer and Internet service, consider using a broadband-based telephone service such as **Skype** (www.skype.com) or **Vonage** (www.vonage.com), which allow you to make free international calls from your computer. Neither service requires that the people you're calling also have the service (though there are fees if they do not).

Money & Costs   Frommer's lists prices in U.S. dollars. The currency conversions quoted below were correct at press time. However, rates fluctuate, so before departing consult a currency exchange website such as **www.xe.com**.

Costs in New Orleans are generally right in the middle of, and sometimes lower than, other midsize U.S. "destination" cities—less than New York, for example, but more than Phoenix. Prices have crept up over the last few years, so it's no longer the great value it once was, and costs vary greatly by season. You can often find good hotel deals in the heat of summer, while prices can soar during big

THE VALUE OF THE U.S. DOLLAR VS. OTHER POPULAR CURRENCIES

US$	C$	£	€	A$	NZ$
1.00	1.08	0.59	0.73	1.07	1.17

WHAT THINGS COST IN NEW ORLEANS	US$
Taxi from airport to the Quarter	33.00 (for 2 people)
Shuttle from airport to the Quarter	20.00 (per person)
Cost of bus/streetcar one-way	1.25
Day pass for bus/streetcar	3.00
Standard room at Ritz-Carlton	259.00–529.00
Standard room at The Chimes Bed & Breakfast	128.00–250.00
Standard room at Drury Inn	119.00–239.00
Order of 3 beignets or cup of café au lait at Café du Monde	2.42
Dinner at Commander's Palace (3 courses)	65.00 (per person)
Dinner at Irene's Cuisine (3 courses)	44.00 (per person)
Muffuletta sandwich at Central Grocery	16.00
Ticket to a show at Tipitina's	10.00–30.00
Cost of a Hurricane at Pat O' Brien's with souvenir glass	12.00
Cost of a Pimm's Cup at Napoleon House	7.00

events. December's **prix-fixe Réveillon deals** can get you into restaurants for dinners that might otherwise be prohibitive.

With a few cash-only exceptions, **major credit cards** are accepted everywhere (some don't accept American Express, Discover, or Diner's Club). Cash is king anywhere, and ATMs are plentiful throughout the city (including inside many bars and souvenir shops). Expect a $2.50 to $4.00 charge to use an ATM outside your network. To avoid the fee, most grocery and convenience stores will allow you to get a small amount of cash back with your purchase (from $10–$100, depending on store policy).

Beware of hidden credit-card fees while traveling. Check with your credit or debit card issuer to see what fees, if any, will be charged for overseas transactions, even if those charges were made in U.S. dollars. Check with your bank before departing to avoid surprise charges on your statement.

Newspapers & Magazines The city has two local papers: **The Advocate** (www.theneworleans advocate.com), which publishes daily; and the **Times-Picayune** (www.nola.com), which publishes Wednesday, Friday, and Sunday editions. **Offbeat** (www. offbeat.com) and **Where Y' at** are monthly entertainment guides with live music,

art, and special event listings. Both can usually be found in hotels and clubs, and get scarce toward the end of the month. **Gambit Weekly** (www.bestofnew orleans.com), which comes out every Sunday, is the city's free alternative paper and has a good mix of news and entertainment information.

Packing What to pack depends largely on what you plan to do while visiting New Orleans. But comfortable walking shoes are a must year-round. A compact umbrella will often be put to use, as will other raingear during the wetter months (and a sun hat for much of the year). A light sweater or jacket is needed even in the hottest weather, when the indoor air can get frigid. Casual wear is the daytime norm, but cocktail wear is appropriate in nicer restaurants, and some of the old-liners require jackets for gentlemen. Also see the suggestions under "Health" and "Safety" in this section.

Passports Every air traveler entering the U.S. is required to show a valid passport (including U.S. citizens). Those entering by land and sea must also present a passport or other appropriate documentation. See www.dhs.gov/crossing-us-borders for more information. For more on passport requirements, contact the Passport Office of your home country. If you need to obtain or renew a passport, do this at least 6 months before your departure.

Pharmacies Pharmacies (aka chemists or druggists) are easily found. Large chain pharmacies, including **Rite Aid, CVS,** and **Walgreens,** operate throughout the city. There are 24-hour pharmacies at the **Walgreens** at 1801 St. Charles Ave. in the Lower Garden District (ⓒ **504/561-8458**) and in Mid-City at 2418 S. Carrollton Ave. (ⓒ **504/861-5033**).

Petrol Please see "By Car" under "Getting Around," earlier in this chapter.

Police Dial ⓒ **911** for emergencies. This is a free call from any phone. Calls from landlines will route to the local emergency dispatch agency. From mobile phones, immediately tell the operator your location and the nature of the emergency.

Safety It's true that New Orleans has a high crime rate. But most (not all) of the serious crime is drug-related and confined to areas where tourists do not go. Still, we urge you to be very cautious about where you go, what you do, and with whom—particularly at night. In short, behave with the same savvy and street smarts you would demonstrate in any big city: travel in groups or pairs, take cabs if you're not sure of an area, stay in well-lighted areas with plenty of street and pedestrian traffic, follow your instincts if something seems "off." Stay alert and walk with confidence; avoid looking distracted, confused, or (sorry) drunk. In fact, avoid *being* drunk—that's just a general good rule. Speaking of which, one way to ensure you will look like a tourist—and thus, a target—is to wear Mardi Gras beads at any time other than Mardi Gras season.

iPhones have become a target of grab-and-run thieves, especially since users, like those who text while walking, are frequently distracted. If you must check something on your phone, stop into a hotel lobby, bar, or shop.

When it's not in use, put that expensive camera out of sight. Use camera cases and purses with a shoulder strap, carried diagonally over the shoulder so a simple tug won't dislodge them. Consider using a money belt or other hidden travel wallet. Ditch the trendy enormous bag and invest in a cute little shoulder-strappy thing for clubbing, one you can dance with rather than leave on your seat (better yet, go purse-free). Never leave valuables in the outside pocket of a backpack and if you must store belongings in a car, store them in the trunk. Leave expensive-looking jewelry and other conspicuous valuables at home. And by all means, **don't look for or buy drugs or engage in any illegal activity.**

On **Bourbon Street** be careful when socializing with strangers, and be alert to distractions by potential pickpocket teams. Use busy Decatur Street to walk from the French Quarter to Frenchmen Street.

Scattered sections of the **Tremé, Bywater,** and the **Irish Channel** section of the Lower Garden District are transitional and may be considered sketchy. This shouldn't dissuade you from visiting, but you should keep on your toes.

Single Travelers Single travelers, both male and female, should feel comfortable in New Orleans. People are generally friendly, and many restaurants, including some of the city's finest, serve meals at the bar—a personal favorite spot when dining solo (Emeril's, Coquette, Cochon, and

Acme come to mind). Still, single women travelers in particular should heed the warnings in the "Safety" section, above.

Smoking Technically, smoking is not allowed in most public places, with some exceptions such as free-standing bars. Restaurants are nonsmoking (though many bars serve some food, and thus smoking is allowed); often the nearest courtyard or street becomes an impromptu smoking section. Hotel lobbies are nonsmoking, but guest rooms can be designated as smoking or non-smoking (be sure to make your preference clear when reserving a room; many hotels are entirely smoke-free). Historically, nightclubs have been smokers' havens, but there's a growing trend toward nonsmoking clubs (see **www.letsbetotally clear.org** for a list of them).

Taxes The United States has no value-added tax (VAT) or other indirect tax at the national level. Every state, county, and city may levy its own local tax on all purchases, including hotel and restaurant checks and airline tickets. These taxes will not appear on price tags. The sales tax in New Orleans is 9.75%; hotel room tax is 13% (for properties with 6 or more rooms). There is also a nightly tax of 50¢ to $3 based on the property's number of rooms.

On the upside, international travelers who purchase goods in Louisiana to take to their home countries

can often get the sales tax refunded in full. When you make your purchase, keep your receipt and also request a "tax back" voucher (you'll be asked to show your passport). Before you leave the state, bring your receipts and vouchers to the **Refund Center** in the Outlet Collection at Riverwalk mall (p. 187) or New Orleans Airport (main lobby of Terminal C; allow time before your flight). You'll be rebated in cash up to US$500. Larger rebates are mailed; see www.louisiana taxfree.com for instructions and more information. Not all stores participate, so ask first.

Also, many original works of art purchased in New Orleans are tax-exempt. Do inquire, as this applies in designated cultural districts only.

Telephones Hotel costs for long-distance and local calls made from guest rooms vary widely. Local calls range from complimentary to astronomically expensive; long-distance calls typically fall into the latter category. Calls to area codes **800, 888, 877,** and **866** are free. If you intend to use the room phone, definitely inquire about phone charges. You may be better off using a mobile phone or a prepaid calling card. Public payphones are rare, but some (for example, at airports) accept credit cards. Most long-distance and international calls can be dialed directly from any phone. **To make calls**

within the United States and to Canada, dial **1** followed by the area code and the seven-digit number. **For other international calls,** dial **011** followed by the country code, city code, and the number you are calling. For **directory assistance** (help finding numbers, aka "Information") in the U.S. and Canada, dial **411.** For other phone services, dial **0** to reach an operator for phone services within the U.S.; dial **00** for assistance with international calls. Also see "Mobile Phones," earlier in this section.

Time New Orleans is in the Central Time Zone (CST), which is 6 hours earlier than Greenwich Mean Time. When it's noon in New Orleans, it's 10am in Los Angeles (PST); 1pm in New York City; 6pm in London (GMT); and 5am the next day in Sydney.

Daylight saving time (summer time) is in effect from 1am on the second Sunday in March to 1am on the first Sunday in November, except in Arizona, Hawaii, the U.S. Virgin Islands, and Puerto Rico. Daylight saving time moves the clock 1 hour ahead of standard time.

Tipping Tips are a very important part of certain workers' income, and the standard way of showing appreciation for services provided (it's not compulsory if the service is poor, but most people would leave a smaller tip rather than none at all). In hotels, tip **bellhops** $1 to $2 per bag ($3 if you have a lot of luggage) and tip the **chamber staff** $5 and up per night (more if you've been extra messy). Tip the **doorman** or **concierge** if he or she has provided you with some specific service (for example, calling a cab for you or obtaining tickets or reservations), $5 to $20 or more depending on complexity. Tip the **valet-parking attendant** $1 every time you get your car; more if you're driving something you need to protect.

In restaurants, bars, and nightclubs, tip **service staff** and **bartenders** 15% to 20% of the check, tip **checkroom attendants** $1 per garment, and tip **valet-parking attendants** $2 to $3 per vehicle. Some restaurants will automatically add a tip to the bill for larger parties (typically 18% for 6 or more guests, but this can vary). Check your bill or ask your server if gratuity has been included in your bill.

As for other service personnel, tip **cab drivers** 15% of the fare, tip **skycaps** at airports at least $2 per bag (more if you have a lot of luggage), and tip **hairdressers** and **barbers** 15% to 20%.

Toilets You won't find public toilets or "restrooms" on the streets in most U.S. cities, but they can be found in hotel lobbies, bars, restaurants, museums, department stores, railway and bus stations, and service stations. Large hotels

and fast-food restaurants are often the best bet for clean facilities. Restaurants and bars may restrict their restrooms to paying patrons.

Tours There are tours geared toward antiquing, literature, history, gay and lesbian culture, ghosts, and Voodoo, along with tours of the fabled, stunning swamps, plantation homes, cemeteries, and various areas of New Orleans. For more on tours, see chapters 7 and 11; 10 for self-guided walking tours.

Travelers with Disabilities Most disabilities shouldn't stop anyone from traveling in New Orleans. Most public places are required to comply with disability-friendly regulations. Almost all public establishments (except a few National Historic Landmarks) and at least some modes of public transportation provide accessible entrances and facilities.

Still, a few places may be inaccessible, with regulatory allowances due to their historic nature. Before you book a reservation, call and inquire based on your needs. The city's newer hotels, restaurants, and shops are fully accommodating, and many older ones have undergone excellent retrofitting.

The city's bumpy and uneven sidewalks (and sometimes potholed or cobblestoned streets) can be challenging for wheelchairs and walkers, though most have curb cuts. The St.

Charles streetcar requires a big step up and does not have a lift; all other streetcar lines do.

For paratransit information and reservations, call **RTA Paratransit** (www.norta.com/accessiblity; ℰ **504/827-7433**).

VAT See "Taxes," earlier in this section.

Visas The U.S. State Department has a **Visa Waiver Program (VWP)** allowing citizens from a long list of countries to enter the United States without a visa for stays of up to 90 days. Even for visitors from VWP countries and others for whom a visa is not necessary, online registration through the Electronic System for Travel Authorization (ESTA) is required before departing for the U.S. They must complete an electronic application providing basic personal and travel eligibility information. Travelers from non-VWP countries and those with certain types of passports, usually older ones, may still be required to get a visa. Some travelers may also be required to present a round-trip air or cruise ticket upon arrival in the U.S. Canadian citizens may enter the United States without visas, but will need to show passports and proof of residence. Citizens of all other countries must have: (1) a valid passport that expires at least 6 months later than the scheduled end of their visit to the U.S., and (2) a tourist visa. For more information, check with the American

Embassy in your home country at least 6 months before your planned departure. More information at **http://travel.state.gov/visa**.

Visitor Information

Even a seasoned traveler should consider writing or calling ahead to the **New Orleans Convention & Visitors Bureau,** 2020 St. Charles Ave., New Orleans, LA 70130 (www.neworleans cvb.com; © **800/672-6124** or 504/566-5011; Mon–Fri 8:30am–5pm). The friendly staff can offer advice and help with decision-making; if you have a special interest, they'll help you plan your visit around it—this is definitely one of the most helpful tourist centers in any major city.

The state of Louisiana's **New Orleans Welcome Center,** 529 St. Ann St. (© **504/568-5661;** daily Tues–Sat 9am–5pm) has walking- and driving-tour maps; booklets on restaurants, accommodations, sightseeing, special tours; and more. **Warning:** Many of the **tour offices** and **visitors centers** scattered around the city are for-profit offices operated by tourism businesses hawking their wares. Rather than unbiased services that will recommend the best tour for you, these are commissioned sales offices.

Water Tap water is safe to drink in New Orleans, although bottled water is still popular.

Wi-Fi See "Internet, Wi-Fi & Computer Rentals," earlier in this section.

Index

See also Accommodations and Restaurant indexes, below.

General Index

A

The Abbey, 182
Accommodations, 51–70. *See also* Accommodations Index
alternate options, 59
best, 4–5
Central Business District, 63–66
French Quarter and Faubourg Tremé, 51–59
Marigny and Bywater, 59–61
Mid-City/Esplanade, 61–63
with outstanding restaurants, 70
Uptown/The Garden District, 67–70
African American Heritage Trail, 236
African-American travelers, 236
Aidan Gill for Men, 195
Airboat Adventures, 156
Airport Shuttle New Orleans, 231
Air travel, 231–232
Algiers Point, 39, 141
Allstate Sugar Bowl Classic, 23
AllWays Lounge, 177
Ambush Magazine, 238
American Bicycle Rentals, 235
American Queen Steamboat Company, 233
American River Cruises, 233
America's Wetland Conservation Corps, 28
Amtrak, 232
A Musing Bicycles, 235
Amusement Park and Children's Storyland, 162
Angela King Gallery, 189
Annie Miller's Son's Swamp and Marsh Tours, 157
Antieau Gallery, 189
Antiques, 187–188
Antiquing tours, 161
Apple Barrel, 171
Arcadian Books, 191
Area code, 236
Armstrong, Louis, Satchmo Summerfest, 26
Art galleries, 189–191
Arthur Roger Gallery, 189
Art markets, 186
Arts and Cultural Center (St. Alphonsus Church), 137
Atchafalaya Experience (Lafayette), 230
Audubon, John James, Oakley Plantation at Audubon State Historic Site (St. Francisville), 223

Audubon Aquarium of the Americas, 121, 125, 162
Audubon Insectarium, 125
Audubon Park, 141
Audubon Zoo, 141–142, 162
Aunt Tiki's, 182
Authentic New Orleans experiences, 2–3
Avenue Pub, 182

B

Bacchus krewe, 47
Backstreet Cultural Museum, 134, 155
Bamboula's, 171, 174
Bank of Louisiana (Police Station), 201
Bars, 178–183
gay, 184
Bar Tonique, 179
Battle of New Orleans, 14, 142
Bicentennial, 24
Bayou St. John, 133–134
walking tour, 212–216
Beauregard-Keyes House, 126, 205
Beckham's Bookshop, 191
Benjamin Button House, 212
Besthoff Sculpture Garden, 136, 162
Best Stop (Scott), 226
Bicycle Michael's, 234–235
Big Easy Metropolitan Community Church, 238
Big Easy Rollergirls, 163–164
Big Lake, boating and biking in, 162–163
Bike Taxi Unlimited, 235
Biking, 234–235
tours, 160–161
BJ's Lounge, 182
Blount Small Ship Adventures, 233
Blue Frog Chocolates, 192
Blue Moon Saloon (Lafayette), 229
Blue Nile, 174
Boat and kayak tours, 159–160
Boating, Big Lake, 162–163
The Bombay Club, 179
Bonomolo Limousine Service, 231
Books, recommended, 17–20
Books A Million, 192
Bookstores, 191–192
Boomtown Casino, 165
Botanical Gardens, 143
Bottom of the Cup Tearoom, 197
Boudin, 226
Bourbon Orleans Hotel, 203
The Bourbon Pub–Parade Disco, 184
Bourbon Street, 32–33, 45
Boutte, John, 169
Bradish Johnson House, 210
Brass bands, 21, 168
Brennan's Restaurant, 201

Brevard-Mahat-Rice House, 210
Briggs-Staub House, 209
The Brulatour Court, 202
Bucktown, 134
Bush Antiques, 187–188
Business hours, 236–237
Bus travel, 235
Bywater, 38
accommodations, 59–61
restaurants, 91–94

C

The Cabildo, 32, 128–129, 162, 206
Café Istanbul, 185
Café Lafitte in Exile, 184
Cajun Country, 224–230
Cajun cuisine, difference between Creole cuisine and, 80
Cajun Encounters, 153, 220
Cajun language, 224
A Cajun Man's Swamp Cruise, 157
Cajun music, 168–169, 179, 225
Cajun Zydeco Festival, 25
Calendar of events, 23–27
Canal Place, shopping, 186
Canal Street/Algiers Ferry, 235
Canal Street Ferry, 162
Canal Street streetcar, 236
Candies, pralines and pastries, 192–193
Candlelight Lounge, 176
Cane & Table, 179
Carl Mack Presents, 193
Carnival Cruises, 233
Carol Robinson Gallery, 189
Carousel Bar, 169
Carousel Bar at the Monteleone Hotel, 179
Carousel Gardens, 142, 162
Carriage Cab, 234
Carroll-Crawford House, 210
Car travel and rentals, 232, 233–234
Casinos, 165
Cat's Meow, 180
Celebration in the Oaks, 27, 162
Cellphones, 239
Cemeteries, 143–147
Cemetery and Voodoo Tour, 157
Central Business District (CBD), 38–39
accommodations, 63–66
restaurants, 99–105
Chalmette Battlefield/Jean Lafitte National Historical Park & Preserve, 142
Champions Square, 165
Charpentier House, 214
Chickie Wah-Wah, 176
Children's Storyland, 142
Christmas, New Orleans Style, 27
Christopher Porche-West, 189
Churches, 137–139
Church of St. John the Evangelist (Lafayette), 228

Accommodations